Rendering to God and Caesar

Manchester University Press

Rendering to God and Caesar

The Irish churches and the two states in Ireland, 1949–73

Daithí Ó Corráin

Manchester University Press
Manchester and New York

distributed exclusively in the USA by Palgrave

Copyright © Daithí Ó Corráin 2006

The right of Daithí Ó Corráin to be identified as the author of this work has been asserted by him in accordance with the Copyright, Designs and Patents Act 1988.

Published by Manchester University Press
Oxford Road, Manchester M13 9NR, UK
and Room 400, 175 Fifth Avenue, New York, NY 10010, USA
www.manchesteruniversitypress.co.uk

Distributed in the United States exclusively by
Palgrave Macmillan, 175 Fifth Avenue,
New York, NY 10010, USA

Distributed in Canada exclusively by
UBC Press, University of British Columbia, 2029 West Mall,
Vancouver, BC, Canada V6T 1Z2

British Library Cataloguing-in-Publication Data is available

Library of Congress Cataloging-in-Publication Data is available

ISBN 978 0 7190 7347 2 paperback

First published by Manchester University Press in hardback 2006

First published by Manchester University Press in paperback 2011

The publisher has no responsibility for the persistence or accuracy of URLs for any external or third-party internet websites referred to in this book, and does not guarantee that any content on such websites is, or will remain, accurate or appropriate.

Printed by Lightning Source

For my parents, Esther and Teddy

Contents

List of figures	viii
Acknowledgements	ix
Terminology and abbreviations	xi
Introduction	1
1 'Hands across the border must be the unfailing principle of our common church life': the Church of Ireland and the border	12
2 'The indivisible island': the Catholic Church and the border	43
3 'A confident minority': the Church of Ireland and the Irish state	70
4 Standing with the people: the Catholic Church and the Northern Ireland state	115
5 'That they may be one': inter-church relations and religious borders in Ireland	182
Conclusion	240
Appendix 1: Church of Ireland archbishops of Armagh and Dublin; bishops of cross-border and Northern Ireland dioceses	244
Appendix 2: Catholic bishops of the Armagh province	247
Bibliography	249
Index	263

List of figures

1 Church of Ireland dioceses   3
2 Roman Catholic dioceses   4

Acknowledgements

This book has grown out of a Ph.D. thesis which was supported by the Irish Research Council for the Humanities and Social Sciences (IRCHSS) and supervised by Professor Eunan O'Halpin. In overcoming serious illness, he provided all his research students with a striking example of fortitude. I am grateful to him for teaching me a great deal about the use of archives, for his encouragement and dry humour. In transferring my thoughts and findings on to paper I have benefited greatly from the advice and drawn on the scholarship and insight of many fellow historians, churchmen and friends, whom I should like to thank. They include: Dr Gearóid Barry, Rev. Patrick Burke, Rt Rev. Donald Caird, Very Rev. Martin Clarke, His Eminence Cardinal Cahal Daly, Most Rev. Edward Daly, J. L. B. Deane, Very Rev. Ian Dickie; Dr Anne Dolan, Most Rev. Joseph Duffy, Keith Dungan, Professor Roy Foster, Dr Louise Fuller, Professor Michael Gallagher, Robin Gibson, Rev. Edward F. Grant, Very Rev. Victor Griffin, Dr Gerard Hogan, Dr Susan Hood, Professor John Horgan, Ms June Howard, Rev. Michael Hurley, Rev. Gabriel Kelly, Dr Michael Kennedy, John Lynch, Very Rev. Robert MacCarthy, Rt Rev. Mgr. Liam MacDaid, Rev. Peter McAnenly, the late Most Rev. Francis MacKiernan, Dr Deirdre McMahon, Seán MacRéamoinn, Dr Eoin Magennis, Dr Kenneth Milne, Ms. J. Montgomery, Kevin Murphy, Mícheál Ó Fathartaigh; the late Risteard Ó Glaisne, Very Rev. Canon George O'Hanlon, Geoffrey Perrin, Rt Rev. Samuel Poyntz, Dr Niamh Puirséil, Dr Raymond Refaussé, Rev. Robin Richey, Peter Rigney, David Sheehy, Dr Katharine Simms, Nicholas Simms, Rev. Albert Stokes, John Walsh, Dr W. E. Vaughan, Rt Rev. Roy Warke and Professor Trevor West. Special thanks are due to Julie O'Donovan for creating the maps used herein.

I thank the following institutions and holders of copyright for access to collections of papers in their care and permission to quote from them: Most Rev. Seán Brady, archbishop of Armagh; Cardinal Desmond Connell, archbishop emeritus of Dublin; His Eminence Cardinal Cormac

Murphy-O'Connor, archbishop of Westminster; Most Rev. Edward Daly, bishop emeritus of Derry; Most Rev. Patrick Walsh, bishop of Down and Connor; Rt. Rev. Michael Mayes on behalf of the House of Bishops; Most Rev. John McAreavey, bishop of Dromore; Most Rev. Leo O'Reilly, bishop of Kilmore; Most Rev. Joseph Duffy, bishop of Clogher; the Director of the National Archives of Ireland; the National Archives, Kew; the National Library of Ireland; the Keeper of the Public Record Office of Northern Ireland; University College Dublin Archives Department; the UCD-OFM Partnership (de Valera Papers); and the trustees of Lambeth Palace Library. I have made far too many demands on the patience and kindness of the staff at the Ó Fiaich Memorial Library and Archive, the Representative Church Body Library and Trinity College Library, as well as those of many diocesan offices, county councils and public libraries.

Many thanks are due to the team at Manchester University Press for their work on this book. My friends in Priory Walk could not have been more understanding during the past few months. My greatest gratitude is to my family and relatives. The Joyce family made my many research trips to London a pleasure. My late grandaunt Bina believed in this book before anyone else did. Aogán Ó hIarlaithe, Máire Ní Iarlaithe and Clare Murphy painstakingly proofread various drafts with surprising enthusiasm. Thanks are inadequate for the unfaltering encouragement of my parents, brothers and particularly my sister, Aoife, who read and reread versions of this book with such astute eyes; for everything, *mo bhuíochas libh*. Any errors of facts or judgement are of course my own.

Terminology and abbreviations

The terms 'North' and 'South' are used throughout this book as synonyms for the territories that became Northern Ireland and the Republic of Ireland. Where the words 'nationalist' and 'unionist' begin with capital letters they refer to political parties and their MPs; the lower case versions refer to individuals or opinions. It should be clear from the text where 'the church' refers to the broader community and where it indicates church authorities. The following is a list of the most commonly used abbreviated terms in the text:

AC	*Anglo-Celt*
BCC	British Council of Churches
BNL	*Belfast News-Letter*
BT	*Belfast Telegraph*
CAB	Minutes of Cabinet Meetings (RoI); Cabinet Conclusions (NI)
CDA	Clogher Diocesan Archives
CJ	Northern Ireland Office
CoIG	*Church of Ireland Gazette*
DCDA	Down and Connor Diocesan Archives
DD	*Dáil Debates*
DDA	Dublin Diocesan Archives
DEA	Department of External Affairs
DerDA	Derry Diocesan Archives
DFA	Department of Foreign Affairs
DO	Dominions Office
DRDS	Derry and Raphoe, diocesan synod reports
DroDA	Dromore Diocesan Archives
DT	Department of the Taoiseach
FCO	Foreign and Commonwealth Office
FO	Foreign Office
GOC	General Officer Commanding

HB	House of Bishops, minutes of meetings
HO	Home Office
ICC	Irish Council of Churches
ICD	*Irish Catholic Directory*
II	*Irish Independent*
IN	*Irish News*
IP	*Irish Press*
IR	*Impartial Reporter*
IRA	Irish Republican Army
IT	*Irish Times*
JGS	*Journal of the General Synod*
JSA	*Journal of the Synod of Armagh*
JUS	Department of Justice
KDA	Kilmore Diocesan Archives
LHL	Linen Hall Library, Belfast
LOL	Loyal Orange Lodge
LPL	Lambeth Palace Library
NAI	National Archives of Ireland, Dublin
NAUK	National Archives UK, London
NIHA	Northern Ireland Hospitals' Authority
NIHT	Northern Ireland Housing Trust
NLI	National Library of Ireland
OD	Other denominations
OFMLA	Ó Fiaich Memorial Library and Archive, Armagh
PACE	Protestant and Catholic Encounter
PREM	Prime Minister's Office
PRONI	Public Record Office of Northern Ireland
RCB	Representative Church Body
RCBL	Representative Church Body Library, Dublin
SD	*Seanad Debates*
SDLP	Social Democratic and Labour Party
SPAC	Sparsely Populated Areas Commission
UCC	University College Cork
UCCC	United Council of Christian Churches and Religious Communions in Ireland
UCDA	University College Dublin, Archives Department
UCG	University College Galway
UDA	Ulster Defence Association
VEC	Vocational Education Committee
WCC	World Council of Churches
WDA	Westminster Diocesan Archives

Introduction

Render unto Caesar the things which are Caesar's;
and unto God the things that are God's. (*Matthew*, 22:21)

Few subjects in contemporary Irish history have attracted more comment than the partition of Ireland, which, in 1920, divided the island into Northern and Southern states. There has been an understandable inclination to examine separately the historical experiences of the two jurisdictions. Even the titles of integrated studies, such as *The Two Irelands 1912–1939* and *Ireland in the Twentieth Century: Divided Island*, bear this out.[1] The idea of 'two Irelands' has been a very effective interpretative framework for various aspects of economic and political history on both sides of the border. However, it is a less appropriate perspective for examining certain cultural, professional and ecclesiastical bodies which have continued to function on an all-Ireland basis. While the constitutional effects of partition have been well rehearsed, the same cannot be said of its social and cultural consequences. These have remained unlighted areas of twentieth-century Irish history. The fixation with political division, hostility, rivalry or even enmity between or within the Irish states has completely eclipsed any consideration of how unitary all-Ireland organisations tried to adjust to, moderate or simply live with partition.

This book concerns two such all-Ireland bodies: the Catholic Church and the Church of Ireland. They were not the only churches to be crossborder in nature; so too were the Presbyterian and Methodist Churches. But whereas these were and are predominantly confined to Northern Ireland, by comparison the Church of Ireland and the Catholic Church have had a far greater demographic and geographical spread throughout the entire island and therefore lend themselves more readily to examination.[2] The accompanying figures illustrate that diocesan boundaries, which date from medieval times, were not coincident with state boundaries. Within each church, the numbers, names and configurations of dioceses and provinces (groups of dioceses) differed.³ But, as can be seen, in both churches there were (and still are) four dioceses, or united dioceses, which straddled the border with a further two located entirely within Northern Ireland. For them, the advent of the border did not occasion ecclesiastical partition, or make obligatory a new organisational beginning, or compel a sharp break with the past. After 1920 their 'map image' and frame of reference remained an all-Ireland one. But the political fault line did mean that henceforth the Church of Ireland and the Catholic Church would have to function in two very different jurisdictions. Consequently, both churches were simultaneously part of a local minority and a local majority religious bloc. They, therefore, had a vested interest in minimising the border's divisive potential as they tried to accommodate the contending and sensitive demands of head and heart.

Rendering to God and Caesar departs from the well-worn depiction of a single or strictly political historical trajectory. It treats the consequences of the border on the Church of Ireland and Catholic Church in the quarter-century between 1949 and 1973. In 1949 the declaration of the Republic of Ireland and the British parliament's Ireland Act (which confirmed Northern Ireland as part of the United Kingdom) reinforced the existence and permanence of the border. This study closes in 1973, a year often remembered for the British government's White Paper and the Anglo-Irish Sunningdale Agreement which led to the short-lived Northern Ireland executive and the unrealised hope of an end to bloodshed in Northern Ireland. But here 1973 is chosen for a different reason. Denomination formed the second border in Ireland and one which frequently coalesced with concerns about maintaining the political boundary. September 1973 witnessed the first official Irish inter-church meeting. This historic event was the product of several international and domestic factors, including, among others, the Second Vatican Council and, in particular, revulsion at the slide into violence in Northern Ireland.

The complex challenge facing the churches was that of maintaining a dual loyalty: to God, on the one hand, and to Caesar, on the other. Faithfulness to God meant determined efforts to ensure that political partition did not fracture or undermine the churches' respective confessional unity. Secondly, in response to developments in international ecumenism and a shared horror of the Northern Ireland Troubles, fidelity to Christian principles also prompted greater inter-church *rapprochement*. Allegiance to Caesar required loyalty to the states in which church members lived and church institutions functioned, but states with very different cultural, economic and political systems. Three interrelated questions arising from an exploration of the churches' dual loyalty have

Figure 1: Church of Ireland dioceses

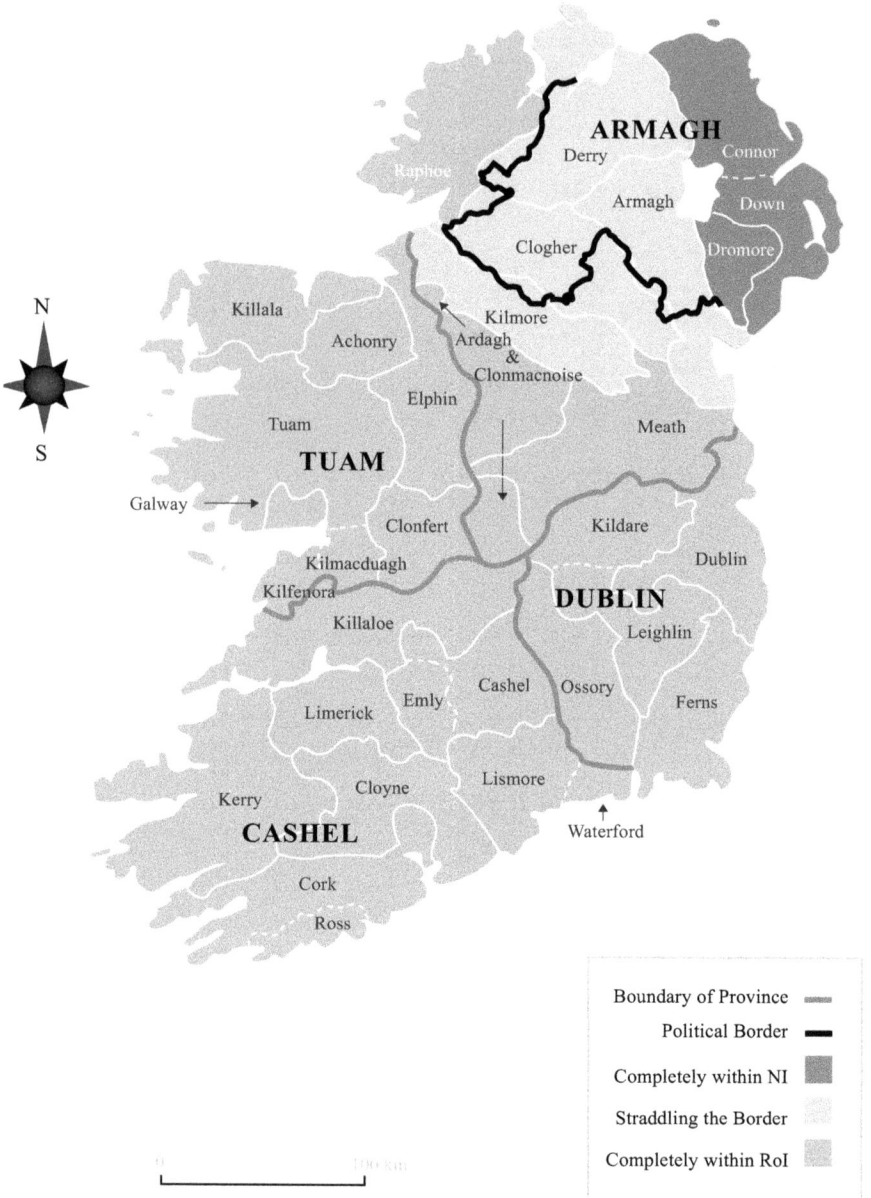

Figure 2: Roman Catholic dioceses

shaped this investigation. Firstly, how did the political border affect the churches' organisation and concerns? Chapters one and two consider the cases of the Church of Ireland and the Catholic Church respectively. Secondly, what was the nature of church–state relations in this period? Chapter three treats the Church of Ireland and the Southern state. Chapter four discusses the Catholic Church and the Northern Ireland government and, following intervention by Westminster in 1969, the Catholic Church and the British government during the opening years of the Troubles. Lastly, what developments occurred in inter-church relations in these years and why is the subject of chapter five. This book examines how the Church of Ireland and the Catholic Church, in their own ways, complied with the biblical injunction to render as appropriate to God and to Caesar.

It might be thought that the historiography of the Irish churches in the twentieth century has been well addressed by historians. If only. For the earlier decades, major contributions have been made to such facets as: the Church of Ireland in the South, the Catholic Church in the North, the Catholic Church and the Treaty, relations between the Vatican and Catholic Church, and inter-church relations.[4] By contrast, the period after the Second World War has attracted much less historical attention. Perhaps historians have been held back by too literal an interpretation of William Faulkner in *Absalom, Absalom!*, that 'the past is not dead. In fact, it's not even past', as journalists, sociologists and political scientists have provided most of what has been written.[5] The most influential work has been John Whyte's classic political science work: *Church and State in Modern Ireland, 1923–1970*. First published as long ago as 1971, *Church and State* remains the standard reference for undergraduate courses, academics and commentators of all shades.[6] It had three aims: to give a general overview of church–state relations since 1923; to examine the most celebrated clash of church and state – the 'Mother and Child' scheme of 1951 when Noël Browne's proposals for free medical care for mothers and children under sixteen were successfully opposed by the Catholic Church and the Irish Medical Association culminating in Browne's resignation; and, to assess the influence of the church on Irish politics. As the title suggests, Whyte judiciously surveyed just one church (the Catholic) in the twenty-six counties (variously styled the Irish Free State/Éire/Republic of Ireland) alone.

Whyte's was a fine beginning and one completed despite considerable clerical disapproval. Yet few scholars have built on his work and this leaves the post-war story of the Irish churches distinctly unbalanced. The other manifestations of church–state relations outlined above in this work's second thematic question have not received enough attention.

Furthermore, Whyte's work was written without recourse to archival material, something of which he made a virtue. Since the appearance of *Church and State*, the few historians who have addressed the subject have tended to rely solely on newspaper and state archival material, although Louise Fuller's *Irish Catholicism since 1950* is a groundbreaking work in its considered exploitation of Catholic journals, church legislative documents, encyclicals and devotional works.[7] One of the main reasons for the paucity of historical studies has been the unavailability of church archives. This has resulted in a tendency, whether intentional or not, to make totems of controversial episodes and strong personalities. Examples *par excellence* include a fixation with the Fethard-on-Sea boycott of 1957 and the episcopacy of John Charles McQuaid, Catholic archbishop of Dublin.

It was as if McQuaid was the only Irish prelate of note. Had he no superiors, colleagues or counterparts? What of Bishop Daniel Mageean, Cardinal John D'Alton or Cardinal William Conway and, in the Church of Ireland, Archbishops John Gregg, James McCann or George Simms, among many others? Likewise, were there no other interesting episodes and issues in the 1950s and 1960s which concerned the churches? What, for instance, was the Church of Ireland's response to the South's withdrawal from the British Commonwealth or the Catholic Church's stance on the IRA border campaign of the late 1950s? How were denominational educational demands pursued by the churches in the two states? What impact, if any, did the Orange Order have on the Church of Ireland? Did the Irish government mark the centenary of the Disestablishment of the Church of Ireland? Why was there no state support for the Mater Hospital in Belfast? How did the *Ne Temere* decree damage inter-church relations? What was the influence and reception of the Second Vatican Council in Ireland? What role did other Protestant churches play in improving inter-church relations? How did church leaders respond to the onset of the Troubles?[8]

That this book has explored such obvious but necessary questions is due to the unprecedently broad range of church *and* state archival material in the Republic, Northern Ireland and Britain which was made available to the author. Some of these sources, particularly in the case of the Church of Ireland printed reports, though always accessible, have been under-utilised. A chief merit of this book is the sizeable array of other church records, such as Catholic diocesan material, which is used for the very first time and adds greatly to historical insight.

Such archival material also facilitates the probing of the many questions listed above from the perspective of the respective benches of bishops. These *dramatis personae* were responsible for the spiritual guardianship of their dioceses. But they also articulated and represented their laities' aspirations and concerns. Bishops often engaged directly with government departments in either an individual capacity or as committee chairmen. Education is a case in point for both churches in both states. Another example was the role played by both sets of bishops during the early years of the Troubles in giving voice to the concerns and anxieties of their laities in public statements and in meetings with the British Home Secretary or his representatives. Therefore, the significance of diocese and the persona of the presiding bishop are interwoven in all aspects of church–state and inter-church relations. In conjunction with state archival material a consideration of the role of church leaders adds an important new layer of historical interpretation and explanation. Detailed appendices have been provided listing key dates for those prelates encountered in the text. Equally significant were the means of decision-making and administrative organisation in each church. These differed markedly and each is outlined in turn, as they functioned during the period 1949 to 1973.

Catholic bishops came together at general meetings of the Irish Episcopal Conference which treated matters concerning Ireland as a whole. These took place in Maynooth in June and October, but a third general meeting, before Easter, was added after 1965 to cope with the increased volume of business. The archbishop of Armagh, the senior ecclesiastic, normally presided. Two secretaries, drawn from the bench of bishops, served the Episcopal Conference, one as general secretary and the other as financial secretary.[9] The general meeting was less a creator of policy than a clearinghouse for decisions forged in the smithies of Standing and *ad hoc* Episcopal Committee meetings. It considered a medley of reports, discussed matters of the day and directed the secretaries on how to answer various correspondences. The influential Standing Committee was composed of the four archbishops as *ex officio* members, the senior bishop by date of episcopal consecration from each of the four Catholic provinces and the episcopal secretaries.[10] Chaired by the archbishop of Armagh, this committee met quarterly but occasionally at other times as circumstances demanded. In terms of the mechanics of decision-making, it was the key caucus for the formulation of hierarchical policy. It was at Standing Committee level that the influence of certain prelates, such as McQuaid, could be brought to bear, often by simply controlling what featured on the agenda. Episcopal committees or commissions formed the next layer of decision-making. In the early 1950s, these appear to have been *ad hoc* in nature rather than permanent, exceptions being the Commission on Finance and the two committees responsible for primary and technical, and secondary and university education. The number of permanent episcopal commissions grew enormously during the 1960s to cater for the diverse range of issues on which the hierarchy was expected to comment. By 1969 there were nineteen commissions divided into nine groups: Education; Universities; Religious Life; Liturgy and Laity; Doctrine; Social Welfare; Justice and Peace; Communication; and Finance. From the mid-1970s, the Standing Committee was reconstituted to reflect the diversity of these committees. Lastly, provincial meetings under the chairmanship of the local archbishop also took place. For instance, there were nine dioceses in the province of Armagh. Approximately four meetings of the nine bishops took place annually. But given the complexities of dealing with the two states, the six bishops with diocesan territory in Northern Ireland consulted frequently, often in Ara Coeli, the Armagh residence of the archbishop.[11]

Church of Ireland bishops had less autonomy than their Catholic counterparts which was due partly to being elected rather than appointed and partly to the nature and extent of the church's administrative framework. Devised in the wake of Gladstone's Disestablishment Act, this structure came into operation in 1871 and transformed the Church of Ireland from a state church to a self-governing voluntary body. At the apex of the organisational triad of parish–diocese–province, supreme legislative authority resided with the General Synod (as it still does). Under the presidency of the archbishop of Armagh, this can be thought of as the church's national parliament. Modelled on Westminster, as it existed in 1870, the General Synod is divided into the House of Bishops and the House of Representatives. During the period under consideration, the former comprised the archbishops of Armagh and Dublin and twelve bishops.[12] Until the mid-1950s, the House of Bishops met six times a year; this subsequently increased to nine meetings, one each month with the exception of January, August and September. The House of Representatives was, and still is, composed of 216 clerical and 432 lay members (a set ratio of one cleric to two lay people). Members were elected triennially by diocesan synods (regional versions of the General Synod); these in turn were elected by parish vestries. In most cases the Houses of Representatives and Bishops sit together but the bishops have the right to meet and vote separately as well as to veto any motion passed by the House of Representatives. The *raison d'être* of a synod, whether at diocesan or national level, is to debate and vote on decisions at least once a year. More specifically, the work of the General Synod may be divided into three categories. It deliberates bills for amendments to the constitution, changes in articles, doctrines, rites and rubrics of the church, or the establishment of special commissions. Secondly, the reports of various boards and committees and their election are considered. Lastly, motions on various subjects are discussed.[13] The proceedings are reported annually in the *Journal of the General Synod*. Day-to-day administrative business at a national level is conducted by the Standing Committee of the General Synod. In the 1950s and 1960s this consisted of the archbishops and bishops, the honorary secretaries of the General Synod, one lay and one clerical representative from each diocese or united diocese, and fourteen co-opted members. This key committee met about eight times a year to consider matters of general interest to the church as a whole and had the power to refer matters to a specialist sub-committee.[14] Similarly, a diocesan council, chaired by the bishop, conducts business during the year at the diocesan level.

Several fascinating and long overlooked themes and personalities get due recognition in these pages as the churches are viewed in their natural all-Ireland context. What clearly emerges is a picture of pragmatic and dexterous church leadership which, for both Church of Ireland and Catholic Church, was determined to transcend the political border in terms of church unity, but at the same time reconcile the local church community to the states in which they lived. As might be expected, this posed different challenges for the Church of Ireland and the Catholic Church. The churches were united in their distaste for any notion of 'two Irelands' in a confessional sense but partition obliged them to live in and adapt to such a political environment. Despite the difficulties involved, they nonetheless endeavoured to render to both God and Caesar.

Notes

1 David Fitzpatrick, *The Two Irelands 1912–1939* (Oxford, 1998); David Harkness, *Ireland in the Twentieth Century. Divided Island* (Basingstoke, 1996). Other works simply provide a separate section on Northern Ireland such as J. J. Lee's, *Ireland 1912–1985. Politics and Society* (Cambridge, 1989).

2 For example, the geographical distribution of the Presbyterian Church in the twentieth century still reflected its seventeenth-century origins with its strongest areas in the counties of Antrim, Derry and Down. In 1961 0.7 per cent of the population in the Republic were Presbyterian. See John Erskine, 'The Presbyterian Church in Ireland', in Norman Richardson (ed.), *A Tapestry of Beliefs. Christian Traditions in Northern Ireland* (Belfast, 1998), p. 47.

3 From 1944 the Church of Ireland had fourteen dioceses or united dioceses: eight in the province of Armagh and six in the province of Dublin. Killaloe was united with Limerick in 1976 and Cashel with Ossory in 1977 to reduce the number to its current total of twelve. The Catholic Church comprises

twenty-six dioceses divided into four provinces: Armagh, Dublin, Cashel and Tuam. From 1954 the diocese of Ross was administered by the bishop of Cork and in 1958 was united with the diocese of Cork.
4 Alan Acheson provides a useful overview in *A History of the Church of Ireland 1691–1996* (Dublin, 1997); Alan Megahey's *The Irish Protestant Churches in the Twentieth Century* (Basingstoke, 2000) is an excellent survey work. Kenneth Milne charts the experience of the Church of Ireland in the new Southern state in 'The Church of Ireland since partition', in Brendan Bradshaw and Dáire Keogh (eds), *Christianity in Ireland. Revisiting the Story* (Dublin, 2002), pp. 220–30; Kurt Bowen provides an influential sociological study in *Protestants in a Catholic State. Ireland's Privileged Minority* (Dublin, 1983). Mary Harris treats the Catholic Church and the Northern Ireland state in the 1920s in *The Catholic Church and the Foundation of the Northern Ireland State* (Cork, 1993). Patrick Murray's pioneering *Oracles of God. The Roman Catholic Church and Irish Politics, 1922–37* (Dublin, 2000) focuses on clerical responses to the Treaty and its aftermath. Dermot Keogh examines relations between the Southern government, Catholic bishops and Holy See in *Ireland and the Vatican. The Politics and Diplomacy of Church–State Relations 1922–1960* (Cork, 1995). Ian Ellis's *Vision and Reality. A Survey of Twentieth Century Irish Inter-church Relations* (Belfast, 1992) and Michael Hurley's *Christian Unity. An Ecumenical Second Spring?* (Dublin, 1998) have reduced the extent of unmapped territory in the field of Irish inter-church relations.
5 Works by journalists include Paul Blanshard, *The Irish and Catholic Power* (London, 1954), and, more recently, John Cooney, *John Charles McQuaid. Ruler of Catholic Ireland* (Dublin, 1999). One of the more influential sociological treatments has been Tom Inglis, *Moral Monopoly. The Catholic Church in Modern Irish Society* (Dublin, 1987). Survey works on the Catholic Church include: Oliver Rafferty, *Catholicism in Ulster 1603–1983* (London, 1994) and Marianne Elliott, *The Catholics of Ulster. A History* (London, 2000).
6 John Whyte, *Church and State in Modern Ireland 1923–1970* (Dublin, 1971). A second edition appeared in 1979 bringing the account up to that date. Tom Bartlett provides an assessment of *Church and State* in 'Church and state in modern Ireland, 1923–1970: an appraisal reappraised,' in Bradshaw and Keogh (eds), *Christianity in Ireland* , pp. 249–58.
7 Louise Fuller, *Irish Catholicism since 1950. The Undoing of a Culture* (Dublin, 2002).
8 Despite the avalanche of research on the Northern Troubles this question is still largely unanswered, Gerald McElroy's survey-based *The Catholic Church and the Northern Ireland Crisis 1968–86* being an exception.
9 These were respectively: James Staunton of Ferns who was succeeded by James Fergus of Achonry in 1952, and William MacNeely of Raphoe who was succeeded by Eugene O'Doherty of Dromore in 1964.

10 Whyte is slightly inaccurate on this point, see *Church and State*, p. 2.
11 Confirmed in conversation with Bishop Edward Daly, April 2002.
12 It currently comprises the two archbishops and ten bishops due to the diocesan amalgamations outlined in note three above.
13 See W. G. Wilson, *How the Church of Ireland is Governed* (Dublin, 1963), p. 46.
14 See J. L. B. Deane, *Church of Ireland Handbook* (Dublin, 1962), p. 154.

1

'Hands across the border must be the unfailing principle of our common church life': the Church of Ireland and the border

If a house be divided against itself, that house cannot stand. (Mark, 3:25)

The efflorescence of writing on community relations in Northern Ireland and relations between North and South, since the late 1960s, has made the expression 'hands across the border' a cliché. Yet, it was certainly not common currency when John Gregg, Church of Ireland archbishop of Armagh, uttered the phrase at the General Synod in 1949, in response to the withdrawal of the newly designated 'Republic' from the British Commonwealth.[1] Gregg's exhortation summed up the inherent importance to the Church of Ireland of ensuring that religious unity across the political border was in harmony with its all-Ireland territorial scope. But it also underlined the challenges that such a 'principle' posed. By 1949, members of the Church of Ireland had lived for almost thirty years in separate states whose cultural, economic and political systems had evolved in different ways. Moreover, given the political loyalties of its members, the consequences of partition were more keenly felt by the Church of Ireland than by its Catholic counterpart, whose members could be broadly described as nationalist irrespective of political jurisdiction. Termination of membership of the British Commonwealth forced the Church of Ireland to alter its state prayers. This episode exposed the difficulties of operating in two states. It illustrated just how pervasive an impact the political border had on a church for which any possibility of 'two Irelands' in the religious sphere was an anathema. This chapter explores some of the consequent apprehensions for the Church of Ireland by asking how 'unfailing' was the core principle alluded to by Gregg and why?

State prayers and liturgical realities

Gregg's very career and leadership embodied the commitment to bind the Church of Ireland, North and South, together. Equipped with experience of both parts of Ireland, he served as archbishop of Dublin, from 1920 until 1939, and as archbishop of Armagh and Primate from 1939 until his retirement in February 1959. He was the undisputed oracle on theological matters at home and abroad. With his natural reserve, rigid adherence to principle and firm chairmanship of General Synod meetings, his stature within the Church of Ireland was immense. He overshadowed Archbishop Arthur Barton of Dublin who, as a noted pastoral bishop, was a foil and adjunct to a Primate with great strengths. Gregg guided his church through an unprecedented period of social and political change during which Ireland was divided into two jurisdictions and endured the difficult years of the Second World War. It was a considerable achievement to hold the Church of Ireland together as a single entity during this trying time and to gain acceptance of the minority in the new Southern state. This was his great legacy. Yet, what is little known is that Gregg reluctantly, but dutifully, accepted translation from Dublin to Armagh in 1939, lest the unity of the Church of Ireland be damaged. In April 1938, he declined the Primacy which devolved instead to Bishop John Godfrey Fitzmaurice Day of Ossory. When Day died five months later, the House of Bishops again elected Gregg, though not unanimously. He received seven votes, Bishop Joseph Peacocke of Derry and Raphoe got three, and Bishop Charles King Irwin of Limerick one.[2] John MacNeice, bishop of Cashel and Waterford, and father of the poet Louis, revealed to Professor Nicholas Mansergh that Gregg contemplated refusing the appointment should he be elected by only a bare majority. Mansergh recorded in his diary that in MacNeice's view any such refusal was 'a great mistake, chiefly because of [the] impression that the Church of Ireland was divided between north and south'.[3] In a letter to George Simms, the future archbishop, Gregg revealed a stoical acceptance of duty:

> The move, which I make in about a month, means a sad wrench after a life of more than eighteen years in Dublin. But it seemed as if the move had to be made this time. I am sure I shall find very great differences between life in the North and in the South, but I have been assured of a welcome from many quarters.[4]

Gregg's presence as an archbishop for almost forty years crucially provided, in the opinion of the *Church of Ireland Gazette*, 'a symbol of stability and permanence' for the Church of Ireland.[5]

The Primate's call for hands across the border in 1949 was thus in character; it came in response to a vexatious liturgical conundrum. Despite Disestablishment in 1871, the liturgy of the Church of Ireland contained prayers for, and references to, the king and royal family. When Bunreacht na hÉireann (the Constitution of Ireland), which replaced the 1922 constitution, was promulgated in 1937, the House of Bishops largely recommended that there be no change to the state prayers as the twenty-six counties remained within the Commonwealth.[6] On 23 December 1948, two days after the Republic of Ireland Act was signed into law, the writer St John Ervine wondered: 'In law, all Episcopalians in Éire, like all other persons domiciled there, will be Republicans. Will the prayers for the King then be seditious?'[7] It was paradoxical that in a republic, prayers would be offered for a foreign king. Logical consistency demanded some form of alteration of the Book of Common Prayer for the South.

Under the shadow of the border, the delicate issue of state prayers had to be treated with great circumspection. While 'crisis' is perhaps too strong a word, the state-prayers problem was viewed gravely by the House of Bishops. The Commonwealth was regarded as a binding agent tying together not only the twenty-six counties to the British Empire but members of the church in the two political jurisdictions on the island. Lack of uniformity in the Book of Common Prayer opened the vista of two Prayer Books, with prayers for the king and Commonwealth in the Northern Ireland version only, and, in a worst-case scenario of schism, perhaps eventually two separate General Synods. Gregg was at pains to ensure that the church's unity would not be fissured. Religious partition would not and could not be countenanced. A. A. Luce, professor of Moral Philosophy and vice-provost of Trinity College Dublin, counselled against being stampeded 'into an orgy of liturgical regicide . . . for liturgical unity with our fellow Churchmen in the North is of first importance. If we are to remain one Church, we must retain the one Prayer Book'.[8] The unfolding debate revealed a generational divide among the Church of Ireland population in the South, which Gregg outlined to Geoffrey Fisher, archbishop of Canterbury from 1945 to 1961, in the following terms:

> It is hard to find anything that suits the conditions in Éire. We have amongst our own people there ardent Republicans who have no wish to hear the King's name – over against them being various of the British regime who will have the King, Republic or no Republic, and, as apart from these extremes, a central body of quiet worshippers who are ready to pray for all, without distinction, who are in authority.[9]

For the Church of Ireland population in the Republic, the state-prayers issue was also a turning point in terms of party political allegiance. Those who had supported Fine Gael in the February 1948 election, because the party was regarded as dependable on constitutional issues, were shocked when as Taoiseach John A. Costello seceded from the Commonwealth.

Bishop John Percy Phair of Ossory found it hard 'to understand why this measure has been introduced, especially since we were told expressly that no such change was contemplated. It has given a shock to many who like myself supported the ruling party at the election. Who is one to trust these days?' Another felt that the 'Government was guilty of breach of promise in the action they have taken'.[10] William Sheldon, an active member of the Church of Ireland, independent TD for Donegal East and future Senator, was bitterly critical of the government in the Dáil:

> To argue, that by going further apart we are getting nearer together, is an insult to the intelligence of those who have been repeatedly assured that Fine Gael desired association with the Commonwealth ... it should be recognised that there is a minority which believes that this nation could find full expression for its national outlook and at the same time remain within the comity of nations called the Commonwealth of Nations.[11]

Sheldon articulated a belief among the Church of Ireland population in the South that membership of the Commonwealth posed no threat to Irish independence and should not have been abandoned. This was reinforced by India's subsequent example of remaining within the Commonwealth as a republic. As Lord Rugby (Sir John Maffey), the first UK representative to Ireland, later expressed it, Costello 'brought about a position in which all the bridges went down between Éire and the Commonwealth'.[12] Confidence in Fine Gael had been previously undermined by a diplomatically unprecedented telegram to the Pope 'desiring to repose at the feet of your Holiness the assurance of our filial loyalty and of our devotion to your August Person'.[13] In a letter to the *Irish Times*, Victor Griffin, then a curate in Derry and future dean of St Patrick's Cathedral in Dublin, protested that the government of a state, which professed to be democratic and republican, should not on election to office 'set about publicising their subservience to a foreign pontiff or to any religious leader'.[14] The 'Mother and Child' débâcle of 1950–51 damaged Fine Gael further.[15] There was a reappraisal of Church of Ireland political opinion, in some quarters, in favour of Fianna Fáil who were seen as 'less supine in the face of ecclesiastical pressure'.[16]

A campaign to retain references to the king was initiated by Hugh Maude, a prominent Dublin layman. He was a member of the General Synod and of the diocesan council of Dublin, Glendalough and Kildare. St John Ervine's letter galvanised him into action lest widespread shock turn to pervasive apathy. His letter to the *Gazette* on 14 January 1949 opened a protracted debate:

> Exceedingly important to us, members of the Church of Ireland, is the possibility of any alteration in the prayers for His Majesty the King and

the Royal Family . . . The King binds us together as one great Christian family. It will be a bitter blow to a very large number in Southern Ireland if the State prayers are altered to preclude the King and the Royal Family.[17]

Maude was the exemplar of the landed, traditional, sentimental and 'British establishment' cohort more common of those born before independence and not at all representative of younger Southern members of the church, or indeed of middle- and working-class Protestants. In his view, kith and kin in the Commonwealth were bound by bonds of blood and religion which could not be severed, whatever the political situation. In a letter to David Wilson, dean of St Patrick's Cathedral, he revealed his fear that there 'is a faction in this country belonging to our own great people, who have become lethargic, I am afraid defeatist too in their outlook towards their Church of Faith, their Country and their King'.[18] Maude saw the state-prayers issue as an opportunity to arrest this lethargy among Southern Protestants.

Those opposed to retaining the state prayers as they stood were often, but not always, of the generation that had come of age since 1922 and had no inherited allegiance to the British crown. For instance, David Webb, the respected Trinity College botanist, accused Maude of doing a disservice to the Anglican Communion by suggesting that it was somehow conterminous with the British Empire and of refusing 'to face facts which, however unpalatable, remain facts'.[19] For others of Maude's ilk, although sentiment wrestled with hard facts, the new constitutional position had to be reflected in the liturgy. F. H. Garrett, a curate in Limerick, was firmly of the belief that 'in this matter facts and not sentiment must be the guide. And the hard facts are that the twenty-six Counties, whether one likes it or not, have become a Republic – a Republic outside the Commonwealth – in whose affairs King George VI has no say.'[20] Others, such as Sir Cecil King-Harmon, feared the entanglement of politics in religious affairs and concluded that one could 'always pray for the King in private'.[21] Similarly, an editorial in the *Irish Times* underlined that

> now a totally different situation has arisen. Henceforward, Irish Protestants in the South must make up their minds that they can have only one political allegiance; they must be unconditionally loyal to the Republic . . . they must not expose themselves to the taunt that they are in the State while not of it. [22]

The need to respond to the new constitutional position was clearly grasped by the House of Bishops, which appointed a sub-committee to investigate the implications as early as February 1949. Indeed, the bishops discussed the issue at their meetings in February, March, May and November 1949. Unlike 1937, there could be no return to the *status quo ante*. While anxious to safeguard church unity, Gregg was alert to the danger, should the political loyalty of the church appear ambiguous, of affronting the government in Dublin. He resolutely told Maude that 'this matter must, to some extent at any rate, be governed by the wishes of those who live in Éire. Change of some kind, I think, there must be'.[23] Each General Synod opens with a keynote presidential address by the Primate which highlights major events or decisions to be faced. Demonstrating firm leadership in May 1949, Gregg chose not to dwell 'on the change which has come over the political scene and which causes the members of this Synod to acknowledge two diverse loyalties'. Instead, he focused on the unity of the church by expressing 'the fervent hope that no change of political conditions will ever be allowed to mar the essential oneness of the Church of Ireland'.[24] He prudently revealed his sensitivity to those whose loyalties were to the Crown, but was nonetheless resigned to the inevitable:

> Many dwellers in the Republic will regret the loss of the familiar words, but what other way out is there? . . . For in our prayers, above all, there must be reality. And if the Republic of Ireland has left the Commonwealth . . . sad as I am sure the hearts of many will be, we must obey the call of our Christian duty, even if it wounds our sentiment.[25]

Other members of the House of Bishops were also careful not to alienate sections of their flock by appearing insensitive to imperial tradition and ties of kin. Bishop Tyner of Clogher told the diocesan synod at Clones, in October 1949, that it would be 'manifestly insincere to suggest that a legislative act of either Church or State could transform treasured and deep-rooted convictions'.[26] Nonetheless, he added that as a church they had an age-long tradition of loyalty to the constitution under which they were governed.

A *via media* had to be found to reflect the external political change in the Order of Public Worship in the Republic, while ensuring that the Book of Common Prayer used in Northern Ireland remained unaltered. Guidance had to be given to the clergy until a final formula was agreed. An interim statute was therefore passed at the 1949 General Synod. It made temporary provision for state prayers in churches outside Northern Ireland until permanent alterations could be introduced at the 1950 General Synod. Outside Northern Ireland, the term 'ruler' replaced 'king' in morning and evening prayer. Instead of a prayer for the king and Commonwealth, the following formula was used: 'Almighty God, who rulest over the nations . . . Grant to thy servants, The President of this

State and The Governor of Northern Ireland, and to all in authority, wisdom and strength to know and do thy will.'[27]

This did not satisfy Maude, who with Ernest H. Lewis-Crosby, dean of Christ Church Cathedral and a former chaplain to the Lord Lieutenant, feared that the House of Bishops might take unilateral action and present their people with a *fait accompli*. They vigorously advocated a round-table consultation before any permanent changes would be decided. After a meeting of like-minded, but unnamed, clergy and laity on 17 June 1949, Maude wrote to Gregg asking the House of Bishops 'to consider seriously authorising a prayer, in the interim period between the Synods, for the King's welfare . . . to be used as an occasional prayer, that would be voluntary, and said at the discretion of the clergy'.[28] However, this contradicted the very reason for an interim prayer, namely to remove discretion from the clergy. Gregg replied from Armagh in forceful terms. He argued that the bishops faced the novel situation, for which there was no constitutional provision, 'of there being *no* King. Accordingly, the only thing they could do was to come to the Synod and ask it to *cut the knot*' because, he continued, 'it would have been unfair to the clergy to leave the matter optional. They would have been under pressure to *pray* or *not* to pray for the King'. The letter's final line was a blunt reminder that 'the Church's governing body has spoken, and the Bishops – who asked it to speak – must obey'.[29]

Maude regarded the Primate's letter as 'an acknowledgement of weakness and of intimidation'[30] At the joint diocesan synod of Dublin, Glendalough and Kildare on 26 October 1949, he argued that 'if we pray sincerely for our country, we should at all times pray for Northern Ireland, the King thereof, and all in authority therein, and throughout the British Commonwealth of Nations'.[31] That the Standing Committee of the General Synod appointed a sub-committee to report on the matter in October 1949 was something of a victory for Maude's coalition. It allowed that faction at least the prospect of influencing what would come before the General Synod in 1950. Joseph Riversdale Colthurst, a retired Dublin clergyman, put it to Maude in military language: 'while we have hitherto been engaged in long-range bombing, we shall now be engaged in hand to hand fighting, having successfully breached the wall of the citadel!'[32]

The twelve-member sub-committee included Archbishops Gregg and Barton and the bishops of Meath, Derry and Ossory. Maude felt that with the exception of his associate Frank Fitzgibbon, a synodsman since 1932, and the bishop of Derry, the committee had been filled by Gregg with those opposed to retention of the state prayers. Archbishop Barton claimed that the nomination of the committee was left solely to Gregg.[33]

Following the death of Archdeacon William Webb in December 1949, Maude was co-opted as a member. The deliberations of the Standing Committee and its sub-committees have not been made public. However, a letter among Maude's papers reveals that it was Robert Boyd, bishop of Derry and Raphoe, who defused protest over the prayer for the king outside Northern Ireland. He ingeniously proposed the addition of the words 'in whose Dominions we are not counted as aliens', which he regarded as 'a reasonable ground why any citizen might pray for the King without imputing disloyalty to his own State'.[34] Thanking Maude the following year, Boyd felt that those attached 'to the older loyalties have much for which to be thankful with regard to the outcome of the Sub-Committee's efforts. For a minority [on the sub-committee] we achieved as much as we could expect, and that without too much tension'.[35]

The result of the sub-committee's deliberations was contained in a bill brought before the General Synod in 1950. In addition to the prayer for the king, the dilemma posed by prayers which contained references to him, such as morning prayer, was solved by the simple expedient of enclosing such references in square brackets prefixed with the letters N. I. Similarly, any words enclosed in square brackets prefixed with R. I. were to be used in the Republic only, where a prayer for the President and all in authority would be read. Thus only *one* Book of Common Prayer was used. Analogous minor amendments were made in the order for prayers and thanksgivings, communion, and catechism. Nevertheless, a residual loyalty to the Crown survived into the 1950s.

When King George VI died on 6 February 1952, the Standing Committee sent a letter of sympathy signed by Gregg on its behalf.[36] However, such sympathy was not simply confined to members of the Church of Ireland. President Seán T. Ó Ceallaigh asserted that the death of the king 'caused an extraordinary outburst of feeling everywhere. Even in Ireland, one could sense the depth of the sympathy that arose spontaneously'.[37] As international courtesy dictated, both the Taoiseach and the President sent letters of sympathy to Winston Churchill and Princess Elizabeth respectively. The government was represented at the funeral by Frank Aiken, Minister for External Affairs, and F. H. Boland, the Irish ambassador in London. On the day of the king's death, Eamon de Valera requested that flags be flown at half-mast on all state buildings and a week later he made a dignified statement in the Dáil, tendering on behalf of the Irish people 'a neighbourly understanding and a neighbourly sympathy'.[38] A memorial service, one of a number which took place in the state, was held in St Patrick's Cathedral on 15 February at which the President was represented by Colonel Ronald Mew and the government by Erskine Childers. One church dignitary recalled his father wearing a black tie to such a service in Tipperary.[39] Preaching in All Saints', Blackrock, County Dublin, on 10 February 1952, the Reverend Harry Dobbs felt that although members of the Church of Ireland were loyal citizens of the Republic,

> loyalty to the sovereign was in our blood . . . It is an imperishable thing, and we older people are not ashamed of our faithfulness, nor of the unchangeable affection we continued to give to the heirs of the English throne, especially to the King . . . [we] who were bound to him by invisible ties which no political revolutions could sever, grieve for his passing as deeply as do his own subjects.[40]

Prior to Queen Elizabeth's coronation, Gregg, who was English by birth, revealed lingering loyalties to the Crown. He began his presidential address at the 1953 Synod with the comment:

> We gather from different parts of this island, with their separate jurisdictions. And while those from Northern Ireland have their minds turned towards the forthcoming Coronation (an interest not wholly unshared by many of those who live in the Republic), Éire has been observing the three weeks devoted to An Tóstal [an Irish tourist festival inaugurated in June 1953].[41]

Asymmetrical demographics and their implications

Part of the anxiety engendered by the state-prayers issue was due to the Church of Ireland's asymmetrical population base. Though an all-Ireland body, in demographic terms the Church of Ireland had to contend with an expanding church population in some Northern Ireland dioceses and a declining minority marooned in the Republic. In 1949 the report of the diocesan council of Down and Dromore concluded with the comment: 'Our beloved Church, at the moment, has much cause for anxiety and much occasion for thankfulness. The increase of its numerical strength in the North cheers us; its continuing decrease in the South and West depresses us, but we are one.'[42] The skewed population base forced a stern and inevitable reappraisal of the Church of Ireland's labour and infrastructural resources and how best to deploy them in the 1950s and 1960s. Firstly, the degree of decline in the South and the reasons for it should be examined.

That population decline predated independence is often overlooked. Numerically, membership of the Church of Ireland declined from 693,357 in 1861 to 576,611 in 1911 prompting Archbishop John Crozier, the Primate, to highlight the 'dwindling population' outside north-east Ulster at the 1912 General Synod. However, whereas the Church of Ireland's population in Northern Ireland subsequently increased from 327,076 in 1911 to 344,800 in 1961 (24.2 per cent of the total population), the South witnessed a steady recession from 164,215 in 1926 to 104,016 (3.7 per cent of the population) in 1961. By 1971, it stood at 97,741.[43] This created a palpable sense of despondency among some members. Much of this decline was urban, in particular urban working-class, thus leaving Protestantism in the South 'a predominantly middle-class phenomenon'.[44] The greatest decline, of nearly a third in relative terms, occurred between the censuses of 1911 and 1926. In Monaghan, for instance, the Protestant population declined by almost twenty-three per cent compared to a decrease among Catholics of four per cent.[45]

These years witnessed the First World War, transition to independence (with the consequent withdrawal of the British army and other public servants and their dependents) and an emigration rate among the Church of Ireland community, estimated by Sexton and O'Leary, of over 15 per 1,000, or twice the contemporaneous rate for Catholics.[46] The rate of migration of Irish Protestants remained higher than that for Irish Catholics until after the Second World War. Brendan Walsh found that subsequently the emigration rate for Church of Ireland members was significantly lower, at all ages, than that among Catholics and other Protestant groups such as the Presbyterians.[47] Although the rate of overall Church of Ireland population decline fell, it still remained higher than that which applied to the population as a whole. Only in the 1970s did the Church of Ireland's population stabilise.[48]

The loss of younger members in the two decades before the Second World War precipitated a dwindling birth rate with the consequence that by the 1950s and 1960s, the age structure of the Church of Ireland in the South was old with a low marriage rate and low fertility. Weak natural increase was confirmed in an ESRI study by Walsh on religion and demographic behaviour for the period 1946 to 1961. It made gloomy reading. The *Ne Temere* decree, by which children of a mixed marriage were brought up as Catholics, was highlighted as the primary factor behind low fertility and declining numbers among the Church of Ireland community (*Ne Temere* is discussed in chapter five). A small, scattered Church of Ireland population in the South increased the likelihood of marriage across traditional religious boundaries. Walsh's study found that almost 200 OD (other denomination) grooms and 125 brides were married to RC partners in 1961, amounting to almost thirty per cent of all OD grooms and twenty per cent of all OD brides. By contrast, mixed marriages accounted for less than two per cent of all Catholic grooms and brides.[49] The most arresting demographic feature of the OD was its sheer weakness. Walsh pessimistically concluded that 'this weakness is far more serious than a mere failure to match the demographic strength of the RC population: any population which experiences a substantial natural *decrease* over a fifteen year period . . . between 1946 and 1961, is obviously in serious danger of eventual extinction'.[50] For many, the alternative to a mixed marriage was celibacy. This was singled out by Archbishop Gregg as a significant cause of population decline among his Southern flock as early as 1939.[51] The 1961 census revealed that over sixty per cent of Protestant males and forty per cent of Protestant women between the ages of twenty and forty were unmarried. However, in a follow-up study Walsh was less convinced that mixed marriages had an impact on the Church of Ireland birth rate and emphasised the Church of Ireland's old age structure and low birth rate.[52]

The steady erosion of the Church of Ireland population in the South had the inevitable consequence of shrinking the church network. A narrowing base had to bear an ever greater financial burden to maintain a superfluity of church property. The Church of Ireland had over twenty-four cathedrals – almost the same number as the Church of England.[53] In 1965 it supported twenty-nine deans, twenty-seven archdeacons and 145 canons in fourteen dioceses. By contrast, Welsh Anglicans had six dioceses with only six deans, fourteen archdeacons and sixty-five canons.[54] The Church of Ireland's *Administration 1967* report cited one area of fifty square miles in which 1,000 people maintained eight churches, six rectories and five halls.[55] Put simply, the Church of Ireland was overchurched in the South and understaffed everywhere but particularly in the North. In 1949 the diocese of Connor had an estimated population of about 107,500 in thirty-two parishes ministered to by twenty-eight incumbents, four curates-in-charge and thirty-five curate-assistants: approximately one clergyman for every 1,600 souls. There were six vacancies in Belfast city alone.[56] In 1965 the Church of Ireland population of Connor stood at 130,400. By contrast there were only 2,200 members in the diocese of Limerick.[57] Falling vocations so exacerbated the situation that by 1965 seven of the thirty-four individual dioceses had a ratio of 680:1 laity to clergy. But in the twenty-seven others, the ratio was 191:1.[58]

The shortage of vocations preoccupied church authorities throughout the 1950s and 1960s. On average only fifteen deacons were ordained which was half the minimum annual requirement.[59] In a pastoral letter on the subject in March 1952, Gregg stressed that the health of the church as a whole was reflected in the extent of its manpower and ability to self-propagate. While three-quarters of the Church of Ireland population lived in Northern Ireland, the Northern *confrères* did not measure up in terms of supplying clergymen with three divinity students for every five from the South. J. E. L. Oulton, regius professor of Divinity at Trinity College, suggested that 'if the North could make it five to three instead of three to five, the problem of manpower for the ministry would largely be solved'.[60] Many regarded inadequate stipends as responsible for falling vocations and these interrelated issues dominated debate at diocesan and national level. A fixed minimum stipend, first introduced in 1920, was augmented by parochial endowments in some parishes so that incomes varied from parish to parish. The Reverend J. F. W. Ruddell, incumbent of Killanne, Enniscorthy in County Wexford, wondered 'who but the wilfully blind would expect a young man to enter a ministry where conditions are such that he will have to devote to the hopeless task of trying to make ends meet the attention he wishes to give to God's service'.[61] Remedial action was taken in 1957 when minimum stipends were raised from £450 to £750 for incumbents and from £250–280 to £400 for curates. Increased again in 1962, the respective stipends were set at £950 and £600 in 1965. It is worth bearing in mind that the basic salary for a female or unmarried male secondary school teacher in the Republic in 1969 was £1,515.[62]

Did the preponderance of Southern born clergymen and clerical mobility complement the Church of Ireland's geographical sense of togetherness? Many Southerners served in Northern dioceses, and clergy in cross-border dioceses served parishes in both jurisdictions. While this undoubtedly bolstered religious unity, most clergy completed their ministerial careers in the diocese to which they were first appointed. Clerical mobility across dioceses, and not simply from North to South or vice versa, was less frequent, though not unknown. For instance, Roy Warke, future bishop of Cork, Cloyne and Ross, spent over two years in Newtownards, County Down before taking up duty in St Catherine's parish in Dublin in 1956.[63] Victor Griffin, a Wicklowman, spent twenty-two years in Derry, followed by twenty-two in Dublin as dean of St Patrick's Cathedral.

In terms of church property, by the mid-1950s it was reluctantly acknowledged that there had to be a trade-off between maintaining ancient or under-utilised buildings in sparsely populated rural parishes in the Republic and church extension in the urban centres in the diocese of Connor and the diocese of Down and Dromore. These dioceses also had to repair churches damaged during Second World War air raids; in Connor this was only completed in 1958.[64] Their diocesan council reports throughout the 1950s and 1960s catalogue the creation of new parishes and sustained church building. For instance, three new parishes (St Dorothea's, Gilnahirk; St Molua, Stormont; and Knocknagoney) were dedicated in Down and Dromore during 1959 alone.[65] Introducing the accounts and report of the Representative Church Body (RCB),[66] Howard W. Robinson warned the General Synod in 1963 that the church would have to tighten its organisation in the Republic to provide further finance and manpower for Northern Ireland.[67] With limited resources, the Church of Ireland had to decide whether it regarded bricks and mortar as more important than souls. This critical issue exerted an almost psychological domination over the General Synod and letter columns of the *Gazette* throughout the 1950s and 1960s.

The thorny issue of uniting small rural parishes was first addressed by the Sparsely Populated Areas Commission (SPAC) between 1956 and 1965, a sparsely populated parish being defined as one with less than fifty parishioners. Committees of enquiry, consisting of four commissioners, investigated the state of each diocese. There were two categories of review: one of areas with genuinely low population numbers, the other of areas where numbers were not especially low but had too many churches in use for that population base.[68] In each case the commission first consulted the diocesan council and then a panel of local commissioners. The subsequent reorganisation was responsible for closing some 144 churches. The City and Town Parishes Commission was the urban equivalent of the SPAC. It faced the modern phenomenon in Dublin of the church population moving from the city centre to the outer suburbs. In 1950 there were 197 churches and places of worship in the united dioceses of Dublin, Glendalough and Kildare for a population of 52,837.[69] Rationalisation in the South was paralleled by equally problematic expansion in the north-east. In 1962 the building fund for new churches and church halls in housing areas, particularly in Belfast, was increased from £200,000 to £250,000.[70] This grant from the RCB was complemented by diocesan development funds in Connor and Down and Dromore to meet the needs of church extension.

Administration 1967 continued the process of review. This committee, chaired by Archbishop Simms, was appointed by the Standing Committee of the General Synod in 1965 to investigate the state of the church at that time, its place in modern society, policy direction and priorities, and reform and reorganisation.[71] Archbishop James McCann, Gregg's somewhat reluctant successor as Primate, reminded his flock that 'the structure of our organisation was formed and adapted to the needs of a time far different from that of today'.[72] Although much fêted, this far-reaching report was poorly received. It 'far exceeded the vision of the General Synod and failed overall to win acceptance.'[73] This was partly due to proposals deemed too radical such as reducing the size of the General Synod, introducing team ministries and reducing the number of canonries and dignitaries. But it was also in part due to the lack of enthusiasm shown by the House of Bishops and to the death, in 1969, of Maurice Dobbin, the report's chief architect and lay honorary secretary to the General Synod.[74]

The responses to the SPAC and *Administration* betray a fixation with immutability. Many members of the Church of Ireland were conservatively and cautiously wedded to the maintenance of the *status quo* and trenchantly opposed the closing of churches. A sense of letting down the flag was understandable. In remote areas the church building itself provided an anchor and rallying point for a thinly spread and outnumbered Church of Ireland population. There were emotional attachments to burial grounds. The action of the SPAC was criticised for accentuating 'the gloom that hangs over many members of the Church in the South' but opposition did not deflect it from its task.[75] Recalibrating the settled parochial system required a change of mindset lest the Church of Ireland be imprisoned by its history. McCann presciently saw that

> to have a future is much more important than to have a past . . . What this Synod is being asked to do is to take a calm look – untinged with sentiment or emotion – at the day-to-day working and administration of our Church in the light of changes in population, money values and more especially in relation to the lives of men and women engaged in the work.[76]

Although serious infrastructural change was regarded as the ecclesiastical equivalent of draining the Shannon, adaptation to the demographic, financial and manpower reality was inescapable. For instance, in the diocese of Clogher there were sixty-three clergy and fifty-seven parochial units in 1947, but by 1965 this was reduced to forty-eight clergy and forty-six units, and by 1973, thirty-six units.[77] Similarly, in Derry and Raphoe the number of units fell from eighty-one in 1948 to sixty-two by 1972.[78]

It would be reasonable to suppose that a declining Church of Ireland population in the Republic with a contracting infrastructural base might have attenuated the ties of unity. However, there were several mediating factors, many stemming from the church's administrative structure, which helped counteract this. The Church of Ireland's long historical pedigree as the Dublin-centred former established church did not simply disappear. Although its demographic centre of gravity in the 1950s and 1960s was firmly in Northern Ireland, since Disestablishment its administrative capital remained in Dublin where the RCB was located. The General Synod met each May in Synod Hall adjacent to Christ Church Cathedral. Church of Ireland ordinands were trained in Trinity College. For 107 years the *Church of Ireland Gazette*, the Church's only national weekly publication and the longest running weekly church newspaper in Great Britain and Ireland, was published in Dublin. Though not an official organ, *faute de mieux* the comment of the *Gazette* was regarded as the touchstone of Church of Ireland opinion, as Andrew Willis (editor from 1955 until 1975) put it, 'not only within the church itself but to the outside world and in particular to the public press'.[79] A combination of financial difficulty and a low readership forced relocation to Belfast in October 1963, and with it a markedly more Northern news focus.

Southern members of the church were, due to population changes since 1868, over-represented at the General Synod. In 1965, for instance, the diocese of Armagh had a population of 41,200 represented by fifteen clerical and thirty lay synodsmen. By contrast, the united diocese of Dublin, Glendalough and Kildare had only 900 more members but thirty-two clerical and sixty-four lay representatives.[80] Although three-quarters of the Church of Ireland population lived in Northern Ireland, they made up only half the members at the General Synod. While demographically unrepresentative this has ensured that the Synod has not become intrinsically Northern in character. This inequity was occasionally highlighted at diocesan synod level. For instance, a member of the diocesan synod of Down and Dromore raised the matter in 1966 but the diocesan council decided not to pursue it. The annual excursion to Dublin, which on a personal and social level was regarded as a highlight of the church year, did not arouse protest from Northern members. Institutional inertia meant that despite being mooted by the *Administration 1967* report, the General Synod was not staged outside Dublin until 1986 when it was held in Belfast.

The General Synod appoints a medley of committees to oversee all aspects of church life. Composed of members from North and South, with various political perspectives, these committees have played a significant but understated role in maintaining church unity. They have enabled a fluidity of interaction of members of different political persuasions throughout the year. In the view of one church dignitary, the Church of Ireland 'holds together and . . . the secret to this is that the committees are cross-border and always have been.'[81]

However, where a political jurisdiction directly impinged on an issue such as education, with two separate educational systems and government departments, sub-committees have been the norm. The General Synod Board of Education, which covers the whole island, met once a year to rubberstamp the findings of its Northern Ireland sub-committee and its Republic of Ireland counterpart. Similarly, in 1961 a Broadcasting Committee was set up to cover the whole island and consisted of a Northern and Southern sub-committee. There have been calls for a stronger committee system, one more representative of the General Synod and the views expressed in it, with an appointments board to oversee this.[82] However, the important point remains that both the committee system and the General Synod helped moderate political diversity and facilitated the appreciation 'that deeply held political views or aspirations are not necessarily incompatible with being a loyal churchman or protestant'.[83]

The 'Ripon affair'

Given that the Church of Ireland acknowledged Ireland to be divided politically but not ecclesiastically, did the increasing salience of the political border in the 1950s and 1960s endanger the principle of hands across the border? During the IRA border campaign, between 1956 and 1962, both the Church of Ireland and Catholic Church endured the disruption of spiked roads. Edward Moore, Church of Ireland bishop of Kilmore, Elphin and Ardagh (which included portions of Cavan, Leitrim and Fermanagh and had a population of 9,200 at that time) articulated such concerns to Seán Lemass in September 1961. The bishop told the Taoiseach of 'a very real fear that these lawless men will not hold any life sacred . . . in the Fermanagh area it has added grave difficulties to my clergy in carrying out their pastoral duties, and damaged bridges and roads have cut off people from the churches.' Moore suggested a review of the Offences against the State Act, believing 'that penalties ought to be imposed in line with the gravity of the offence, particularly where the sovereignty of our state is being challenged, and you and your government are being flouted if not mocked'.[84] Lemass instructed Nioclás Ó Nualláin, secretary to the government, to liaise with Peter Berry, secretary of the Department of Justice, as well as the Attorney General, before drafting a reply. The Taoiseach shared Moore's 'concern at the Border outrages and their unhappy consequences for all our people'. He assured the bishop that all was being done to bring to an end the IRA's futile campaign, which the government had 'repeatedly condemned as conducive to the perpetuation instead of the abolition of the Border'.[85] This exchange illustrates the challenges for a diocese and a church that operated across political jurisdictions at a time when the legitimacy of Northern Ireland was contested. It was therefore not surprising that the Church of Ireland, just as the other major denominations, welcomed the ground breaking meeting between Lemass and Terence O'Neill, the Northern Ireland Prime Minister, in January 1965. The General Synod unanimously supported a motion by Canon Henry Lamb, rector of Lisnadill, County Armagh, in favour of cross-border talks and harmony between people of all religious and political affiliations.[86]

For the most part, members of the Church of Ireland were able to set aside their religious and political allegiance at General Synods and committee meetings. However, fault lines were exposed where these adherences intersected. This was particularly so with regard to the Orange Order which was distasteful to many in the South. The 'Ripon affair' in 1967 illustrates that despite ecclesiastical unity there was no affinity between Southern and Northern members *vis-à-vis* the proper influence of the Orange Order.

John Moorman, bishop of Ripon, served as senior Anglican observer at the Second Vatican Council. He was invited to St Anne's Cathedral, Belfast on 6 February 1967 to address the Irish Church Association on the conversations between Canterbury and Rome. Founded in 1935, the Irish Church Association was a body of Church of Ireland clergy and laity representative of a cross-section of Church of Ireland opinion which met periodically in Belfast for lunch and the presentation of a paper. The threat of an outbreak of violence by the Orange Order and extreme Protestants prompted Cuthbert Peacocke, the dean of St Anne's, to withdraw the invitation at the behest of the Northern Ireland government which could not guarantee that the police would be able to maintain the peace.[87] Moorman himself received numerous menacing letters, one threatened to shoot him if he made a Belfast address. The incident revealed a sinister and uncompromising opposition to ecumenism headed by Ian Paisley, who labelled Moorman 'the Pope's quisling'.[88] It exposed the inherent contradictions of a dual loyalty to the Church of Ireland and the Orange Order (who denied responsibility for the cancellation) and opened a charged debate, on the Orange Order's relationship with the Church of Ireland, that persists to this day.[89] Brian Harvey, canon theologian of St Anne's Cathedral, felt it necessary to tell a congregation on Sunday 5 February 1967, on which day Moorman was due to preach, that

> The Orange Order itself has no constitutional relationship with the Church of Ireland; and no one must ever think that the Orange Order has any constitutional right to dictate or even give the impression of dictating about what the Church of Ireland or any Church of Ireland group does.[90]

The withdrawal of Moorman's invitation was extremely damaging to the reputation of the Church of Ireland and through it to the Primate. Even before 1967, Archbishop McCann was seen to capitulate to Low Church criticism. When the infamous canon 36, which forbade a cross to be placed on or behind the holy table, was amended in 1964 by 273 votes to sixty-three, McCann continued to forbid a cross in the churches of his diocese lest he be accused of 'Romish' leanings. A meeting of the

House of Bishops on 14 February discussed the circumstances surrounding the cancellation of Moorman's lecture and produced a statement for publication. This meek response did not mention the Orange Order by name and was a weak effort to contain the damage. Expressing its 'deep concern' that the threat of organised disturbance had prevented a bishop of the Anglican Communion addressing a meeting, the bishops' statement unconvincingly reaffirmed the belief in 'freedom of speech throughout the community' and 'the right of our Church to order its own affairs without let or hindrance'.[91] Surprisingly, the affair was not on the agenda of the Standing Committee of the Church of Ireland, even though Bishops Elliott of Connor and Mitchell of Down and Dromore both had seats in St Anne's and would have been expected to comment.[92] It fell to J. L. B. Deane, the prominent Cork layman and Standing Committee member, to have the Ripon affair debated. Deane argued that the subtext of the Ripon incident was 'whether the affairs of the Church of Ireland are to be settled by the competent authority in its free and unfettered judgment or whether decisions are to be forced on it by threats, by bullying, or by pressure groups'.[93] Dismayed at the lack of episcopal comment, he believed that silence merely encouraged the bully to try again. The *Gazette* also seemed afraid to speak out. However, the daily press in Northern Ireland was more openly critical. The *Belfast Telegraph* upheld the right to speak and even the pro-unionist *Belfast News-Letter* spoke of 'regret at the weakness that has led us into this latest débâcle of dishonour. The hope must lie with the future, that this distasteful affair will be the last retreat. If it is not, then spiritually, socially and economically God help Ulster.'[94]

The appearance of weakness and timidity by the House of Bishops was deeply unsettling for Southern members of the Church of Ireland who expressed a sense of shame. T. J. Thompson, diocesan secretary and treasurer of Leighlin, Killenane and Bagenalstown, asked:

> Why is there no condemnation of Orangeism? Surely if the Orange Order takes upon itself, as it has done in this instance, to dictate to the Irish Church as to whom it may or may not invite to occupy its pulpits, the time has come for a firm declaration that membership of this organisation is incompatible with membership of the Church of Ireland. Principle is more important than numbers.[95]

Following the resignation of Dick Ferguson, Unionist MP for South Antrim, in October 1969, ostensibly because he had parted company with the Orange Order, an editorial in the *Irish Times* wondered

> how happy, in the present circumstances is the Most Rev. Dr Simms to have among his clergy members of the Orange Order? It is not good enough for

him to call for restraint and moderation, if clergymen of his own discipline, by that membership alone, are siding with provocation and aggression.[96]

The following year another editorial felt the most fitting celebration of the centenary of Disestablishment would be to 'disestablish all connection between clergy of the Church of Ireland and this distressful organisation'.[97] While the overall number of Church of Ireland members of the Orange Order was small, many Northern clergy and indeed some bishops were members. Robert Elliott, bishop of Connor from 1956 to 1969, was a Grand Chaplain of the Grand Lodge of Ireland and marched each year in 12 July processions. Ironically, Gregg refused to join either the Masonic or Orange institutions as he felt that their members 'forfeited independence of judgment'.[98] However, Victor Griffin argued that if this moderate element left it 'would mean the complete surrender of the Order to the extremists . . . [who] will gain a tremendous advantage in using the whole set-up to propagate their views, especially among the young people of the country areas'.[99] In response to a query from the British Council of Churches, Eric Gallagher, a leading Methodist, suggested the critical problem for church leaders was that the

> vast majority in the Order have never worked out the implications of membership. They equate loyalty to their Faith (or to the faith) which can be a good thing with the assumption that it is to be defended by pressures, activities, selectivity in employment, housing etc. and direct representations on the Unionist Party Council. They have an obsessive fear that the future of Protestantism in Northern Ireland is in great jeopardy.

Gallagher believed that it was necessary to 'develop a ferment of thought and a crisis of conscience inside the Order itself'.[100]

Archbishop McCann seemed over-anxious to avoid controversy. There was a sense that the warm-hearted but self-effacing Primate felt inadequate, squeezed between Gregg's shadow and Simms's rising star. Writing to Simms in 1970, McCann referred to his incumbency in Armagh as being a 'caretaker, nothing more – and not even a very worthy one'.[101] In his last address as President of the General Synod, he appealed for the Church of Ireland to 'be seen to be firmly opposed to all forms of fanaticism – religious or political. There must be no compromise with those who stand for intolerance, bigotry or hatred.'[102] But the burden of leadership had become too great for him and he resigned in July 1969. At the diocesan synod of Cork, Cloyne and Ross, in October 1969, a motion by J. A. D. Bird – that the bishops of Northern Ireland 'must get the clergy out of the Orange Order which is an anachronism and has no place in Ireland today' – was overwhelmingly carried.[103] Captain Lawrence Percy Orr, Imperial Grand Master, MP for South Down and leader of the Unionist MPs at Westminster, argued that the Orange Order was the best guarantee for justice, peace and prosperity in Ulster and accused Bird of being misled. But the *Belfast Telegraph* felt that it was Orr who was misinformed.[104]

The Orange Order was unbending, even towards members of the House of Bishops. The career of Richard Hanson as bishop of Clogher is a case in point. Educated in Trinity College Dublin, Hanson was an old friend of George Simms. He was professor of Christian Theology at Nottingham University when he accepted the see of Clogher offered to him by the House of Bishops in December 1969. After his consecration on St Patrick's Day 1970, he wrote to Simms expressing the hope that his archbishop would 'have no reason to regret [his] act'.[105] Ill-fatedly this did not prove so. A man of great integrity and intellectual prowess, the progressive and liberal-minded Hanson was fearless, if brusque, in both his sincere commitment to ecumenical dialogue and condemnation of extremism. Addressing the diocesan synod in May 1971, he exhorted those present to

> throw off this unworthy spirit of fear and of unthinking conservatism. We must play our part confidently as a middle and mediating tradition between Roman Catholicism and Protestantism . . . If we succeed in this, we shall not only have found integrity, honesty and a true role as a Church, but we shall have deserved well of all communities and both the states in Ireland.[106]

But in the conservative rural diocese of Clogher such a bishop was the proverbial square peg in a round hole. Decrying the political crisis and the indiscriminate disregard of life, limb and property in Northern Ireland the following year, he called on Christians and churchmen to refrain from marching and flag-waving. At an Irish Association gathering in Virginia, County Cavan, on 30 September 1972, Hanson, apparently unaware of the presence of reporters, tongue-in-cheek compared the Orange Order to the Mafia and a Sunday school. This was misrepresented in the press and a storm of vituperation and vilification was unloosed on him which led inexorably to his resignation.

In an explanatory letter to Simms, Hanson stressed that his criticism centred on the public utterances and unrelenting hostility to the Catholic Church displayed by leaders of the Order. In the bishop's view

> whether the Order intended this or not, it made for religious division. I do not think that this amounts to destructive or unfair criticism. I believe that members of the Orange Order must take account of the fact that their Order is being criticised severely by an increasing number of people in Ireland, both North and South of the Border.[107]

That was not how the outraged select vestry of Rossorry parish, which represented a significant number of members of the Church of Ireland around Enniskillen, saw it. A letter signed by fifteen members accused Hanson of attempting 'to discredit and distort the political aspirations of the vast number of the Church of Ireland people living in Ulster, of both those within and without the Orange Order.'[108] In their opinion, the bishop had betrayed his clergy and people who would no longer welcome him or regard him as their spiritual leader. Letters pouring scorn on Hanson's comments from equally indignant Orangemen filled the letter columns of the *Impartial Reporter* during October. One letter pointed out that Hanson's predecessor Richard Tyner had been Grand Master of the Grand Black Chapter of County Monaghan.[109] One senses what Hanson endured by his reply to a suggestion by G. B. Newe, the former Minister of Community Relations, at a meeting of Protestant and Catholic Encounter (this is discussed in chapter five) in November 1972, that clergy should be more courageous in their preaching. For a clergyman to do what Newe suggested would, Hanson believed, result in disturbing the laity, forfeiting income, losing both standing in the diocese as well as the goodwill of fellow clergymen and might entail becoming the 'target of vilification, attack, distrust, hatred and direct insult for an indefinite period.'[110] Such action would be akin to undergoing a martyrdom of sorts. By the end of March 1973, Hanson could endure the martyr's fire no longer and resigned his bishopric to return to academia as professor of Historical and Contemporary Theology at Manchester. In a mildly defiant farewell address, Hanson acknowledged that in his public utterances he did not always give credit for the fellowship and friendship of the people. But he told them to be confident enough in the security of their own position to be understanding and open towards others, 'for their church to commit itself publicly to one particular line in politics was to deny its catholicity and to brand their church a sect.'[111] His three-year tenure in Clogher was the shortest of any incumbent in the twentieth century in that diocese. In a most poignant letter to Simms, symbolically written on Good Friday 1973, Hanson admitted that he had not been a successful bishop, being too intellectual and without the common touch:

> Because it was mainly at your persuasion that I came originally, I feel I have particularly betrayed you in leaving so soon. But I think that had I had to endure another summer or so of Orange parades and Orange flags flown on Churches in [the] Clogher diocese I would have had a nervous breakdown and been no use to you anyway . . . I shall miss greatly the companionship of the Episcopal bench.[112]

Tellingly, Hanson's replacement, Robert Heavener, rector of Monaghan, was a member of the Orange Order.

The role of the Church Committee

The 'Ripon affair' did, however, have both short and longer term consequences. On being consecrated bishop of Derry and Raphoe in January 1970, Cuthbert Peacocke resigned from the Orange Order of which he had been a member for more than forty years. That the *Gazette* felt it necessary to applaud this decision as 'wise, courageous and properly episcopal' and an example to the clergyman 'uncertain about the rightness of his continued membership' of the Orange Order indicates the degree to which the relationship was hitherto unquestioned.[113] However, Peacocke's appointment generated controversy. Members of the diocesan synod of Cork, Cloyne and Ross regarded it as a pay-off for the cancellation of Moorman's visit in 1967.[114] Representations were made to Alan Buchanan, archbishop of Dublin from 1969 to 1977, for a forum to discuss such matters. This appears to have coalesced with a growing demand for a specialist committee to consider the church's position with regard to political, ethical and social issues affecting its members, North and South. The result of this grassroots pressure was the formation of the Role of the Church Committee at the instigation of, and presided over by, Archbishop Buchanan.

Appointed by the Standing Committee in 1970, the Role of the Church Committee presented influential annual reports to the General Synod. It also commissioned appendices on specific issues for the Church of Ireland clergy and laity. The Committee was high profile in media terms and high powered in composition.[115] Its fifteen members included prominent laypeople such as J. L. B. Deane and John A. Young, both honorary secretaries to the General Synod; the bishops of Connor, Derry, Down and Dromore; two future bishops in Samuel Poyntz and Robin Eames; and Dean Victor Griffin. The latter felt that the members 'were not the conservative element of the Church of Ireland.'[116] The Committee met about seven times a year to consider the work of its sub-committees which met about once a month.[117] Eric Elliott, incumbent of St Thomas's in Belfast, was honorary secretary. The Role of the Church Committee was soon seen to act as 'a think-tank for the Primate of All-Ireland and the House of Bishops, briefing others, meeting political leaders, identifying and interpreting public issues, preparing statements and helping to co-ordinate the Church's response.'[118] The demand for comment on an increasing number of social and ethical issues had escalated in the late 1960s.

Given the traumatic political situation in Northern Ireland from 1969 onwards, the Role of the Church Committee 'was equally committed to the problems facing the Church of Ireland, North and South'.[119] The Troubles forced the Church of Ireland to reconsider the interpenetration of politics and religion. Andrew Willis intimated his 'very definite impression as an observer with a foot on either side that we have steadily grown apart over the past 25 years. I mean the two parts of [the] C of I'.[120] He did not avoid solemn self-criticism or provide self-absolution in the pages of the *Gazette*. He believed the Church had failed to improve community relations, rather 'we have paddled in the political puddle. We have compromised and temporised and played the party game. We have, at best, generalised and platitudinised. And we cannot shirk our share of the blame or wash our hands of the consequences.'[121] The Troubles heightened the disharmony among the Church of Ireland exposed by the 'Ripon affair', as Southern members tried to distance themselves from events in Northern Ireland. In August 1969, a notice in the press by Colonel and Mrs O'Callaghan-Westropp of O'Callaghan's Mills, County Clare declared that they were 'so thoroughly ashamed of our co-religionists in the Six Counties of Northern Ireland that we no longer wish to be considered Protestants'.[122] Dean F. K. Johnson of Cork articulated a similar sentiment and declared that fifty years of Unionist government in Northern Ireland had 'produced the present holocaust', whereas Southern Protestants 'have been fairly and honourably treated as first class citizens and have been happily integrated into the community'.[123]

The advent of the Troubles fuelled a concern that divergent political partisanship threatened the Church of Ireland's collective religious unity. The first annual report of the Role of the Church Committee in 1972 opened by referring to the civic, social and political tensions of the time which were 'still more formidable for us, since our members live in two States within one island.'[124] That this anxiety was writ large is hardly surprising given the Northern background of many members. This included Archbishop Buchanan, the chairperson, who, as bishop of Clogher from 1958 to 1969, had first hand experience of dealing with two political jurisdictions within one diocese. Tellingly, one of the final recommendations of the 1972 report emphasised the importance of developing 'personal contacts and dialogue between members and organisations of the Church of Ireland in parishes north and south of the border.'[125] They were not the only Church of Ireland body to do so. The same point was raised some months before, in September 1971, at a meeting of the Armagh Board of Social Responsibility. Two types of split were feared: firstly, at parish level, where discontented people might establish a free Church of Ireland, and secondly, a rupture between the Church of Ireland in the Republic and that in Northern Ireland. The Board emphasised that 'such a situation can hardly be contemplated and everything possible will have to be done to ensure that the danger is eliminated' and it endorsed especially the need for greater understanding between members of the church, North and South.[126] Its members considered it important for Southern members of the church to understand that the vast majority of their brethren in the North were loyal subjects of the Crown but not necessarily members of the Unionist Party. Addressing the Kilmore Clerical Association on 23 November 1971 at Kildrumferton Rectory, County Cavan, on whether the Church of Ireland was threatened by a schism, Eric Elliott underlined the 'fear in the North that the rift up there might easily be reflected in the Church as well.'[127]

As will be seen in chapter three, the first report of the Role of the Church Committee was highly critical of mixed marriages and family planning in the Republic, almost to the exclusion of the inequalities and problems in Northern Ireland. One member attests that these were well-aired and that consequently criticism of the Republic was intended to provide some form of balance to redress perhaps unwarranted complacency in the South.[128] Criticism of the Republic was also reassuring for the majority of the Church of Ireland who resided in Northern Ireland and endorsed their claim for retaining the Union.

Against this backdrop, the Committee welcomed the establishment of an interdepartmental unit within the Department of External Affairs by the Minister on 28 May 1970. This comprised representatives of the Departments of External Affairs, Taoiseach and Finance. It had a brief of staying abreast of all aspects of Anglo-Irish relations having a bearing on Northern Ireland, the study of short-term problems and long-term solutions and advising on the creation and maintenance of contact with various responsible groups in Northern Ireland.[129] It was not a policy-making unit but reported to the Taoiseach. The Role of the Church Committee furnished the interdepartmental unit with copies of General Synod policy statements. It also met the All-Party Oireachtas Committee on the Implication of Irish Unity[130] on 23 January 1974, to discuss the position of Protestants in the Republic, family-planning, border security and mixed marriages, as well as individual politicians such as John Hume, Brian Lenihan and Charles Haughey.[131]

In terms of unity across the two political jurisdictions, the reports of the Role of the Church Committee in the early 1970s provided a sort of palliative for the concerns of the Church of Ireland's Northern members. It may, therefore, as Kenneth Milne argues, have 'provided a safety-valve for members from the North at a time of high feelings'.[132] The Committee helped deepen the understanding among its members of differing political standpoints across the Church of Ireland and the reasons for them, hitherto often poorly understood. It thus ensured that religious unity would not be compromised by competing political aspirations.

It is arresting to reflect on the often understated impact of partition on the Church of Ireland. A twenty-five per cent minority was dramatically transformed into being simultaneously a five per cent minority and part of a two-thirds majority in the respective political jurisdictions. That political, economic and cultural divergences had distanced members on either side of the border is incontrovertible. Nevertheless, the Church of Ireland has remained an all-Ireland church devoid of religious borders. Precisely because it is not itself partitioned, the Church of Ireland has proudly regarded itself as a unifying factor between the political jurisdictions.[133] The importance to the Church of Ireland of maintaining its religious unity was no subsidiary theme and religious unity was the watchword throughout the quarter century from 1949 to 1973. Though tested, this has never been subverted. This was in part structural as the Church of Ireland's administrative organisation reflected a desire to accommodate and moderate political diversity within an all-Ireland framework. It was also in part demographic. Though small in number, Southern members were not simply adjuncts to a predominantly Northern church. The significant size of the church's Northern Ireland population was tempered by the nominal nature of some of its membership. Reacting angrily to suggestions made in the *Gazette* of a North-South division in terms of church work, Charles Tyndall, bishop of Derry and Raphoe from 1958 to 1969 and previously bishop of Kilmore, Elphin and Ardagh, pointed out that he personally knew both sides of the border intimately and both kinds of church work: 'There is one ministry, one Church, one people, North, South, East and West and the cure of souls is equally valid and equally necessary whether numbers are large or small.'[134] Lastly, unity was in part a guiding principle. For these reasons, the Church of Ireland held together despite stern challenges at both ends of the period discussed. After mid-century, the state-prayers issue removed public expressions of loyalty to the Crown in the South as a unifying factor. By 1973, the volatility of the Northern political situation threatened to hollow out this religious union. Indeed for some, political friction lent only greater piquancy to religious unity. The Irish historian, J. C. Beckett, argued that if the Southern minority disappeared

> the prospects of a lasting peace in Ireland would be greatly reduced. The Northern Protestants would feel, not without reason, that he was right in regarding the border as a necessary bulwark against Rome; and the chances of cordial co-operation between the two parts of the country, not very good at present, would disappear altogether . . . It is hardly an exaggeration to say that the future of Ireland depends upon the future of the Church in the Republic.[135]

The enduring and unshakeable ties of creed have ensured, perhaps despite the odds, that two branches of Anglicanism, one on either side of the political border, have not developed.

Notes

1 *Journal of General Synod* (henceforth *JGS*) *1949*, President's address, 10 May 1949, p. lxxxiii.
2 House of Bishops, Minutes of Meetings (henceforth HB), vol. ii, meeting of 27 April 1938, p. 3; meeting of 15 December 1938, p. 13.
3 Diary entry: 'Wednesday December 14th 1938 (Dublin)', Diana Mansergh (ed.), *Nationalism and Independence. Selected Irish Papers by Nicholas Mansergh* (Cork, 1997), p. 133.
4 Representative Church Body Library (henceforth RCBL), Simms Papers, MS 238/1/7, Letter Gregg to Simms, 24 January 1939.
5 *Church of Ireland Gazette* (henceforth *CoIG*), 19 December 1958, p. 1.
6 *JGS 1939*, 'Report of Proceedings of Standing Committee', pp. 209–10.
7 RCBL, Maude Papers, MS 262/1/2, Copy St John Ervine's letter to *The Times*, 23 December 1948. The Republic of Ireland Bill was introduced into the Dáil on 18 November 1948, signed by the President on 21 December and came into operation on Easter Monday 18 April 1949. See Ian McCabe, *A Diplomatic History of Ireland, 1948–49. The Republic, the Commonwealth and NATO* (Dublin, 1991).
8 *CoIG*, 28 January 1949, p. 9.
9 Lambeth Palace Library (henceforth LPL), Fisher Papers, vol. 72, fol. 302, Letter Gregg to Fisher, 3 January 1950.
10 RCBL, Maude Papers, MS 262/1/1/2/1, Letter bishop of Ossory to Lord Templemore, 10 December 1948; MS 262/1/1/2/39, Letter ('private') Edward Grant to Maude, n.d.
11 *Dáil Debates* (henceforth *DD*), vol. 113, cols. 442–3, 24 November 1948.
12 University College Dublin Archives Department (henceforth UCDA), de Valera Papers, P150/2940, Letter Rugby to de Valera, 18 May 1957.
13 Cited in Dermot Keogh, 'The role of the Catholic Church in the Republic of Ireland 1922–1995', in *Building Trust in Ireland. Studies Commissioned by the Forum for Peace and Reconciliation* (Belfast, 1996), p. 130.
14 Victor Griffin, *Mark of Protest. An Autobiography* (Dublin, 1993), p. 82.
15 For recent research on the 'Mother and Child' scheme, see Finola Kennedy, *Cottage to Crèche. Family Change in Ireland* (Dublin, 2001) and John Horgan, *Noël Browne. Passionate Outsider* (Dublin, 2000).
16 Kenneth Milne, 'Brave new world', in Stephen R. White (ed.), *A Time to Build. Essays for Tomorrow's Church* (Dublin, 1999), p. 21.
17 RCBL, Maude Papers, MS 262/1/1/2/11, Copy letter Maude to *Gazette*, 5 January 1949; printed in *CoIG*, 14 January 1949, p. 10.
18 Ibid., MS 262/1/1/2/17, Draft letter Maude to Wilson, 19 January 1949.
19 *CoIG*, 28 January 1949, p. 9.

20 *Ibid.*
21 RCBL, Maude Papers, MS 262/1/1/3/56, Letter Cecil King-Harmon to Maude, 7 May 1949.
22 *Irish Times* (henceforth *IT*), 14 May 1949.
23 RCBL, Maude Papers, MS 262/1/1/2/26, Letter Gregg to Maude, 4 February 1949.
24 *JGS 1949*, p. lxxxiii.
25 *Ibid.*, pp. lxxxiii–iv.
26 *Impartial Reporter* (henceforth *IR*), 6 October 1949.
27 *JGS 1949*, p. cxxxviii.
28 RCBL, Maude Papers, MS 262/1/1/3/94, Copy letter Maude to Gregg, 17 June 1949.
29 *Ibid.*, MS 262/1/1/3/98, Letter Gregg to Maude, 22 June 1949. Gregg's emphasis.
30 RCBL, Maude Papers, MS 262/1/1/4/101, Copy letter Maude to Rina Ingram, 29 June 1949.
31 *Ibid.*, MS 262/1/2, Speech to the joint diocesan synod, 26 October 1949.
32 *Ibid.*, MS 262/1/1/4/137, Copy letter Colthurst to Maude, 24 October 1949.
33 RCBL, Maude Papers, MS 262/1/1/5/156, Copy letter Maude to Frank Fitzgibbon, 10 November 1949; RCBL, General Synod 2/16, Standing Committee sub-committee on state prayers, Letter Barton to John Briggs (assistant secretary of the General Synod), 24 October 1949.
34 RCBL, Maude Papers, MS 262/1/1/5/178, Letter bishop of Derry to Maude, 3 December 1949. The prayer for King George VI read: 'Almighty God, the fountain of all goodness, we humbly beseech thee to behold they servant, King GEORGE the Sixth, in whose dominions we are not accounted strangers. Endue him with thy Holy Spirit; enrich him with thy heavenly grace; prosper him with all happiness; and bring him to thine everlasting kingdom; through Jesus Christ our Lord', *JGS 1950*, p. xcv.
35 RCBL, Maude Papers, MS 262/1/1/5/193, Letter bishop of Derry to Maude, 10 March 1950.
36 *JGS 1952*, 'Report of Proceedings of Standing Committee', p. 92.
37 National Library of Ireland (henceforth NLI), Shane Leslie Papers, MS 22848, Letter Ó Ceallaigh to Leslie, 25 February 1952.
38 National Archives of Ireland (henceforth NAI), Department of the Taoiseach (henceforth DT) S 15256A, Minute by Nioclás Ó Nualláin (assistant secretary DT), 6 February 1952; Minute of 7 February 1952; *DD*, vol. 129, col. 410, 13 February 1952.
39 Interview with Very Rev. Robert MacCarthy, February 2002.
40 RCBL, Crawford Papers, MS 402/6, Copy of sermon delivered by Dobbs on 10 February 1952.
41 *JGS 1953*, President's address, 28 April 1953, p. lxxxiii.
42 *Report of the Down and Dromore Diocesan Council to the Diocesan Synod 1949*, p. 21.

43 Thomas Keane, 'Demographic trends', in Michael Hurley (ed.), *Irish Anglicanism 1869–1969* (Dublin, 1970), p. 169; Acheson, *A History of the Church of Ireland*, p. 251.
44 Martin Maguire, 'The Church of Ireland and the problem of the Protestant working-class of Dublin, 1870s-1930s', in Alan Ford, James McGuire and Kenneth Milne (eds), *As by Law Established. The Church of Ireland since the Reformation* (Dublin, 1995), p. 202.
45 Terence Dooley, *The Plight of Monaghan Protestants 1912–26* (Dublin, 2000), p. 47. For Protestant population decrease by county between 1911 and 1926, see Enda Delaney, *Demography, State and Society. Irish Migration to Britain, 1921–1971* (Liverpool, 2000), appendix 6, p. 305.
46 J. J. Sexton and Richard O'Leary, 'Factors affecting population decline in minority religious communities in the Republic of Ireland', in *Building Trust in Ireland*, p. 263. Bowen estimates that the withdrawal of the British army accounted for a quarter of the decrease in Irish Anglican numbers, see *Protestants*, p. 22. Delaney highlights the impossibility of establishing *exact* figures but suggests that at least over 60,000 Protestants who were not directly connected with the British administration left the South between 1911 and 1926. See Delaney, *Demography*, pp. 71–3.
47 Brendan M. Walsh, 'Trends in the religious composition of the population in the Republic of Ireland, 1946–71', *Economic and Social Review*, 6: 4 (1975), p. 555.
48 Sexton and O'Leary, 'Factors affecting population decline', pp. 260–2.
49 Brendan M. Walsh, *Religion and Demographic Behaviour in Ireland* [ERSI Paper No. 55] (Dublin, 1970), pp. 27–8. Bowen estimated that between sixteen and twenty-two per cent of Irish Anglicans were marrying Catholics in the 1960s, see *Protestants*, p. 41.
50 Walsh, *Religion*, p. 34. Walsh's emphasis.
51 *JGS 1939*, pp. lxxviii–ix.
52 Walsh, 'Trends in the religious composition', pp. 554–5.
53 Megahey, *Irish Protestant Churches*, p. 9.
54 *Administration 1967*, appendix T, p. 123.
55 Ibid., p. 49.
56 *CoIG*, 20 May 1949, p. 7
57 *Administration 1967*, p. 48.
58 Ibid., p. 36.
59 HB, vol. ii, meeting of 17 February 1955, 'Candidates for the Ministry. Preliminary report, October 1954', p. 128.
60 *CoIG*, 25 November 1955, p. 5.
61 *CoIG*, 19 November 1954, p. 9.
62 R. B. McDowell, *The Church of Ireland 1869–1969* (London, 1975), p. 129; NAI, DT 2001/6/25, Proposals of the minister for Education on Teachers' Salaries and Allowances.
63 Roy Warke, *Ripples in the Pool* (Dublin, 1993), p. 37.
64 *Report of the Connor Diocesan Council for 1957*, p. 2.

65 *Report of the Down and Dromore Diocesan Council for 1959*, p. 8.
66 This was incorporated in 1870 to administer the temporalities of the disestablished church. It acted as trustee of money and property at the church's disposal in the absence of state intervention. The RCB was composed of the bishops as well as one cleric and two laymen elected by each diocesan synod for a three year term. Its most important committee was the Finance Committee which met about twenty times a year in the 1950s and 1960s.
67 *IT*, 17 May 1963.
68 HB, vol. ii, meeting of 14 May 1956, pp. 146–7; *Commission for the Sparsely Populated Areas. Reports to the General Synod 1957–1965*, 'Report to the General Synod, 1957', p. 6.
69 *Report of the Dublin Diocesan Council and the Glendalough and Kildare Diocesan Councils to the Diocesan Synods*, 23 October 1951, p. 23.
70 *JGS 1962*, pp. xcii–iii.
71 *JGS 1965*, 'Report of Proceedings of Standing Committee', p. 67.
72 *Ibid.*, President's address, 11 May 1965, p. xlvi.
73 Lesley Whiteside, *George Otto Simms. A Biography* (Gerrards Cross, 1990), p. 113.
74 HB, vol. iii, p. 54. 'Observations on *Administration 1967*', 18 December 1967; confirmed in conversation with J. L. B. Deane, April 2002.
75 *CoIG*, 26 September 1958, p. 5; confirmed in conversation with J. L. B. Deane, one of two surviving members of the SPAC.
76 *JGS 1967*, President's address, 9 May 1967, p. xlvii.
77 James Mehaffey, *One Family* (Dublin, 1983), p. 23; Letter Thomas Moore to author, 4 February 2003.
78 Calculated from *Derry and Raphoe Diocesan Synod Reports* (henceforth *DRDS*).
79 *The Church of Ireland Magazine*, 5: 1 (1970), p. 1.
80 *Administration 1967*, p. 48; Wilson, *How the Church of Ireland is Governed*, p. 30.
81 Interview with Very Rev. Victor Griffin, April 2002.
82 J. L. B. Deane, 'General Synod: retrospect and prospect', *New Divinity*, 1: 1 (1970), p. 18.
83 RCBL, Clerical Society of Ireland, MS 142/3, Minute Book 1938–1971, *Problems and Opportunities for the Church of Ireland*', presented at A. G. M., 17 November 1971.
84 NAI, JUS 8/1133, Copy letter Moore to Lemass, 5 September 1961.
85 *Ibid.*, Letter Lemass to Moore, 9 September 1961.
86 *JGS 1966*, p. lxiii; *Irish Press* (henceforth *IP*), 12 May 1966.
87 *Belfast News-Letter* (henceforth *BNL*), 15 February 1967; LPL, Diaries of John Moorman, MS 3655, entry for 27 January 1967.
88 LPL, Diaries of John Moorman, MS 3655, entry for 20 January 1967; Michael Manktelow, *John Moorman: Anglican, Franciscan, Independent* (Norwich, 1999), p. 72.

89 On the current debate, see Earl Storey, *Traditional Roots. Towards an Appropriate Relationship between the Church of Ireland and the Orange Order* (Dublin, 2002).
90 *CoIG*, 10 February 1967, p. 1.
91 HB, vol. iii, meeting of 14 February 1967, p. 19.
92 Interview with Rt Rev. Roy Warke, April 2002 and with J. L. B. Deane, April 2002.
93 RCBL, Deane Papers, MS 438/20, Copy of introduction to a motion for the Standing Committee.
94 *Belfast Telegraph* (henceforth *BT*), 30 January 1967; *BNL*, 4 February 1967.
95 *CoIG*, 3 March 1967, p. 3.
96 *IT*, 8 October 1969.
97 *Ibid.*, 13 May 1970.
98 See George Seaver, *John Allen Fitzgerald Gregg Archbishop* (London, 1963), p. 334.
99 RCBL, *Irish Anglicanism*, MS 487/1/14, Letter Victor Griffin to Michael Hurley, 26 August 1969.
100 RCBL, Simms Papers, MS 238, Copy letter Eric Gallagher to Kenneth Sansbury (general secretary British Council of Churches), 25 June 1971.
101 RCBL, Typescript by Roy Warke, *A Sixties Man. Some Reflections on the Primacy and Retirement of the Most Rev. James McCann* (2001), p. 4–1.
102 *JGS 1969*, President's address, 20 May 1969, p. xlvii.
103 *IT*, 31 October 1969.
104 *BT*, 7 November 1969.
105 RCBL, Simms Papers, MS 238/1/8, Letter Hanson to Simms, 22 March 1970.
106 *IR*, 3 June 1971.
107 RCBL, Simms Papers, MS 238/1/8, Letter Hanson to Simms, 6 October 1972.
108 *Ibid.*, Copy of letter John F. Clanachan (honorary secretary select vestry) to Hanson, n.d.
109 *IR*, 26 October 1972.
110 *Ibid.*, 9 November 1972.
111 *Ibid.*, 5 April 1973.
112 RCBL, Simms Papers, MS 238/1/8, Letter Hanson to Simms, 20 April 1973.
113 *CoIG*, 30 January 1970, p. 2.
114 Interview with J. L. B. Deane, April 2002. Peacocke's wife, Helen, was a prominent member of the Unionist Party and his brother, Anthony, was Inspector-General of the RUC in 1969.
115 Victor Griffin felt that it had a higher profile than the Standing Committee itself. Interview with Victor Griffin, April 2002.
116 *Ibid.*
117 *Ibid.*
118 Letter Samuel Poyntz to author, 13 March 2002. Bishop Poyntz was a member from the beginning and later acted as chairperson of the

Committee from 1978–1995. Buchanan was succeeded as chairperson by Bishop Gordon Perdue in 1976. The Committee was replaced by the Church in Society Committee in June 2001.
119 *Ibid.*
120 RCBL, *Irish Anglicanism*, MS 487/1/13, Letter Willis to Michael Hurley, 22 August 1969.
121 *CoIG*, 29 November 1968, p. 2.
122 *Irish Independent* (henceforth *II*), 20 August 1969.
123 *BT*, 18 August 1969 cited in Megahey, *Irish Protestant Churches*, p. 165.
124 *JGS 1972*, 'Report of the Role of the Church Committee 1972', p. 250.
125 *Ibid.*, p. 255.
126 RCBL, Simms Papers, MS 238, Copy letter Douglas J. Crozier (general secretary Armagh Board of Social Responsibility) to the board, 4 September 1971.
127 RCBL, Kilmore Clerical Association, MS 403, 'Minutes 1963–77', 23 November 1971.
128 Interview with Victor Griffin, April 2002; see also report of a sermon by Griffin, *IT*, 5 July 1971 in which he attests that in the Republic a blind eye is turned to the 'shambles in their own backyard'.
129 NAI, DT 2001/6/549, Letter Nioclás Ó Nualláin to private secretary Minister for External Affairs, 28 May 1970.
130 This was an informal committee established to find common ground between political parties 'on the constitutional, legal, economic, cultural, social and other relevant implications of a united Ireland' and to make recommendations to this end. [See NAI, DFA 2000/14/462, Copy statement by Jack Lynch in Dáil Éireann, 4 May 1972]. It was to meet all important sectors of public opinion in the Republic and Northern Ireland. Fianna Fáil was represented by Michael Kennedy (chairperson), Patrick Smith, Vivian de Valera and Frank Carter; Fine Gael by Thomas F. O'Higgins, Richie Ryan and Patrick Harte; Labour Party by James Tully and Conor Cruise O'Brien. The committee was re-established by Liam Cosgrave after the 1973 election. The membership remained the same but with the addition of Joe Brennan for Fianna Fáil; Garret FitzGerald and Declan Costello replacing O'Higgins and Ryan and Barry Desmond replacing James Tully. Patrick Harte was chairperson.
131 *JGS 1974*, 'Report of the Role of the Church Committee 1974', p. 248; letter Samuel Poyntz to author, 13 March 2002; interview with Victor Griffin and J. L. B. Deane, April 2002.
132 Milne, 'Brave new world', p. 23.
133 See for example Stephen A. Cave, *Our Church in History* (Dublin, 1954), pp. 36–7.
134 *IR*, 30 September 1965.
135 *CoIG*, 31 July 1970, p. 5. For an appraisal of Beckett's own inclusivist political philosophy, see Alvin Jackson, 'J. C. Beckett: politics, faith, scholarship', *Irish Historical Studies*, 33: 130 (2002), pp. 129–50.

2

'The indivisible island': the Catholic Church and the border

Ut Christiani ita et Romani sitis. (Book of Armagh)

To commemorate the fifteenth centenary of the death of St Patrick, the Catholic Church declared 1961 a Patrician Year. Expressing thanks to President Eamon de Valera for attending the St Patrick's Day celebrations in Armagh, William Conway, auxiliary bishop to Cardinal John D'Alton and future Primate of All-Ireland, revealed his belief that the occasion symbolised 'the spiritual unity of Ireland'.[1] Furthermore, he felt that the 'delay in achieving political unity' did not matter 'so long as the deeper sense of unity of the Irish nation remain[ed]', which was important 'not only for the nation but also for the Church.'[2] For the Catholic Church, unlike the Church of Ireland, there was never the same pressing sense of having to keep a Northern and Southern wing united. However, in the 1950s and early 1960s the Catholic hierarchy's ideal of an 'indivisible island' was by no means a foregone conclusion.[3] The bishops had to meet the challenge of the IRA 'border campaign' which was carried out, for the most part, in those dioceses that straddled the border. Under the adroit leadership of Cardinal John D'Alton, their response contributed in a very significant way to a re-evaluation of the national question, though this has not received the historical attention that it merits. The supra-state aspect of ecclesiastical unison, alluded to by Conway, also had to be safeguarded in the Catholic Church's relations with the Holy See. In this it was supported by the Irish government, whose foreign policy dealings with the Vatican were informed by the fusion of the political and the geographical image of 'the indivisible island'. This helped ensure that the Holy See would neither recognise partition in the ecclesiastical sphere nor downgrade the standing of the archbishop of Armagh, who, as leader of the Irish church, was seen as a unifying figure across the border.

Responses to partition and the border campaign

The appointment of John D'Alton, a native of Mayo, as archbishop of Armagh in 1946 was a departure from modern tradition. He was the first Connacht-born bishop to be appointed to the see of Armagh since Anthony Blake in 1758. The *Leader* argued that a non-native of Northern Ireland could see, perhaps more objectively, 'all the forces of division and of unity' in a diocese which straddled the border, and play 'more successfully the unifying role which history has imposed upon the occupant of the See of St Patrick'.[4] As will be seen in chapter four, there was a notable thaw in relations between the hierarchy and the Northern Ireland government during D'Alton's seventeen-year episcopacy. In a letter of congratulations and welcome, Austin Quinn, parish priest of Drogheda and later bishop of Kilmore from 1950 until 1972, remarked: 'No doubt a partitioned Diocese with one government none too friendly will present problems, but as far as the priests are concerned I think I can assure you that you will find a very friendly atmosphere.'[5] At his enthronement on 13 June 1946, D'Alton spoke of the 'tragedy of partition'. He contrasted the 'Primatial See of Armagh [which] happily knows no artificially created boundaries' with 'the political partition of this island of ours which God intended to be one and undivided'.[6] Such a reference to partition was not unusual for an episcopal consecration in the 1940s. Neil Farren, bishop of Derry from 1939 until 1973, referred in his enthronement address to 'the mutilation of our country'.[7] Similarly, Eugene O'Callaghan, bishop of Clogher from 1943 until 1969, spoke of 'the evil of partition' which he deemed 'in the eyes of the world as the very negation of statesmanship . . . stupid in conception' and militating 'against the possibility of good citizenship'.[8]

It would be unhistorical to ignore the point that the older bishops such as Daniel Mageean, bishop of Down and Connor from 1929 until 1961, Bishop Eugene O'Doherty of Dromore and Bishop O'Callaghan were Northerners who were born, reared, educated and ordained before the onset of partition in 1920. But as bishops, they were the second generation of prelates since partition and were, therefore, less emotive and more pragmatic on the national question than perhaps it was emotionally possible for their predecessors to have been. For instance, Charles McHugh, bishop of Derry from 1907 to 1926, was so implacably opposed to partition that he claimed he and his fellow Northern bishops would prefer another fifty years of British rule to 'a divided Ireland'.[9] Nevertheless, Mageean et al. were old enough for the unity of Ireland to be an underlying and deeply felt reality that could not be gainsaid. Indeed, during the Anglo-Irish negotiations in 1938, Mageean, among others, issued a 'strongly-worded letter' to de Valera rejecting partition and highlighting the grievances of the minority.[10] The sentiments expressed in the enthronement addresses above simply reflected the traditional nationalist view of partition which placed the blame on Britain for engineering an artificial division of an island which geographically was one entity comprising one nation.

Politically this unquestioned orthodoxy was embodied in the North in the Anti-Partition League, founded in Dungannon on 14 November 1945, and in the South in the umbrella All-Party Anti-Partition Conference established in January 1949. The latter asserted the 'right of the Irish people to the ownership and control of all the national territory', and repudiated 'the right of Britain to carve up the Irish nation or to occupy any portion of it'.[11] The object of the Anti-Partition Campaign was naive: create a hurricane of propaganda at home and abroad so as to compel the British to leave Ireland. The banging of the anti-partition drum in the international arena at the Council of Europe – the so-called 'sore thumb' policy – did little to elevate Irish reunion and much to demean Irish foreign policy. Indeed it was inimical to Irish unity. As John Bowman put it, 'such was the nature of Partition that frontal pressure tended only to reinforce it'.[12] In one of his 'Reports from the North', Séamus McCall privately commented that 'the greatest service it [the Anti-Partition League] could render to the cause of Irish unity would be to commit hari-kari'.[13] The monotonous chorus-line of 'partition must go' led into a political cul-de-sac. Irish insistence on making partition a European issue found little sympathy among continentals, who regarded Britain as a liberator from wartime tyranny.[14] Clare O'Halloran is correct in her assessment that a 'striking characteristic of the campaign was its timelessness, its reiteration of the anti-partitionism of previous decades'.[15] However, it is too simplistic to argue that the received wisdom on partition did not alter in substance, as opposed to tone, in the latter part of the 1950s and 1960s. It is equally facile to fall into what Eithne MacDermott calls 'the trap of hindsight history . . . the superimposing of current attitudes and outlooks on former contexts' by deriding all nationalists for being uncompromisingly irredentist.[16] How could those born before partition be otherwise?

It is important to recognise that the bankruptcy of the Anti-Partition Campaign, which exhibited a surfeit of sentiment but not enough common sense, followed by the general condemnation and failure of the IRA border campaign contributed to a change of outlook with regard to the partition issue from the late 1950s. Throughout that decade, individuals such as Ernest Blythe strenuously argued that the very underpinning of the anti-partition campaign, British culpability, was incorrect or at least misleading. In the opening sentence of *Briseadh na Teorann* (the smashing of the border), Blythe states that partition was a symptom of Northern Protestant opposition to a united Ireland, rather than its cause *per se*.[17] As early as 1949, a cycling holiday in Northern Ireland convinced Seán Ó Nualláin of the strength of the Protestant fears of religious discrimination and economic loss and

> how little our people in the South know of the interests and activities of their fellow countrymen across the Border . . . so far as the generation that has grown up since 1920 is concerned, the Six Counties is a place apart, almost a foreign country.[18]

The Northern Catholic bishops played an important, but understated role, in the recalibration of attitudes towards a realisation of the need for reconciliation and cooperation between North and South. In May 1959 Bishop O'Callaghan described partition as a cancer damaging Ireland through duplication of public services and the consequent dissipation of national effort and resources.[19] At a political level, as Michael Kennedy illustrates, anti-partitionist rhetoric gave way to the necessity of economic cooperation as the 1950s progressed. On this foundation the Lemass-O'Neill meeting would later occur.[20] It is in this context that Cardinal D'Alton's proposed federal solution to partition in 1957, which is discussed below, must be viewed. Tellingly, bishops enthroned in the 1950s no longer spoke of the tragedy of partition because the IRA campaign and loss of life changed the valency of the national question. However uncomfortable the hierarchy may have been with the dismemberment of the island unit, it was unshakeably opposed to physical force nationalism.

The opposition of D'Alton, who was made a cardinal in January 1953, and his brother bishops to partition was less emotionally profound than that of their predecessors. D'Alton was unequivocal in his condemnation of the IRA, which the previous archbishop of Armagh – Cardinal Joseph MacRory, labelled a 'rabid anti-Partitionist' – found difficult, even during the trying years of the Second World War.[21] In a Christmas letter to Mageean in 1942, MacRory admitted that for a long time he had

> been troubled about the IRA but I think it would do more harm than not to attempt to pull them up. We are unable to pull up their aggressors, against whose injustice they act. That most of them have no scruple of conscience about what they do and these [*sic*] would continue their course in spite of anything we might say. The whole matter is very annoying and . . . it is all down – and for centuries – to the unjust interference of another nation in our country's affairs.[22]

Over a decade later, D'Alton had no hesitation in 'pulling up' the IRA after an attack on Gough Barracks in Armagh on 12 June 1954 when fifteen men carried off 300 guns. This was in contrast to somewhat sympathetic opinion elsewhere. For instance, two members of Cavan County Council, Councillors Sheridan and O'Reilly, congratulated the fifteen raiders.[23] Further incidents followed. The military barracks in Omagh was attacked on 17 October 1954, and Fianna Uladh, a republican splinter group led by Liam Kelly, raided Roslea RUC station on 27 December 1956.[24] Preaching on Christmas Eve 1954, Cardinal D'Alton therefore appealed

> to our young men not to have recourse to methods of violence in their eagerness to end the unnatural division of our country. The injustice of Partition is so glaring that it cannot continue. But every true lover of Ireland should pray that it will end in an atmosphere of goodwill. There is surely sufficient good will on both sides to bring about a settlement that will be satisfactory to all, that will respect honestly held convictions, and help to remove old prejudices and allay fears, however ill-founded they may seem.[25]

There is no archival evidence to suggest that the Cardinal was prompted by the Northern Ireland administration. His thoughtful statement, welcomed by the *Belfast Telegraph* as 'wise advice', recognised the strength of opinion on partition, but was unambiguous in its condemnation of violence as a means to its end and sought to transmute this brand of nationalism.[26] This encapsulated the hierarchy's line on the national question for the remainder of the 1950s. It reaffirmed the second inter-party government's abjuration of force as a solution of the problem of partition.[27] The consent of the majority in Northern Ireland would be required for any potential reunification. John Charles McQuaid, archbishop of Dublin, was also utterly opposed to physical force nationalism. A rare insight into his thinking is provided in a letter of reply to Gerald O'Hara, the papal nuncio, who alerted McQuaid to the visit of Father Lodge Curran, a maverick anti-partitionist American priest whose rash statements had displeased the American hierarchy and his superior, Bishop Thomas Molloy of Brooklyn. McQuaid informed O'Hara that 'in the present discipline of the Diocese, I do not permit any priest to make any political pronouncements.'[28] Furthermore, he expressed the view that

> the anti-Partition campaign in the United States has been in very poor taste, ill-advised and, to a great extent, destructive of the aim that it would achieve. The invasion of this country by American agitation can (again, in my own view) have but one effect in the long run: the secret promotion of violent methods, in substitution of constitutional methods that will inevitably appear to the young people to be slow and ineffective.[29]

During 1955 both political and ecclesiastical authorities were concerned at a recrudescence of Sinn Féin-IRA support and activity. Sinn Féin named candidates for all twelve Northern Ireland seats in the 1955 Westminster election. It secured the nationalist seats of Mid-Ulster and Fermanagh-South Tyrone, where the Nationalist Party did not stand against their candidates. Sinn Féin received a total of 152,310 votes, nearly fifty thousand greater than the anti-partition vote of 1949.[30] In tandem with this electoral success went a military campaign called 'Operation Harvest', which persisted sporadically from 1956 until 1962 with guerrilla-style attacks on military and economic targets in Northern Ireland. This campaign was conducted in the border counties and deeply concerned the Northern bishops.

Their response was to launch a campaign of their own on both an individual and collective basis, to moderate and restrain the frustrations felt by those who believed their misfortunes stemmed from the perceived injustices of partition. The bishops' chief weapon was the public statement, particularly the Lenten pastoral and Christmas sermon. Throughout the border campaign this weapon was not allowed to rust or lose its uncompromising edge. Violence was the antithesis of God's law. In an opening salvo in St Patrick's Cathedral Armagh on Christmas Eve 1955, D'Alton repeated his appeal to young men for calm.[31] In St Eugene's Cathedral, Derry, Bishop Farren prayed for peace: 'Injustice and wrongdoing cannot be righted by further wrong-doing, and I would urge those who have influence with the young people today to encourage patience and turn their backs on force as a means of settling our difficulties here in Ireland.'[32] These statements were similar in logic and tone to the warnings of de Valera against the understandable but counterproductive resort to violence with its potential loss of life.[33]

The centrepiece of the hierarchy's offensive came in early 1956. The previous September, D'Alton floated the idea to Bishops Farren and Mageean of issuing 'a statement at the October meeting regarding Unauthorised Armed Forces, without mentioning the IRA. The statement . . . might stress in particular the basis of State Authority, and the sole competence of the State to raise an army and declare war.'[34] A joint statement by all members of the hierarchy was drawn up but, for unmentioned reasons, publication was postponed until 29 January 1956. Read at all masses throughout Ireland, the statement set down the precise conditions under which it was lawful to wage a just war and declared it a mortal sin to belong to a secret organisation:

> No private citizen or group or organisation of citizens has the right to bear arms or to use them against another state, its soldiers or citizens . . . it is a

mortal sin for a Catholic to become or remain a member of an organisation or society which arrogates to itself the right to bear arms and use them against its own or another state; that it is also sinful for a Catholic to co-operate with, or express approval of, or otherwise assist any such organisation or society, and that, if the co-operation or assistance be notable, the sin committed is mortal.[35]

This was not the first time that physical force nationalism met the wrath of the Catholic hierarchy, as condemnations of the Fenians in 1863 and Republicans in October 1922 testify. But neither was it the first time that such condemnation was ignored, even by ardent Catholics such as Seán South. A member of the Legion of Mary and *Maria Duce* (an extreme Catholic group discussed in chapter three), South was killed in the IRA raid on Brookeborough barracks in 1957.[36] Sir Gilbert Laithwaite, former British ambassador in Dublin and Permanent Under-Secretary of State for Commonwealth Relations, put it to Frederick Boland, the Irish ambassador in London, that the 'type of young man concerned was not, however, likely to be unduly deterred by ecclesiastical opposition.'[37] This encapsulated the chief difficulty confronting the hierarchy.

Twelve months later, the outpouring of national sympathy following the deaths of South and Fergal O'Hanlon in an attack on Brookeborough barracks in County Fermanagh on New Year's Day 1957 manifested a popular sympathy for, and ambivalence towards, the IRA campaign. The advice of the hierarchy had been completely disregarded, if not defied. Jeremiah Kinane, archbishop of Cashel, thought it 'a scandal' that those so killed 'should be getting High Masses'.[38] To show its disquiet at the recalcitrant minority who continued to fight against partition by joining a secret organisation, the Standing Committee of the hierarchy republished the 1956 pastoral at a meeting on 15 January 1957. D'Alton further added that 'while deploring with the general body of our countrymen the effects of partition, no matter how good and desirable the ending of partition may be, the use of unlawful means to bring it about would not be justified'.[39] The statement continued, 'those who express sympathy with them share to some extent in their guilt, encourage their continuance, and endanger the peace of the whole community and preservation of ordered government, which is the most important safeguard of that peace'.[40] For their part, the Church of Ireland bishops also issued a statement, in February 1957, deploring 'the campaign at present being waged against Northern Ireland which involves the illegal and immoral use of force and which has resulted in loss of life and widespread destruction of property'.[41]

Of the Northern dioceses, Clogher, which comprises parts of Monaghan and Fermanagh, was most acutely affected by the IRA campaign. Fergal O'Hanlon was a twenty-year-old from Monaghan town who worked as a County Council clerk. His family received a vote of sympathy from Monaghan Urban District Council and County Council. His funeral in St Macartan's Cathedral, on 4 January, attracted a large crowd which included the two local Fianna Fáil TDs, Patrick Mooney and Eddie Kelly.[42] Bishop O'Callaghan was gravely concerned by these events. In an address at Roslea Church, three days after the O'Hanlon funeral, he asked his priests to read the bishops' statement of January 1956 at all masses, on Sunday 13 January, lest there be any ambiguity.[43] This was followed by a considered and subtle analysis of the situation in a lengthy Lenten pastoral in March 1957. In what the *Northern Standard* regarded as a 'masterly treatment of [an] all-important subject', O'Callaghan did not deny that 'there is an injustice to the nation, imposed from without and supported by a minority within', or that all were 'painfully aware' that 'there is obstinate and subtle discrimination against Catholics and nationalists in the separated counties'.[44] Like his brother bishops, he was adamant that any

> solution of the national problem is the right and duty of the freely elected representatives of the people, not the self-imposed task of any lesser group or organisation, however determined in character or sincere in purpose. No upsurge of emotion, no expression of popular sympathy for youth sadly and unwisely sacrificed for an ideal can blind us to principles or absolve us from the obligation of pronouncing what we believe to be the law of God ... We have the constitutional means to redress our grievances, and if our progress along these lines is too slow for our more impetuous citizens that is not a sufficient reason for disowning the methods of peace and exposing the whole population to the turmoil and confusion of internecine strife ... The border is not merely a geographical division. It is a spiritual division of minds and hearts which physical force cannot heal, but only aggravate.[45]

His closing statement reflects a deepening analysis of the national question. We see in embryonic form what became known during the Troubles, as a 'divided society' paradigm. The general election in March 1957, which served as a barometer of the popular mood in the Republic of Ireland portion of his diocese, increased O'Callaghan's anxiety. Eineachán Ó hAnnluain, brother of the late Fergal, was elected for Sinn Féin with 4,791 votes, coming second in the poll behind James Dillon of Fine Gael who received 5,894 first preferences. This was one of four seats won by abstentionist Sinn Féin candidates and the first time since 1932 that Fianna Fáil had won only one of the three Monaghan seats.[46]

If the laity's appetite for heroic sacrifice had grown, then the hierarchy's response was to cut off further feeding by constantly reminding that, in D'Alton's words, 'acts of violence will not advance the cause they have at heart'.[47] The Northern bishops relentlessly warned that membership of any secret organisation was a mortal sin. Furthermore, they stressed that wanton destruction of property was a breach of justice. Farren told a Confirmation congregation in May 1960, that such damage even if done 'in the name of patriotism by organisations, which in the eyes of, and by a declaration of the Church, are illegal and immoral, makes it nonetheless sinful, nor does it remove the obligation of restitution'.[48] On the very subject of patriotism, Bishop William Philbin of Clonfert rejected the notion that patriotism and nationalism were indistinguishable. He argued that the bedrock of all patriotism was serving the people of the country and 'since they can be helped in other ways than by alteration in the structure or status of the state, it follows that patriotism can take other forms than the political'.[49] Foremost in his mind was economic patriotism to help raise living standards in Ireland. Interestingly, two years later, Seán Lemass also linked patriotism with economic success.[50] In tandem with condemning violence as a means of ending partition, Cardinal D'Alton similarly tried to give a positive lead in the other direction by advocating a federal solution to the partition conundrum in February 1957.

The 'D'Alton plan'

Such a proposition by the Cardinal was unprecedented. It indicates not only a concern to move beyond physical force's dialectic of promise and failure, but also a desire to sanctify cooperation between North and South, despite his belief that it 'would certainly be a tremendous relief to us here in the Six Counties if the border disappeared'.[51] Given his office, D'Alton, though he claimed to speak solely in a personal capacity with 'no desire to enter the arena of party politics', instantly commanded recognition from the press, the laity, his fellow bishops and the governments.[52] His pragmatic and considered views appeared in an exclusive interview (the text of which appears to have been prepared in advance) with journalist Douglas Hyde on 19 February 1957. This was first published in the *Observer* on 3 March and subsequently in the Irish daily press on 4 March. Citing the example of cooperation between France and Germany, who moderated their concept of sovereignty to their mutual advantage, the Cardinal argued that a 'spirit of good will' and a 'sympathetic understanding of the other's point of view' would ameliorate 'the deplorable condition of things caused by partition'.[53] His first proposal was that each of the six counties be allowed decide whether it wished to remain under the Northern Ireland parliament or come under Dublin's jurisdiction, with those preferring the *status quo* retaining their parliament in Belfast. If the Northern government agreed to unite with the South, D'Alton proposed as a *quid pro quo* that Ireland 'associate itself with the Commonwealth as an independent Republic on the same basis as India'.[54] This link, he felt, would safeguard the shipbuilding industry, while linen production would profit on the US market as a united Ireland commodity. He presciently raised the question of the European free market and the contribution a united Ireland could make to it. Referring to greater interdependence among western nations, he even suggested that 'a reunited Ireland should offer bases to NATO'.[55] However, there were prerequisites if a satisfactory solution were to be found to partition. In particular, the Cardinal mentioned 'the ending of the present system of gerrymandering and of unfair discrimination against the minority, which are the sources of much bitterness and irritation'.[56] In return he believed that the nationalist minority should give their full cooperation to the Northern parliament in solving the problems of Northern Ireland. 'The policy of keeping step by step with England', D'Alton argued, 'has not to my mind, contributed greatly to their solution'.[57] He concluded his interview with the rider that despite his hesitation at giving the interview for fear of being misunderstood, the suggestions were necessary to break the current deadlock.

Cardinal D'Alton's intervention was generally well received as a constructive move in the right direction and was reported widely in the press at home and abroad.[58] The *Irish Times* felt that he

> set a high minded example to political leaders on both sides of the Border, and has established – or rather, lifted out of obscurity and neglect – terms of reference which now will be less easily ignored than heretofore. His words are a reminder that bitterness will do nothing to solve Ireland's problems, which can be tackled only by taking objective thought, compounded of realism – a sense of things as they are – and of vision – a sense of things as they ought to be.[59]

Oddly, the *Irish Press* was too busy recording business at the polls on 5 March to comment on D'Alton's proposals. The *Irish Catholic* also did not comment. Sir Graham Larmor, President of the Irish Association, described the Cardinal's comments as the 'outstanding contribution' towards the solution of Ireland's problems in recent months and praised their clarity and attitude of realism.[60] The *Leader* similarly regarded D'Alton's contribution as 'the only statesmanlike solution so far proposed for partition in terms of Irish duties as well as Irish rights . . . He put the onus on both sides to recognise that they were living in the twentieth century, not the sixteenth'.[61] One commentator in the *Spectator* thought that the proposals were not 'remotely practicable for the present', but felt that the Cardinal had 'done something to break the stranglehold on Irish public opinion of a nationalism better suited to the battles of the past than to the needs of the future'.[62] The *Belfast Telegraph's* major objection, which it made on behalf of both Protestants and Catholics, was that the proposal jeopardised the standard of living in Northern Ireland.[63]

As one might expect, D'Alton's brother bishops were very supportive. Bishop Joseph Rodgers of Killaloe congratulated him on his 'very practical and courageous proposals'.[64] Bishop Austin Quinn argued that it was

> obvious that rethinking is needed, and I feel that it will have to be done along the lines you have suggested. Whether any of us will live to see your words bear fruit may be questioned, but I have no hesitation in saying that you will never regret them.[65]

Archbishop Joseph Walsh of Tuam thought 'the body of the people are delighted with your pronouncement . . . you have done a very good work and we are all proud of you'.[66] William Conway reported that in both Maynooth and Dublin he 'heard nothing but the highest praise of it as a superb concept excellently expressed and I feel . . . to the credit of the Church'.[67] D'Alton's proposal was also transmitted privately to members of the US hierarchy by Sir Shane Leslie of Glaslough, County Monaghan. Author and convert to Catholicism, Leslie was a privy chamberlain to Pope Pius XI and regularly corresponded with D'Alton. During a six-month lecture tour in the US in 1957–58, Leslie met the cardinals of Los Angeles and Chicago and delivered D'Alton's greetings and copies of his proposals 'for temporarily settling the irritation on the Ulster border' to them. He left further copies 'with other sympathetic Archbishops'.[68]

Government reaction was cool in the North, sceptical in London and cautious in the South. To Unionist ears, it seemed that Cardinal D'Alton's proposal inferred the bartering of Northern Ireland within a Commonwealth context. It was hardly surprising, therefore, that Brian Faulkner, Unionist Party Chief Whip, thought that the suggestion was irrelevant for Northern Ireland because it had always been part of the United Kingdom.[69] Basil Brooke, the Northern Ireland Prime Minister, also dealt roughly with the suggestions. Speaking in Belfast, he argued that 'even if 100 per cent of the English people thought that partition was wrong and we in Northern Ireland decided we were going to maintain partition, it is for us to decide it'.[70]

Sir Alexander Clutterbuck, the British ambassador in Dublin, regarded the Cardinal's ideas as an 'unexpected development', but considered there was much that was 'courageous and sensible' in them, as they demanded 'concessions from both sides'.[71] He was generous enough to believe that D'Alton would have taken 'careful soundings' before making his suggestions and 'it may be therefore that there are persons of influence here who would not be totally unreceptive to such suggestions and would welcome a break from present rigid patterns of thought'.[72] However, Clutterbuck poured cold water on the likelihood of any Irish political party seriously considering re-entry to the Commonwealth, especially during an election campaign in the Republic.[73] His major criticism of D'Alton's plan was that it was based

> on the old fallacy, so common here, of sketching the end result without considering the ways and means of working towards it. The real truth is that reunion cannot suddenly come about on the basis of a blue-print, however ingenious and imaginative; there has first to be a desire for reunion on both sides, or at least a willingness to look at it as an eventual goal. [74]

This, he deemed, totally lacking in Unionist circles and was something that would have to be induced and encouraged.

Although the Cardinal's plan prompted only one question in the House of Commons to C. J. Alport, the Under-Secretary of State for Commonwealth Relations, it did have a significant impact on the thinking of Frank Pakenham (Lord Longford), the former Minister of Civil Aviation, First Lord of the Admiralty and future Lord Privy Seal, Secretary of State for the Colonies, leader of the House of Lords and biographer of de Valera.[75] He raised the Cardinal's proposals with Harold Macmillan, the Prime Minister, in August 1957.[76] It appeared to Con Cremin that Pakenham toyed with the idea of initiating moves to end partition on the British side based on the Indian formula. Pakenham sounded out the Taoiseach in an interview on 6 September 1957 and was informed by de Valera that there could be no unilateral step to rejoin the Commonwealth that was not concomitant with the ending of partition.[77] Pakenham was not the only peer to advocate re-entry to the Commonwealth as a means of forging closer economic and cultural links. Four months previously, Lord Rugby suggested that de Valera get his 'knees under a table in London where you could feel your way. I fully recognise that the terms of admission would be in conformity with a republican status.'[78] Although de Valera regarded Rugby's proposition as 'impractical', in the context of a united Ireland, the Indian formula was not dismissed out of hand and Bowman considered that de Valera was quite open on the issue when interviewed in London by *The Times* in March 1958.[79] Pakenham backed the Cardinal's unity proposals in a lecture on Anglo-Irish relations in Cork in December 1957.[80] He again referred to the D'Alton plan in a House of Lords motion put down by the Liberal peer Lord Windlesham (apparently at the behest of Lord Rea, leader of the Liberals in the Lords) on Anglo-Irish relations and the desirability of closer economic and cultural relations between the Republic and the UK on 14 December 1960.[81] Pakenham requested background material for the debate from Hugh McCann, Irish ambassador in London, to whom he intimated that he would mention the Cardinal's proposals.[82] In the event, focusing on the political aspect of the question, he commended D'Alton's suggestion and argued for voluntary unity within a Commonwealth framework, and pending such a resolution called for closer economic cooperation between both parts of Ireland and between Ireland and Britain.[83] This was followed a month later by an article in the *Sunday Observer* entitled: 'Ireland and the New Commonwealth: must she stay out?' Pakenham mooted an 'Indian' solution in a Commonwealth which was no longer, he maintained, 'the Britain-dominated, imperialist setup which Ireland made such sacrifices to escape'.[84] An editorial in the *Derry Journal* questioned the realism of such an approach and argued that the Unionist Party's

> only real loyalty is to its own vested interests and that [its] allegiance to such institutions as the former British Empire is a secondary matter, conditional on those sacred vested interests being safeguarded. It is wishful thinking at its worst to believe that, by becoming one of the Commonwealth 'family' the Twenty-Six Counties could bring the removal of the Border, with Unionist consent, a single day nearer. [85]

Strangely, the D'Alton plan has never been regarded as part of the re-evaluation of approaches to partition. Yet, even a cursory glance at Irish government files reveals that warfare, whether verbal or actual, was seen to have failed. The idea of encouraging cooperation and friendship began to percolate to the surface and gain common acceptance both inside and outside government. Commenting on a memorandum by Blythe on partition, Conor Cruise O'Brien of the Department of External Affairs felt that the logical implication of ruling out force as a solution was 'to do everything we can to diminish the tensions which make it impossible at present even to launch, let alone to carry through, any campaign of persuasion'. To do so required the cessation of anti-Stormont propaganda abroad, the crushing of border raids and a statement that 'we hope and believe the Six Counties will one day rejoin us, but that we accept that they are free to stay out as long as a majority in the Six Counties so desires'.[86] O'Brien felt that 'such a new lead can, however, take us somewhere only if it starts from a realistic and complete acceptance of the fact that Partition cannot be ended as long as it is supported by the overwhelming majority of the Protestants of the north'.[87] In November 1957, de Valera ruled out force as a solution to partition at the Fianna Fáil Ard Fheis (Annual Conference) and concluded that only closer relations in areas of common concern between North and South would unlock this dilemma.[88] Church and state authorities in the South were united in this stand. Bishop Cornelius Lucey of Cork asked: 'Why do we not try to win over these counties to unity, instead of trying to force them to unity', and prayed 'the hand of friendship would be grasped if it were extended . . . Love is a more cohesive force than either force or hate, whether between nations or within one and the same nation.'[89] Within another two years, the contention that 'the campaign of sporadic violence in the vicinity of the Border serves only to help and strengthen those whose purpose is to keep the nation divided by perpetuating the animosities and tensions on which the case for partition has always rested' had become the official government line.[90]

One plausible explanation for the lack of recognition of the part played by Cardinal D'Alton lies in his leadership or managerial style. In a Shakespearian sense, he did not bestride his church like a colossus, as may be said of Archbishop Gregg. With his 'gentle and kindly bearing', the unassuming Cardinal rarely led a delegation.[91] He assigned this responsibility to Archbishop McQuaid of Dublin or Bishop Mageean of Down and Connor, who, in effect, acted as his plenipotentiaries. In popular mythology McQuaid was the pre-eminent prelate, as a recent biographer put it the 'ruler of Catholic Ireland'.[92] However, such a claim must be put in context. The head of the Catholic Church in Ireland was the archbishop of Armagh. Weight of Catholic numbers and proximity to the seat of government in Dublin made McQuaid a powerful figure and the natural choice to meet members of the Southern administration. But had McQuaid, for all his intellectual ability, administrative zeal and uncompromising commitment to the faith, presided in Ireland's smallest diocese of Clonfert (with a Catholic population of only 36,491), he would have been as well known as Bishop John Dignan or Thomas Ryan.[93] Under canon law each bishop is autonomous within his own diocese but unless McQuaid had permission from the chairperson of the hierarchy, he could not claim to represent the views of his colleagues. It is often overlooked that on an all-Ireland basis, Mageean, who had a warm personal relationship with D'Alton, was just as pivotal as McQuaid in terms of access to the Northern Ireland government. Both Mageean and McQuaid were powerful figures not alone because they were the incumbents of Ireland's two largest dioceses with strategic proximity to government, but also due to D'Alton's preferred non-interventionist role. His successor, William Conway, could not have been more different. He was energetic, in good health and only fifty when appointed archbishop in 1963. He was thirteen years younger than D'Alton when he became archbishop in 1946 and eighteen years younger than McQuaid, who was sixty-eight in 1963. It was not simply on age grounds that McQuaid appeared less prominent or less powerful in the 1960s. Similarly, William Philbin for all his youth and many public statements seemed less pivotal in Belfast than his predecessor, Bishop Mageean. If D'Alton had a presidential managerial style, then Conway ruled as a hands-on chief executive who personally approached the governments, North and South. Whereas D'Alton was a background mover, Conway preferred the foreground. Of course, they operated in very different milieux. As we will see in chapter four, the climate in Northern Ireland in the late 1960s was far removed from D'Alton's era.

Relations with the Holy See

In their relations with the Holy See, both the hierarchy and the Irish government utilised the symbolic importance, if not moral force, of Ireland's ecclesiastical geography. In their all-Ireland purview, the territoriality of the Catholic Church conveniently buttressed the national question. While exhibiting an almost obsequious deference to the Holy See, the hierarchy exhibited a prickly defensiveness if papal pressure threatened independence of domestic action. When the Vatican proposed, in 1958, that the statutes regulating general meetings of the hierarchy be revised, and that, critically, the archbishop of Armagh be made honorary rather than effective president, the political division of the island was advanced as a pretext to resist any change. An unusually assertive letter on behalf of the hierarchy to Alberto Levame, the papal nuncio, stressed that

> owing to the partition of our country against the will of the Irish people as a whole – one part being subject to the jurisdiction of the Republic, while the other part owes allegiance to the Queen of England – it is of the utmost importance that the Chairman should be one who is fully conversant with conditions on both sides of the Border and who can be regarded as representing Catholic interests in both parts of the country.[94]

There was no insincerity or lack of conviction in the hierarchy's equation of the role of the archbishop of Armagh and representation of 'Catholic interests in both parts of the country'.

That the island of Ireland had one ecclesiastical jurisdiction but two political administrations led to a diplomatic arrangement with the Vatican which was *sui generis*. Although accredited to the Irish state, the papal nuncio's delegated ecclesiastical jurisdiction covered the entire island, both North and South. A nuncio has two discrete functions. He is a diplomat accredited to a head of a state. Secondly, he is a senior ecclesiastic, the local eyes and ears of the Vatican, with powers *vis-à-vis* the local church. In normal circumstances both areas would be coterminous. This was not so in Ireland and neither the Irish hierarchy nor the Dublin government wished to see this arrangement altered. In 1953 Frederick Boland, Irish ambassador in London, became concerned at suggestions that the status of the Apostolic Delegation in the UK, which was established in 1938, would be raised to that of an Inter-Nunciature with the implication that the latter would be responsible for Northern Ireland. This was presaged by the appointment of the former Irish nuncio, Gerald O'Hara, to London, and rumoured in the English press. O'Hara succeeded William Godfrey who became archbishop of Liverpool. It was felt unlikely that Queen Elizabeth would accept a letter of credence from Godfrey because he was a British subject. However, as Boland viewed the situation, with Godfrey's translation to Liverpool and the arrival of O'Hara, an American, this catch was removed.[95] Joseph Walshe, Irish ambassador to the Holy See, registered his government's concerns in the Vatican in December 1953. He stressed that any extension to Ireland of the jurisdiction of an Apostolic Delegate 'would be considered by the Irish people, in the whole world, as an act destined to confirm and perpetuate English tyranny in Ireland'.[96] Con Cremin, Walshe's successor, was likewise instructed in 1954 by the Department of External Affairs to raise the matter because 'it would be clearly unacceptable to the Irish Church and public opinion if the Holy See's representative for the Primate of All-Ireland and the other Bishops of the Six Counties should be accredited to the English monarch.'[97] Cremin met Monsignor Dell'Acqua, Substitute Secretary of State for Ordinary Affairs, on 3 November 1954. Dell'Acqua assured him that there was 'no real possibility' of this at the present time, but should there ever be such a development, full consideration would be taken of Irish concerns. The special importance the Holy See attached to Ireland was emphasised to the Irish ambassador.[98]

In 1956 Boland became concerned again that the issue was being revived. The Catholic Church in England had grown steadily since 1920. Numbers grew after the Second World War with an influx of Polish and Irish emigrants. By 1961, ten per cent of the population were practising Catholics who 'had established a strong institutional presence in London, Oxford, Cambridge and the principal cities of the south, but had done this without losing its grip on its old provincial strongholds of the north'.[99] As Boland saw it, the danger was that if the Vatican decided to limit an Inter-Nuncio's jurisdiction to Great Britain and if consequently the British government demurred to this as implying an intervention by the Holy See in the Partition question, the Holy See – depending on the extent of its anxiety to have full diplomatic representation in Great Britain – may be tempted to revive the present arrangement and give the Inter-Nuncio some measure of jurisdiction in respect of the Six Counties.[100]

To do so, of course, would amount to recognising partition and would scuttle the image of an Ireland one and undivided in the eyes of the majority church and the Holy See. A visit to the Pope, in February 1956, by the Duke of Norfolk, President of the Catholic Union and effective head of the English Catholic laity, heightened speculation regarding the status of the English delegation. The Minister for External Affairs, Liam Cosgrave, instructed Cremin to make 'discreet enquiries on the matter'.[101] In a *démarche* on 14 March 1956, Leo McCauley, who succeeded Cremin as ambassador to the Holy See in 1956, was assured by Dell'Acqua that there had been no developments. In a further interview with Domenico Tardini, Pope Pius XII's Under-Secretary for External Affairs and subsequently Secretary of State under Pope John XXIII, McCauley explained the government's interest in the subject. Tardini assured him that should a problem arise it would be approached in the light of the Vatican's 'most friendly dispositions' for Ireland.[102]

In June 1957, McCauley learned from Sir Marcus Cheke, British minister to the Holy See, that political representations prevented his government taking any action for fear that it would lead to embarrassment at home.[103] However, the issue refused to die and the question of an Inter-Nunciature had been making progress in 1959 until Edward Heath, the Conservative Party Chief Whip, shelved it lest it damage his party's electoral fortunes.[104] The political-geographical image of Ireland as one entity was an article of faith in Irish foreign policy in general, but particularly for McCauley as a Catholic from Derry. In September 1960, we glimpse the depth of this commitment. He forcefully explained to Dell'Acqua

> how deeply we were interested in this matter and how strongly all Irish Catholics would feel if those in the Six Counties were placed under the jurisdiction of a Nuncio or Internuncio in London, adding that the Six County Catholics, of which I was one, would view the possibility of such an arrangement with special bitterness. For them it would be a blow full in the face.[105]

Ecclesiastical unity was regarded as a heaven-sent means to bolster political policy on partition. The growing rapport between the Holy See and Canterbury in the ecumenical summer of the mid-1960s caused the British representative to the Holy See, Sir Peter Scarlett, to suggest that there were 'surely no valid reasons left for withholding diplomatic status from the Pope's representative in the United Kingdom'. It seemed anomalous to him that relations 'with some Communist satellite should be conducted at normal Ambassadorial level while those with the Holy See – an enduring force for good in the world – are neither reciprocal nor up to that level'.[106] This, allied to Pope Paul's ambition to increase the Holy See's diplomatic presence abroad, caused Frank Aiken as Minister for External Affairs to review the position in May 1966 as a precaution. Significantly, Thomas Commins, Irish ambassador to the Holy See, reported to Hugh McCann, the new secretary of the Department of External Affairs, that

> By reference to any precedents which I have been able to consult, it does, as a matter of fact, seem to be the case that in the matter of its diplomatic relations it has been the constant usage of the Holy See to avoid altering an already existing situation where such alteration would have the effect of conveying recognition or seeming recognition to boundaries or areas in dispute in the matter of *de jure* jurisdiction unless and until the contending parties have first definitely settled up the matter by agreement between themselves. Cases in point are e.g. Germany and Portugal-India.[107]

The *sui generis* diplomatic arrangement with the Vatican remained unaltered, even when a Pro-Nunciature was established in Britain in 1982.

Cardinal D'Alton died on 1 February 1963. The question of representation at his funeral caused some unease in London due to the positioning of the diocese of Armagh in the United Kingdom. There was no such difficulty for the authorities in the Republic. The Taoiseach, Seán Lemass, in the traditional practice, issued a statement of condolence in the Dáil on 5 February 1963.[108] He and Frank Aiken represented the government at the funeral. Permission was granted, pursuant to Article 12.9 of the Constitution, for President de Valera to leave the state to attend the obsequies of the Cardinal who was his former classmate at Blackrock College in Dublin.[109] On the British side, consideration was given as to whether Queen Elizabeth should be represented. When Cardinal Bernard Griffin, the archbishop of Westminster, died in August 1956, she sent a message of condolence but no representative attended the funeral. This attracted much negative comment from the English Catholic laity in the Catholic press.[110] When Cardinal William Godfrey (Griffin's successor) died in January 1963, the protocol was re-evaluated. The Home Office considered that 'the climate of opinion has changed since 1956. Relations between the Catholic and other churches are more friendly and it is by no means obvious that the earlier precedents should be followed.'[111] It recommended representation as did the archbishop of

Canterbury. Indeed, the Queen herself wanted to be represented; Lord Eldon performed this function.[112] However, the Home Office regarded the requiem mass in Westminster for Cardinal D'Alton in a different light and advised against:

> As the Roman Catholic Church in Ireland covers the whole of that country, only a small part of which is within the United Kingdom, and having regard to the religious divisions within Northern Ireland, it appeared that the case for the Queen's representation was very much weaker than the case for representation at Cardinal Godfrey's funeral had been.[113]

Heavy snow prevented the Northern Ireland government from being represented.[114] There is no indication from Northern Ireland cabinet minutes that Cardinal D'Alton's death was discussed by the government.

The Irish government's concern about an Inter-Nunciature in London was compounded by even deeper anxiety *vis-à-vis* D'Alton's successor. Whatever their private thoughts on the merits and demerits of Archbishop McQuaid gaining the cardinal's hat, departmental records reveal the government's concern that it should go North. With few exceptions, the archbishop of Armagh was normally created cardinal.[115] The demise in rapid succession of Godfrey and D'Alton in the opening two months of 1963 reduced the members of the Sacred College to eighty-three and gave rise to speculation of an early consistory. Were this to occur during the interregnum at Armagh, the obvious, and perhaps only, Irish candidate was McQuaid. Commins advised Hugh McCann that should the government have any considerations they wished taken into account by the Vatican, 'it would be well, in my view, to let them be known to the powers that be here as early as possible . . . so as to avoid any possibility of being suddenly faced with a *fait accompli* which might, possibly, prove embarrassing'.[116] The reply, a handwritten letter from McCann marked 'top secret', is highly significant. It asked the ambassador to convey to the Vatican authorities that:

> The Irish Government are strongly of the view that everything possible should be done to maintain the importance of the See of Armagh. If His Holiness intends to elevate an Irish ecclesiastic to the Sacred College of Cardinals, the Government humbly pray that the nominee should be appointed to fill the vacant See. The marking of Armagh as the first-ranking See is not only of vital importance to sustaining the morale of the Catholic minority in the North but to emphasise the unity of the Irish Church and to advance the cause of political unity.[117]

Clearly, the second reason took precedence in government reasoning. Any diminution of the standing of the see of Armagh would damage church unity and, by implication, aspirations of political unity. When, on

1 March 1963, Commins communicated his government's instruction to Cardinal Samoré and Cardinal Cicognani (who succeeded Tardini as Secretary of State), he was given the impression that a consistory and the appointment of a new Irish cardinal were some way off and that Armagh would be filled after Westminster.[118]

President Seán T. Ó Ceallaigh revealed to Shane Leslie that D'Alton told him that he wished Conway to succeed him.[119] But was it a foregone conclusion that D'Alton's mitre would devolve to his auxiliary? Conway's name along with that of Philbin and, to a lesser extent, Austin Quinn, who was regarded as a safe candidate, were mentioned in non-official circles. There was nothing new in such conjecture. What Commins did find surprising was the automatic assumption that Armagh would be 'hattable' and the 'remarkable absence of mention of Dublin, or indeed of Archbishop McQ as Cardinal, even in Armagh'.[120] Professionally disinclined to be impressed by such logic, Commins prepared an *appunto* with two key points for transmission to the Cardinal Secretary of State on 14 September 1963. Firstly, that the Irish government considered that in the current political climate, a new cardinal other than the archbishop of Armagh would 'have the most deleterious political effects' and be interpreted at home and abroad as impeding Irish unity. Secondly, it reaffirmed unification of the country as 'the fundamental objective of Irish policy'.[121] An earlier draft accounted for the 'unprecedented political significance' vested in the see of Armagh as 'the only landmark left of the former undivided Ireland' and a symbol of faith for Irish people that 'the historic Irish nation will eventually be restored to unity'.[122] Commins also argued that chief among the internal domestic consequences of transferring the cardinal's hat to the Republic would be the justification it would give the IRA to renew violent action, because it would be 'obvious that from the international standpoint the partition of the country was here to stay and that continued reliance on constitutional methods to achieve the reunification of Ireland was therefore pointless'.[123]

Bizarrely, the ambassador was not informed that during his very meeting with the Cardinal Secretary of State, on 14 September 1963, William Conway was named as archbishop of Armagh. Before leaving Ireland in 1967 to take up a new appointment in Portugal, Giuseppi Sensi, the papal nuncio, claimed credit in an interview with Aiken for Conway's appointment.[124] This did not mean an end to the 'hat question', which Commins discussed with Sensi at the end of September 1963. The nuncio responded to the political considerations raised with the question: 'how can the AB of D be passed by?'[125] Commins steered away from personalities. He stated that the government would not pretend to enter into the question of whom the Holy See should honour, yet conveyed to the nuncio, as the latter understood it, that 'it is the interests of the country which should predominate'.[126] There the matter rested until December, when Hugh McCann instructed Commins to make no further representations. If asked whether the hat should be given to Conway or McQuaid, the ambassador was to reply that the government 'has never expressed any opinion for or against either of the individuals concerned'.[127] Pope Paul VI announced the names of twenty-seven new cardinals on 25 January 1965. It was Conway who would be created Irish cardinal at the consistory on 22 February 1965.[128] There was no *deus ex machina*. The government's partiality and the conditions it laid down proved decisive.

There was never any question that the political border would compromise the religious unity of the Catholic Church. Although the Northern bishops came together to treat matters pertaining solely to Northern Ireland, they were fully integrated with their colleagues, as the morphology of the Catholic Church was both an all-Ireland and an indivisible one. Ecclesiastically, spiritually and organisationally the Catholic Church was united across the border. There was no compartmentalisation of dioceses by political jurisdiction. The contention of the political geographer M. W. Heslinga that the Irish land boundary represented an important spiritual divide is only accurate if one is contrasting different denominations.[129] Indeed the title of Frank Gallagher's book, *The Indivisible Island*, seems more applicable to the Catholic Church, than to the political situation he describes. The Northern bishops were nationalist, the border did mean the inconvenience of divided dioceses and parishes, but they were trenchantly and unapologetically opposed to physical force efforts to end partition. Their stance was an important, but underestimated, element in the reassessment of the national question at the end of the 1950s, from a simplistic one-nation concept towards a two-nation one. In terms of the relations between the Vatican, the Catholic Church and the Irish government, the 1950s bear witness to an unusual commingling of ecclesiastical reality and political objective. Heslinga suggests that to many Irishmen 'it is almost a dogma that the Creator has predestined Ireland to be a national and political unit, because it is "a perfect geographical entity"'.[130] If so, then the Creator's representatives in Ireland pressed this case. As for their secular colleagues in the Irish government, ecclesiastical unity ran as the woof through their dealings with the Holy See, in respect of a mooted Inter-Nunciature in London and the appointment to the see of Armagh. In contrast to the political map of the island, on which Northern Ireland was painted a different colour to its Southern neighbour, the territoriality of the Catholic

Church ensured that only one colour was necessary on the ecclesiastical map of Ireland.

Notes

1 UCDA, de Valera Papers, P150/2868, Letter Conway to de Valera, 22 March 1961.
2 Ibid.
3 This is a reference to Frank Gallagher's classic anti-partitionist work, *The Indivisible Island. The History of the Partition of Ireland* (London, 1957).
4 *Leader*, 4 May 1946, p. 7.
5 Ó Fiaich Memorial Library and Archive (henceforth OFMLA), D'Alton Papers, Box 16, Appointment, Folder 1, Letter Quinn to D'Alton, 26 April 1946.
6 *Ibid.*, Folder 3, Draft of enthronement address, 13 June 1946.
7 *Irish Catholic Directory* (henceforth *ICD*) *1940*, p. 667 cited in Finbar J. Madden and Thomas Bradley, 'The diocese of Derry in the twentieth century, c.1900–1974', in Henry A. Jefferies and Ciarán Devlin (eds), *History of the Diocese of Derry from Earliest Times* (Dublin, 2000), p. 254.
8 Clogher Diocesan Archives (henceforth CDA), O'Callaghan Papers, Reply by O'Callaghan to addresses from public bodies of County Monaghan and representatives from Fermanagh and Tyrone, 4 April 1943.
9 Bartlett, 'Church and state in modern Ireland', p. 252. On the generally positive response of the Northern bishops to the Treaty, see Murray, *Oracles of God*, ch. 7.
10 Earl of Longford and Thomas P. O'Neill, *Eamon de Valera* (Dublin, 1970), p. 319 cited in Deirdre McMahon, *Republicans and Imperialists. Anglo-Irish Relations in the 1930s* (New Haven and London, 1984), p. 260.
11 *IP*, 28 January 1949 cited in Clare O'Halloran, *Partition and the Limits of Irish Nationalism* (Dublin, 1987), p. 183.
12 John Bowman, *De Valera and the Ulster Question, 1917–1973* (Oxford, 1982), p. 276.
13 UCDA, Aiken Papers, P104/4591, Letter MacUgo (assistant secretary DT) to Aiken, 13 December 1950 enclosing copy of McCall's 'Report from the North', 4 December 1950.
14 See Lee, *Ireland*, p. 301.
15 O'Halloran, *Partition*, p. 185.
16 Eithne MacDermott, *Clann na Poblachta* (Cork, 1998), p. ix.
17 Earnán de Blaghd, *Briseadh na Teorann* (Dublin, 1955), p. 7: 'Tá an CHRÍCHDHEIGHILT ANN toisc gur éiligh Protastúnaigh na tíre í, go mórmhór Protastúnaigh an Tuaiscirt.' For a discussion of new thinking on partition in the 1950s, see Ó Corráin, 'Ireland in his heart north and south': the contribution of Ernest Blythe to the partition question', *Irish Historical Studies*, 35: 137 (2006).

18 UCDA, Aiken Papers, P104/4602, Letter Frank Gallagher to Aiken, 4 August 1949, enclosing Ó Nualláin's account, 18 July 1949.
19 *Northern Standard*, 8 May 1959.
20 See Michael Kennedy, *Division and Consensus. The Politics of Cross-Border Relations in Ireland, 1925–1969* (Dublin, 2000), ch. 7.
21 Roosevelt Papers, PSF 56, Letter David Gray to Roosevelt, 25 September 1940 cited in Bowman, *De Valera*, p. 253, n. 62. MacRory was bishop of Down and Connor (1915–1928) and then archbishop of Armagh (1928–1945).
22 Down and Connor Diocesan Archives (henceforth DCDA), Mageean Papers, E.P. 1942, Letter MacRory to Mageean, 21 December 1942.
23 Cavan County Council, Minutes of monthly meeting, 10 July 1954.
24 National Archives UK, Kew (henceforth NAUK), Dominions Office (henceforth DO) 35/4984, Copy memo 'Diary of principal events and conversations concerning the Irish Republic', n.d.; Peadar Livingstone, *The Monaghan Story* (Enniskillen, 1980), pp. 452–3.
25 OFMLA, D'Alton Papers, Box 20, Instructions and Sermons, Folder: Sermons 13, Armagh Cathedral, Christmas Eve 1954.
26 *BT*, 27 December 1954.
27 UCDA, McGilligan Papers, P35C/198, Secret memorandum for government: 'A solution of partition problem by peaceful means', 29 January 1956.
28 Dublin Diocesan Archives (henceforth DDA), McQuaid Papers, AB8/B/XVII/05, Draft letter ('personal') McQuaid to O'Hara, 29 December 1952.
29 *Ibid.*
30 Thomas Hennessey, *A History of Northern Ireland 1920–1996* (Dublin, 1997), pp. 104–5.
31 *ICD 1957*, p. 630.
32 *Derry Journal*, 28 December 1955.
33 Bowman, *De Valera*, pp. 288–90.
34 Derry Diocesan Archives (henceforth DerDA), Farren Papers, 'Letters to/from Bishops', Letter D'Alton to Farren, 16 September 1955.
35 *ICD 1957*, p. 632.
36 See Whyte, *Church and State*, p. 321.
37 NAUK, DO 35/4985, Copy memo ('top secret') of conversation between Boland and Laithwaite, 22 February 1955.
38 OFMLA, D'Alton Papers, Box 6, Hierarchy III, Folder: Hierarchy Statements 1946–61, Letter Kinane to D'Alton, 10 January 1957.
39 *Ibid.*, Minute of Standing Committee Meeting, 15 January 1957 with additional notes in D'Alton's hand.
40 *Ibid.*
41 HB, vol. ii, meeting of 19 February 1957, p. 159.
42 *Northern Standard*, 4 January 1957; Livingstone, *The Monaghan Story*, p. 453.

43 CDA, O'Callaghan Papers, Diary entry 7 January 1957.
44 *Northern Standard*, 8 March 1957; CDA, O'Callaghan Papers, Lenten pastoral, 24 February 1957.
45 CDA, O'Callaghan Papers, Lenten pastoral, 24 February 1957.
46 Brian M. Walker, *Parliamentary Election Results in Ireland 1918–92* (Dublin and Belfast, 1992), p. 196; Livingstone, *The Monaghan Story*, p. 454.
47 *ICD 1958*, p. 639.
48 *II*, 25 May 1960.
49 Linen Hall Library (henceforth LHL), NI Political Collection, William Philbin, *Patriotism* (Dublin, 1958), p. 12. This sixteen-page pamphlet was originally delivered as a lecture on 7 August 1957 to the Social Studies Summer School held at Mount Melleray Abbey, County Waterford.
50 *IP*, 11 November 1959 cited in Brian Girvin, *From Union to Union. Nationalism, Democracy and Religion in Ireland – Act of Union to EU* (Dublin, 2002), p. 206.
51 OFMLA, D'Alton Papers, Box 19, D'Alton Plan 1957, Copy letter D'Alton to Father Allen, 12 July 1959.
52 *Ibid.*, Text of interview given to Douglas Hyde, 19 February 1957.
53 *Ibid.*
54 *Ibid.* For discussion of the impact of Irish withdrawal on India, see Deirdre McMahon, 'A larger and noisier Southern Ireland: Ireland and the evolution of dominion status in India, Burma and the Commonwealth, 1942–9', in Michael Kennedy and Joseph Morrison Skelly (eds), *Irish Foreign Policy 1919–1966. From Independence to Internationalism* (Dublin, 2000), pp. 155–91.
55 OFMLA, D'Alton Papers, Box 19, D'Alton Plan 1957, Text of interview given to Douglas Hyde, 19 February 1957.
56 *Ibid.*
57 *Ibid.*
58 For instance the *Quebec Chronicle-Telegraph* carried the story on 2 April 1957 under headline 'Archbishop Proposes Union in Ireland'.
59 *IT*, 4 March 1957.
60 *II*, 20 May 1957.
61 *Leader*, 13 September 1958.
62 *Spectator*, 15 March 1957.
63 *BT*, 4 March 1957.
64 OFMLA, D'Alton Papers, Box 19, D'Alton Plan 1957, Letter Rodgers to D'Alton, 25 March 1957.
65 *Ibid.*, Letter Quinn to D'Alton, 9 March 1957.
66 *Ibid.*, Letter Walsh to D'Alton, 8 March 1957.
67 OFMLA, D'Alton Papers, Box 8, NI Government A, Folder 3, Letter Conway to D'Alton, 29 March 1957.
68 OFMLA, D'Alton Papers, Box 34, Miscellaneous B, Letter Shane Leslie to D'Alton, 15 April 1958.

69 *IT*, 5 March 1957.
70 *II*, 7 March 1957.
71 NAUK, DO 35/7845, Letter ('confidential') Clutterbuck to A. W. Snelling (Commonwealth Relations Office), 7 March 1957.
72 *Ibid.*
73 This question surfaced again in 1965. Following the Commonwealth Prime Ministers' Conference (17–25 June 1965), Sir Saville Garner, Permanent Under-Secretary of State in the Commonwealth Relations Office, intimated to J. G. Molloy (Irish ambassador in London) that he would like to see the Republic return to the Commonwealth. See NAI, DT 97/6/422, Confidential memo Molloy to secretary of the Department of External Affairs (henceforth DEA), 5 July 1965.
74 NAUK, DO 35/7845, Letter ('confidential') Clutterbuck to Snelling, 7 March 1957.
75 *Hansard*, vol. 566, col. 1306, 14 March 1957. Philip Bell asked if discussions would be opened with the governments in the Republic and in Northern Ireland on foot on the Cardinal's proposals.
76 NAI, Department of Foreign Affairs (henceforth DFA) P203/2A, Secret report Con Cremin to Seán Murphy (secretary DEA), 20 August 1957.
77 *Ibid.*, Letter ('secret') Cremin to Murphy, 19 September 1957 with enclosed of conversation between Cremin and Lord Pakenham.
78 UCDA, de Valera Papers, P150/2940, Letter Rugby to de Valera, 18 May 1957.
79 *Ibid.*, Letter de Valera to Rugby, 8 June 1957; NAI, DFA P203/2A, Letter Cremin to Murphy, 19 September 1957 with enclosure 'Secret report of conversation between Cremin and Lord Pakenham'; Bowman, *De Valera*, p. 292.
80 *IP*, 12 December 1957.
81 NAI, DFA P332, Confidential letter Hugh McCann (Irish ambassador) to Cremin (secretary DEA), 21 November 1960; DFA 313/31F, Confidential report McCann to Cremin on Irish motion before the House of Lords 15 December 1960.
82 NAI, DFA P332, Confidential letter McCann to Cremin, 8 December 1960.
83 NAI, DFA 313/31F, Confidential report McCann to Cremin on Irish motion before the House of Lords 15 December 1960.
84 *Sunday Observer*, 8 January 1961.
85 *Derry Journal*, 10 January 1961.
86 NAI, DT S 9361G, Letter Patrick Lynch to Maurice Moynihan, 6 May 1957 with comments by Conor Cruise O'Brien on Ernest Blythe's 'Appeal to leaders of Nationalist opinion in the North.' Blythe's memorandum is discussed in Ó Corráin, 'Ireland in his heart north and south'.
87 *Ibid.*
88 *IP*, 20 November 1957.
89 *Ibid.*, 6 April 1959.

90 NAI, DT S 9361K/61, Speech by Lemass to south Louth *comhairle ceantair* (branch) of Fianna Fáil, Drogheda, 5 February 1961. At the Fianna Fáil Ard Fheis in January 1962, Frank Aiken called on Irishmen 'of all classes and creeds to work together through democratic institutions to achieve reunification of our country', see UCDA, Aiken Papers, P104/1974.
91 NAI, DT S 15405 B/63, Telegram of sympathy Lemass to Conway, 1 February 1963.
92 Cooney, *John Charles McQuaid. Ruler of Catholic Ireland* (Dublin, 1999).
93 Ryan had worked in the Roman diplomatic service, was part of Pope John XXIII's entourage and was supposed to have taught the pope English. He became well known nationally after an ill-judged intervention on the *Late Late Show*, which gave rise to 'the Bishop and the Nightie' headline.
94 OFMLA, D'Alton Papers, Box 3, Apostolic Nunciature, Folder: Archbishop Levame 1954–59, Copy letter William MacNeely and James Fergus to Apostolic Nuncio from the June Meeting 1958.
95 NAI, DFA 313/31, Confidential report Boland to Seán Nunan (secretary DEA), 15 June 1954.
96 NAI, DFA 313/6A, Letter ('secret') Walshe to Nunan 18 December 1953 with memo on Inter-Nuncio, 15 December 1953. Walshe first alerted Vatican authorities to this danger in January 1947, see NAI, DFA 14/21/1, Copy secret and confidential letter Walshe to secretary DEA. Walshe's career as ambassador has been considered by Keogh in *Ireland and the Vatican*.
97 NAI, DFA 14/21/1, Letter ('secret') secretary DEA to Cremin, 4 October 1954.
98 *Ibid.*, Secret report Cremin to Cosgrave, 6 November 1954.
99 Adrian Hastings, *A History of English Christianity 1920–1990* (3rd edn, London, 1991), pp. 475–6.
100 NAI, DFA P278A, Confidential report Boland to Seán Murphy (secretary DEA), 28 January 1956.
101 NAI, DFA 14/21/1, Confidential letter Cosgrave to Cremin, 1 February 1956.
102 NAI, DFA P278A, Copy secret report by Con Cremin, 20 March 1956.
103 *Ibid.*, Confidential report McCauley to secretary DEA, 24 June 1957.
104 *Ibid.*, Secret report Hugh McCann to secretary DEA, 19 Nov 1959. The issue is not mentioned in Heath's autobiography, *The Course of My Life* (London, 1998).
105 *Ibid.*, Confidential report McCauley to secretary DEA, 8 September 1960.
106 NAUK, Foreign Office (henceforth FO) 371/183258, Confidential dispatch Peter Scarlett to Michael Stewart (Secretary of State for Foreign Affairs), 15 April 1965.
107 NAI, DFA P12/2(a) II, Report ('highly confidential') Commins to McCann, 7 May 1966.
108 NAI, DT S 15405 B/63, Minute by Ó Nualláin for Taoiseach, 4 February 1963.

109 NAI, Government Minutes, vol. G 3/27, entry for 5 February 1963, G.10/71.
110 NAUK, Home Office (henceforth HO) 304/13, Letter Michael Adeane (private secretary to the Queen) to Home Secretary, 23 August 1956.
111 NAUK, HO 304/14, Memorandum by R. J. Guppy on representation of the Queen at funeral of Cardinal Godfrey, 24 January 1963.
112 *Ibid.*, Minute Home Secretary to Secretary of State, 24 January 1963; Letter John Hewitt to Guppy, 28 January 1963; *Catholic Herald*, 1 February 1963.
113 NAUK, HO 304/17, Memo on attendance at funerals of church dignitaries, 18 February 1963. When Cardinal Conway died in April 1977, Lord Glentoran represented Queen Elizabeth, see *IT*, 23 April 1977.
114 NAUK, HO 304/17, Memo on attendance at funerals of church dignitaries, 18 February 1963.
115 Three archbishops of Dublin have been created cardinal: Paul Cullen on 22 June 1866, Edward McCabe on 12 March 1882 and Desmond Connell on 21 February 2001.
116 NAI, DFA P104BI, Letter ('strictly confidential') Commins to McCann, 19 February 1963.
117 *Ibid.*, Copy letter ('top secret') McCann to Commins, 22 February 1963.
118 NAI, DFA P104BI, Letter ('secret') Commins to McCann, 1 March 1963; Letter ('secret') Commins to McCann, 18 May 1963.
119 NLI, Shane Leslie Papers, MS 22849, Letter Seán T. Ó Ceallaigh to Leslie, 14 March 1963.
120 NAI, DFA P104 BI, Letter ('secret') Commins to McCann, 18 May 1963.
121 *Ibid.*, Copy *appunto*, 13 September 1963.
122 *Ibid.*, Draft memorandum (in Commins's hand), n.d.
123 *Ibid.*
124 NAI, DFA 98/2/6, Copy memo ('most secret') of meeting between Dr Sensi and the Tánaiste, 19 July 1967.
125 NAI, DFA, P104BI, 'Summaries of ambassador's reports', report of 26–28 September 1963.
126 *Ibid.*
127 NAI, DFA P104 BI, Letter ('top secret') McCann to Commins, 21 December 1963.
128 *Ibid.*, Report Commins to secretary DEA, 2 February 1965.
129 M. W. Heslinga, *The Irish Border as a Cultural Divide* (3rd unrevised edn, Assen, 1979), p. 78.
130 *Ibid.*, p. 41.

3

'A confident minority': the Church of Ireland and the Irish state

No need to spin the penny again. Harp it is. (Lionel Fleming, *Head or Harp*)

There has been a tendency to portray church–state relations in the Republic in a monochromatic way as solely involving the Catholic Church. Equally, studies of the Church of Ireland have focused morbidly and excessively on the interrelated issues of numerical decline and social isolation in the opening decades of the new state.[1] The perception carried over from these years of the Church of Ireland being regarded, and at times regarding itself, as a nervous or cautious minority existing 'with increasing unobtrusiveness' (as Hubert Butler phrased it) has been pervasive.[2] But it would be anachronistic to contend that this remained the case into the late 1950s and 1960s. Apart from the obvious institutional field of education, formal contacts between the Church of Ireland and the Irish government have remained at the periphery of historical attention. How did they engage with one another at official church ceremonies or state functions? The state prayers issue underlined the House of Bishops' commitment to accept pragmatically the reality of living in the Republic. But if so, how well do the following popular assumptions (or misconceptions) stand up to scrutiny: that the Church of Ireland was reluctant to contribute to national life and that its members endured discrimination? As will be seen, the government was anything but partial in its treatment of the Church of Ireland. This chapter will illustrate that in the Irish state of the 1950s and 1960s, the Church of Ireland was not the alienated minority of caricature, but was, in the words of Bishop Arthur Butler, more aptly characterised as a confident one.[3]

Arresting the 'tendency towards defeatism'

The House of Bishops was not simply a bench of churchmen. In a broader sense, the Church of Ireland bishops were also leaders of their community. The air of despondency referred to by Hubert Butler did not go unnoticed or unchallenged by them. As early as 1936 Gregg warned of a 'tendency towards defeatism, which is exactly what we have to fight against.'[4] Yet for all his ability as an administrator and legislator, by the 1950s Gregg, in his old age, was more comfortable warning of a decline in morals and spiritual values than in providing fresh ideas.[5] Therefore, the translation of George Simms from Cork to Dublin, following the retirement of Arthur Barton in 1956, was vital in recovering confidence and optimism in Church of Ireland circles.

Simms was marked out from an early point in his career as a man of great potential. Fearful of losing him to the Church of England in 1937, when he took a post as chaplain in Lincoln Theological College, Gregg wrote personally hoping his young protégé might soon come back to Ireland.[6] In late 1939 Simms returned as dean of residence in Trinity College and chaplain secretary of the Church of Ireland Training College, responsibilities he held for twelve years. Following the death of Bishop R. T. Hearn in 1952, Simms was elected bishop by the synod of Cork, Cloyne and Ross by an enormous majority. At forty-two, he was the youngest to be appointed to a bishopric since Gregg, at the same age, became bishop of Ossory, Ferns and Leighlin in 1915. Henry McAdoo, dean of St Fin Barre's Cathedral (future bishop of Ossory and later archbishop of Dublin), likened Simms's arrival in Cork to 'springtime' in the diocese.[7] In contrast to Gregg, who was formidable and distant, Simms was ever approachable, a man of great scholarship, spirituality, humanity, full of ideas and energy. An insightful letter from Frank Jacob, a prominent Cork businessman and active synodsman, recounted how Simms was leaving 'a re-vitalised and active diocese' in Cork. It captured the importance of Simms's elevation as archbishop of Dublin:

> You will be able to inspire the whole church in the Republic (not only in Dublin) in the way that you lifted us up in our small diocese. You will make an impact on all the inhabitants of Dublin that will do the utmost good for the Church of Ireland.[8]

The appointment was timely. Only days before, the *Gazette* glumly suggested: 'We should keep ourselves to ourselves and, if we speak, confine our remarks to platitudinous exhortations on non-controversial subjects ... lest such attention should result in material or social disadvantages.'[9] The new archbishop's conception of the role of his church could hardly have been more different. His enthronement address concluded with an encouraging and positive exhortation:

> It is all too easy for a Church to feel fearful and to live a life apart from public and civic concerns. After today let us remind ourselves that our

Church allegiance, our beliefs, and our way of worship will not hinder, but will rather help, anything we can contribute in public service, in the field of education, in matters cultural and communal.[10]

During his twelve years in Dublin, Simms became the best-known leader of the Church of Ireland both domestically and internationally. By word and action he taught the Church of Ireland population in the Republic how to be Anglican and Irish. If Gregg had been a reassuring presence from the 1920s to the 1950s, then Simms was heir to this accolade. He forged common ground with the Catholic community who saw in him 'a face of the Church of Ireland that many of them had never encountered before: deeply respectful of their religious and political traditions, while unshakeably Anglican himself'.[11] By the time of his translation to Armagh, in July 1969, the morale of the Church of Ireland in the Republic had never been higher. This Donald Caird, archbishop of Dublin from 1985 to 1996, ascribed to Simms above all others.[12]

Church–state relations

That relations between the churches and the Irish government were genial was *de rigueur*. Of the Protestant churches, the Church of Ireland had the strongest relationship. This was not just a consequence of its greater demographic strength in the Republic. In 1961 the Church of Ireland accounted for 3.8 per cent of the population compared to 0.8 per cent Presbyterian, the largest concentration being in Donegal, and 0.2 per cent Methodist.[13] Neither was it exclusively due to having its administrative centre in Dublin. Also significant was its episcopal structure which allowed bishops to remain in position for a number of years and develop a personal rapport with political and civic leaders. Particularly important in this respect was the archbishop of Dublin. The minutes of the House of Bishops reveal that he was the natural choice to represent the views of his colleagues to the government by memorandum or in person. By contrast, the Presbyterian and Methodist Churches lacked this element of sustained corporate identity as a new Moderator of the General Assembly and President of the Methodist Conference were appointed annually.[14] Consequently, as Kurt Bowen notes, the Church of Ireland, rather than other Protestant churches, 'shaped the basic outlook and style of the Protestant community in the South'.[15]

Given their ceremonial importance, episcopal enthronements provide a rarely used indicator of the government's *bona fides* towards the Church of Ireland. As no archiepiscopal enthronement had taken place since 1920, there was no precedent for official government representation when both Armagh and Dublin fell vacant in 1939. It was, therefore, highly significant that Senator D. L. Robinson represented the government at the installation ceremonies of both Gregg as archbishop of Armagh on 25 January 1939, and Barton as archbishop of Dublin on 25 March.[16] De Valera also sent a telegram congratulating Gregg, for which kind message the Primate was 'very much obliged.'[17] President Douglas Hyde, a member of the Church of Ireland, attended Barton's enthronement in Christ Church Cathedral. By acknowledging the solemnity of such ceremonies, government representation set an important and reassuring precedent for Church of Ireland authorities.

On a personal level there was a deep mutual respect, and indeed physical resemblance, between Gregg and de Valera such that during the War of Independence, Gregg was temporarily placed under house arrest in a case of mistaken identity! It is well established that de Valera consulted and acted on Gregg's suggestions when drafting Bunreacht na hÉireann.[18] When the Primate retired in 1959, de Valera personally thanked him for his 'great kindness on every occasion on which I had, as Head of the Government here, to call on you for co-operation or assistance'.[19] For his part, Gregg could 'look back with pleasure to the various occasions when our paths crossed, and I am glad to think of the kindliness of our mutual relations'.[20]

Despite the absence of Archbishop Barton's personal papers, a number of archival snippets reveal an agreeable relationship with the government of the day. When de Valera lost office in February 1948, the archbishop wrote to him in appreciation of 'the unfailing courtesy which you have always shown to me personally since I returned to Dublin eight years ago, and the fairness with which you have always treated the minority community'.[21] Barton went on to assure de Valera of the Church of Ireland's appreciation of the government's 'fairness and helpfulness in connection with our educational and other problems . . . There is no minority to acknowledge this better.'[22] More surprising is a letter from Seán MacBride, the former inter-party Minister for External Affairs, to Barton in 1951 which refuted an allegation by Noël Browne at the time of his resignation. Browne suggested that he was the subject of 'an envenomed attack' by MacBride for being photographed with the archbishop. MacBride was deeply regretful that the distortion of a private remark might have caused embarrassment to Barton:

> Throughout the discharge of my public duties and in all my utterances, I have always done my best to ensure that absolute fair play should prevail in regard to the religious minorities . . . It was because of my anxiety to ensure that the religious minorities should have their interest properly safeguarded . . . that I now again write to Your Grace, placing my services at Your Grace's disposal.[23]

This letter poses an interesting counterbalance to MacBride's well-known and obsequious letter to Archbishop McQuaid in 1947, in which he hoped that McQuaid would not hesitate to avail of his services as a Catholic and public representative, should the occasion arise.[24] These correspondences, albeit limited, demonstrate a cordial relationship between the archbishop of Dublin, the senior Church of Ireland ecclesiastic in the South, and the government.

When Archbishop Simms was translated to Armagh in July 1969, Jack Lynch warmly expressed the hope that 'Your Grace's elevation will not involve the severance of all your links with Dublin and that we will continue to see you here from time to time in the years to come.'[25] As was the case when Simms became archbishop of Dublin, the Taoiseach was not represented at the ceremony of installation on 26 September 1969 because no approach was made by Armagh regarding representation.[26] But Colonel Ronald Mew, Director of the Irish Army's Engineer Corps and a member of the Church of Ireland, represented President de Valera. Sir Norman Stronge, Lieutenant of Armagh, represented the Governor of Northern Ireland.[27] In a letter of thanks to de Valera, Simms recalled with characteristic *bonhomie* the 'happy occasions' at de Valera's 'hospitable home and also much wise counselling which you so readily gave in problems concerning Church and State in which there were constantly decisions to be made.'[28]

The Second Vatican Council's Decree on Ecumenism permitted the attendance of Catholic public representatives at the official ceremonies of other churches. The Taoiseach accordingly attended in person, for the first time, the installation of Alan Buchanan, Simms's successor as archbishop of Dublin, on 22 November 1969; likewise the President. In a letter of thanks, Dean Salmon of Christ Church, felt that Lynch's presence 'both personally and as Taoiseach added much to the dignity of the ceremony'.[29] Buchanan promised to do his 'utmost to be a friend to the whole community. If ever it lies in my power to be of service to the Government, I shall count it a privilege.'[30]

It should also be noted that the government was regularly represented at the installation of Church of Ireland bishops and not simply archbishops. For example, Lieutenant-Col. R. W. Bunworth, a member of the Church of Ireland, represented Lemass at the consecration of Henry McAdoo as bishop of Ossory on 11 March 1962. An army officer was not always chosen as representative. Lionel Booth TD, a Methodist, occasionally did the honours such as at the memorial service for John F. Kennedy in St Patrick's Cathedral in November 1963.[31] In May 1967, he represented the Taoiseach at the installation of Samuel Poyntz as vicar of St Anne's. Booth believed that such 'small tokens of mutual concern and respect [were] of very real value.'[32] Despite the oft-rehearsed condemnation of the government's deportment at the funeral of Douglas Hyde, it was in fact regularly represented at funerals. When Gregg died on 2 May 1961, Lemass sent a message of sympathy to Mrs Gregg and arranged that Lieutenant-Col. Bunworth would represent him at a memorial service in St Patrick's Cathedral on 5 May.[33]

Courtesy towards church dignitaries was equally in evidence at local government level. A cursory examination of votes of sympathy and messages of congratulations in the minutes of Cavan and Monaghan County Councils, for instance, reveals an impartial treatment of Catholic Church and Church of Ireland notables. On becoming bishop of Kilmore, Elphin and Ardagh in 1950, Cavan County Council wished Frederick Mitchell 'a long and fruitful administration of the duties of his episcopal office' and undertook to present an address on the day of his consecration.[34] The Council also presented formal addresses of welcome in 1956 to Charles Tyndall, Mitchell's successor, and in 1959 to Edward Moore who succeeded Tyndall.[35] Similarly, Monaghan County Council unanimously extended its good wishes to Alan Buchanan on his appointment as bishop of Clogher in 1958 and on his accession as archbishop of Dublin in 1969.[36] Votes of sympathy to the local bishop on the death of a clergyman were just as even-handed. There was no ebbing of courtesy in the turbulent opening years of the 1970s. Indeed, at a civic reception in November 1973 by Monaghan Urban District Council to honour Bishop Heavener's appointment, Heavener described 'community relations in Monaghan as a model for the rest of the country.'[37]

These examples illustrate a respect for men of the cloth, irrespective of denomination, by representatives of both national and local government. By contrast, it is worth bearing in mind how inconceivable it would have been for the Northern Ireland government to be represented at the enthronement of a Catholic bishop or archbishop. At a more fundamental level, as late as June 1968 the Grand Orange Lodge expelled Phelim O'Neill, the Unionist MP for North Antrim and cousin of the Prime Minister.[38] He was guilty of attending a service in a Catholic church in Ballymoney during Civic Week two years previously, of doing, in his own words, his 'minimum inescapable public duty'.[39] Even the *Belfast News-Letter* was shocked by the 'ultra-conservative, even reactionary' stance of the Orange Order.[40]

Apart from episcopal enthronements, the government was equitable in granting state receptions to mark other important church occasions. This was admirably demonstrated in 1961. A state reception was held in honour of the Catholic Church's Patrician year on 22 June 1961.[41] In April a state reception was held for the visit of the British Council of

Churches (BCC), the regional equivalent of the World Council of Churches of which the Irish Protestant churches were members. This is noteworthy because it was the first state reception by the government for a Protestant inter-church group or meeting. The April 1961 meeting of the BCC was not the first in Ireland as a meeting was held in Belfast in April 1952, but it was the first held in the Republic. Though not strictly a Church of Ireland affair, it was the most involved. Archbishop Simms was chairperson of the BCC 'Dublin Visit Committee' and Samuel Poyntz, vicar of St Anne's and future bishop of Cork and later Connor, was honorary secretary.[42] Among the four hundred delegates were Archbishop Geoffrey Fisher of Canterbury, a number of bishops of the Church of England and leaders of other Christian communities in Britain. Given their prestige, the possibility of a state reception was raised with Frank Aiken, Minister for External Affairs.[43] The Minister privately discussed the matter with Lemass who decided to hold a reception in Iveagh House, Dublin on 25 April 1961.[44] Intriguingly, and unknown to the organising committee, in consultation with Skentelbery of External Affairs and Con Cremin, secretary of that Department, Aiken proposed inviting Archbishop McQuaid and the nuncio! Not unexpectedly, given the infancy of inter-church relations before the Second Vatican Council, Monsignor Storero, secretary at the Nunciature, admitted to Cremin his doubts as to 'whether the Nuncio or the Archbishop would regard it as proper to be present – primarily because of the possibility that their presence might be interpreted by the general public as implying approval of the Council of Churches or its programme on the part of the Catholic Church'.[45] Kenneth Slack, general secretary of the BCC, informed Lemass that the Council agreed 'with acclamation' that its gratitude be conveyed to the government for its 'gracious hospitality'.[46] 'The reception, and the beauty of Iveagh House', he continued, 'was a most memorable feature of a visit to Dublin which will make this particular Council meeting to be long recalled as one of the most remarkable which we have held'.[47] Both Simms and Poyntz similarly appreciated 'the delightful reception' and 'the excellent arrangements'.[48] The President also entertained a number of delegates, including Archbishop Fisher, at a luncheon at Áras an Uachtaráin.[49]

Despite the trauma of the political situation in Northern Ireland, the Church of Ireland celebrated the centenary of Disestablishment in 1970 with events in Dublin and Belfast. The Irish government made two tasteful gestures to honour the occasion. The Department of Finance, which had taken over responsibility for official entertainment, responded positively to a suggestion from Robert Wyse Jackson, bishop of Limerick and chairperson of the Disestablishment Committee, that the government host a reception on 12 May 1970.[50] Among the 900 guests were the four Catholic archbishops as well as representatives of the Methodist and Presbyterian Churches and the Jewish Congregation.[51]

Secondly, the government facilitated a volume of essays in tribute to the Anglican contribution to Irish life entitled: *Irish Anglicanism 1869–1969*. This *festschrift* was the idea of Michael Hurley SJ, the leading Irish Catholic ecumenist. He secured a grant towards the cost of publication from Jack Lynch who prevailed on Pádraig Faulkner, the Minister for Education. Though anxious 'not to create a precedent', the Department of Education sanctioned a grant of £3,000.[52] Similar efforts to get assistance from the Northern government proved unsuccessful.[53] For publication reasons, the volume was presented to Archbishop Simms at an inter-denominational ceremony, televised on RTÉ, at Gonzaga College, Dublin on 15 April 1970, instead of at the Government reception. This was attended by the Taoiseach, who proposed the toast to the Church of Ireland.[54] The government's generous approach contrasted sharply with that of the Catholic hierarchy and, in particular, with that of Archbishop McQuaid. Invitations had been issued to all religious leaders including Gaetano Alibrandi, the papal nuncio. When he sought McQuaid's advice on the matter, the archbishop had 'no hesitation' in counselling the nuncio not to attend. McQuaid himself had refused an invitation along with his two auxiliaries because one had to 'take very carefully into account the effect on the ordinary Catholics of the whole country of attending such a function . . . Ordinary people, who form the overwhelming majority of our Faithful, cannot understand any appearance of mitigating heresy.'[55] In the end, Peter Birch, Catholic bishop of Ossory, was the only Catholic bishop to attend the presentation.[56] While acknowledging that 'misunderstandings did not disappear over night', the *Irish Press*, in an aptly titled editorial: 'Disestablished and Integrated', complimented the wise leadership of successive Church of Ireland primates and the impartiality of successive governments.[57]

The insistence by the government that each major denomination, without distinction, mark state occasions such as the opening of a new Dáil or the fiftieth anniversary of the 1916 Rising has been conveniently overlooked by political scientists.[58] It was customary for special services to be held on the day the Dáil assembled after a general election. For instance, the assembly of the 17th Dáil, on 11 October 1961, was marked by a Solemn Votive Mass in the Pro-Cathedral and separate Divine Services by the Church of Ireland, the Methodist Church, the Presbyterian Church and the Dublin Jewish Congregation. In 1937 and 1938 the Taoiseach was represented at such Church of Ireland services, and the President in 1943, 1944, 1948 and 1951.[59] However, in 1954 de

Valera decided that the government should be represented by Erskine Childers, Minister for Transport and Power, as well as the President, a practice which continued throughout the 1960s. The assembly of the 18th Dáil, on 21 April 1965, and the 19th Dáil, on 2 July 1969, saw the main Protestant churches come together for a joint service in St Patrick's Cathedral at which Childers represented the government, and an army officer, the President.[60]

The commemoration of the fiftieth anniversary of the Rising saw all the churches cooperating with the government's desire to venerate suitably the event. In March 1965, initial approaches were made, with the exception of the Catholic hierarchy, to the local (i.e. Republic of Ireland) head of all the main denominations and congregations.[61] Archbishop Simms brought a letter from Lemass to the attention of the House of Bishops. The government subsequently changed the proposed date from Sunday 24 April to Sunday 10 April. Both Church of Ireland and Catholic Church authorities expressed concern, on liturgical grounds, that 10 April was Easter Sunday, and so favoured Easter Monday 1966 instead.[62] The House of Bishops authorised special services of commemoration in diocesan cathedrals in the Republic, with a united Protestant service in St Patrick's Cathedral at which Childers represented the government.[63] All the churches were represented by their respective heads at the government reception in St Patrick's Hall, Dublin Castle on Sunday 17 April 1966.

Education

Education was the key area of interaction between the Irish state and Church of Ireland authorities for whom the school was second only to the church as a mainspring of community cohesion. The Church of Ireland was certainly not a fearful minority in its educational demands, rather a self-assertive one. In contrast to Northern Ireland, church–state relations in the educational sphere in the Republic were, by and large, harmonious. The Irish government played an enabling role actively, but even-handedly, reinforcing a parallel system of denominational education. In June 1954, the report of the Council of Education recommended that 'explicit recognition' be given to the

> denominational character of the schools and, in accordance with Article 44.2.4 of the Constitution, to provide that the Rules shall not discriminate between schools under the management of different religious denominations or be such as to effect prejudicially the right of any child to attend a National School without attending religious instruction at that school.[64]

At the opening ceremony of the new £26,000 Bandon Grammar School on 2 May 1958, Tarlach Ó Raifeartaigh, secretary of the Department of Education, felt that 'while the state is neutral in the sense that it tries to deal fairly with all Church authorities, it is not neutral in the sense that it has a particular interest in the welfare of the various denominations as denominations'.[65]

On balance, the Department of Education did well by the Church of Ireland. Ó Raifeartaigh's contention that the government tried to be 'a little generous towards the schools of the minority' was a fair one and frequently acknowledged by the Church of Ireland bishops.[66] Evelyn Charles Hodges, bishop of Limerick, Ardfert and Aghadoe from 1943 until 1960, spoke about education at the 1958 Lambeth Conference, the decennial consultative assembly of bishops of the Anglican communion first initiated in 1867. Hodges commended his government for being 'meticulously honourable in carrying out its undertaking'. He highlighted that the state bore seven-eighths of the cost of maintenance but allowed the Church of Ireland appoint teachers and manage its schools. He also praised the transport scheme that delivered Protestant children to their own schools 'having passed several Catholic schools'.[67] As a prominent member of the Board of Education and former principal of the Church of Ireland Training College, Hodges was well placed to make such an observation.

The Church of Ireland Board of Education was responsible for general policy on education and related issues such as school transport, supply of teachers and religious education curriculum. It comprised the archbishops and bishops as *ex-officio* members, one lay and clerical representative from each diocese and about twenty co-opted members representing teachers. Throughout the 1960s, the House of Bishops also nominated three bishops as representatives to the executive committee of the Board, which was the main agent for negotiation with the government.

A transport scheme to convey children to schools under Church of Ireland management first came into operation in 1934. It was overseen by the Transport Sub-Committee of the Board of Education. Representations to the Minister for Education secured a grant increase from £5 to £8 per child in the 1954–55 school year.[68] The total cost involved was spread across the Department of Education, the Board, as well as the local diocese and parish. In Kilmore, for example, there were six so-called No. 1 schemes in operation in the late 1950s. The Arvagh scheme, which catered for twelve children in north Cavan, cost £170 6s. The Department contributed £90, the Board of Education almost £41, the diocese £24, and the parish of Arvagh itself over £15.[69] Kilmore diocesan educational funds were augmented in this period by donations from individuals and subscriptions from organisations, particularly Orange lodges. David Fitzpatrick has calculated that there were about 700 lodge members in Cavan and Monaghan in 1965.[70] Such donations in 1962 included £2 from the Kilmore LOL, £191 11s from the Women's Grand LOL and £8 from the Cavan Women's LOL.[71] Other cross-border dioceses such as Clogher also received contributions towards school transport from the Orange Order.[72] Indeed, seconding the Clogher diocesan council report in 1961, Archdeacon R. T. Farrell of Clogher felt that such strenuous efforts to provide school transport from all quarters of the diocese demonstrated 'the unity and the oneness of their Church'.[73]

School closures and amalgamations tended over time to markedly increase the cost involved, as larger numbers of children were ferried longer distances. In 1962 over 700 children were conveyed at an annual cost of £17,000. But this figure excluded as many as 400 children, in isolated areas, who needed greater assistance.[74] However, in this year a new scheme (known as a No. 2 scheme) was sanctioned by the Department of Education, whereby children living over three and a half miles from school, hitherto out of reach of public transport, were to receive a grant of £14 per child. These No. 2 schemes catered for groups with an average of less than five children. In 1968 there were four such schemes in Kilmore and seven in the united dioceses of Dublin, Glendalough and Kildare.[75] From 1 April 1967 the Department of Education undertook to pay for all the No. 1 transport schemes, subject to a nominal contribution from the local education authority.[76]

The government's commitment also extended to teacher training. The Church of Ireland did not have to contend with the same acute shortage of teachers in the Republic as it did in Northern Ireland, but a shortfall nonetheless. Bishop Hodges secured a concession from the Minister for Education which allowed married women, prohibited from teaching in primary schools under the marriage bar of 1932, to be appointed in a temporary capacity in extreme circumstances where no teacher fully qualified in training and religion was available.[77] The unpalatable alternative, a danger raised by Robert Heavener, future bishop of Clogher, was that Catholics would teach Protestant children.[78] Less successful was a recommendation that teaching experience gained outside Ireland be recognised. When it was decided to build a new Church of Ireland Training College in Rathmines, to replace the facility at Kildare Place, the government agreed, in November 1966, to guarantee the required loan of £535,000 under the State Guarantees Act (1954).[79] Church authorities intended to borrow £200,000 from the RCB and the remainder from a consortium of insurance companies. However, this did not materialise and the government stepped in by providing a direct capital grant of £259,600. The Department of Education also awarded a grant of £13,797 towards running expenses, which by 1970 had increased to £24,931.[80] Thanking President de Valera for attending the opening on 13 March 1969, Archbishop Simms remarked that 'the College is a magnificent building and the Departments of Finance and Education have been most helpful all through the days of planning and construction'.[81]

Two curricular issues were particularly problematic. The question of suitable textbooks was largely solved in the 1920s and 1930s by the provision of *Saorstát Readers* and lists of books approved by the Department. Doubts about the 'general tendency' of textbooks, particularly in history, persisted into the late 1950s.[82] The second and more complex issue was the position of the Irish language in primary schools. Was the Church of Ireland openly hostile to the Irish language? Or, as Terence Brown posits, was the language revival policy an assault on their English language cultural identity?[83] However true this may have been in the 1920s, a report by a sub-committee of the Board of Education in October 1949 was at pains to distinguish between the prerequisites of pedagogical efficiency *per se*, and attitudes to the Irish language: 'Virtually no hostility to Irish as such was noted, but general dissatisfaction is expressed with regard to the methods employed to extend the use of Irish as a known and used language.'[84] The response of the Board to the Report of the Council of Education similarly sought to decouple teaching methods, which placed the main burden on infants, from attitudes towards the language.[85] The Dublin, Glendalough and Kildare diocesan board of education was less diplomatic. It believed Pearse's 'murder machine' had been merely painted green and deemed the revival effort a failure because the motive behind the method of teaching sprang 'from political rather than educational roots, from sentiment rather than from common sense'.[86] Individual members of the Church of Ireland were supportive of the language. The Irish Guild of the Church (*Cumann Gaelach na hEaglaise*) was founded as early as 1914 to promote the use of Irish.[87] An Irish translation of the Prayer Book was provided in 1931 and services in Irish were held each month in St Patrick's Cathedral. Indeed many members of the House of Bishops were Irish speakers, among them Simms, McAdoo and Caird, all of whom served as archbishop of Dublin. Returning to Brown's thesis, there was little fear in the reports of the Board of Education that the Irish language policy would erase the Church of Ireland's cultural identity. Brown's argument could only make sense if the language revival policy was very successful. It was not. Moreover, this impractical government policy applied to all school children and to argue that the Church of Ireland was somehow more aggrieved than other denominations in the 1950s is fanciful.

Both churches faced the challenge posed by the necessary reorganisation of one-teacher primary schools. In the early 1960s, over half of the 740 one-teacher schools in the Republic were under Church of Ireland management, in a scattered network.[88] One-teacher schools accounted for twenty-seven out of a total of thirty-five schools in the Glendalough and Kildare area of the diocese of Dublin, Glendalough and Kildare alone.[89] This not only put pressure on the supply of teachers but also made increasingly difficult the provision of adequate teaching facilities. In some schools one teacher had to teach six to seven divisions with children ranging in age from four to fourteen years. In June 1962, Senator John C. Cole raised the issue of educational standards at the Kilmore diocesan synod and argued that a better standard of education in Britain was one of the reasons why families emigrated.[90] He pressed for the centralisation of schools and proposed that a committee be appointed to investigate the matter.

An Advisory Committee on Primary Education, with Archbishop Simms as chairperson, was established by the Board in November 1963. It studied Cole's proposals for Kilmore and recommended that similar schedules be prepared for Monaghan and Donegal.[91] By June 1964, in line with the Advisory Committee, the House of Bishops favoured the general idea of centralisation where practical, provided the government would finance school transport.[92] This foreshadowed the recommendations of the survey team set up by the Department of Education and OECD in their monumental 1965 report, *Investment in Education*. This influenced the thinking of George Colley, Minister for Education, for whom untrained staff, modern sanitation, building standards and the degree of attainment were equally pressing concerns. He therefore advocated larger central schools with three or more teachers.[93] Colley met the Advisory Committee in July 1965 and expressed his approval of the decision of the General Synod to adopt the policy of school centralisation. The Minister appreciated the concerns of the committee and gave reassurances that the brunt of the cost of transport would be borne by the state.[94]

Unsurprisingly, the policy of amalgamation met with resistance in some quarters. There was a reluctance to give the *coup de grace* to what in the past was an essential element of parish life. But this sentiment had to be balanced by economic and pedagogic realities. One Church of Ireland teacher told Michael Viney: 'These schools are a disgrace. They exist for the prestige of the Church, rather than for the education of the children. They exist so that the country parson can still talk of "my little school, my teacher."'[95] Disinclination was even greater in Catholic circles. Bishop Michael Browne of Galway clashed publicly with Colley in September 1965 and again the following February over the proposed closure of two-teacher schools.[96] But Colley was not deterred and the policy continued. Between January 1966 and 1972, more than 900 one and two-teacher schools of all denominations were closed.[97] One Church of Ireland central school in Monaghan replaced eight neighbouring schools when it opened in 1968.[98] In Clogher there were fifty-seven Church of Ireland schools in 1967, forty-one fewer than in 1955.[99] An interesting feature of this reorganisation was, in stark contrast to earlier decades, the necessary coming together of various Protestant denominations to build joint primary schools. One of several examples was the opening in April 1965 of a new Presbyterian-Church of Ireland school in the village of Convoy, County Donegal. The Donegal Education Committee of the Derry and Raphoe diocesan synod regarded such schools as 'symptomatic of the new spirit of interdenominational thinking in Donegal with regard to education'.[100]

Turning now to secondary education, the General Synod established a committee to 'make a thorough investigation' in 1962.[101] A stark realism is evident in the reports of the Board of Education during this period. Radical steps had to be taken to improve the scope as well as the infrastructure of secondary education if Protestant children were to receive an education equal to European and national standards, a point emphasised by Archbishop McCann at the General Synod in 1967.[102] Just as for primary education, this would require fewer and larger schools. A number of developments emanating from the Department of Education both facilitated and necessitated change. In 1964, Patrick Hillery, the Minister for Education, introduced a scheme of building grants for secondary schools under which the state provided a grant of sixty per cent of the cost of providing new secondary schools or additions to or reconstruction of existing schools. By the end of the decade many prominent Church of Ireland schools had been redeveloped. In Dublin, the High School moved from Harcourt Street to a new site in Rathgar and Alexandra College moved to Milltown, while in Cork the Grammar School and Rochelle School merged in 1970.

Less straightforward was the concept unveiled in May 1963 by Hillery of a comprehensive school, where entry would be comprehensive (i.e. not selective and open to all regardless of ability) to cater for children living in areas not served by either a secondary or vocational school.[103] Though largely favoured by the Board of Education, the working out of the practicalities in a denominationally satisfactory way led to much histrionics by both churches. At a time when the educational landscape was being altered in several spheres conjointly, each church had its own vested interests and suspicions. There was tension between the desire to preserve denominational education in the Republic, in order to protect the Church of Ireland community's solidity, and the government's plans. This was further complicated by a notable dissatisfaction among Protestant parents that the price they were being asked to pay by the Board for denominational education, day or boarding, was too high, when from 1967 onwards the government offered 'free' education.

There was grave apprehension among church authorities that all vocational schools would be amalgamated with existing secondary schools to form new comprehensives. The Department was at pains to allay such fears.[104] The Church of Ireland bishops were for the most part happy with the vocational system under which boards of management were interdenominational and chaplains were provided for Church of Ireland students. But they feared that comprehensives would be under Catholic control. In Cootehill, the first comprehensive to be opened, the board of management which came into operation in April 1966, consisted of a nominee of Austin Quinn, the Catholic bishop, who would act as chairperson; a nominee of the Minister for Education; and a nominee of the Vocational Education Committee (VEC), who would act as Chief Executive Officer.[105] The Catholic hierarchy pressed for an assurance that the consent of the bishop's representative on the board would always be required for the appointment of non-Roman Catholics to teaching posts.[106] Sensing a misunderstanding, the Department of Education stated clearly that it did not favour positive discrimination but wanted any Protestant application fairly considered so that the best-qualified teacher could be hired.[107]

The introduction of free secondary education by Donagh O'Malley from September 1967 resulted in a rapid increase in the number of post-primary students from just over 152,000 in 1967 to over 185,000 in 1969.[108] New secondary schools were needed to meet this growing demand. The Department proposed a development of the comprehensive school model – the community school, which could be formed from the amalgamation of secondary and vocational schools. This came to light when the text of a working document was published by the *Irish Times* in November 1970.[109] The Catholic hierarchy had been consulted but no one else. A storm of protest ensued. The Board of Education was alarmed at the proposed composition of the boards of management. The Catholic hierarchy wished to explore the possibility of having a clause in the Trust Deed which would safeguard the Catholic character of such schools.[110] Pádraig Faulkner, the Minister for Education, failed to offer reassurance in a statement in May 1971 and it appeared that Catholic interests would dominate the trusteeship and management. For this reason at the Clogher diocesan synod later that month, Bishop Richard Hanson described the legislation as 'a deplorable move'.[111] Bishop Edward Moore told the Kilmore diocesan synod that if the intention of the Minister was not sectarian, then he should at once withdraw the scheme and a resolution sharply critical of the proposals was passed.[112] Alarmed at the misunderstanding aroused by the proposals, Cardinal Conway denied the assertion that the Catholic Church was anxious to gain control of the entire vocational school system. He pointed out that the government, not the Catholic Church, decided where amalgamations were to occur. In this regard, the rule that schools of fewer than 400 had to amalgamate only applied to Catholic schools; Protestant schools could have a much lower enrolment.[113] He further outlined that if Protestant church authorities had a comprehensive school, they were entitled to have three of the five members appointed by the local Protestant bishop or Board of Education. This was the case with the amalgamation of the Royal School in Raphoe and the Prior School in Lifford to form the Royal and Prior Comprehensive School, which from September 1971 served the Protestant community in east Donegal.[114] Conway thought it only proper that Protestant parents seek that their children be 'brought up in a school which corresponds to the religious ethos and atmosphere of their own homes.'[115] Faulkner was forced to alter his proposals and in early 1972 suggested new arrangements. The composition of the six-member board of management would henceforth be divided equally between representatives of the secondary school, the VEC and parents.[116] The trustees in whom the school was vested would be appointed by the Minister on the nomination of the school authorities and not by the Catholic bishop as was originally proposed.[117] This was noted with 'appreciation' by the Board of Education.[118]

The Church of Ireland broadly welcomed O'Malley's secondary education initiative and mourned his sudden death in 1968.[119] A new interdenominational Protestant body known as the Secondary Education Committee was established in 1965 to represent the educational interests of all Protestant children. The Church of Ireland was the dominant member of this lobby group with Gordon Perdue, bishop of Cork, as chairperson. The Committee inspired similar cooperation between Protestant denominations at a local level such as in Donegal.[120] The Secondary Education Committee and the government haggled over the size of grants in the late 1960s. Perdue was not slow to load the pleadings in favour of the minority so as to reinforce the moral and legal obligations of the State. Notably, he rarely approached the Departments of Education and Finance. Instead, he utilised his local TD, the Taoiseach Jack Lynch, with whom he had a warm relationship. Under O'Malley's original blueprint, on the basis of a projected seventy-five per cent participation rate by Catholic pupils, the Secondary Education Committee would be entitled to a block grant of £70,000 or £25 per day-pupil. The actual participation rate for Catholic pupils was ninety-two per cent. Consequently, Perdue's committee calculated an entitlement of £86,500 to be disbursed on the basis of a means test.[121] Even though the Department of Education paid £78,400, the Committee allocated funds to its schools on the basis of their estimation and were thus caught awkwardly in the red. Perdue subsequently had an interview with Lynch and sought the shortfall of £6,000 from the Department, as well as administration costs of £3,000.[122] Lynch approached Brian Lenihan, Minister for Education, to ask if he 'could manage this?'[123] Both Lenihan and Lynch then made representations to Charles Haughey, the Minister for Finance. He was unsympathetic because the discrepancy between the actual block grant paid and the estimate by the Committee rested on the exclusion by the Department of non-recognised pupils, such as those not taught Irish or under twelve years of age. Given that the criteria for eligibility were clearly communicated, Haughey was 'satisfied that he would not be justified in allocating a further sum'.[124] Neither did he entertain the suggestion that the administration costs be reimbursed because, as he saw it, the funds for free secondary education 'must be confined to what is strictly needed for tuition fees'.[125] However, there appears to have been a change of heart in December 1968. Lynch informed Perdue that having reviewed the matter the Department of Finance would pay the £8,500 sought by the Secondary Education Committee.[126]

O'Malley's scheme required some modification in view of the number of Protestant boarding pupils and the distance travelled by day pupils. A block grant of £60,000 was originally proposed for boarders. Haughey honoured O'Malley's commitment in a once-off gesture even though the Department of Education recommended £54,000 for the 1967–68 school year based on the number of eligible boarders. The following year £55,000 was allocated with a grant of £82,225 for day pupils based on an anticipated three per cent increase in numbers of Protestant pupils.[127] Haughey felt on the whole that 'the Protestant community is being very fairly treated under the free education scheme and I do not think that we could, in equity, make any further concessions than those already indicated.'[128] Thanking Lynch for his efforts, Perdue informed the Taoiseach that having met a Church of Ireland delegation, Lenihan was 'fully aware of our disappointment at the amount of the grant suggested for boarding pupils for the coming year'.[129] He reported growing unrest among poorer Protestant parents towards the end of the year and expected 'a major eruption'.[130] This was dissimulation in that unrest came from parents favouring a local comprehensive in Cork. In reality, the bishop feared the government was stealing his thunder by opportunistically offering free education. Perdue's energetic lobbying paid dividends. In January 1969, it was announced that the boarding grant would be increased by almost sixty-four per cent to £90,000 for the 1969–70 school year.[131] This represented a *per capita* increase per Protestant boarder from £25 to £41 in comparison to £19 for non-Protestant boarders.[132] At this point, Lenihan felt that both block grants should be amalgamated to prevent increases in one being used to justify increases in the other. Henceforth, there would be one payment to the Committee for use as it saw fit, which in 1969–70 was £186,000.[133]

Nonetheless, for certain members of the Church of Ireland this was not enough. A resolution at the General Synod in 1969, proposed by Frank Jacob and seconded by Bishop McAdoo, welcomed the advances in the educational field but called on the government to remove disadvantages encountered in the areas of transport grants, staff remuneration, boarding grants and assistance in aid of capital expenditure for the provision of boarding accommodation. McAdoo felt the fact that 'these disabilities were not intended, does not affect their existence or their reality . . . if our children are to receive the same benefits as others do, they must have the right to be educated in their own schools'.[134] This helps explain the importance attached to boarding grants, particularly for children outside Dublin where Church of Ireland schools were not so plentiful. Jacob estimated that 4,500 children lived outside the range of day schools under Protestant management.[135] The strict application of free transport for secondary pupils within specific catchment areas was, therefore, resented as some Church of Ireland children were not eligible for free transport to a Protestant secondary school slightly further away, or in another direction. Jacob ended his speech by proclaiming his credentials as a Protestant Republican and an Irishman, lest anyone misconstrue his 'criticism of the government of the Republic as an attack on the Republic itself'.[136] In July 1971, the Secondary Education Committee agreed to a number of comprehensives in the Dublin area. This was on condition that such schools did not exceed 500 pupils and that grants towards fees were available for parents of limited means who wished to continue to send their children to the existing post-primary schools in Dublin.[137]

To its credit, the government tried to meet these concerns. In the 1971–72 school year, the block grant was raised by £4,050 to £195,000.[138] Also in this year, Protestant pupils qualified for free transport to the nearest Protestant secondary school irrespective of whether an adequate vocational school was within three miles of their home. In effect, this meant that all Protestant pupils within an economic range of transport were given free transport to a Protestant school.¹³⁹ But a Catholic child would have to self-finance the journey if s/he wished to attend a school other than the local vocational. Protestant pupils outside the range of transport qualified for remoteness grants, where the school fee was £250 or less.¹⁴⁰ All things considered, in the field of education the Church of Ireland was treated with generosity and goodwill by the government. As one parent expressed it, a willingness to accept a comprehensive school indicated 'more clearly than words the real confidence and trust which Protestants have in the basic fairness and democratic principles on which the Republic of Ireland is founded.'¹⁴¹

Contributing to national life

In June 1964 Bishop Edward Moore proudly claimed that by their industry and integrity the Church of Ireland community made a contribution to national life greatly in excess of their numbers.¹⁴² In the 1961 census other denominations (OD) accounted for 4.9 per cent of the population, Catholics 94.86.¹⁴³ However, this relatively weak demographic position did not translate as under-representation in the labour force. In several categories the representation of OD was substantially above their demographic proportion. Of male farmers: 13.4 per cent had holdings of 100–200 acres and 22.6 per cent over 200 acres. In the commercial occupations, OD accounted for 8.7 per cent of proprietors and managers in addition to 18.3 per cent of commercial travellers and agents. Of the professions, OD accounted for 13.9 per cent of dentists, doctors and surgeons; 8.5 per cent of male teachers and 10.8 per cent of female teachers. However, the most dominant economic sector was that of company directors, managers and executives with 30.8 per cent.¹⁴⁴ A report by Viney in 1965 found that 6.5 per cent of Protestant men were directors, managers and company secretaries with a further 8.3 per cent in professional and technical jobs. The respective figures for Catholics were 0.9 per cent and 4.3 per cent.¹⁴⁵ A survey by the *Irish Times* in 1973 claimed that twenty-four per cent of senior executives in Irish business were Protestant.¹⁴⁶

In popular unionist mythology the Irish language proviso for entry to the civil service was regarded as discriminating against Southern Protestants.¹⁴⁷ But the assertion that Protestants were conspicuous in the Irish civil service by their absence has little foundation. In 1961, 89 of the 1,970 male officials in senior grades in the civil service and local authorities were Protestant. This amounts to a participation of 4.5 per cent, which was not much less than their proportion of the population as a whole.¹⁴⁸ This omits the career of Thekla Beere, the daughter of a

Church of Ireland clergyman, who in 1959 became the first woman to head a government department in the newly established Department of Transport and Power. Such evidence supports Jack White's belief that there was a stronger inclination among Protestants towards private business as opposed to some feeling of alienation engendered by the necessity of requiring Irish for the civil service.[149] Only 140 of the 8,500 members (1.65 per cent) of the Defence Forces were Protestant and all but 50 of the 6,400 Gardaí (99.2 per cent) at rank of sergeant or below were Catholic.[150] This reflected career choice rather than any institutionalised discrimination. Significantly, in the Defence Forces provisions for religious and spiritual welfare were the same for members of the Church of Ireland as for Catholics. The local clergyman in whose parish members of the Defence Forces were stationed normally acted as 'officiating clergyman' on the authority of his bishop. The exception was the Curragh where chaplains were formally employed by the Department of Defence with the bishop's licence, their stipend part-paid by the Department and the parishes where they were rectors.[151]

At the opening of Bandon Grammar School in May 1958, the Reverend J. W. McKinney, President of the Methodist Church and principal of Gurteen Agricultural College, highlighted the perception that 'as a Protestant community [we] have very often been slow to play our full part in public life and in helping to contribute to the well-being of the nation as a whole. It is time that error was corrected.'[152] Yet taking the upper house of the Oireachtas, it is seldom recollected that in the eleven Seanads between 1938 and 1973 members of the Protestant churches regularly featured in the Taoiseach's list of nominees. This was unconnected with the contribution of the Trinity College senators. For example, in 1948 John A. Costello nominated Captain Edward Richards Orpen; Denis Ireland, a writer and broadcaster who was a Northern Presbyterian and the first resident of Northern Ireland to become a member of the Oireachtas; and James Green Douglas, a prominent Quaker businessman.[153] In some cases, such nominations were a means of rewarding the party faithful. For instance, de Valera nominated Michael B. Yeats, son of the poet, to the sixth Seanad, which sat between 1951 and 1954. Yeats had been a party member since 1943 and stood unsuccessfully for Fianna Fáil in Dublin South-East in 1948 and 1951.[154] He lost his Seanad seat when the second inter-party government took office in 1954, but regained it in 1961. On his re-nomination in 1965, Yeats promised to do all in his power 'to further the interests of Fianna Fáil, both inside and outside the House' and in 1969 he became Cathaoirleach.[155] Similarly, Liam Cosgrave nominated Billy Fox in 1973 when he failed to be re-elected Fine Gael TD for Monaghan. Perhaps more surprising was the nomination of John C. Cole to the Seanad in 1961 and 1965. Cole was a Presbyterian from Cavan whose father, John, had been an independent TD for Cavan. Both father and son also served as Grand Master of Cavan.[156]

Did aspirant Seanad nominees stress their denominational background? 'Disliking any kind of interference in such matters', Archbishop Barton asked de Valera in 1951 to give consideration to R. G. L. Leonard, who missed out on election for Trinity.[157] Leonard was chancellor of the diocese of Dublin, Glendalough and Kildare, a member of the diocesan council as well as the General Synod, editor of the *Constitution of the Church of Ireland* (1946) and apparently a Fianna Fáil supporter.[158] This did not sway de Valera. On Costello's return to office, Barton again apologetically put forward Leonard's name: 'On general principles I dislike making any such suggestion, but Mr Leonard has given so generously of his time and energy to the legal work of the Church of Ireland that I feel I must break my rule in this case.'[159] For a second time Leonard was overlooked in favour of Henry Eustace Guinness and James Green Douglas.[160] However, such lobbying by churchmen was rare.

Turning to the lower house, that numbers of TDs of one particular denomination or another were few proves very little. In the Irish political context, the Dáil in the 1950s and 1960s was not the equivalent of the Knesset with political cleavages on religious grounds. As Hubert Butler cogently argued, minority opinion was not *ipso facto* confined to the Protestant community. He felt that the number of Protestant public representatives was low 'not because the electoral system is unfavourable to minorities, but because in the last few decades our minority has got out of the way of nominating candidates. We simply don't stand for election.'[161] Edna Longley wryly observed that there was an almost inadmissible element of self-exclusion or self-seclusion among the Church of Ireland community at that time.[162] Church of Ireland bishops encouraged participation in public life. At the Derry and Raphoe diocesan synod, in June 1958, Bishop Boyd hoped that those 'who have the capacity to serve the community in this way will not hesitate to go forward'.[163] Similarly, Archbishop McCann reminded the laity at the diocesan synod of Armagh of the 'necessity of taking a full share in public life, in the work of administration in County Councils and in all other Committees appointed to deal with the government of our local affairs'.[164]

Faith was by no means a bar to career advancement for those of the Church of Ireland who served as political representatives. In 1962 Senator John C. Cole was unanimously elected chairperson of Cavan County Council. Patrick Reilly TD, the outgoing chairperson, felt this exemplified the spirit of tolerance in the county (which had a Protestant population of 5,146) and in the Republic generally, as well as serving as an example to Northern Ireland.[165] Henry and Maurice Dockrell were Fine Gael TDs. Maurice was Lord Mayor of Dublin in 1961. He dismissed any notion of Protestants voting solely *qua* Protestants or of any reluctance on the part of his Catholic constituents to seek his help and thought 'a young Protestant could enter politics now without feeling his faith was going to be an issue'.[166] He himself demonstrated this when on 17 June 1961 he read an address 'with great pleasure . . . both personally and as Lord Mayor' welcoming Cardinal Agagianian, the Papal Legate, to the Dublin Congress of the Patrician Year.[167] He even kissed Agagianian's ring to the dismay of some of his co-religionists. However, Dockrell acted in his representative capacity and not as a private member of the Church of Ireland. He revealed to Viney that this decision had been made prior to the ceremony 'in tribute to the wonderful Catholicism of the Irish people'.[168] At a national level, Erskine Childers not only held a number of ministerial portfolios, including being Tánaiste under Jack Lynch, but was elected fourth President of Ireland on 31 May 1973 – the second member of the Church of Ireland to hold the office of first citizen. In a letter to Seán MacEntee in 1948, Childers expressed disbelief at Robert Barton's hinting that a Protestant was unlikely to be appointed a Fianna Fáil minister.[169] His career proved Barton's suggestion unfounded. By comparison, it was only in October 1971 that a Catholic first held a ministerial position in the Stormont administration. But when G. B. Newe became a Minister of State in the Department of the Prime Minister he was a non-elected, non-party minister in a government of which the future was a matter of considerable speculation.

The caveat should be added that several Protestants contested elections and that the political parties were aware of the mobilising potential of denomination. Sacks's analysis of the 1969 election showed that Bertie Boggs, an Inishowen Protestant and Fine Gael candidate in Donegal North East, won a cross-cleavage vote in Inishowen and a largely Protestant vote outside his home area but failed to make the quota.[170] In 1965 Fine Gael ran Billy Fox in Monaghan where Erskine Childers was the Fianna Fáil candidate. He failed to reach the quota by a mere 235 votes but was elected in 1969. When Lionel Booth, Fianna Fáil TD for Dún Laoghaire-Rathdown from 1957 until 1969 and a Methodist, retired, Neville Keery was put forward as the Fianna Fáil candidate. Protestants also ran for Labour. For instance, in 1948, Archie Heron contested Dublin North-East and Arnold Marsh, Dún Laoghaire-Rathdown. The floating Protestant vote was attracted to Fianna Fáil in the aftermath of Costello's withdrawal from the Commonwealth.

However, by 1973 there appeared to have been a return to Fine Gael as suggested by the party's confidence in running Protestant candidates in all of the then four Ulster constituencies.

It is well recognised that members of the Church of Ireland were appointed to the highest ranks of the judiciary. For instance, Theodore Kingsmill Moore was a judge of the Supreme Court. Less well known is that members of the Church of Ireland were routinely appointed to the governing bodies of the university colleges. Government minutes for the years 1949 to 1973 consistently show that the Minister for Education put forward the local Church of Ireland bishop as one of the three government appointees.[171] The local Catholic bishop was also usually nominated along with the president of the student union. For instance, in 1950 Thomas Hearn, Church of Ireland bishop of Cork, Cloyne and Ross, was nominated for University College Cork (UCC) and John Winthrop Crozier, Church of Ireland bishop of Tuam, for University College Galway (UCG) along with their Catholic counterparts, Daniel Cohalan and Michael Browne.[172] The bishops, or their successors, were customarily reappointed at the end of each triennial term of office. Thus Simms and Cornelius Lucey were nominated to the governing body of UCC in 1953.[173] The exception to this practice was University College Dublin. The government nominated four out of twenty-seven members to the governing body.[174] A Church of Ireland dignitary was not appointed perhaps because in Dublin in those years Protestant students traditionally attended Trinity.

While nominally pluralist institutions, the reports of the Catholic deans of residence in UCC and UCG reveal the colleges' small number of non-Roman Catholic students. In UCC during the 1966–67 session, there were only 27 from a total student body of 2,644: 1 Methodist, 1 Buddhist and 25 members of the Church of Ireland. In UCG there were 2,232 Catholic students but only 3 others who were not. By comparison, in Queen's University there were 1,100 Anglican students in 1969 compared to 1,246 Catholics (27.2 per cent of full time undergraduates).[175] Given the miniscule number of Church of Ireland students in Cork and Galway, the appointment of the local Church of Ireland bishop to the governing body was a significant gesture by the government, and one that might well not have been made if a rigid *pro rata* scheme linking denominational strength to nomination was employed.

Aside from participation on university boards, members of the House of Bishops did not shirk the responsibility of speaking out on pressing national problems such as emigration. The pronouncements of the Catholic hierarchy, particularly those of Archbishop McQuaid and Cornelius Lucey, received widespread coverage. However, the 'flight from the land' and government inaction on emigration were also frequently mentioned in presidential addresses to diocesan synods.[176] In the context of a declining Church of Ireland population in the diocese of Kilmore, Bishop Frederick Mitchell perceptively drew attention to the reluctance of many farmers to improve living conditions in their homes or allow their adult children succeed them. This 'selfish, unchristian and murderous policy' had the inevitable consequence of driving their offspring to urban centres or to emigrate.[177] Mitchell's successor Edward Moore was a noted proponent of the agricultural sector in both his presidential addresses to the diocesan synod and in representations to the government.[178]

Discrimination in the Republic?

It is generally considered that the Protestant population in the South had been treated fairly since 1922. The *Gazette* expressed the view that 'members of the Church of Ireland were treated as Irishmen entitled to their religious and political opinions by all except a limited number of extremists. The worship of the church has been continuous and unhindered.'[179] Several members of the laity and clergy attested to impartial and tolerant treatment of their church. In a letter to the editor of the *Irish Times*, David Webb maintained that 'the Protestant minority here is protected by excellent guarantees that are honourably kept'.[180] Preaching in Christ Church Cathedral in November 1951, George Seaver, dean of Ossory and biographer of Gregg, felt that the Church of Ireland enjoyed a

> toleration, a consideration and I will add, a respect, such as our forefathers were very far from according to their [Catholic] forefathers . . . Our fellow-countrymen of the Roman Communion have shown themselves to be charitable and forgiving when they might have been vindictive. Gone are the days of religious persecution and ostracism; we are free to conduct our worship in our own churches and in our own way.[181]

Perhaps it is for this reason that the Meath Hospital affair in 1949 and, more especially, the Fethard-on-Sea boycott in 1957 have become *causes célèbres*, remarkable because they were exceptions. In both cases, the government set its face against any organised action which was perceived to be inimical to the Church of Ireland.

The Meath Hospital affair was essentially a clash between the Knights of St Columbanus and the Freemasons who competed to gain positions of influence for their members. Membership of the Knights, who earned popular notoriety as exponents of Catholic Action, was drawn from all sectors of the labour force and in December 1952 stood at 5,108.[182]

They gained a majority of the votes at the Meath Hospital's AGM, at which the governing body was elected, by exploiting lax membership rules. They unseated the old management and installed their own members. A High Court action by the old board failed to reverse this. However, the government came to the rescue with a private bill – the Meath Hospital Act (1951). This replaced the new committee with a body consisting of six nominees of Dublin County Council, six from Dublin Corporation, four from the essentially Protestant medical board, four elected by subscribers, two from the General Council of County Councils and two co-opted members.[183] Senator W. B. Stanford of Trinity College felt that the Act 'gave reason for the religious minority to feel reassured that they would not be allowed to be victimised by militant sectarian organisations'.[184]

A boycott by Catholics of their Protestant neighbours in the small Wexford village of Fethard-on-Sea began on 12 May 1957 apparently at the prompting of William Stafford, the local Catholic curate.[185] It was triggered by a belief that local Protestants had connived at, financed, or colluded in the disappearance of Sheila Cloney and her two daughters on 27 April 1957. A Protestant, she was married to Seán Cloney, a Catholic farmer. She left her home due to alleged clerical pressure to educate her children at the local Catholic school. Under the *Ne Temere* decree children of an inter-church marriage had to be raised as Catholics. The decree was the root cause of the boycott and is discussed in chapter five. Adrian Fisher took charge of the Fethard-on-Sea union of parishes on 9 May 1957. Prior to this Canon M. Talbot fulfilled pastoral duties in a temporary capacity. As a measure of thanks the parishioners decided to make a presentation to him and a fund was opened. Edward Grant, rector in Fethard from March 1946 to November 1956, suggests that contributions to this fund, made in public view in Gardiner's hardware shop, may have been retrospectively misinterpreted as contributions to finance the Cloneys' flight.[186]

The Protestant community was greatly affected by the boycott, in particular the two Protestant businesses in the village: Gardiner's hardware and general merchant store and Betty Cooper's post office-cum-news agency. The local Protestant school, with eleven pupils, was forced to close when Anna Walsh, the Catholic temporary teacher, resigned.[187] The elderly music teacher, Miss Knipe, lost all of her ten pupils and was later forced to appeal to the Fethard Relief Fund, a hardship fund established by Adrian Fisher. Similarly, Protestant farmers lost both Catholic labour and business. William Cruise would normally have sold from £50 to £100 worth of corn but in 1957 had only £15 worth for market.[188] There were more sinister overtones as the boycott continued. Fisher received an anonymous letter, bearing a Wexford postmark, which opened with the comment: 'You may have to be removed from Fethard.'[189]

Reports of events in Fethard-on-Sea did not appear in the national press until the last week of May 1957. The matter was informally considered by the government on 31 May. Memoranda by Maurice Moynihan, secretary to the government, disclose that de Valera discussed the issue with Archbishop McQuaid on 21 June.[190] The archbishop requested that the meeting should be 'strictly confidential' and Moynihan was instructed not to keep a record. However, he does divulge that McQuaid

> appeared to agree, generally, with the Taoiseach's views as to the inadequate justification, or lack of justification, on the available information for the attitude taken up by members of the Catholic community at Fethard and as to the damaging effect on the national reputation for religious tolerance and fair play which is likely to result from the publicity given to the matter.[191]

In a draft letter to James Staunton, Catholic bishop of Ferns, which does not appear to have been sent, de Valera urged him to use his influence to bring the boycott to an end. The Taoiseach felt that it was a source of scandal outside the country and greatly damaging to Catholicism within, 'as if we were a people who when we have numbers on our side can be tyrannical, cruel and unjust'.[192] Stanford recalled during an interview with de Valera that the Taoiseach was 'furious' at the boycott.[193] He was not alone. John Percy Phair, Church of Ireland bishop of Ossory from 1940 until 1962, in whose diocese Fethard-on-Sea was situated, claimed to have received many letters from individual Catholics appalled at the boycott (many of whom also contributed to Fisher's Relief Fund).[194] Dónal Barrington told the Social Study Congress in Dublin on 25 June 1957 that 'while we have great sympathy with them [the Catholic community], we consider that what they are doing is an unjust and terrible thing'.[195] For many people in Northern Ireland, the boycott was a paean to the adversity their co-religionists suffered at the hands of the Catholic Church and grist to the mill of those who argued that their way of life would not be tolerated in the South. It was a gift to Northern politicians keen to exploit the issue as proof 'that the vaunted religious tolerance of the twenty-six counties is little more than skin-deep'.[196] Comment on Fethard-on-Sea during the marching season was therefore as acerbic as it was predictable. Whatever the culpability of the Catholic Church, the Irish government was anxious to minimise the impression that Fethard-on-Sea was demonstrative of a general lack of tolerance of Protestantism in the Republic.

De Valera's public condemnation, in response to a parliamentary question from Noël Browne, on 4 July 1957 was unequivocal:

> I regard this boycott as ill-conceived, ill-considered, and futile for the achievement of the purpose for which it seems to have been intended; that I regard it as unjust and cruel to confound the innocent with the guilty; that I repudiate any suggestion that this boycott is typical of the attitude or conduct of our people . . . I beg of all who have regard for the fair name, good repute and well-being of our nation to use their influence to bring this deplorable affair to a speedy end.[197]

Among the many letters of support de Valera received was one from Bishop Phair who expressed 'deep appreciation' for the Taoiseach's 'helpful pronouncement' which offered 'very real encouragement' to the bishop's people.[198] Despite de Valera's denunciation, the boycott was never officially called off. It fizzled out towards the end of 1957 and the Cloneys were reunited. The government's response demonstrated a firm commitment to non-sectarianism in the Republic. Church of Ireland bishops who commented on the boycott blamed the Catholic Church, not the government. Bishop Charles Tyndall of Kilmore vowed to continue 'to teach Protestant Irishmen that they are not resident aliens but citizens of the country'.[199] Acknowledgement of the fairness and generosity of the government was as plentiful in the years after 1957 as before the boycott. For instance, at the opening of a new £6,000 school in Killarney in September 1959, in the presence of Bishop Hodges, Senator Stanford said minorities had good reason to be thankful for living where justice prevailed.[200] Indeed from the mid-1950s, the Department of the Taoiseach maintained a series of files entitled 'religious toleration in Ireland', which indicates a concern to ensure fair play.

But was Fethard-on-Sea indicative of a latent and subterranean anti-Protestantism merely coming to the surface? Speaking on 'The Reconciling of Conflicts Between and Within Nations' at the 1958 Lambeth Conference, Archbishop McCann seemed to suggest this by distinguishing between what happened at a government level from that of 'parish pump'. Although treated 'fairly and impartially' by the government, McCann maintained that his community was nevertheless afraid, not of their fellow Irishmen, but of 'unseen forces'.[201] He referred in particular to Catholic Action and one of its exponents: *Maria Duce* ('under Mary's leadership'). This was an ultra-Catholic group, a 'lunatic fringe', founded by Denis Fahey in 1945.[202] It came to prominence in 1950 with a hopelessly unsuccessful campaign to have Article 44 amended so as to recognise the Catholic Church as the one true church. McCann believed *Maria Duce* was characteristic of 'authoritarian autocracy, theological and ecclesiastical' or as he also expressed it, Catholic 'totalitarianism'.[203] Such a contention is tendentious. Like Fethard-on-Sea, commentators have placed too great an emphasis on the oddity that was *Maria Duce*.[204] While it is true that Fahey believed a Judeo-Masonic conspiracy threatened the Catholic Church, it is wholly inaccurate to overstate *Maria Duce's* influence or to claim its views were widely representative. Enda Delaney has redressed this by estimating a predominantly Dublin-based membership of around one hundred which 'represented the extremities of Irish Catholicism in the post-war era'.[205] The death of Fahey in January 1954 removed the movement's ideological mainstay and McQuaid subsequently suppressed it. However genuine McCann's fear of underlying anti-Protestantism, he could only invoke one example. As for the unseemly Fethard-on-Sea boycott, it was one localised incident which was swiftly condemned by the government and was not repeated.

Could it be said that specific legal provisions enshrining Catholic values, including the prohibition on the sale of contraceptives or aspects of Bunreacht na hÉireann, such as Article 41.3.2 which banned divorce, impinged on or strained relations between Church of Ireland authorities and the government in the 1950s and 1960s? Commentary on such a complex issue has suffered from two limitations. Firstly, there has been a failure to outline the House of Bishops' position on contraception and divorce in these years. Secondly, there has been a tendency to view legislative and constitutional change retrospectively, solely through the prism of the Northern Troubles.

Lionel Pilkington has refuted the persistent view that Irish Protestantism was *ipso facto* more liberal and more progressive than Irish Catholicism.[206] Concern about moral laxity, alcoholism, gambling and the 'craze for pleasure' during the 1950s was not solely the province of the Catholic hierarchy. The pronouncements of the Church of Ireland authorities articulated the same issues in strikingly similar language. For instance, the House of Bishops was as dubious as the Catholic bishops about proposed changes in the licensing laws in 1959.[207] The tone of the Catholic hierarchy's public statement on the matter, in June 1959, differed little from the report of the Dublin, Glendalough and Kildare Temperance and Social Welfare Society.[208] Both decried the economic, moral and social implications of alcoholism. Another persistent contention is that censorship alienated the Protestant population in the Republic more than their fellow Catholics. But surely interest in literature, theatre and film did not depend on denomination! Brian Fallon argues that the operation of Irish censorship was inefficient and many works were obtainable. He also underlines that censorship in Ireland was by no means unique in European terms and that Ireland was, nonetheless, highly literary and theatre-conscious throughout the 1950s.²⁰⁹

More specifically, how objectionable did the House of Bishops regard the tenets of the constitution on divorce and Article 44.1.2, the 'special position' of the Catholic Church? It was ironic in the light of the future furore over Article 44 that at the 1958 Lambeth Conference, Bishop Hodges paid tribute to the sub-clause which recognised other churches (the Church of Ireland being listed first).²¹⁰ Two years later, in a précis on religious liberty in Ireland prepared for the World Council of Churches, Archbishops McCann and Simms stressed that officially both governments were 'at pains to insure [sic] that there shall be fairness towards minorities; it is at the local level that difficulties arise'.²¹¹ Article 44 of Bunreacht na hÉireann was gently praised by them, as were generally friendly relations between Catholics and those of other religious affiliations.

If Article 44 was not such a bone of contention, then what of divorce? All Irish Protestant churches disapproved of divorce to varying degrees even though it had been available in Northern Ireland since 1939. Speaking on 'The Family in Contemporary Society' at the 1958 Lambeth Conference, Bishop Arthur Butler of Tuam felt that the lack of divorce in the Republic meant 'the moral backbone of people living under that system [was] very much better'.²¹² A pastoral letter from the House of Bishops on mixed marriages in 1966 made clear its stance on the 'unity and indissolubility' of marriage.²¹³ Family planning was also considered at Lambeth where Mitchell, Simms and Tyndall contributed to the drafting of a resolution.²¹⁴ Deliberations were continued at the 1968 Lambeth Conference under the theme of responsible parenthood. The Anglican Communion arrived at the conclusion, in the words of Archbishop Buchanan, that

> the responsibility of deciding the number and frequency of children has been laid by God upon the consciences of parents everywhere: that this planning, in such ways as are mutually acceptable to husband and wife in Christian conscience, is a right and important factor in Christian family life.²¹⁵

Official government concern that aspects of the constitution might be offensive to non-Roman Catholics did not manifest itself until the all-party committee to 'review the constitutional, legislative, and institutional bases of Government' in 1966.²¹⁶ In turn this stimulated greater commentary from the respective churches. The establishment of the committee was influenced by the Second Vatican Council's Decree on Religious Liberty (*Dignitatis humanae*) with its emphasis on protecting and promoting the inviolable rights of the individual.²¹⁷ In a letter to

Brian Lenihan, the Minister for Justice, Seán Lemass wondered if the decree obliged the State to change the law 'so as to allow divorce and remarriage for those of our citizens whose religion tolerates it?'[218] The Taoiseach was undeterred by the warning from the Catholic chancellor of the Dublin diocese, in February 1966, that there would be 'violent opposition from the Hierarchy to any proposal to allow divorce in the State'.[219] Lemass personally oversaw the establishment of the twelve-member cross-party committee, on which he himself served after his retirement in November 1966.[220] From the outset, Fine Gael insisted that recommendations be non-binding on participants.[221] The committee, chaired by George Colley, conducted a systematic review of the Constitution during the course of seventeen meetings, between 12 September 1966 and December 1966, when a final report was produced. While the report covered many aspects of the Constitution, only the proposals on divorce and the 'special position' clause need be considered here.

The reasoning behind the recommendations that divorce should be permitted for members of those churches which accepted it and that Article 44.1.2 be deleted was remarkable for its time as well as for its unanimity. The report highlighted the possible legal paradox of conflict between the recognition of a marriage in church and civil law where, for instance, a valid marriage, in civil law terms, was dissolved or nullified by the Catholic Church.[222] The Hunt case in 1945 was such an example.[223] Secondly, with relation to non-Roman Catholics, several arguments were advanced including the claim that the 'Constitution was intended for the whole of Ireland and that the percentage of the population of the entire island made up of persons who are Roman Catholics though large, is not overwhelming.'[224] Furthermore, it was felt that the prohibition on divorce was 'a source of embarrassment to those seeking to bring about better relations between North and South since the majority of the Northern population have divorce rights under the law applicable to that area'.[225] Deletion of Article 44.1.2 and Article 44.1.3 (which listed the other recognised churches and congregations) was proposed, as neither had juridical effect. The report argued that Article 44.1.2 referred to a statistical fact, or what one periodical later described as a type of Catholic 'TAM [Television Audience Measurement] rating', and that it was not intended to give any privilege to the Catholic Church.[226] Article 44.1.3 was criticised for not taking account of religious denominations which did not exist in Ireland when the constitution came into operation in 1937. Significantly, it was recognised that these provisions 'give offence to non-Catholics and are also a useful weapon in the hands of those who are anxious to emphasise the differences between North and South.'[227]

Although the members of the all-party committee were not bound to implement such recommendations, that these were made public was significant, and from press reports unexpected and even 'revolutionary'.[228] Just as noteworthy was the fact that during their deliberations, the committee did *not* consult the churches. This suggests a genuine and unprompted concern that public law should not be used to impose private religious morality. The response of the Catholic and Church of Ireland bishops to the report is instructive. In a draft letter to Colley, the Catholic bishops expressed their 'astonishment' firstly at not being approached and, secondly, that the 'authority of Vatican Council II, which describes divorce as a "plague" and which teaches that the marriage relationship . . . is a lasting one' should be invoked in favour of the proposal. Notably, there was no principled objection to the deletion of the special position clause, to the extent that 'no reference to it need be made in the letter to Mr Colley.'[229] Archbishop Simms ringingly reiterated the Anglican position on the indissolubility of marriage.[230] Lady Gwendolene Hort, President of the 17,500–member Mothers' Union, a flag bearer of mainstream Protestant opinion, was equally forthright. She informed Lynch that the Mothers' Union 'deplore that the Government of Éire who have always stood for the permanence of the marriage bond should now propose to lower its standard.'[231] It was in this light that Cardinal Conway's comment should be judged: 'One must have the greatest possible respect for the tenets of our fellow-Christians. Yet, in fact, comparatively few of them believe in divorce and still fewer of them want it'.[232] McQuaid too asserted that the demand for divorce among churches other than the Catholic Church was 'v. unlikely'.[233] The church authorities were united in their distaste for divorce.

The context in which the delicate topics of constitutional and legislative change were considered changed dramatically with the onset of the Troubles in 1968, which accelerated a reappraisal of the causes of partition. The locus of opposition to a united Ireland was now placed squarely on the shoulders of Northern Protestants. In *Towards a New Ireland*, Garret FitzGerald diagnosed the Irish problem as

> quite simply the fruit of Northern Protestant reluctance to become part of what they regard as an authoritarian Southern Catholic State. This is the obstacle to be overcome. It is *their* fears that have to be resolved if tensions in the North are to be eased.[234]

Thus the well-meaning, but simplistic, argument was to expunge those overtly confessional aspects of the constitution and legislation in the Republic, thereby creating the conditions for a pluralist society and reassuringly removing the root of Northern qualms. Such obsession with

Northern fears ignored the reality, as the *Irish Independent* warned, that constitutional change would little alter 'the beliefs of a people emotionally committed to another alliance'.[235]

This was made more complex still because two other overlapping groups, who pushed for domestic legal and constitutional change, hitched their claims to the debate on the national question. Those who viewed the legalisation of contraception as a human rights issue, irrespective of the Northern situation, included the three University senators – Mary Robinson, John Horgan and Trevor West – who introduced a private members' bill in 1971 to liberalise the 1935 law prohibiting the importation and sale of contraceptives. In a letter to Jack Lynch, West suggested that it was wrong 'that those people who have no moral objections to family planning should be forced to break the criminal law to indulge in this basic civil right.'[236] The second group regarded the 1937 document as a dated product of its time, moulded by the domestic pressures and prevailing Catholic social teaching of the 1930s, and therefore in need of modernisation. This was the view of Lemass and the rationale behind the all-party review in 1966.

It was ironic, but reflective of the change of attitude, that Article 44, the very article on which all the churches agreed in 1937, was amended in December 1972, with barely a dissenting voice in the Dáil or among church leaders. As early as September 1969, Cardinal Conway famously claimed that he would not 'shed a single tear' if Article 44.1.2 was rescinded. Ambassador Commins reported from the Vatican that 'the Holy See will not make any difficulty about it and indeed will understand the necessity for it in present developing circumstances, which envisage the eventual emergence in Ireland of a significantly pluralistic society'.[237] Archbishop Simms felt that his church would be happy if the relevant subsections disappeared altogether.[238] Despite reams of newsprint to the contrary, its removal made little difference to Northern Protestants. To the *Belfast Telegraph* it was 'even more a misconception now than it was before the troubles escalated' to think that a change to Article 44 would alter Northern attitudes to a united Ireland.[239] The *Irish Times* regarded the 84.4 per cent approval of the referendum as 'not a major step towards better understanding on this island, but it is a first step'. The *Gazette* received the result 'with quiet satisfaction'.[240] In truth, there was nothing lost or gained by the removal of a legal item that merely articulated a sociological fact which would nonetheless remain.

The Civil Rights campaign in Northern Ireland had the unintended effect of refocusing attention on civil rights in the Republic. It was inevitable that proponents of divorce and the sale of contraceptives would play the government's concern for the rights of the minority in the

North against its apparent lack of concern for civil rights in the Republic. The waters were muddied still further by the *Ne Temere* decree, even though this was more an inter-church issue (as discussed in chapter five). These tendencies were particularly evident in the thinking of the Church of Ireland's Role of the Church Committee. Its report in 1972 was highly critical of aspects of life in the Republic, so much so that the *Irish Independent* summed up its findings with the headline 'Nine Points of Criticism'.[241] It denied a claim made on 23 September 1971 by Patrick Hillery, Minister for External Affairs, that members of the Church of Ireland in the Republic were 'satisfied'. While it felt it would be 'churlish if Protestants failed to acknowledge the courtesies, goodwill and kindness experienced at civic, social and personal levels', the report continued, 'at the same time Protestants are not wholly satisfied with all aspects of life in the Republic'.[242] As discussed in chapter one, the Committee was predominantly Northern in membership. Its reports should be seen as a safety valve at a time of high feeling and as an attempt to moderate political diversity. It would be misleading to conclude that calls for legislative change in the area of private morality were indicative of widespread unhappiness on the part of the Church of Ireland in the South. In the light of the Northern situation, thirty-two individual members of religious minorities in the Republic, including among others Bruce Arnold, Professor W. J. Jessop, Professor W. B. Stanford and Justice Kingsmill Moore, issued a public letter. While they acknowledged their reservations about the lack of provision for divorce and contraception, they forcefully asserted 'the basic fairness of our political institutions and, what is more important, the basic goodwill toward us of the community of which we form part'. But looking North, they saw

> a society where sectarian barriers are tending to harden rather than dissolve ... since many of us share a common background, heritage and outlook with our Protestant brothers in the North, we can speak mostly closely to them. And to them most urgently we say: If your sectarian animus and suspicion are in any way motivated by fear, then we beg you to abandon them for, as may be judged from our experience, your fear is groundless.[243]

This was a deserved acknowledgement of fair treatment of Southern Protestants. Neither the Catholic Church nor the Church of Ireland bishops entertained the naïve argument that provision of divorce facilities or the permitted importation and sale of contraceptives in the Republic would somehow eliminate opposition to a united Ireland. In McQuaid's view, himself a native of Cootehill in County Cavan: 'One must know little of the Northern people, if one can fail to realise the indignant ridicule with which good Northern people would treat such an argument. It would indeed be a foul basis on which to attempt to construct the unity of our people.'[244] However, there was an acknowledgement that if and when a united Ireland came about a new situation would exist, which would require constitutional and legislative changes.

The campaign to liberalise the 1935 Criminal Law Act made its political debut in March 1971 and remained a contentious and divisive question until 1979. Archbishop Buchanan welcomed efforts to decriminalise the sale of contraceptives, which he believed was a matter for conscience rather than state control. He did add the caveat that this was a very distinct issue from divorce or abortion and that those who described the contraception debate as a Catholic-Protestant controversy greatly oversimplified the problem.[245] At issue for the Church of Ireland was not so much the absence of free sale of contraceptives or the provision of divorce, but the test on which these were based: the moral law as enunciated by the Catholic Church. While Buchanan underlined that although his church had set its face against divorce even to the point of seeming to lack compassion for hard cases, he wanted the Church of Ireland (as did the House of Bishops) to stand its ground 'without being buttressed by the State'.[246]

The views expressed by the Role of the Church Committee and individual Church of Ireland bishops fed into a general re-evaluation of aspects of life in the Republic by political and administrative elites, which were perceived to impede North-South reconciliation. As outlined in chapter one, the interdepartmental unit established in 1970 was important in this regard. Writing to the papal nuncio, McQuaid regarded this development as 'very serious' and saw it as inevitable that 'legislation that would placate the Northern non-Catholics, especially in regard to divorce, birth prevention, censorship and the position of the Church in the Republic' would be considered.[247] So it proved. The seventh meeting of the unit considered the confessional aspects of the constitution, which were deemed to constitute 'a serious stumbling block to reconciliation and reunification'.[248] It recommended the repeal of laws relating to contraceptives and family planning so as to remove the existing disabilities. On this point, Jack Lynch did not dispose as the hierarchy proposed and as early as December 1969 stated in an RTÉ interview his belief that the use of contraception was a matter of conscience.[249] His government agreed in principle to change the law with regard to the sale of contraceptives in March 1971.

The Catholic hierarchy responded with a statement on 12 March 1971. This asserted that 'civil law on these matters should respect the wishes of the people, who elected the legislators, and . . . that the legislators themselves will respect this important principle.'[250] The individual response of McQuaid, the senior Catholic prelate in the Republic, was nothing short of apoplectic. On 28 March 1971 he issued a vehemently worded pastoral to be read in all churches. He argued that any 'contraceptive act is always wrong in itself. To speak then, in this context, of a right to contraception . . . is to speak of a right that cannot even exist.' He felt that such a measure would 'prove to be gravely damaging to morality, private and public; it would be, and would remain, a curse upon our country'.[251] This intervention did much to reaffirm the crude caricature of Catholic reaction with which McQuaid has been associated since his death in 1973. Public reaction to the pastoral was unprecedented. Newspaper reports record that eight women walked out of the Pro-Cathedral in protest. In a livid editorial, the *Irish Times* disingenuously tried to draw a parallel between the campaign for civil rights in the North and freedom to use contraceptives in the Republic with references to 'ecclesiastical batoning'.[252] The House of Bishops was careful not to publicly criticise McQuaid. However, in the midst of the furore the private members' bill was denied a first reading and the issue was shelved until 1973.

If McQuaid's intervention had seemingly torpedoed legislative change, it was but a Pyrrhic victory. It eventually fell to the courts to take decisive action as a result of *McGee v Attorney General* in 1973. Interestingly, both the Church of Ireland and Catholic bishops were invited by the Attorney General to nominate a representative to give evidence in court, if necessary, as to their views on the matter. Both politely refused.[253] In a watershed judgement, the Supreme Court upheld the plaintiff's argument that the provisions of the 1935 Act violated her personal right to marital privacy under Article 40. This sanctioned a major change in the law and was greeted with an editorial in the *Belfast Telegraph* entitled: 'Good riddance'.[254] Sensationally, the Taoiseach, Liam Cosgrave, and six Fine Gael deputies voted against their own Control on Importation, Sale and Manufacture of Contraceptives Bill in July 1974, which consequently was not passed. There the matter lay, despite the McGee ruling, until Haughey's 'Irish solution for an Irish problem' in 1979 made contraceptives available on prescription to married couples. It is significant that in a pastoral letter in November 1973, the hierarchy openly acknowledged that the State should not be the guardian of private morality: 'There are many things which the Catholic Church holds to be morally wrong and no one has ever suggested, least of all the Church herself, that they should be prohibited by the State.'[255] The Catholic hierarchy had altered its position considerably from one of dogmatic command in 1971 to one of allowing public morality be decided by the people.

Bishop Butler's phrase 'a confident minority' not only captured the Church of Ireland's self-assurance in the practice of its religion and place in Irish society, but it challenged the lionisation by Northern Protestants and self-styled, but unrepresentative, liberals in the Republic of an apparently repressed religious minority south of the border. Such a claim was as misguided as bald suggestions of a Catholic Church-inspired theocracy in the Republic. If the Church of Ireland population withdrew into itself in the decades immediately following independence, then the corner had been decisively turned by the late 1950s as the mindset of decline gave way to a positive outlook. The Church of Ireland bishops played a determining role in reversing the fixation harboured by certain sections of their community that they were merely tolerated. Such a view was outmoded by the beginning of the 1960s. The House of Bishops enjoyed a cordial relationship with the government. The state did not impinge on the Church of Ireland, other than to hear with respect and meet with sincerity its concerns. Neither was in conflict with the other; neither was subservient or subordinate to the other. Denominational identity and state affiliation were not mutually exclusive. Hence, during the centenary of Disestablishment, the *Irish Press* fittingly commented on how 'natural it was to be at once a Protestant and an Irishman'.[256]

Notes

1 For example, Terence Brown, 'Religious minorities in the Irish Free State and the Republic of Ireland 1922–1995', in *Building Trust in Ireland*, pp. 217–31.
2 Hubert Butler, 'Portrait of a minority', in *Escape from the Anthill* (revised edn, Mullingar, 1986), p. 114. This essay first appeared in *The Bell* in June 1954.
3 Title of sermon by Bishop Arthur Butler on eve of General Synod, 13 May 1963, *CoIG*, 17 May 1963, p. 9.
4 *CoIG*, 14 February 1936, p. 106.
5 Seaver, *Gregg*, p. 250.
6 RCBL, Simms Papers, MS 238/1/7, Letter Gregg to Simms, 23 September 1937.
7 Acheson, *A History of the Church of Ireland*, p. 230.
8 RCBL, Simms Papers, MS 238/1/11, Letter Frank Jacob to Simms, 5 December 1956.
9 *CoIG*, 30 November 1956, p. 1.
10 *IT*, 26 January 1957.
11 Milne, 'Brave new world', p. 23.
12 Donald Caird, 'A man greatly loved', *CoIG*, 22 November 1991, p. 1.
13 Michael Viney, 'The five per cent: 3', *IT*, 24 March 1965.

14 However, throughout the period the Moderator paid an annual courtesy call on the Taoiseach of the day and the President. From 1965 onwards the President received an invitation to attend the annual General Assembly to which he sent a representative, as did the Governor of Northern Ireland.
15 Bowen, *Protestants*, p. 4.
16 NAI, DT S 10714 A/1, Memorandum by Maurice Moynihan (secretary to government), 20 January 1939; minute, 24 March 1939.
17 *Ibid.*, Letter Gregg to de Valera, 26 January 1939.
18 See Dermot Keogh, 'Church, state and society', in Brian Farrell (ed.), *De Valera's Constitution and Ours* (Dublin, 1988), p. 117.
19 UCDA, de Valera Papers, P150/2855, Copy letter de Valera to Gregg, 18 February 1959.
20 *Ibid.*, Letter Gregg to de Valera, 25 February 1959.
21 UCDA, de Valera Papers, P150/2854, Letter Barton to de Valera, 23 February 1948.
22 *Ibid.*
23 NLI, Seán T. Ó Ceallaigh Papers, MS 27686, Copy letter MacBride to Barton, 4 June 1951.
24 Cooney, *McQuaid*, p. 216.
25 NAI, DT 2000/6/149, Copy letter Lynch to Simms, 18 July 1969.
26 *Ibid.*, Secretary's minute, 26 September 1969.
27 *CoIG*, 3 October 1969, p. 1.
28 UCDA, de Valera Papers, P150/2856, Letter Simms to de Valera, 27 September 1969.
29 NAI, DT 2000/6/149, Letter Salmon to Lynch, 27 November 1969.
30 *Ibid.*, Letter Buchanan to Lynch, 11 September 1969.
31 NAI, DT 98/6/172, Letter Booth to R. Foley (principal DT), 27 November 1963.
32 NAI, DT 98/6/173, Letter Booth to Lynch, 25 May 1967.
33 NAI, DT S16767/61, Minute by R. Ó Foghlú (R. Foley), 3 May 1961; Letter Mrs Lesley Gregg to Lemass, 6 May 1961.
34 Cavan County Council, Minutes of monthly meeting, 22 August 1950.
35 *Ibid.*, 9 June 1956; 21 March 1959.
36 Monaghan County Council, Minutes of meeting, 10 November 1958; minutes of special meeting, 13 October 1969.
37 *II*, 23 November 1973.
38 *Ibid.*, 13 June 1968.
39 *IT*, 28 May 1968.
40 *BNL*, 16 June 1967.
41 OFMLA, D'Alton Papers, Box 31, Patrician Year 1961 Dublin, Folder 1, Letter McQuaid to D'Alton, 12 November 1960.
42 Letter Samuel Poyntz to author, 13 March 2002.
43 NAI, DT S 16989/61, Secretary's minute, 12 Jan 1961.
44 *Ibid.*, Secretary's minute, 13 January 1961; copy letter Ó Nualláin to Cremin, 13 January 1961.

45 *Ibid.*, Copy confidential memo by Cremin, 29 March 1961; Letter Poyntz to author, 13 March 2002.
46 NAI, DT S 16989/61, Letter Slack to Lemass, 4 May 1962.
47 *Ibid.*
48 NAI, DT S 16989/61, Letter Simms to Lemass, 1 May 1961; Letter Poyntz to Lemass, 13 May 1961.
49 UCDA, de Valera Papers, P150/2856, Letter Simms to de Valera, 1 May 1961; Letter Poyntz to author, 13 March 2002.
50 HB, vol. iii, meeting of 15 July 1969, p. 122; NAI, DT 2001/6/426, secretary's minute, 15 July 1969.
51 NAI, DT 2001/6/426, Minute, 30 April 1970 with attached guest list.
52 RCBL, *Irish Anglicanism*, MS 487/3/4, Letter Hurley to H. O'Dowd (private secretary to Taoiseach), 26 July 1969; MS 487/3/9, Letter S. Mac Gearailt (secretary Department of Education) to Hurley, 15 August 1970.
53 Interview with Rev. Michael Hurley, April 2002.
54 NAI, DT 2001/6/426, Letter Hurley to Ó Dubhda, 20 August 1969; copy letter Ó Dubhda to Hurley, 10 March 1970.
55 DDA, McQuaid Papers, AB8/B/XVII/11, Copy letter McQuaid to Alibrandi, 6 March 1970.
56 Interview with Michael Hurley, April 2002.
57 *IP*, 11 December 1969.
58 See, for example, Bill Kissane, 'The illusion of state neutrality in a secularising Ireland', in John T. S. Madeley and Zsolt Enyedi (eds), *Church and State in Contemporary Europe. The Chimera of Neutrality* (London, 2003), p. 76.
59 NAI, DT 97/6/334, Copy minute on official representation at non-Catholic services, 11 February 1957.
60 *Ibid.*, Letter J. W. Armstrong (dean of St Patrick's) to T. Ó Cearbhaill (assistant secretary DT), 20 March 1965; NAI, DT 2000/6/453, Letter Victor Griffin to D. Ó Súilleabháin (assistant secretary DT) 26 May 1969; copy letter R. Ó Foghlú to private secretary Minister for Transport and Power, 20 June 1969.
61 NAI, DT 97/6/157, Draft letter to religious leaders, 3 March 1965.
62 NAI, DT 97/6/158, Letter Simms to Lemass, 17 June 1965; Letter Bishop James Fergus (secretary to the Irish hierarchy) to Lemass, 25 June 1965.
63 HB, vol. ii, meeting of 15 June 1965, p. 363.
64 OFMLA, D'Alton Papers, Box 7, RoI Government, Department of Education, Folder 2', Copy of memorandum: 'Primary Education Proposed Changes – Statement by the Minister for Education', n.d.
65 *IT*, 3 May 1958.
66 *Ibid.*
67 LPL, Lambeth Conference Papers 1958, vol. 192, fol. 318.
68 *JGS 1955*, 'Report of Board of Education', p. 109.
69 *Report of the Kilmore Diocesan Council*, 'Diocesan Board of Education Annual Report 1959', summary of transport costs.

70 David Fitzpatrick, 'The Orange Order and the border', *Irish Historical Studies*, 33: 129 (2002), p. 66.
71 *Report of the Kilmore Diocesan Council*, 'Diocesan Board of Education Annual Report 1962', p. 49.
72 See, for example, *Report of the Clogher Diocesan Council to the Synod of 1968*, 'Clogher Diocesan Board of Education', p. 55.
73 IR, 5 October 1961.
74 *JGS 1962*, 'Report of Board of Education', p. 126.
75 *Report of the Kilmore Diocesan Council*, 'Kilmore Diocesan Board of Education Annual Report 1969', p. 51; 'Report of the Dublin and Glendalough and Kildare Diocesan Board of Education to the Joint Synods 1968', p. 2.
76 *JGS 1968*, 'Report of the Board of Education', p. 98.
77 *JGS 1955*, 'Report of Board of Education', p. 112.
78 IR, 4 October 1951.
79 NAI, DT 2001/6/383, Memorandum for the government, 6 February 1970, 'Accounts of the Church of Ireland Training College for year ended 31 August 1969.'
80 NAI, DT 99/1/602, Memorandum for the government: 'Accounts for Church of Ireland training college for year ended 31 August 1967'; NAI, DT 2001/6/383, Memorandum for the government, 6 February 1970, 'Accounts of the Church of Ireland Training College for year ended 31 August 1969'.
81 UCDA, de Valera Papers, P150/2856, Letter Simms to de Valera, 14 March 1969.
82 See Séamus Ó Buachalla, *Education Policy in Twentieth Century Ireland* (Dublin, 1988), p. 244.
83 Terence Brown, 'Religious minorities', p. 227. See also his *Ireland. A Social and Cultural History 1922–1979* (London, 1981), pp. 189–93.
84 *JGS 1950*, 'Report of the Board of Education', p. 186. For a discussion of the language issue in the 1920s and 1930s, see D. H. Akenson, *A Mirror to Kathleen's Face* (Montreal and London, 1975), pp. 123–34.
85 *JGS 1955*, 'Report of Board of Education', p. 116.
86 *Report of the Dublin and Glendalough and Kildare Diocesan Board of Education to the Joint Synods 1955*, p. 4.
87 RCBL, Irish Guild of the Church, MS 131, Minutes and papers.
88 *JGS 1964*, 'Report of Board of Education', pp. 96–7.
89 *Report of the Dublin and Glendalough and Kildare Diocesan Board of Education to the Joint Synods 1965*, p. 6.
90 *Anglo-Celt* (henceforth *AC*), 30 June 1962.
91 HB, vol. ii, meeting of 9 March 1964, p. 300 'Interim report of Advisory Committee on Primary Education.'
92 *Ibid.*, meeting of 15 June 1964, p. 312.
93 NAI, DT 96/6/355, Letter Colley to Lemass, 24 September 1965, with enclosed memorandum on 'the general question of small schools.'

94 HB, vol. ii, p. 368, 'Advisory Committee on Primary Education. Report on discussion with the Minister for Education', 16 July 1965.
95 Viney, 'The five per cent: 1', *IT*, 22 March 1965.
96 See Seán O'Connor, *Troubled Sky. Reflections on the Irish Educational Scene 1957–1968* (Dublin, 1986), pp. 101, 125–8.
97 NAI, DFA 2003/17/383, 'Recent Developments in Ireland', lecture by Tomás Ó Floinn (assistant secretary Department of Education), 1972.
98 *JGS 1968*, 'Report of the Board of Education', p. 97.
99 *Report of the Clogher Diocesan Council 1956*, 'Report of Diocesan Board of Religious Education', p. 65; *Report of the Clogher Diocesan Council to Synod of 1967*, 'Report of Clogher Diocesan Board of Religious Education', p. 62.
100 *DRDS 1966*, 'Report of County Donegal Education Committee', p. 23.
101 *JGS 1962*, 'Report of the Board of Education', p. 121. On these developments, see Kenneth Milne, 'The Protestant churches in independent Ireland', in James P. Mackey and Enda McDonagh (eds), *Religion and Politics in Ireland at the Turn of the Millennium* (Dublin, 2003), pp. 71–2.
102 *JGS 1965*, 'Report of the Advisory Committee on Secondary Education', p. 143; *JGS 1967*, Presidential address, 9 May 1967, p. xlv.
103 See O'Connor, *Troubled Sky*, pp. 78–9. For the background to Hillery's scheme, see John Horgan, *Seán Lemass. The Enigmatic Patriot* (Dublin, 1997), pp. 293–5.
104 KDA, Quinn Papers, AQ\77, Letter S. Ó Conchobhair (assistant secretary Department of Education) to Bishop Quinn, 5 October 1964.
105 *Ibid.*, Letter Colley to Quinn, 30 Dec 1965.
106 *Ibid.*, Copy letter James Fergus (on behalf of the Standing Committee) to Colley, 9 May 1966; Letter Cardinal Conway to Quinn, 18 May 1966.
107 *Ibid.*, Letter Ó Conchobhair to Quinn, 10 May 1966; NA, DT 99/1/387, Letter Colley to Lemass, 24 May 1966.
108 Fuller, *Irish Catholicism*, p. 155.
109 *Ibid.*
110 KDA, Quinn Papers, AQ\58, Minutes of General Meeting of Irish Hierarchy, 8–11 March 1971.
111 *IR*, 3 June 1971.
112 *AC*, 2 July 1971.
113 KDA, Quinn Papers, AQ\79, Statement by Cardinal Conway, 30 January 1972.
114 *JGS 1968*, 'Report of the Board of Education', p. 99; *DRDS 1972*, 'Report of County Donegal Education Committee', p. 22.
115 KDA, Quinn Papers, AQ\79, Statement by Cardinal Conway, 30 January 1972.
116 *DD*, vol. 258, col. 813, 27 January 1972.
117 *Ibid.*, col. 2116, 17 February 1972.
118 *IP*, 22 February 1972.

119 *JGS 1968*, 'Report of the Board of Education', p. 97.
120 See for example *DRDS 1967*, 'Report of County Donegal Education Committee', p. 21.
121 NA, DT 99/1/124, Letter Haughey to Lynch, 15 May 1968.
122 *Ibid.*, Copy letter Lynch to Lenihan, 28 March 1968.
123 *Ibid.*
124 NA, DT 99/1/124, Letter Haughey to Lynch, 15 May 1968.
125 *Ibid.*
126 NA, DT 99/1/124, Copy letter Lynch to Perdue, 13 December 1968.
127 NA, DT 99/1/124, Letter Haughey to Lynch, 15 May 1968.
128 *Ibid.*
129 NA, DT 99/1/124, Letter Perdue to Lynch, 19 June 1968.
130 *Ibid.*, Letter Perdue to Lynch, 16 December 1968.
131 *Ibid.*, Copy letter Haughey to Perdue, 9 January 1969.
132 NA, DT 2001/6/79, Memorandum for Taoiseach: 'Scheme for free post-primary education in relation to Protestants', n.d.
133 NA, DT 99/1/124, Letter Lenihan to Lynch, 13 January 1969.
134 *Ibid.*, Letter John Briggs (assistant secretary to General Synod) to Lynch, 27 May 1969 enclosing copy of resolution and speeches by bishop of Ossory and Frank Jacob.
135 *Ibid.*
136 *Ibid.*
137 HB, vol. iii, meeting of 14 September 1971, 'Resumé of discussion on Education by archbishop of Dublin to members of the House of Bishops, 9 July 1971', p. 207.
138 *JGS 1972*, 'Secondary Education Committee of the General Synod', p. 128.
139 NA, DT 2001/6/79, Memorandum for Taoiseach: 'Scheme for free post-primary education in relation to Protestants', n.d.
140 *Ibid.*
141 Letter Lesley Hackett to editor *IT*, 11 October 1969.
142 AC, 13 June 1964.
143 Calculated from Sexton and O'Leary, 'Factors affecting population decline', pp. 317–8; 1,107 respondents entered 'no religion' and 5,625 nothing at all.
144 NAI, DFA 2000/5/8, 'Ireland 1961 Census – selected figures relating to occupations and religion'.
145 Viney, 'The five per cent: 2', *IT*, 23 March 1965.
146 *IT*, 31 July 1973 cited in Jack White, *Minority Report. The Protestant Community in the Irish Republic* (Dublin, 1975), p. 162.
147 See, for instance, Edmund Curran, 'The minority in the republic', *BT*, 22 October 1969.
148 White, *Minority Report*, p. 162.
149 *Ibid.*
150 Viney, 'The five per cent: 2'.
151 Letter Roy Warke to author, 19 May 2003.

152 NAI, DFA 20/54/5, Memorandum: 'Recent statements recording treatment of religious minorities in Ireland'.
153 NAI, DT S 15660, Memorandum: 'Membership of the Fifth Seanad (1948–1951) nominated by the Taoiseach', n.d.
154 Michael B. Yeats, *Cast a Cold Eye. Memoirs of a Poet's Son and Politician* (Dublin, 1998), pp. 48–50.
155 NAI, DT 99/1/445, Letter Yeats to Lemass, 11 June 1965.
156 Fitzpatrick, 'The Orange Order', p. 65.
157 NAI, DT S 15025, Letter Barton to de Valera, 16 June 1951; letter Barton to de Valera, 15 August 1951.
158 *Ibid.*, Letter Seán Ó hUadhaigh to de Valera, 25 June 1951.
159 NAI, DT S 15719A, Letter Barton to Costello, 28 May 1954.
160 NAI, DT S 15660, Statement listing Taoiseach's nominees to Seanad, 19 July 1954.
161 *CoIG*, 26 August 1955, p. 1.
162 Colin Murphy and Lynne Adair (eds), *Untold Stories. Protestants in the Republic of Ireland 1922–2002* (Dublin, 2002), p. 119.
163 *DRDS*, President's address, 25 June 1958, p. 65.
164 *Journal of the Synod of Armagh* (henceforth *JSA)*, President's Address, 10 October 1962, p. 11.
165 *AC*, 30 June 1962; Thomas Keane 'Demographic trends', p. 170.
166 Viney, 'The five per cent: 2'.
167 Dublin City Archives, Minutes of a Special Meeting of the Dublin City Council, 17 June 1961, p. 182.
168 Viney, 'The five per cent: 2'.
169 UCDA, MacEntee Papers, P67/298, Letter Childers to MacEntee, 11 February 1948.
170 Paul M. Sacks, 'Bailiwick, locality, and religion: Three elements in an Irish Dáil constituency election', *Economic and Social Review*, 1: 4 (1970), pp. 531–54.
171 The UCC governing body of consisted of 21 members: 4 *ex officio* (UCC President and Lord Mayors of Cork, Limerick and Waterford); Academic Council elected 6, graduates 5, Cork Limerick and Waterford County Councils 1 each. UCG governing body consisted of 19 members: UCG President *ex officio* member; Academic Council elected 4, graduates 4, Galway, Sligo, Leitrim, Roscommon, Mayo and Clare County Councils and Galway Corporation elected 1 each. See NAI, DT S 3162E/94, Memorandum for the Government, 9 January 1959.
172 NAI, Government Minutes, vol. G 3/15, entry for 30 January 1950, G.5/130.
173 *Ibid.*, vol. G 3/18, entry for 2 Feb 1953, G 6/134.
174 The Lord Mayor of Dublin and the president of the college were *ex officio* members. The Academic Council elected six representatives as did graduates; the Council of the County of Dublin elected one and the General Council of County Councils eight. See NAI, DT S 3162E/94, Memorandum for the Government, 9 January 1959.

175 DDA, McQuaid Papers, AB8/B/XV/b/06, Hierarchy Meetings 1967(2), 'Annual report on the Catholic Chaplaincy in UCC for 1966–67'; 'UCG report of the Dean of Residence 1966–67' 'Report of the Dean of Residence Queen's University Belfast, 1966–67'; *Report of the Down and Dromore Diocesan Council for 1969*, p. 26.
176 For example Robert Tyner, bishop of Clogher, *IR*, 1 October 1953 and Robert McNeill Boyd, bishop of Derry and Raphoe, *DRDS*, President's address, 26 June 1957, p. 66.
177 *AC*, 9 July 1955.
178 See for instance *AC*, 16 July 1960 and NAI, DT 2000/6/321, Letter Moore to Lynch, 1 March 1968.
179 *CoIG*, 6 May 1949, p. 1.
180 *IT*, 11 August 1950.
181 *IT*, 19 November 1951 cited in Frank Gallagher, *Indivisible Island*, pp. 197–8.
182 OFMLA, D'Alton Papers, Box 24, Organisations B, Folder 6A, Supreme Registrar's Report ('confidential') June 1953.
183 See William Bedell Stanford, *Stanford: Regius Professor of Greek, 1940–80, Trinity College, Dublin: Memoirs* (Dublin, 2001), pp. 129–30; John H. Whyte, 'Political life in the South', in Hurley (ed.), *Irish Anglicanism*, p. 150.
184 Stanford, *Memoirs*, p. 131.
185 UCDA, Fisher Papers, P164/35, Typescript notes by Mrs Pam Fisher.
186 RCBL, PC52, Typescript by Edward Francis Grant: *The Fethard Boycott*, p. 11.
187 *IT*, 3 June 1957.
188 UCDA, Fisher Papers, P164/15(6), Letter Lucie Knipe to Fisher, 2 September 1957; P164/15(8), Letter William Cruise to Fisher, 25 September 1957.
189 UCDA, Fisher Papers, P164/8, Anonymous letter to Fisher, 12 August 1957.
190 NAI, DT S 16247, secretary's memo, 31 May 1957; memo, 5 June 1957; memo, 21 June 1957.
191 *Ibid.*, memo, 25 June 1957.
192 *Ibid.*, Draft letter de Valera to Staunton, n.d. [marked 'not sent'].
193 Stanford, *Memoirs*, p. 143.
194 *IT*, 8 June 1957; from author's observations of 259 letters to Relief Fund, e.g. UCDA, Fisher Papers, P164/13(85), Note of contribution of £2.13.0. from Pamela Hinkson (Monkstown, Co. Dublin).
195 *IP*, 26 June 1957.
196 *IT*, 11 June 1957.
197 Quoted in Keogh, 'The role of the Catholic Church', p. 146.
198 NAI, DT S 16247, Letter Phair to de Valera, 19 July 1957.
199 *AC*, 6 July 1957.
200 *IP*, 21 September 1959.

201 LPL, Lambeth Conference Papers 1958, vol. 192, fol. 304.
202 John A. Murphy's expression in *Ireland in the Twentieth Century* (Dublin, 1975), p. 91 cited in Enda Delaney, 'Political catholicism in post-war Ireland: The Revd. Denis Fahey and Maria Duce, 1945–54', *Journal of Ecclesiastical History*, 52: 3 (2001), p. 505.
203 LPL, Lambeth Conference Papers 1958, vol. 192, fols 305–6.
204 For instance, Keogh devotes a section to *Maria Duce* in 'The Role of the Catholic Church', pp. 135–42.
205 Delaney, 'Political catholicism', p. 511.
206 Lionel Pilkington, 'Religion and the Celtic tiger: The cultural legacies of anti-Catholicism in Ireland', in Peadar Kirby, Luke Gibbons and Michael Cronin (eds), *Reinventing Ireland: Culture, Society and the Global Economy* (London, 2002), pp. 125–33.
207 HB, vol. ii, meeting of 14 May 1962, p. 247.
208 DDA, McQuaid Papers, AB8/B/XVIII/02, Government Box 3, Draft statement on Intoxicating Liquor Laws, n. d. [but June 1959]; *ICD 1960*, p. 688; *Dublin, Glendalough and Kildare Temperance and Social Welfare Society. Annual Report for the year 1959–1960*, p. 2.
209 Brian Fallon, *An Age of Innocence. Irish Culture 1930–1960* (Dublin, 1999), chs. 15, 20.
210 LPL, Lambeth Conference Papers 1958, vol. 192, fol. 318.
211 *JGS 1960*, 'Report of Proceedings of Standing Committee', p. 92.
212 LPL, Lambeth Conference Papers 1958, vol. 192, fol. 346.
213 RCBL, Simms Papers, MS 238, Church of Ireland pastoral letter on marriage 1966.
214 See LPL, Lambeth Conference Papers 1958, vol. 193, fols 696–7, 709–10 (for contribution of Tyndall); fols 780, 801, 806–7 (Simms); fols 807–9 (Mitchell).
215 *JGS 1971*, p. cxii.
216 *Report of the Committee on the Constitution* Pr. 9817 (Dublin, 1967), p. 1.
217 See in particular *Dignitatis humanae*, para. 6 in Austin Flannery (ed.), *Vatican Council II. The Conciliar and Post Conciliar Documents* (revised edn, Dublin, 1992), p. 804.
218 NAI, DT 96/6/364, Copy letter Lemass to Lenihan, 25 September 1965.
219 *Ibid.*, Letter Lenihan to Lemass, 17 February 1966.
220 See Horgan, *Lemass*, p. 340.
221 NAI, DT 97/6/515, Letter Liam Cosgrave to Lemass, 5 July 1966.
222 *Committee on the Constitution*, para. 125, p. 44.
223 See Girvin, *From Union to Union*, p. 113.
224 *Committee on the Constitution*, para. 123, p. 43.
225 *Ibid.*
226 *Feasta, Samhain* [November] 1969, p. 3.
227 *Committee on the Constitution*, para. 136, p. 47.
228 *IT*, 14 December 1967.

229 DDA, McQuaid Papers, AB8/B/XV/b/07, Hierarchy Meetings 1968(1) Minutes of Meeting of the Standing Committee of the Irish Hierarchy, 9 January 1968.
230 *IT*, 16 December 1967.
231 NAI, DT 96/6/364, Letter Lady Hort to Lynch, 29 February 1968.
232 OFMLA, Conway Papers, 18/8–1, Comment on Committee on Constitution, 14 December 1967.
233 DDA, McQuaid Papers, AB8/B/XVIII/10, Government Box 3, Note by McQuaid, 14 February 1966.
234 Garret FitzGerald, *Towards a New Ireland* (London, 1972), p. 88.
235 *II*, 4 March 1971.
236 TCD, Trevor West Papers, MS 11034/1/2/2/2, Letter West to Lynch, 30 April 1971.
237 NAI, DFA 2001/20/338, Copy report ('personal and highly confidential') Commins to McCann (secretary DEA), 15 November 1972.
238 *IT*, 23 September 1969.
239 *BT*, 26 October 1972.
240 *IT*, 7 December 1972; *CoIG*, 10 November 1972, p. 2.
241 *II*, 18 May 1972.
242 *JGS 1972*, 'Report of the Role of the Church Committee 1972', p. 255.
243 *IP*, 2 October 1969.
244 *IT* 29 March 1971.
245 *CoIG*, 26 March 1971, p. 1.
246 *Ibid*; HB, vol. iii, meeting of 11 May 1970, p. 156.
247 DDA, McQuaid Papers, AB8/B/XVIII/04, Letter McQuaid to Alibrandi, 16 July 1970.
248 NAI, DT 2001/6/549, Minutes ('confidential') of seventh meeting, 21 December 1970.
249 NAI, DT 2001/6/323, Extract from interview with the Taoiseach broadcast by RTÉ, 28 December 1969.
250 KDA, Quinn Papers, AQ\58, Minutes of General Meeting of Irish Hierarchy, 8–11 March 1971; *IT*, 12 March 1971.
251 *IT*, 29 March 1971.
252 *Ibid*.
253 HB, vol. iii, p. 242, copy letter House of Bishops to Chief State Solicitor, 17 June 1972; KDA, Quinn Papers, AQ\59, Minutes of General Meeting of Irish Hierarchy, 19–22 June 1972.
254 *BT*, 20 December 1973.
255 *IT*, 26 November 1973.
256 *IP*, 11 Dec 1969.

4

Standing with the people: the Catholic Church and the Northern Ireland state

> Politics is not the art of the possible. It consists in choosing between the disastrous and the unpalatable. (J. K. Galbraith, *Ambassador's Journal*)

Not unlike the case of the Catholic population in Bismarckian Germany, the Northern Catholic bishops had a political importance as spokespeople for a minority. Their relationship with the Northern state was thus somewhat ambiguous. They were obeisant to the civil authority, rendering unto Caesar what was Caesar's, but Christ's injunction was tempered by a feeling that they were not of the state. This was more complex still, given the different levels of government – local, central and, particularly after 1969, imperial – which comprised the 'state'. At the lowest level, relations with local government were virtually non-existent. The bishops regarded local bodies as gerrymandered, unaccountable and prejudiced. Distrust of local government was an *idée fixe* which pervaded their consideration of legislation across the spectrum from education to health.

This resulted, *faute de mieux*, in a pragmatic view of relations with central government between 1945 and 1968. A blanket policy of non-cooperation was simply unfeasible. Whereas Cardinal MacRory had been openly hostile towards the Northern administration throughout the 1930s and early 1940s, Cardinal D'Alton was conciliatory, accommodating and sought some sort of *modus vivendi*. His was a more refined variant of traditional nationalism. It was characterised by if not an acceptance of the political *status quo*, then a determination to use it to the Catholic community's advancement. The extension of the welfare state, after 1945, brought such practical considerations to the fore. The manner of the Cardinal's response to the ascension of Queen Elizabeth, in June 1953, demonstrated this change of stance. He declined an invitation to a ceremony by the Privy Council, but generously hoped that

> Irishmen of all shades of opinion, with their innate sense of chivalry, will join in good wishes to the young Queen who was called to the throne in

circumstances of great personal sorrow . . . and that her reign may be the opening of a new era of prosperity for her people.[1]

Tentative trust in Stormont's ministries was not tantamount to a constantly harmonious working relationship. It did not mean *de jure* recognition of the Northern Ireland state by the Catholic bishops. D'Alton still hoped that Queen Elizabeth's reign would see Ireland 'restored to its natural unity'.[2] For its part, the Stormont government did not go out of its way to be cordial. When D'Alton was made cardinal in January 1953, no official message of congratulations was received from the Northern government. Brian Maginess, Minister of Home Affairs, expressed his congratulations rather than those of the government.[3] The bishops stood with their people first, for whose benefit they engaged in the politics of incremental gain with central government. It was not simply the case, as Sabine Wichert suggests, that in the years after the Second World War the minority combined complaints about social, economic or political grievances with demands for the reunification of the island.[4] This statement is broadly true. The ending of partition remained a fundamental objective, but, while it existed as a necessary evil, greater effort was quietly focused by the leaders of Catholic opinion on improving the prevailing conditions for their community *within* Northern Ireland. In this sense there was a decoupling of the national question from practical socio-economic issues. In 1962, several years after it had become the tacit line of the Northern bishops, Con Cremin, then secretary of the Department of External Affairs, made this very point to John Molloy, the newly appointed Irish ambassador in London. To Cremin's mind, ending partition seemed

> to have acted as an obstacle in the way of action designed to improve the position of the minority on the ground, that any steps in that direction could be held to imply acceptance of the permanence of the division of the country. I have the impression, however, that there may have been a change in public opinion, both here and elsewhere, in recent years which would diminish, if not entirely eliminate, the risks of such an implication being read into any action of that kind taken today.[5]

The aftermath of October 1968, conventionally regarded as the beginning of the Troubles, unlocked a Pandora's box and ushered in an intensely difficult period for the Northern bishops. They had the invidious task of distancing their church from a campaign of violence which shared the same memories of discrimination and injustice. Along with the Catholic community generally, the bishops steadily lost all faith in the Northern Ireland administration. Instead, they hoped that redress might be more forthcoming from London. During the first half decade of the

Troubles the bishops played an important, if somewhat thankless, role in supporting Westminster's policy of reform and excoriating all violence.

Welfarism and the concept of subsidiarity

Just as in the Republic, the major areas of interaction between church and state were in the fields of education and health. Both were highly contentious issues due to the restructuring occasioned by the welfare state and the reluctance of the Catholic Church to give up its voluntary status. There was much to be gained, but also a lot to lose. In the implementation of welfare state policies, the Northern government accepted the principle of 'parity' with Britain. This step-by-step approach required a volte-face in its anti-socialist attitude as Stormont quickly realised that only massive state intervention could surmount Northern Ireland's economic and geographical disadvantages. For the Catholic Church, however, the case was not so straightforward. It would be an oversimplification to conflate its moral teaching (or *magisterium*) and social teaching. The *magisterium* had the duty to prescribe and proclaim the moral law. By contrast, social teaching was less prescriptive. Its purpose was to offer general principles and guidelines on socio-economic matters, as the increasingly omni-competent state became involved in areas of traditional church interest.[6] The social teaching of the Catholic Church had a profound influence on the nature of the Northern bishops' reaction to changes in education and health legislation.

Episcopal statements and pastorals in the late 1940s and early 1950s give the impression of a polarised, even antagonistic, relationship between the Catholic bishops and government ministries at Stormont. This was not just a clash of religious and national identities made even more fraught by Unionist resentment of a Catholic population which had refused as a group to join the war effort. Neither was it due simply to government suspicion of the Anti-Partition Campaign in the South. Contesting social policy paradigms, an aspect rarely afforded the significance it merits, was at the heart of this antagonism. Catholic social thought did not pervade the thinking of the Northern Ireland government or the shaping of policy. It was simply not the case, as Whyte observed of the Republic, that 'churchmen and statesmen were moulded by the same culture, [and] educated at the same schools'.[7] Therefore, to fully comprehend relations between the Catholic Church and the Northern state, it is necessary to consider the underlying philosophical context of episcopal pronouncements in the 1950s.

Pope Pius XI's seminal encyclical, *Quadragesimo anno* (1931) largely shaped Catholic social thought until the Second Vatican Council.

It marked the fortieth anniversary of Pope Leo XIII's landmark *Rerum novarum* (1891) which was the first encyclical to commit the church to addressing the social problems that had intensified in the industrial age. *Rerum novarum* was a critique of both capitalism and socialism, stressing the rights and duties of both employers and workers. It also warned of abuses in society which the state ought to remedy, in particular protecting the right to a living wage. While warning against an over-expansion of state power, the encyclical stated that the state ought to play a role in the social field. *Rerum novarum* introduced, in embryonic form, the principle by which this should be implemented: subsidiarity, that the higher social entity should assist the lower and weaker.

This concept was made more explicit in *Quadragesimo anno*. In the interests of distributive justice and the public good, the state should grant subsidium (assistance, help or support) to component parts of society, especially the family as the pre-eminent social unit, but within strictly delineated limits.[8] While the state had its responsibilities, *Quadragesimo anno* warned that it was 'an injustice, a grave evil and a disturbance of right order, for a larger association to arrogate to itself functions that can be performed efficiently by smaller and lower societies'.[9] Under the principle of subsidiarity, the state would never normally replace the individual, or these smaller societal units, all of which had to work harmoniously to promote the common good. The state's duty was, as Cardinal D'Alton put it, 'to supplement, not to supplant'.[10]

Quadragesimo anno reinvigorated Catholic Action, the Catholic social movement, which gave rise to Christian democratic parties in Europe after the Second World War. In Ireland, the hierarchy established a chair of Sociology and Catholic Action in Maynooth in 1937 which was first held by Father Peter McKevitt. Individual bishops, such as Michael Browne of Galway and Cornelius Lucey of Cork, were interested in developing the vocational organisation of society which was seen as a middle road between capitalism and socialism. Browne had 'no objection' when proposed by de Valera as vice-chairperson of the Commission on Vocational Organisation between 1939 and 1943.[11] It was only with Pope John XXIII's encyclical, *Mater et magistra*, in 1961, that the Catholic Church's approach to social issues was reappraised. The church moved from condemnation of state involvement to greater endorsement of it.[12] Notably, *Mater et magistra* reaffirmed subsidiarity as the state's guiding principle and individual human beings as 'the foundation, the cause and the purpose of every social institution'.[13]

The response of the Northern bishops to the welfare state, in the aftermath of the publication of the Beveridge Report in 1942, was hewn from the dogmatic bedrock of subsidiarity. For Daniel Mageean, bishop of

Down and Connor, the omni-competent state created the danger of creeping totalitarianism, whereby 'the human person will be treated ... as a mere chattel of the state. The rights, liberties, and independence of the individual are to be drastically curtailed, and he is to come under the control of the state at every stage of life, from the cradle to the coffin.'[14] Suspicion of state interference merged with, and was heightened by, the suppression of organised religion in Eastern Europe under communist regimes, the threat of this in Western Europe, as well as more amorphous fears that state welfarism would unleash 'the virus of secularism and materialism' on St Patrick's island.[15] Many Northern bishops moved almost seamlessly from denouncing communism to criticising welfarism. In a Lenten pastoral in 1952, D'Alton warned of a

> milder form of Totalitarianism, known as the Welfare State, which in its own way tends to undermine the foundations of human liberty ... A system of social services, which began by assisting the needy, ends by being made compulsory for all. The State thus makes unwarranted inroads on the family, and usurps functions that properly belong to parents.[16]

Bishop Eugene O'Doherty of Dromore similarly deplored 'those encroachments of the State on the sacred domain of parental rights'.[17]

Some of this trepidation was also shared by the Church of Ireland. At the diocesan synod of Armagh in October 1948, Archbishop Gregg regarded as dangerous the tendency towards control over the individual. He felt that it was the duty of the church

> to see that this ever tightening control does not degenerate, or harden, before we know it, into a tyranny ... The State is not, in the last resort, its own dictator and law-giver ... the individual is not created for the purpose of the State – it is more true to say that the State exists for the benefit of each individual within it. And so freedom must be guarded with all diligence, not only freedom from external attack, but freedom within the State.[18]

Four years later, he warned the same assembly that a 'system of planned materialism', which dealt with individuals by the tens of thousands, would make them 'little better than ciphers'.[19] A consideration of the state and the individual in 1949 by the United Council of Christian Churches (an Irish Protestant inter-church grouping further discussed in chapter 5) noted the benefits of welfare legislation. But it also highlighted the dangers of a 'menace to individual freedom', 'lessening of the sense of personal responsibility' and 'the further development of impersonal bureaucratic government'.[20] These examples demonstrate that admonition of the welfare state leviathan was not the sole prerogative of the Catholic Church.

Defending voluntary schools

As self-appointed guardians of a tight, self-conscious community, defined by its Catholicism, the Northern bishops were particularly active in the field of education. Indeed several bishops had backgrounds, at different times, as heads of prestigious educational institutions. Both Bishop Farren and Bishop O'Doherty, for instance, had been presidents of St Columb's College in Derry. The hierarchy's approach to educational change was philosophically grounded in adherence to subsidiarity and more practically rooted in defence of voluntary control of its schools. The intensity of the education question is captured in the title of Donald Akenson's classic study: *Education and Enmity*.[21] The key issues in all four pieces of legislation that fashioned the education system in Northern Ireland (1923, 1930, 1947 and 1968) were those of control and funding. In contrast to the South, where one gets an impression of a Catholic Church casting a long shadow over education policy, in Northern Ireland the Ministry, the local authorities and the churches all vied with one another.

It is first necessary to outline briefly developments before the 1947 Education Act. In the tense opening years of the state, the Catholic bishops refused to participate on the Lynn Committee, appointed by Lord Londonderry, the first Minister of Education, to report on primary education which it sought to make secular, compulsory and free. Its recommendations formed the basis of the 1923 Education Act, which divided primary schools into three categories with the allocation of public funding being proportional to the amount of control by local education committees. Class I schools were transferred to local education committees. Control by a local authority, rather than a clerical manager, was abhorrent to the Catholic hierarchy, despite the contribution of the Catholic taxpayer to their upkeep. Class II schools were managed by four representatives from the trustees of the school and two from the education authority. The so-called 'four and two' committees were rejected out of hand as the thin end of a gerrymandered wedge, which would eventually appropriate control of Catholic schools. Class III were voluntary and were not given a contribution for capital expenditure, but teachers' salaries and half the running expenses were paid from public funds.[22] The vast majority of Catholic primary schools came under this category. Consequently, inadequate financial provisions posed a perennial dilemma for the Northern bishops who jealously guarded full control of their voluntary schools. Their response to the 1923 Act set the tone for almost the next fifty years, during which there was no attenuation of hierarchical opposition to 'four and two' committees.

Catholic and Protestant authorities could only agree that there would be no miscegenation, so to speak, in education. Mary Harris argues that this prevented 'endless conflict over appointment of teachers and curriculum'.[23] Neither group was pleased with the secular component of the 1923 Act. A heated campaign by the Protestant churches and the Orange Order secured amendments in 1925 and 1930 with the result that bible instruction became mandatory in schools run by local education authorities.[24] The secular state schools envisaged by the Lynn Committee were now *de facto* Protestant. For their part, the Catholic hierarchy squeezed a concession of fifty per cent capital funding under the 1930 Educational Amendment Act.

After the Second World War English precedents provided the blueprint for Northern Ireland's social policy developments in general and advances in secondary education in particular. Under the Butler Education Act (1944), all children in England and Wales were to receive post-primary education to the age of fifteen. Samuel Hall-Thompson, the Northern Ireland Minister of Education, recommended these proposals in a White Paper, *Educational Reconstruction in Northern Ireland*, on 11 December 1944. He proposed three types of secondary school. Intermediate, or junior secondary school, would be free and provide a non-academic education. Grammar, or senior secondary, school would be fee-charging and provide an academic education for pupils who passed the 'eleven-plus' examination at the end of primary school. Lastly, technical intermediate schools would be non-fee paying, but would only take pupils at the age of thirteen.[25] Hall-Thompson proposed to increase capital grants from fifty to sixty-five per cent for voluntary secondary schools and primary and junior secondary schools, with the added incentive of full heating, lighting and cleaning expenses if, and only if, Catholic managers placed their schools under 'four and two' committees.

The White Paper aroused bitter controversy. Bishop Mageean led the defence of the Catholic position in a lengthy and cogent Lenten pastoral in February 1945, the thrust of which was essentially repeated the following month in a joint pastoral by the Northern bishops. The hierarchy played both the subsidiarity and besieged minority cards. The delineation of rights among the agents of family, church and state *vis-à-vis* education was made clear. The state should play an enabling role, encouraging and assisting the family and the church. Where it went beyond this province by forcing

> either physically or morally, neutral or mixed State schools upon a section of the community against the dictates of their conscience, or to extinguish the free denominational schools by refusing them adequate financial

assistance, she violates the twofold duty that devolves upon her from her obligations to pursue the common good.[26]

In such an instance, Mageean was under no doubt that the state would be acting both 'tyrannically' and 'unjustly'.[27]

While the Catholic bishops welcomed the White Paper's assurances that religion would get its proper place in the education system, they were deeply critical of its financial and managerial aspects. They continued to believe that 'four and two' committees would lead inexorably to non-denominational state schools and even educational deicide. To countenance such committees would be the end of the voluntary principle which not alone ensured full control of schools, but importantly safeguarded their Catholic ethos. Mageean regarded the White Paper as stepping up the 'starving process' by using 'the financial position as a lever to force them [voluntary schools] into submission'.[28] Financial carrots, however attractive, would not induce the bishops to surrender managerial control to 'the representatives of the gerrymandered County Councils'.[29] The contention that the state would, in effect, penalise parents and children for their 'conscientious convictions' by imposing a hefty financial burden became the *cri de coeur* of the Northern bishops for the next twenty years. Lest the hierarchy find themselves presented with a *fait accompli*, Mageean and Farren headed a delegation of representatives of the Northern Catholic dioceses at a meeting with the Minister of Education, in September 1945, of which there is no official record.

For the Irish hierarchy, no less than for the English Catholic hierarchy, a Catholic ethos was the *sine qua non* of a 'proper' education, a fundamental principle and an essential matter of conscience for all Catholics. Mageean put this forcefully in his 1946 Lenten pastoral: 'It is the conscientious conviction of Catholics that education, if it is to be true and genuine education, should have a moral and religious foundation.'[30] Similarly, Farren regarded education as 'not merely the handing out of knowledge' but 'the training in character and the almost imperceptible day-to-day inculcation of Christian virtues'.[31] This insistence was not peculiar to the Catholic Church in Ireland or England and Wales. Alarmed at growing secularism, in November 1953 the American hierarchy felt it essential that education inculcate a religious and moral outlook because 'education of the soul is the soul of education'.[32] But given the polarised nature of society in Northern Ireland, school ethos had even greater import as a means of sustaining a community that was both Catholic and nationalist, or conversely Protestant and unionist. Bishop O'Doherty neatly captured both aspects of group reinforcement:

'Whatever the cost, we have no intention of allowing our youth to be deprived of those spiritual aids so necessary to equip them to carry on the traditions for which our forefathers laboured, and fought, and died.'[33] It is worth recalling Marianne Elliott's observation of the 1961 census, that only 348 out of a population of 1.5 million did not accept a religious identity.[34]

Church of Ireland bishops were also concerned about school ethos and protective of the voluntary principle. Bishop Robert McNeill Boyd of Derry and Raphoe thought it

> well to remember that when a school is transferred to the public authority, there is being handed away not only a building . . . [but] the children of our Church. For the moral and spiritual education of these, neither parents nor the Church can lightly divest themselves of God-imposed responsibilities . . . which the State can lighten by giving material assistance, but if it aims to usurp them, it will do so to the detriment of the child, and of the community.[35]

Like their Catholic counterparts, managers of Church of Ireland voluntary schools were finding it increasingly difficult to meet the costs of repairs and renovations. Out of financial necessity, most managers placed their schools under 'four and two' committees.[36] Of even greater worry to Protestant church authorities was the 'conscience clause', outlined in the White Paper, which excused teachers from religious instruction if they were conscientiously opposed. The theoretical danger was that if bible instruction was not mandatory under a teacher's contract, then should Catholics ever form a majority on an education committee they could appoint Catholic teachers to Protestant schools and forbid such teachers giving bible instruction.[37] For the government and Hall-Thompson the Education Act was a double-edged sword because 'in increasing its grants to Roman Catholic schools, [the government] suffered the venom of the extreme Protestants while reaping precious little gratitude from the Roman Catholics'.[38] With the backing of Basil Brooke, the Northern Ireland Prime Minister, Hall-Thompson was able to push through what was a transformation of Northern Ireland's education system despite opposition from cabinet colleagues and backbenchers. The Bill received the royal assent almost in its entirety on 27 March 1947. Significantly, the capital grant was raised from fifty to sixty-five per cent without insistence on 'four and two' committees.

The direct financial implications of maintaining the voluntary principle were severe. One third of the cost of each new extension or school building still had to be raised by the Catholic community. In Derry, for instance, the cost of new schools in 1954 came to £600,000, of which

£200,000 had to be provided by the Catholic community.[39] But this did not deter Bishop Farren from an extensive programme of school and church building. Indeed, opening St Patrick's Voluntary Intermediate School, Dungiven, in June 1963, he proudly proclaimed that 'the Catholic people, who provided one-third of the cost of their schools, could avoid that cost by jettisoning their rights, but they were prepared to make sacrifices to ensure a Catholic education for their children'.[40] Between 1950 and 1956, the dioceses of Armagh, Clogher, Derry, Dromore, and Down and Connor spent almost £1,245,766 on new buildings, alterations, equipment and interest payments.[41] To meet this, dioceses embarked on various fund raising schemes. Farren had each parish report on the availability of sites and the state of parochial funds. In Clogher, Secondary School Projects Committees were established in many parishes, whereas in Dromore weekly collections were started to acquire the vital one-third.

The financial burden was increased by a number of factors. The proposal to raise the school leaving age to fifteen by 1 April 1951 meant considerable additional expense. Space in existing secondary (grammar) schools had to be found to cater for children up to this age and in many cases new secondary intermediates had to be built.[42] The first Catholic boys' intermediate school in Belfast only opened in August 1955.[43] Secondly, Catholic school children made up the largest denominational group in Northern Ireland and one which continued to increase. At the beginning of 1949 there were 75,083 Catholic primary school children, who comprised forty-one per cent of the total number of school children. By 1960 this figure had increased in absolute and proportional terms to 93,564, or 46.53 per cent of the total.[44] In the diocese of Dromore alone, the number of primary school pupils increased by almost 1,700 between 1954 and 1960.[45] Thirdly, new Catholic schools required additional teaching staff. The provision and financing of training facilities became a battleground of its own. The scale of the undertaking facing the Northern bishops was therefore vast.

By the end of the Second World War there was a severe shortage of teachers, especially Catholic male teachers. This was exacerbated by the lack of training facilities in Northern Ireland. Between 1922 and 1941, Northern Catholic male teachers were trained at St Mary's College, Strawberry Hill in Middlesex. However, in 1945 the college authorities informed the Ministry of Education that owing to insufficient accommodation, they would only be able to take four Northern students. The Northern Ireland government would not entertain any suggestion of teachers being trained in the South.[46] The Ministry of Education therefore proposed a temporary arrangement to have male students trained in

Belfast at either Stranmillis (the Protestant training college) or St Mary's College (the Catholic female teacher college) with a view to providing a separate male training college when normal conditions resumed. The Northern bishops rejected any suggestion of lectures at Stranmillis.[47] It seemed that a Catholic ethos was just as indispensable for a teacher training college. Instead, it was decided to create a separate department for male students at St Mary's, with the first intake in 1946–47.

There still remained the important issue of student accommodation. Mageean favoured a communal setting rather than private lodgings. He sought to have Trench House in Andersonstown, which had been his former residence and was requisitioned by the War Office in 1938, de-requisitioned to provide hostel accommodation. Privately, he was most

> indignant at the attitude of the military authorities. I feel that we have been very patient during the years of emergency, that the European war is now over and that the responsible authorities should recognise that peace has brought a new kind of emergency with its own pressing problems which should be met with the same drastic determination as those of war.[48]

An urgent appeal, in August 1945, to the Director of Quartering at the War Office met with a refusal to release the property; it was finally de-requisitioned on 16 November 1945. During the summer of 1947 it was decided to transfer the male student department to Trench House which underwent considerable redevelopment with the provision of lecture rooms and a residential block at a projected cost of over £95,500.[49] It opened its doors on 22 September 1947. The remaining challenge for Mageean was to have this recognised by the Ministry, so as to receive sixty-five per cent of the cost from the government under Section 59 of the 1947 Education Act. This was granted in 1949. In addition, Cardinal D'Alton promised to alleviate the remaining thirty-five per cent on a *pro rata* basis of the Catholic population of Northern Ireland.[50] Student numbers grew from an intake of 106, in 1947–48, to 199 in 1954–55. Therefore, Mageean requested that the Ministry consider the establishment of a separate college under voluntary management for the training of male student teachers. In 1957 the cabinet approved in principle underwriting sixty-five per cent of the cost of providing residential accommodation for eighty students, as well as new buildings.[51] For Mageean the opening, in December 1961, of St Joseph's College was 'the dream of half a lifetime'.[52] Less successful was an attempt to secure full government support for an extension to St Mary's. This was despite the pleas of Cardinal D'Alton, who contrasted the generous treatment of the

Church of Ireland training college in the Republic with the stony response of the Northern government.[53]

Two questions must be asked before considering the 1968 Education Act. Did the bishops' relationship with the Ministry of Education retard the development of Catholic schools, and why was their fear of local education authorities so great? Whereas local education authorities made available 28,000 places for Protestant children in the decade after 1947, only 10,000 new voluntary primary school places for Catholics were created. The contrast was even more pronounced at second level. As Michael McGrath illustrates, education committees provided 30,000 secondary intermediate school places with an additional 4,000 places in new grammar schools for Protestant pupils but Catholics acquired only 8,000 places.[54] Bureaucratic jersey-pulling aside, the bishops recognised that the Ministry played a vital enabling role, even if a separate, and not always equal, approach was employed. While decrying the financial burden, prelates often thanked the Ministry as protocol dictated. William Conway commented privately that such speeches were the 'customary address of courtesy', to which too much importance should not be attached.[55] However, the *realpolitik* of the situation meant the bishops had little choice.

Of the ten Ministers of Education between 1944 and 1972, the bishops had most contact with Samuel Hall-Thompson and William Long, who oversaw the implementation of major pieces of legislation in 1947 and 1968 respectively. McGrath suggests that Hall-Thompson, who was unusual for not being a member of the Orange Order, was the most liberal Minister of Education in the history of the state.[56] Given the political circumstances, the 1947 Education Act was as accommodating as possible, a feat which Patrick Shea argues demonstrated Hall-Thompson's courage and that of Reginald Brownell, permanent secretary of the Ministry, one of its chief architects.[57] But by such accommodation Hall-Thompson signed his political death warrant. Two years later, he introduced a bill whereby the Ministry would pay the employers' share of teachers' National Insurance contribution in voluntary schools for the good reason that the state paid teachers' salaries. This led to a revolt from the Unionist backbenches headed by Harry Midgley. Fearing for the unity of the Unionist Party and the survival of the new education policy, Brooke sought a political scapegoat. The intervention of the Grand Orange Lodge in December 1949 forced the resignation of Hall-Thompson. The shabby manner of his removal and the appointment of Midgley as his successor greatly alarmed the hierarchy. In a carefully worded sermon on New Year's Day 1950, vetted by Mageean, Cardinal D'Alton urged the congregation to pray for 'the safety of our Catholic schools', because

Recent developments give one an uneasy feeling that sinister influences are at work with the object of undermining the agreement reached under the Education Act of 1947 . . . It is difficult to imagine that an agreement honourably entered into, and hitherto scrupulously respected by all concerned, will be sacrificed to the clamours of those who look with disfavour on Voluntary Schools in general, and particularly on Catholic Voluntary Schools.[58]

It would not be stretching a point to say that the staunchly anti-Catholic Midgley was the Minister of Education least trusted by the Northern bishops. Their misgivings were notably *ad hominem* in nature, rather than departmental. Deep hostility to the Catholic Church was an integral part of Midgley's worldview. After the Second World War, Midgley's career began 'to slide almost inexorably into the politics of Protestant exclusivism', as he became, in the expression of his biographer, 'a unionist evangelist'.[59] He received the Unionist whip, joined the Orange Order and Royal Black Preceptory and threw himself into the war of words with the Anti-Partition League 'to earn his Unionist "spurs" with impeccably Orange-flavoured orations'.[60] When he accepted the education portfolio he had to swallow his pride and implement what was an agreed government policy. This was no easy task, particularly when the Minister and his permanent secretary were at cross-purposes.[61]

Rather than mellow in office, Midgley's anti-Catholicism intensified. He frequently compared the 'propaganda methods employed by Moscow and Rome' and was bitterly critical of the Republic, where the 'Mother and Child' controversy merely replenished his strident anti-Catholic lexicon. His electoral manifesto in October 1953, which warned of the need for vigilance 'against our enemies within and without', was anything but reassuring to the hierarchy.[62] Playing to the gallery at a unionist meeting in Belfast, in February 1955, Midgley charged 'the ecclesiastical leaders of the minority in the Six Counties with promulgating and preaching a policy of narrow nationalism, denominational separatism, and professional and educational discrimination and differentiation'.[63] When Cahir Healy, Nationalist MP for South Fermanagh, asked, in November 1951, whether the Minister believed in the voluntary school system, Midgley replied that he recognised the fact that it was there, but would not go out of his way 'to add to it and extend it.'[64] He was true to his word. McGrath's analysis of school building shows that in Midgley's last year 720 voluntary secondary intermediate places were provided. During the first year of Morris May's tenure, Midgley's successor and no liberal, voluntary secondary intermediate schools attained over 2,000 places.[65]

The Northern bishops' intransigence on the issue of local education authorities was the product of two interrelated fears: that their composition would be gerrymandered so as to be inimical to Catholic interests and that local bodies were infiltrated by the Orange Order. Numerous allusions were made to the baleful influence of the Orange Order. A motion tabled in the Northern Ireland Commons, in June 1956, by Unionist MP Nat Minford, and seconded by Independent MP Norman Porter, sought to reduce future grants to voluntary schools to fifty per cent, unless such schools adopted 'four and two' committees. Cardinal D'Alton intimated to Dean Quinn, chairperson of the Catholic Managers of Northern Ireland, that this was the fruit of 'a small clique noted for its bigotry and intolerance'. If the Minford motion succeeded, it would merely confirm 'the opinion widely held, not only among Catholics but among non-Catholics, that Government policy is in the last resort being dictated by a body whose chief desire seems to be the resurgence of strife and disorder in this part of Ireland'.[66] In the event, the government did not accept the motion. In a joint statement in 1957, the Northern bishops maintained that while 'four and two' committees worked satisfactorily in England, to their sorrow the

> official climate in England is very different from that of Northern Ireland, where Catholics are frequently the victims of intolerance and unfair discrimination. Though to some our fears may seem groundless, we are honestly convinced that under existing conditions the system of Four and Two Committees could be utilised to undermine our authority over our schools, and ultimately to destroy their Catholic character, which it is our sacred duty to maintain at the cost of heavy sacrifices.[67]

In 1959 Senator George Clark, Grand Master of the Grand Orange Lodge, and Brookeborough (Basil Brooke was made a viscount in 1952) publicly rebuked Sir Clarence Graham, chairperson of the standing committee of the Ulster Unionist Council, and Brian Maginess, the Attorney General, for daring to suggest that Catholics be admitted to the Unionist Party. This naturally did little to dispel the hierarchy's anxieties.[68]

The opening years of the 1960s briefly suggested a warmer and more hopeful climate. The IRA's border campaign finally died out in March 1962. The papacy of John XXIII, and the announcement of an ecumenical Council, generated hopes of greater inter-church understanding. In Northern Ireland there was a changing of the political and ecclesiastical guard. In March 1963 Brookeborough, who had been Prime Minister for twenty years, resigned on grounds of ill health. He was replaced by Terence O'Neill. In the same year, William Conway succeeded Cardinal D'Alton as archbishop of Armagh. Following the death of Daniel

Mageean in January 1962, William Philbin became the new bishop of Down and Connor. His appointment was somewhat unusual given his relative youth, short episcopal experience and non-Northern background. He broke sharply with tradition by paying a courtesy call on the Lord Mayor of Belfast, Alderman Martin Wallace, on 1 October 1962, the first such visit by a Catholic bishop since partition.[69] More remarkably, an offer in August 1962 by Gerry Lennon, vice-president of the Ancient Order of Hibernians and future Nationalist leader in the Senate, to meet Orange Order and Unionist leaders to discuss religious discrimination and unemployment in Northern Ireland was accepted by George Clark.[70]

Hopes of new beginnings were short-lived. The so-called 'Orange-Green' talks took place in Belfast on 17 October 1962. But these were shipwrecked the following year on the reef of 'the constitutional position', recognition and acceptance of which was non-negotiable for the Orange Order.[71] Any perceived progress was sharply reversed by Captain Lawrence Orr, Clark's successor as Grand Master, who stated publicly that the 'Order must continue to dominate and control the Unionist Party.' To Philbin's mind, this implied that the ruling party was 'openly declared to be controlled by a politico-religious society working in the Protestant interest', a concern he made known to the Governor of Northern Ireland.[72] The insensitive location of the new University of Ulster in Coleraine rather than in Derry, drew both communities in that city together, but aroused dark suggestions of a hidden hand from, ironically, Derry unionists as well as nationalist spokespeople. Bishop Farren waited several months before claiming, in February 1966, that 'there would be harmony in Derry and greater employment in Derry, if non-Catholics in Derry were only allowed to act as they know the proper way to act and were not dragooned by some hidden force'.[73]

Educational reform in Northern Ireland did not end with the 1947 Act. The Northern bishops maintained a sharp eye on developments in England. In June 1959, Geoffrey Lloyd, the UK Minister of Education, introduced a bill which raised the maximum rate of grant on voluntary school building work from fifty to seventy-five per cent. It also offered a maximum of seventy-five per cent for new aided secondary schools needed wholly, or mainly, for the continued education of children from aided primary schools of the same denomination. Aided schools were those where the church retained a majority on the managing body, controlled the appointment of teachers and where religious instruction was denominational. The majority of English Catholic schools (1,960) came under this category; the corresponding figure for the Church of England schools was

3,378.[74] In 1965 the churches in England and Wales agreed to government proposals, firstly, to increase the rate of grant to all approved aided and special agreement schools from seventy-five to eighty per cent and, secondly, to enlarge the scope of exchequer grants to cover completely new schools or enlargements of existing ones not previously eligible.[75]

Motivated by these developments, in April 1966 Cardinal Conway wrote to William Fitzsimmons, the Minister of Education, on behalf of the Northern bishops. The Cardinal called for capital grants to be raised to not less than eighty-five per cent. McGrath powerfully demonstrates that thousands of Catholic children were still denied the opportunity of a full secondary education by the end of the 1960s.[76] Given the plumbline of 'step by step', the bishops might have expected the White Paper, *Local Education Authorities and Voluntary Schools*, to meet their concerns when it was published on 19 October 1967. This was not the case. The old chestnut of school management was once again the divisive issue, but one on which the Catholic bishops were forced to concede ground.

William Long, who succeeded Fitzsimmons in October 1966, matched the English proposals on condition that 'four and two' committees were accepted, even though, as Conway pointed out in May 1967, the Westminster measure did not alter the management system.[77] Furthermore, all entirely new schools had to accept maintained status to qualify for aid. In a memorandum for the cabinet, Long was certain that he would be charged with being less liberal than Hall-Thompson was in 1947. Nonetheless, he was resolute in his desire to 'break' the exclusively clerical control of Catholic schools. He believed that 'mounting pressure from the Roman Catholic laity might now force the hand of the Hierarchy within a few years into acceptance of "four and two" committees'.[78] So it proved. The Northern government had never before imposed such a harsh alternative on the Catholic hierarchy. This Hobson's choice demonstrated that behind Terence O'Neill's veneer of liberalism there was, as several commentators note, no such 'reforming zeal'.[79] To reject 'four and two' committees would mean no capital funding for new schools. To accept would allow local education authorities a role in the management of Catholic schools which had always been emphatically, if not fanatically, opposed by the bishops.

Without the benefit of either diocesan or public records for these years, McGrath argues, on the basis of press reaction, that it was only in the aftermath of the White Paper's publication that Conway modified his position of absolute opposition to any form of school committee.[80] In fact this was not so. In response to a confidential outline of the White Paper's proposals in July, the Northern bishops underlined their disquiet 'at the measure of increased control over Catholic schools which it would be proposed to give to local authorities, whose general attitude towards, and treatment of, the minority in Northern Ireland can be well documented.'[81] Significantly, the hierarchy feared *local* rather than *central* government interference in the running of their schools, but not school committees *per se*. In a further affront, the Ministry refused, on the pretext of parliamentary privilege, to give an advance copy of the White Paper to the hierarchy.[82]

Conway was in Rome when the White Paper was published. Rather than wait until his return, Philbin rushed the fences. He issued a statement, in a personal capacity, which vigorously criticised the proposals as an attempt to invade the established system of Catholic school management by taking advantage of their grave financial needs.[83] In retrospect, the bishop's statement seemed out of touch with lay opinion. While not ignoring the validity of Philbin's concerns, many lay Catholics did not share his apprehension about local education authorities or perceive the proposals as a devious attempt to subvert Catholic education. Significantly, Nationalist politicians were slow to denounce the White Paper and the Northern executive of the Irish National Teachers Organisation gave it their qualified support, before eventually rowing in with the hierarchy.[84] As early as the summer of 1964, Conway was surprised to learn from Bishop O'Doherty that several priests and lay people in the diocese of Dromore were in favour of 'four and two' committees. An opinion poll in the *Belfast Telegraph* in December 1967 revealed that eight out of ten people favoured acceptance of the eighty per cent grant and public representatives on school management committees.[85] For many members of the Catholic community, the financial imperative was too strong to ignore. According to McGrath, by the mid-1960s they paid more than £10 million per annum for their schools in 1996 prices.[86] These arguments were well aired in the letter pages of the Northern press and in direct approaches to Philbin. Furthermore, the Second Vatican Council advocated greater lay involvement in church affairs. This coalesced with a growing interest in integrated education in Northern Ireland, something which notably predated the Troubles. Digressing momentarily from the discussion of the 1968 Act, Conway consistently argued against the proposition that integrated schooling would somehow solve the Northern Ireland Troubles. He cited the examples of denominational education in the Republic, Holland, the US, Britain and Germany which were in no way a divisive factor in community relations. The divisions in Northern Ireland were, he felt, 'due to deep historical, social and political causes'.[87]

Conway issued a statement on 1 November 1967, which acknowledged that elements of the White Paper were acceptable. This was followed by a meeting with Long on 16 November. Key to the Cardinal's strategy was, firstly, to reunite the Catholic lobby and, secondly, to suggest a parallel system of school boards. He told Long that 'four and two' committees would be acceptable subject to two conditions: that the two public representatives should be nominees of the Minister of Education not of the local authority, and, secondly, that the legal right to maintain and equip the schools should rest with the 'four and two' committee not with the local authorities.[88] The cabinet regarded the hierarchy's counter-proposals as 'a textbook definition of apartheid.'[89] Even so, this represented a ground-breaking change of stance by the Northern bishops. Long was unmoved and the White Paper was adopted *in toto*. The essence of the government's proposal was, Long informed Conway, to reduce the influence of the Ministry and individual voluntary schools by augmenting the status of the local education authorities. These would be responsible for maintenance of buildings, employment of ancillary staff and the appointment of one-third of the members of school management committees. Any suggestion that he, as Minister, should appoint the public representatives did not, to Long's mind, 'provide a satisfactory basis for further consideration'.[90] Between the debate on the Bill at the end of November 1967 and the second reading at the end of January, a personal assurance that the denominational character of the schools would not be altered was all the Minister offered.[91] More out of show than realistic prospects of success, the bishops published a half-hearted statement on the evening of 7 January 1968. It underlined their misgivings at the curtailment of voluntary control but hoped that the efforts to 'reach an agreed solution' would be 'reciprocated'.[92]

Compared to the attitude of Craigavon and Brooke *vis-à-vis* the Education Acts of 1930 and 1947, O'Neill and Long were far more unyielding and corralled the hierarchy into acceptance.[93] On the credit side of the ledger, the 1968 Act reduced the voluntary contribution from thirty-five to twenty per cent and abolished the voluntary contribution for maintenance. At the opening of the annual Ulster Teachers' Association conference in April 1971, Long was 'happy to say' that 'over 60 per cent of the voluntary primary schools and about 90 per cent of the voluntary secondary intermediate schools are now in the maintained school category.'[94] By 1974 only two of the 177 intermediate secondary schools were not maintained, which is indicative of the financial cross Catholic schools had had to bear. However, on the negative side, the hierarchy failed to get Ministry representation for school committees. They could only agree with good grace to give the new system 'a fair trial . . . in the interests of harmony and goodwill'.[95] It was ironic that having fought and resisted for so long, Catholic authorities finally succumbed to the middle route originally offered in 1923.

The Northern Ireland Bill (1962)

A dichotomous view of central and local government also existed in fields other than education. In January 1957 the replacement of the Charities Branch of the Ministry of Finance with a Board of Commissioners for charitable bequests was mooted. In his assessment of the pros and cons, William Conway tellingly favoured the *status quo*, because Catholics

> get fairer treatment from government Ministries than from bodies, such as local councils, on which they are in a minority. Catholics would certainly be in a minority of at least one in three and possibly one in four, on the new Board. If the record of similar bodies in the past is any guide the danger of unfair treatment of Catholics is greater with such a body than with a government department.[96]

The concerns highlighted in this vignette were amplified in 1962 by the little known, but significant, Northern Ireland Bill. This measure was intended to equip the Northern Ireland government with powers to make laws with regard to matters prohibited under Section 5 of the Government of Ireland Act (1920) in respect of compulsory purchase of property for the purpose of slum clearance and housing development. Clause 13 of the Bill, published on 26 January, included property belonging to religious and educational bodies. During the Bill's second reading in the House of Lords, on 1 February, Lord Longford asked the Lord Chancellor, Lord Kilmuir, how the educational and religious bodies concerned viewed Clause 13. Incredibly, they had not been consulted even though the Northern government had appointed a committee chaired by Brian Maginess as far back as October 1956 to consider items the Bill might contain.[97] It only came to the attention of the Northern Catholic bishops from press reports.

Worried by the proposed legislation, Cardinal D'Alton intimated to Cardinal Godfrey, archbishop of Westminster, that there was 'something sinister about the way it is being introduced'.[98] D'Alton dispatched Conway and O'Doherty to London, where they were ably assisted by Godfrey and, in particular, his secretary Monsignor Derek Worlock, the future archbishop of Liverpool. Worlock arranged a meeting between Longford and the Irish bishops at Archbishop's House, Westminster on 9 February 1962, and another with representatives of the Lord Chancellor that evening. The bishops made clear to Kilmuir that they had no prior opportunity for consultation and informed him that Cardinal D'Alton intended to make a public protest against Clause 13.[99] The following day they met Longford and Lord Craigmyle, another Catholic peer, to urge them to move an amendment to the Bill.

In anticipation of the third reading of the Bill, D'Alton's statement was released simultaneously in London and Armagh on 11 February. Worlock sent copies to the BBC, Independent Television News, the Press Association, Reuters and to National Dailies to redress the 'glorious unawareness [in Britain] of the situation in Northern Ireland'.[100] The statement highlighted the lack of consultation and the bishops' 'profound' apprehension that such powers were open to abuse. While recognising the need for modern social development schemes, D'Alton felt that

> such powers take on an entirely different significance when transferred to the context of Northern Ireland, where the past forty years have witnessed a sustained use of power, particularly by local authorities, to discriminate against Catholics in the exercise of the franchise, in housing, in public employment and in many other fields.[101]

Not for the first time, the bishops singled out local authorities as the least trustworthy branch of government. The statement closed by stating the importance of Section 5 of the Government of Ireland Act. D'Alton regarded it as a pledge by Britain, no less important in 1962 than in 1920, to safeguard the property and rights of the religious minority. In a letter to Shane Leslie, the Cardinal suggested that political measures lay at the secret heart of the Bill. Its measures would, he believed, 'give very dangerous powers to the Stormont Government, which would certainly be abused by some of the local authorities.'[102] The statement was covered well by both the Irish and English press, with an editorial in *The Times* entitled 'Diluting a Guarantee'. In contrast to this Machiavellian tone, the *Belfast Telegraph* carried an editorial entitled: 'Overstated Fears'.[103] Con Cremin informed Sir Ian Maclennan, British ambassador in Dublin, of the Irish government's anxiety:

> We are satisfied that the Northern Ireland Government have not in all cases used the powers they already possess in a non-discriminatory manner ... We would therefore urge that provision should be made in the Bill for guarantees that the powers to be conferred cannot be exercised in an unfair or discriminatory fashion.[104]

The Commonwealth Relations Office bluntly felt that Dublin had no standing in the matter, as Section 5 was not enshrined in the Schedule to the Irish Free State (Agreement) Act 1922.[105]

Longford and Craigmyle moved the rejection of Clause 13 at the committee stage on 13 February. This was only withdrawn on the undertaking from Kilmuir that he would receive the Irish bishops. At a meeting on 16 February, Conway and O'Doherty made clear to the Lord Chancellor and Charles Cunningham, Permanent Under-Secretary of State, that they had no objection to slum clearance or housing development, but they feared that such powers could be used to discriminate against Catholics through their schools, churches and ecclesiastical property. By this time, the Bill had also attracted the attention of the principal Protestant churches to which the Home Office had written.[106] Representatives of seven Protestant churches sought a redrafting of Clause 13, an action approved by the House of Bishops.[107] Kilmuir met these difficulties with an amendment at the report stage, which exempted from compulsory acquisition powers 'the property of a religious denomination or educational institution used by it exclusively for a religious or educational purpose and the curtilages thereof'. This was more than Conway expected.[108] Both D'Alton and Conway were loud in their praise of the assistance received from the archdiocese of Westminster. Conway assured Worlock that 'none of the Northern Bishops is in any doubt as to how much we owe your good self. We have told them quite simply that we could not even have got off the ground but for your untiring help.'[109] D'Alton was also indebted to Lord Longford, in whom the Northern bishops 'had a very reliable champion in the House of Lords'. Conway, too, was praised by the Cardinal as 'a tower of strength' during what was one of the most serious legislative proposals to confront the hierarchy.[110] The Northern Ireland administration had to acquiesce and their concerns turned to avoiding any impression that the amendment could be interpreted as a rebuff from London.[111]

Health and social services

Social service legislation in Northern Ireland also mirrored that in Britain. The Social Services Act (NI) 1949 ensured the annual receipt by the Northern Ireland exchequer of £5 million from Westminster towards the cost of the health service, children's allowances and old age pensions. The Northern bishops tirelessly and vigorously defended their community's right to such benefits. Children's allowance was the subject of acrimonious debate in 1956 when Major Ivan Neill, the Northern Ireland Minister of Labour and National Insurance, sought to depart from the UK position. Westminster increased allowances from 8s per week for the second and subsequent children to 8s for the second and 10s for those thereafter. This increase of 2s to all children after the second child was not replicated in Northern Ireland which proposed 1s 6d per week to the second and third child only, and 8s thereafter. The Ministry of Pensions in London suggested that the discrepancy was potentially contrary to the 1949 Act, but the Northern government maintained that while the rates might differ, the total cost would be the same.[112] Given the Catholic community's higher rate of unemployment and larger family size, it was no surprise that the bishops interpreted Neill's proposal as discriminatory and stoutly defended parity with Britain. In an unpublished letter, D'Alton regarded the measure as 'a counsel of despair, sinister in its import, and inexplicable except as a fresh attempt to discriminate against one section of the population'.[113] The General Assembly of the Presbyterian Church also strongly condemned the proposal. The government backed down by announcing, on 12 July 1956, their intention to maintain uniformity with Britain.[114]

Health was the second great battleground in the Catholic hierarchy's pursuit of incremental gain. The Health Services Act (NI) 1948 established the Northern Ireland Hospitals' Authority (NIHA) which came into being on 5 July 1948. Its working relationship with the hierarchy was testy and distrustful. Relatively minor proposals often led to protracted and strained negotiations. For instance, the NIHA proposed a prayer of dedication at the opening ceremonies of new hospital accommodation. Cardinal D'Alton suggested that the person opening the hospital conclude with the words: 'I declare this Hospital open, and I pray that the Blessing of God may be ever with it, its staff and patients, so that the work of healing carried out herein may redound to the honour and glory of the Almighty.' This inoffensive formula was acceptable to Archbishop Gregg and the Reverend Robert John Wilson, Moderator of the General Assembly of the Presbyterian Church when the matter was considered in April 1958, but not to the NIHA. Its proposal was in turn disagreeable to the Cardinal, who decided not to take part in public dedication ceremonies and to have mass on another day instead.[115] The public relations conundrum for the Northern bishops was captured succinctly by Bishop O'Doherty. He felt that the Cardinal 'would be asked whether "non-participating" is to be considered as equivalent to "abstention". Anything that would look like a boycott of the dedication ceremonies is very liable to be misinterpreted and I can see it being used against us later.'[116] Suspicion of the NIHA was reinforced by its composition. In 1961 Father Michael Kelly, dean of residence at Queen's University, claimed that only two of twenty-four members of the NIHA were Catholic. Secondly, only twelve per cent of those on the thirty-one hospital management committees, which ran seventy-five hospitals, were Catholic and the secretary of only one management committee was Catholic. Lastly, only thirty-five (or six per cent) of the 573 hospital consultants in Northern Ireland were Catholic.[117] Consequently, it seemed to the hierarchy that equity was in short supply.

The greatest running sore concerned the position of the Mater Hospital, Belfast which was established by the Mercy Order of Catholic nuns in 1883. In 1948 the new Health Act intended to introduce the National Health Service to Northern Ireland in line with arrangements in Scotland, England and Wales. The three acts were very similar. However, they differed in their treatment of voluntary hospitals, which wished to remain outside the state scheme, in two respects. In England and Wales, 210 hospitals opted out but still received state grants, as did twenty-two hospitals in Scotland.[118] There was no such provision in the Northern Ireland Act. Secondly, the NIHA had a policy-making role denied to English regional boards. In addition, safeguards to protect the religious character of the institutions were not regarded as safe enough in the Northern Ireland legislation.[119] The proposal to bring the Mater into the scheme met with a storm of protest. In an address to St Peter's Holy Family confraternity, Bishop Mageean resisted any attempt to filch the Mater: 'We stand where we always stood. We hold our hospital. We hold our endowments and we will continue in the future to serve our Catholic people and the whole community as we have done in the past.'[120] The bishop would not be stampeded into capitulation. As chairperson of the governing body, he requested, in February 1948, that the hospital be exempted from the Act lest its ethos be jeopardised. The Mater therefore received no public money for treating patients who would otherwise have been treated at public expense. Neither did its medical staff receive salaries from the state for their services. An appeal to the Ministry of Health and Local Government, in January 1949, to have specialists' services remunerated under Section 21 of the Health Services Act fell on deaf ears. The central issue, captured in a legal opinion sought on behalf of the medical staff, was that the consultative staff, as well as the Catholic community generally, was prejudiced against because the Northern Ireland Act treated Catholic hospitals less favourably than the English and Scottish Acts. While the Mater could fit into these schemes, there was no such provision in the Northern Ireland legislation.[121]

Never one to rely solely on the persuasive power of public statements, Mageean established a committee to press the case that the Mater, as a voluntary hospital, was entitled to the same financial treatment as exempted hospitals in England. To safeguard the voluntary principle, the Catholic hierarchy of England and Wales pressed for an amendment to the National Health Services Bill. This demanded that the rights of ownership, endowments and trusts of voluntary hospitals continue to be vested in the trustees or management committee, which should have freedom of action with regard to medical and nursing appointments and deployment of funds.[122] Furthermore, the English and Welsh bishops insisted that any hospital transferred under the Act to the Ministry of

Health should be entitled to have a Catholic management committee and to treat Catholic patients.[123] In Northern Ireland William Grant, the Minister of Health and Local Government, set an unbending rule that the Mater had to be either one hundred per cent *in* or one hundred per cent *out* of the scheme. By contrast, Aneurin Bevan, his English counterpart, sensibly felt that the 'circumstances of one hospital will be quite different from those of another . . . it would be both premature and unsatisfactory to attempt to lay down at this stage any hard and fast rules intended to be applicable to all Catholic hospitals'.[124] In June 1954 a Health Services Advisory Committee, chaired by H. G. Tanner, was appointed to review the operation of the health service. The Board of Management of the Mater made a submission which stressed that the position of the Mater was a legal anomaly given that the state levied taxes 'from all citizens without distinction' to provide free hospital treatment. Moreover, it was felt that 'a square deal for the Mater Hospital would do much to foster a desirable spirit of co-operation amongst all sections of the community'.[125] A delegation from the Board met the Tanner Committee on 29 November 1954. It turned down a request to give public representatives an input into medical appointments and another to contract a number of beds to reduce NIHA waiting lists.[126] The Tanner Report of May 1955 was short on concrete remedies. However, in paragraph 178 it did acknowledge the significant role the Mater played, without which the burden on the NIHA would be unmanageable.[127]

Loss of public funding had grave implications for the financially precarious hospital. As early as December 1948, medical staff privately admitted that the hospital could not 'continue to exist outside the scheme as a first class hospital', as it would not be able to maintain a comparable level of service.[128] Its status as the only Catholic teaching hospital in association with Queen's University was also under threat. Without investment in new equipment and staff, the Mater would lose patients and acquire third class status. It was not surprising, then, that Mageean, and later Philbin, protested vociferously at the lack of funding for their hospital. In an outspoken criticism on 15 November 1960, Mageean condemned the government for boasting 'of being step by step with England, but England gives help to voluntary hospitals while they do not'.[129] Indeed the Mater was technically not regarded as a hospital within the meaning of the Northern Ireland Act. Philbin informed the Minister of Health and Social Services in April 1965 that the Mater survived only through the continued voluntary efforts of a whole complex of charitable organisations both inside and outside Northern Ireland.[130] Church and door-to-door collections were supplemented by voluntary contributions. Key to survival in the lean 1950s and 1960s was the innovative Young Philanthropists (YP) football pools. In July 1954 Mageean sent Father P. J. Mullally, the diocesan secretary, and Thomas Cairns to Dublin to meet John A. Costello, the Taoiseach, to ensure provisions were made to allow the YP Pools continue in the Republic.[131] The extent of the fund-raising effort involved demonstrated the significance to the Catholic community of the religious, educational and ethical interests centred in the Mater.

By the mid-1960s it was widely felt that the anomalous position of the Mater should be rectified. An editorial in the *Belfast Telegraph*, in February 1964, argued that if the Mater treated both Protestant and Catholic patients, and was well regarded by both communities, then the official attitude should reflect this.[132] A cabinet meeting in January 1964 revealed an awareness of growing middle class Protestant opinion in favour of some measure of aid. Yet this was tempered by a fear of electoral repercussions. At a subsequent meeting in May 1964, the Prime Minister again felt that any proposed solution would have to command party support.[133] However, prior to this William Morgan, Minister of Health, had suggested to Philbin that informal talks be held without commitment. Representatives of the Board of Management and the Ministry of Health and Social Services subsequently exchanged views on 17 April and 1 May 1964. Discussions were revived in early 1965 with Morgan in favour of reaching an equitable solution.

At a cabinet meeting on 27 January 1965, Ivan Neill, Minister of Finance, proposed a different approach, that any further move be deferred until general legislation on hospital administration be introduced in which the legal standing of the Mater could be tidied up.[134] Morgan was aware that such legislation might take a year to prepare, but bowed to Neill's suggestion which had the backing of the majority of cabinet. When this was revealed in a speech on 9 March 1965, Philbin was mystified at the Minister's u-turn, from a line that 'seemed to be that of high statesmanship' to the substitution of 'a legalistic approach for one of conciliation and understanding'.[135] To bring maximum public attention to this, the bishop went as far as to enquire of Seán Lemass whether the Irish Embassy in London could assist his representative, Father Michael Kelly, in securing publicity for an open letter to the Minister in the English press.[136] The Embassy provided Kelly with contact details of newspaper editors in London. Philbin's letter and articles on the Mater appeared in the *Tablet*, *Universe* (Britain's largest Catholic newspaper), and *Catholic Herald*. The bishop was pleased with the results and informed Lemass that 'nothing was done to harm the better climate of relations here: rather, the result is more support for a charitable institution of ours from people of goodwill of all points of view'.¹³⁷ However, John Kelly, London editor of the *Irish Independent*, confirmed the ambassador's opinion that Father Kelly did not succeed in achieving any great publicity due to poor preparation, short notice and the dominance of the Race Relations Bill in the British press.¹³⁸ In this regard, Frank Soskice, the Home Secretary, ironically believed that the Northern Ireland government would not wish for the Race Relations Bill to be applied in their state lest the issue of religious discrimination be raised. Moreover, this would greatly complicate matters in Westminster. Predictably, the Northern Ireland government saw no reason to extend the provisions of the Race Relations Bill to their political jurisdiction.¹³⁹

Morgan wrote privately to Philbin on 7 May 1965, stressing that the discussions were in abeyance rather than terminated.¹⁴⁰ Philbin was more conciliatory in a major speech at a nurses' prize-giving ceremony in the Mater on 24 November 1966. He stated that the Mater's interests were 'religious, medical, educational – all factors that cannot but make for goodwill and harmony if they could enjoy the atmosphere of encouragement an institution of this kind has a right to expect.' On this basis, he argued that the government had within its grasp the means to free all concerned from 'this wretched controversy'.¹⁴¹ Another year elapsed before Morgan felt that the way was clear for a resumption of discussions in tandem with the coming into operation of the Health Services (Amendment) Bill in August 1967. He had a private meeting with Philbin in June 1967. This was the beginning of a protracted period of negotiation. That great strides had been made is clear from Morgan's claim, in December 1968, that 'the protection of character and associations is the end to be secured, and upon this there is no difference of view between us. The issue therefore concerns not the end, but the means to that end.'¹⁴² Philbin accepted terms for bringing the Mater into the state service in June 1969. The state undertook the hospital's running costs, which for the year ended 31 December 1969 amounted to an excess of expenditure over income of over £73,000.¹⁴³ This compromise was without loss of the Mater's Catholic ethos. The long running saga came to an end with the transfer of the hospital to the state on a 999–year lease at nominal rent on 1 January 1972.¹⁴⁴

The pursuit of social justice

The Catholic bishops reaped the benefits of the welfare state. Criticism of central government was therefore tempered by the need to find accommodation in the fields of education and health. But as default spokespeople for the Catholic community, the bishops had to highlight the social injustices experienced by their flock. John Whyte's examination of the Stormont regime reveals that gerrymandering, public employment and regionally based housing allocation provided sustainable instances of discrimination.[145] One of the most outspoken bishops was Eugene O'Callaghan of Clogher. Speaking in Roslea, County Fermanagh on 6 May 1959, he claimed that 'bigotry and religious discrimination have reached deplorable heights' and that Catholics 'must be prevented, it seems, by every means, from ever becoming sufficiently strong numerically to insist on their rights.'[146] This alluded to county boroughs which had the power to regulate their own ward structure for local government elections. Despite post-war electoral reforms at Westminster, the company vote and ratepayer suffrage were retained in Northern Ireland. This meant that in 1961 only 73.8 per cent of the adult population had the local government vote. Put another way, some 220,000 Westminster electors in Northern Ireland could not vote in local government elections in 1967.[147] Limitation of space does not permit a survey of the bishops' views on every category of complaint. The allocation of housing was one of the most demonstrable examples of discrimination on denominational lines. It was a key catalyst of the civil rights campaign and will be taken as a litmus test of the bishops' stance on the attainment of social justice.

Despite the establishment of the Northern Ireland Housing Trust (NIHT) in 1946 to supervise the construction of public housing, housing did not become an issue until well into the 1950s. It was only then, when public housing actually became available for allocation, that allegations of discrimination were made. Indeed, in 1952 Bishop Boyd of Derry and Raphoe felt that a programme of house-building was far more urgent than the £2.5 million scheme of school-building announced by the Minister of Education.[148] In addition to the NIHT, local authorities also provided housing. Even though a Catholic was not appointed to the NIHT until January 1968, local authorities became the central focus of complaint. Criticism was of two varieties: that Catholics were simply not allocated housing and, secondly, that they were confined to certain wards so as not to disturb the electoral balance.

In the first category, Fermanagh, where Catholics formed a slight majority of the population, was one of the worst offenders. One report found that in the early 1960s only two nationalists compared to 177 unionists were allocated houses in the four housing estates around Enniskillen. Yet, more than 300 nationalists were living in slum conditions and faced a wait of at least three years before being re-housed.[149] Speaking in St Macartan's Cathedral, Monaghan, in January 1964, Bishop O'Callaghan felt it incumbent on his office to speak 'on behalf of those Catholics of Enniskillen who are being condemned to live in some of the worst slums of Northern Ireland through the Council's policy of discrimination'. However, not wishing to recriminate or cite the injustices of the past, he called for 'peace and harmony among all the people of the town', and urged the heads of other denominations to support this appeal.[150] This prompted the mayor, Alderman W. F. Bryson, to seek a meeting with church leaders. On 29 January 1964 he met O'Callaghan and his Vicar General, Monsignor P. J. Flanagan, along with representatives of the Protestant churches in Enniskillen Town Hall. The meeting, held *in camera*, lasted an hour and forty minutes.[151] But however historic this encounter, nine months later the *Irish News* reported that out of a total of 231 houses erected by Enniskillen Borough Council in the previous twenty years, only twenty had gone to Catholics.[152]

In County Tyrone, Omagh and Dungannon were examples of the second type of complaint. Catholics were almost exclusively re-housed in the west wards in an effort, as Cardinal D'Alton expressed it, 'to effect a new plantation'.[153] This also occurred in Fermanagh. George Elliott, a member of Enniskillen Borough Council, captured this attitude in an infamous statement: 'We are not going to build houses in the South Ward and cut a rod to beat ourselves later on. We are going to see that the right people are put into these houses, and we are not making any apologies for it.'[154] Another alleged means of maintaining the electoral balance was simply to build as few houses as possible. Lisnaskea Rural District Council, in which Catholics, according to the 1961 census, outnumbered all other denominations by 3,000, spent less money on housing than any other local authority in Northern Ireland.[155]

Cardinal Conway vigorously promoted housing throughout the 1960s. Speaking in Dungannon, County Tyrone, in May 1965, he temperately prayed that 'a day will come when a man's religion will not be the deciding factor as to whether or not he is to get a decent home for his wife and family'.[156] He therefore welcomed the decision to set up machinery to investigate complaints of discrimination at local government level. But he also warned that to be effective, such machinery would have to determine not simply discrimination in single cases, but 'a pattern of discrimination' which could often only 'be clearly inferred from a number of cases taken together'.[157] That allocation of housing should be taken out of the hands of the local authorities, whether Catholic-controlled, elected or not, and run on a national basis, was one of the very first issues raised by Cardinal Conway during his first meeting with Oliver Wright, the British government representative in Northern Ireland. In October 1969 public housing came under the new Northern Ireland Housing Executive. The following year the Macrory report recommended the abolition of the existing structure of urban and rural district councils and county councils, and their replacement with twenty-six single-tier authorities, which were to retain only the functions carried out by 'lower tier' authorities in the rest of the UK.[158]

There is little evidence from diocesan archives to determine the collective attitude of the Northern bishops to the emergence of the Civil Rights movement. Ciarán de Baróid records that Philbin instructed the clergy of Connor in 1968 not to allow church or school property to be used for Northern Ireland Civil Rights Association meetings.[159] Whether this was circumspection or not, as the pace of the Civil Rights campaign increased the bishops read the signs. Their initial hesitancy was not unlike that of their American colleagues, whose sympathy for the cause of civil rights was moderated by unease with the confrontational methods employed by civil rights leaders to dramatise their objectives.[160] A pastoral by the Northern bishops in January 1968 was severely critical of local authorities:

> In the arrangements for their election, in their composition, their nomination of committees and their record in such matters as employment and housing, very many local authorities in Northern Ireland have manifested a bias against Catholics which is undeniable ... We must regretfully insist that these are not idle charges.[161]

Following the confrontation between Civil Rights marchers and police in Derry on 5 October 1968, Conway appealed to those in government not to misconstrue the recent happenings in a purely political way, but to realise that the causes were social and grew out of a frustrated desire for houses, employment and equitable representation. This was a line of argument often repeated by the Cardinal. As Gerald McElroy argues, by emphasising the social nature of the civil rights movement, Conway in effect challenged the belief of many unionists that the Civil Rights campaign was really a republican plot to destabilise Northern Ireland.[162]

The hierarchy firmly supported the Civil Rights campaign in its response to the loyalist attack on Civil Rights marchers at Burntollet Bridge, outside Derry, on 4 January 1969. On 20 January the bishops issued a major joint statement which drew attention to the existence, for many decades, of serious injustices in the field of civil rights. That this had become widely recognised by people of different faiths and political affiliations, both in Ireland and internationally, was, in the bishops' view, due in considerable measure to the Civil Rights movement. The remainder of the statement set out in detail the bishops' certainty that the movement was essentially non-violent and non-sectarian. Attention was drawn to 'small groups of subversive militants who have associated themselves with the Civil Rights movement for their own ends'.[163] Distinguishing between the vast majority who sought to remedy their grievances by non-violent means, on one hand, and the small minority who did not, on the other, became a feature of many subsequent statements by the hierarchy. The statement welcomed the decision to appoint a commission of inquiry in March 1969 headed by the Scottish judge, Lord Cameron, to uncover the root of recent disturbances. Bishop Farren was invited to make a submission in April 1969. His eight-page document championed the demands of the Civil Rights movement. He stressed that Catholics were not demanding 'any privileges, but merely the same rights and opportunities as everyone else'.[164] The bishop of Derry listed several grievances: gerrymandered constituencies and the perception of undue influence by the Orange Order in local politics; overcrowded living conditions; an unemployment rate which rarely fell below twelve per cent; the failure to site the new university in Derry; the flaunting of the Union Jack; police brutality in October 1968 and January 1969. Before considering the opening years of the Troubles, it is necessary to consider briefly the response of the Church of Ireland bishops to the deteriorating Northern situation.

While social grievances in Northern Ireland may have been discussed informally at meetings of the House of Bishops during the 1960s, they did not form specific agenda items or prompt public statements. By October 1968, the Northern Church of Ireland bishops could no longer avoid comment and a statement was issued on 25 October. Intended to 'strengthen the hands' of the Prime Minister, the statement stood 'unequivocally for the ideal of justice for all, without distinction' and supported the prioritisation of housing. The bishops stated their belief that there was 'massive support for a policy based on a fair deal.'[165] A minority of individual Church of Ireland bishops also took a firm stand. The previous month, Alan Buchanan told the Clogher diocesan synod that everyone had the right to life, which 'includes a right not to be deprived of the means of livelihood through the operation of bigoted or partisan policies. It includes the right to a decent home, not to its denial in circumstances that mock the concept of fair play and justice.'[166] In his last presidential address to the Derry and Raphoe diocesan synod, Charles Tyndall perceptively warned that 'there are subversive forces at this moment in our midst seeking to tear us apart. There are extremists dividing us from doctrines of magnanimity, tolerance and love and inflaming susceptible minds with doctrines of hatred. There are wolves getting in amongst the flocks and devouring the faithful.'[167] The following week, at a Remembrance Day service in Tamlaght O'Crilly Church Lower in the Derry diocese, Tyndall utterly condemned the loyalist march to the Diamond in Derry on 9 November 1968, led by Ian Paisley and Major Ronald Bunting. He courageously asked: 'Did I see the march of men dedicated to religious genocide? Did I see the rise of an ideological force based on cultivated hatred and invective?'[168] The Irish Council of Churches (ICC) was also a default instrument through which Protestant churches commented on the issues convulsing Northern Ireland. Its annual report in May 1970 did not exonerate member churches from blame:

> For far too long manifest grievances have been ignored, and sincerely held fears remained unexamined. True religion in Ireland will suffer irreparable damage if we do not quickly come to terms with the need to spell out what it means to be a Christian in a divided community such as ours.[169]

By the summer of 1969, it appeared that the existence of the Northern Ireland state was under threat. A parade by the Apprentice Boys in Derry, on 12 August, led to violent clashes with residents of the Bogside. The police responded with armoured vehicles and CS gas culminating in the so-called 'Battle of the Bogside'. Rioting spread throughout Northern Ireland. In Belfast over 1,500 Catholic and 300 Protestant families were left homeless. At the end of the month, the register of the Refugees Relief Co-ordination Centre at Trench House recorded 3,590 people living in fourteen emergency centres in schools or church halls and 4,400 sheltered in private homes.[170] This excluded those who had gone to Britain or to the Republic, where over 650 people were sheltered in temporary military centres manned by the Irish army.[171] On 14 August the British government accepted the Northern Ireland government's request that troops be deployed. This was the background to several personal and joint statements made by Cardinal Conway in an effort to avoid an escalation of violence. He appealed to all Catholics not 'to be swept away by emotion – however natural and understandable such emotion may be – but to keep cool heads and realise that a general eruption of violence would seriously weaken the Civil Rights movement.'[172] He questioned excessive police force in Derry but sensibly refrained from apportioning blame. Cardinal Conway clearly emerged as the key source of leadership among the Northern Catholic bishops. A native of Belfast and by training a canon lawyer, he penned most of the joint episcopal statements and was greatly distressed by the descent into violence.

If Conway led the Northern Catholic bishops by example in his constant advocacy of peace and reform, what of the Church of Ireland bishops? With the exception of the diocese of Kilmore, there was an almost complete turnover of Church of Ireland bishops in the Northern dioceses in the summer and autumn of 1969. George Simms became archbishop of Armagh. Arthur Butler went to Connor, Richard Hanson to Clogher, Cuthbert Peacocke to Derry and Raphoe, and George Quin to Down and Dromore. The heaviest responsibility was shouldered by Simms as Primate, and Butler and Quin as bishops of over half of the Church of Ireland population. Despite having spent almost his entire ministry in the South, Simms was the obvious and perhaps only choice to succeed Archbishop McCann in 1969. Raymond Jenkins, rector of Grangegorman and a long-time friend of Simms, believed his 'qualities would be stultified in the harsh irrational northern scene'.[173] Indeed, most of the hostility he encountered in his eleven years as Primate came not from Catholics, but from extreme Protestants. As his biographer observed, the Primate's passive style of leadership meant that for all his great intellectual ability, learning, personal warmth and charm, he was never fully accepted in the North in the way he was embraced in the Republic.[174] It resulted in the criticism that he was too urbane, too quick to equivocate on difficult questions, too concerned to avoid giving offence 'when gentleness might be interpreted as moral cowardice'.[175] To Simms's credit, he led the Church of Ireland with dexterity, fortitude, good judgement and a tireless promotion of peace and reconciliation. His pronouncements echoed the calls for restraint voiced by Cardinal Conway. While these were not always deemed the most newsworthy, Simms quietly worked to further the cause of reconciliation and promote understanding. For instance, at a diocesan level he redefined the duties of the Armagh Diocesan Board of Temperance and Social Welfare. Renamed the Board of Social Responsibility in early 1971, under his chairmanship it considered at length, in the early years of the Troubles, how to improve community relations.[176]

Throughout the latter part of 1969 and in the months that followed, both sets of bishops and their clergy played an important role in attempting to lower the political temperature and counsel patience among their respective communities. Simms cleaved to safe ground at his first General Synod as President in 1970. He paid tribute to the 'faithful and tireless' work of his clergy, whose 'emergency action and steadying influence' might not have made headline news, but was recognised by the affected localities.[177] Church leaders were united in urging their laities to renounce prejudice, bigotry and enmity. For instance, Cardinal Conway told a funeral congregation in August 1969 to remember that the majority of Northern Protestants were 'God fearing people and a great deal of the tension on their part at the present time comes not from hatred but from fear. The fact that we regard these fears as groundless does not make them any less real for them.'[178] At the Synod of Derry and Raphoe, in October 1971, Bishop Peacocke highlighted the political, social and moral dangers of allowing 'the canker of hatred and distrust' to grow.[179] The churches also organised relief for victims from donated funds.

Catholic donors included Pope Paul VI, who allocated £3,000, and Archbishop McQuaid, who quietly contributed £1,000 to the Irish government's fund to help refugees in Belfast through the Red Cross.[180]

Any remaining confidence the Catholic hierarchy may have had in the Northern administration to restore peace, or tackle the underlying causes of the unrest had evaporated by the end of August 1969. In a hard-hitting statement on 23 August, the bishops expressed horror at the events that had taken place. They were dismayed that the true picture had been 'greatly obscured by official statements and by the character of the coverage given in certain influential news media'.[181] They dismissed out of hand allegations that the troubles had originated in an armed insurrection. That the 'virtually defenceless' Catholic communities of the Falls and Ardoyne were 'swept by gunfire and streets of Catholic homes were systematically set on fire' was underlined. The terror meted out in Derry was also highlighted. Recognition of these facts was seen as a necessary precondition for the restoration of confidence. The statement asked 'all concerned to realise that among Catholics belief in the impartiality of the Ulster Special Constabulary is virtually non-existent. The future can hold out no hope whatever unless the whole community is able to trust the forces of law and order.'[182] Henceforth, Conway and his brother bishops placed their faith in the British government.

The 'Callaghan strategy'

Church–state relations in Northern Ireland became triangular when Westminster intervened in August 1969. The Downing Street Declaration of 19 August 1969 was the product of an emergency two-day meeting between the British and Northern Irish governments. To reassure the unionist population, it reaffirmed that Northern Ireland would not cease to be part of the UK without the consent of the people of Northern Ireland. To appease nationalists, it committed the British government to ensure that 'in all legislation and executive decisions of government every citizen of Northern Ireland is entitled to the same equality of treatment and freedom from discrimination as obtains in the rest of the United Kingdom, irrespective of political views or religion.'[183] The two governments also agreed to the unusual appointment of a special UK Representative to Northern Ireland. The net result was that the 'Northern Ireland government would exist for the foreseeable future as a client regime, under constant supervision both at ministerial and official levels.'[184] Oliver Wright was dispatched to work within the Cabinet Office and Alex Baker to work within the Ministry of Home Affairs. Wright was no mid-ranking civil servant. A former ambassador to

Denmark, with an impressive record of service, he was seconded to the Home Office and 'grabbed with both hands' by James Callaghan.[185] Wright regarded his appointment 'in nature rather more than ambassadorial and rather less than gubernatorial, it represented the increased concern which the UK Government had necessarily acquired in Northern Ireland affairs through the commitment of the Armed Forces in the present conditions.'[186] But it also indicated London's lack of knowledge of Northern Ireland, which came under the ambit of the Home Secretary. Of the Labour Home Secretaries since 1964, Frank Soskice visited once; Roy Jenkins, despite his image as a liberal reformer, not at all; and James Callaghan only after the eruption of violence in August 1969.[187] Wright, therefore, played a pivotal role in analysing and reporting the situation on the ground from August 1969 until March 1970.

Church leaders were cultivated by Callaghan and Reginald Maudling, who succeeded him as Home Secretary. After the prorogation of Stormont, in March 1972, William Whitelaw, the first Secretary of State for Northern Ireland, did likewise. But given the political vacuum in the Catholic community before the emergence of the Social Democratic and Labour Party (SDLP) in 1970, the Catholic Church and, particularly, Cardinal Conway were regarded as essential, if the 'Callaghan strategy' – the introduction of reform through the Unionist government – was to be successful. Callaghan met Conway, and several other leaders of opinion, during his visit to Northern Ireland in August 1969. The reforms announced by him, including the Hunt Committee on police reform and the Scarman Tribunal into the causes of the riots, were welcomed by the Cardinal as 'an enormous step forward'. Nonetheless, he insisted that justice remained 'the foundation of peace'.[188] On the Church of Ireland side, the House of Bishops approved a statement to be issued by the Standing Committee of the General Synod, on 12 May 1970, welcoming the programme of reforms, but acknowledging that legislation on its own could not change society.[189]

Oliver Wright's reports offer a unique insight into Cardinal Conway's concerns. The removal of barricades, which had sprung up in areas of Belfast and Derry since mid-August 1969, was the delicate and complex issue which dominated Wright's attention on arrival in Northern Ireland. In the eyes of the Northern cabinet the barricades symbolised public defiance of all established law and order and might be construed as undermining its position.[190] During their first meeting at Ara Coeli (the residence of the archbishop of Armagh) on 30 August, Conway informed Wright that the primary motive for the barricades was a real fear of further physical attack.[191] What was not justifiable in the Cardinal's view was the use, in the current circumstances, of 'the barricades for political or social objectives'.[192] Wright's appraisal of the situation, in his first formal dispatch in September 1969, was stark but fair. An urgent programme of reform was necessary. The key instrument for implementing the reform programme was, in his view, the Stormont government.[193] The Irish government also hoped that James Chichester-Clark, who succeeded Terence O'Neill as Prime Minister in April 1969, would accomplish this because there was 'no more attractive short-term alternative'.[194] There was also the additional benefit, from London's perspective, of adhering to the conventional wisdom of keeping the affairs of Northern Ireland at arm's length.[195] Hence, the great concern in Westminster that Stormont's authority would be sustained rather than undermined. To the Home Secretary, the barricades were 'inconsistent with the normal concepts of law and order', which in Wright's view was 'the essential pre-requisite to the establishment of justice'.[196] The influence the Cardinal could bring to bear on the Catholic community to sell this policy was therefore crucial in the British government's scheme. Wright did, however, distinguish between the nature and purpose of Catholic and Protestant barricades. He did not need a Scarman report to observe that the Catholic barricades were erected by those genuinely afraid for their lives and property, whereas the Protestant barricades were largely a protest against the Catholic ones. He took cognisance of extremists on both sides who, for different reasons, hoped that the reforms would not succeed. Conway was just as alive to this, particularly of 'ultra-left political elements' exploiting a tense situation for their own ends. Similarly, in a Lenten pastoral the following February, Bishop Philbin also warned against being 'led by Reds'.[197]

To Conway's mind, dismantling the barricades resolved itself into two difficulties. Firstly, adequate protection in the affected areas had to be provided by the military. Secondly, those behind the barricades had to be convinced that the protection was adequate and the danger thereby eliminated.[198] In this regard, a key role was played, on Conway's authority, by Father Pádraig Murphy, parish priest of St John's on the Falls Road, and Bishop Philbin in reassuring people that once the danger had passed the barricades would have to come down. Wright felt that, in the last resort, force would have to be used against the Catholic barricades, 'if that is the only way we can get justice for them'. He left Callaghan under little illusion that 'Ulster is still what one might call a stone's throw from anarchy.'[199]

Efforts to expedite the issue had an inauspicious start. On 9 September 1969, a brusque speech by Chichester-Clark, to the effect that the barricades must go immediately, was leaked before Wright had an opportunity to brief Cardinal Conway. Speaking on behalf of an irate Philbin,

Father Murphy informed Wright that the impression was given that the barricades 'would be removed at once without regard for ensuring adequate arrangements for protecting the Roman Catholic community'. Furthermore, it was rumoured that the powers of the Royal Ulster Constabulary (RUC) and Ulster Special Constabulary would be restored to implement this, which would cause terror among the Catholic community and would amount to an act of war.[200] During a five hour meeting on 11 September, a nationalist delegation headed by Gerry Fitt made clear to the Home Secretary their perception of Chichester-Clark's statement as a betrayal and raised concerns about the provision of adequate protection by the army.[201] Wright had to retrieve the situation. He telephoned the Cardinal on the night of the 9 September to apologise. When they met in Ara Coeli the following morning, Conway insisted that the barricades be dismantled gradually, that the army provide 'absolute security' afterwards, and that the Special Powers Act not be invoked for 'those who had been defending their homes'.[202] Wright gave assurances on the first two issues, and promised to do his best on the third. In the event, he sought the Cardinal's approval by telephone of the wording of a statement in which the Northern Ireland government affirmed that the Special Powers Act would not be invoked. Conway issued a statement to the press urging those behind the barricades not to be manipulated into conflict with the army and hoping that the promise of military protection would be fulfilled.

The general situation in Northern Ireland was discussed in Downing Street, on 15 September, at a meeting attended by General Freeland, the GOC, Wright and the Home Secretary. Wright was interrupted by a telephone call from Harold Black, secretary to the Northern Ireland cabinet, with news of an apparent crisis *vis-à-vis* the barricades. The Belfast Central Defence Committee issued an ill-judged statement, on the lunchtime news, stating that there could be no negotiation on the removal of the barricades unless certain key preconditions were met. By the time the Defence Committee issued a clarifying, and far more moderate, statement that afternoon, the Northern Ireland government had unanimously decided they would have to issue a strong counterstatement stating a timetable for removal of the barricades, if it was to retain its credibility.[203] The Home Secretary telephoned Chichester-Clark and outlined that there could be no negotiation of political issues with a body of people who had no political standing. He advised against any mention of timetables lest, in a worst case scenario, it would lead to an urban guerrilla war of which the British army had no experience, and stressed the safety of those behind the barricades.[204] In the meantime, Conway had been in touch with Austin Wilson of the Office of the UK

Representative in Belfast, and appealed for both the UK and Northern Ireland governments not to take the statement of the Defence Committee at face value. He had been assured by Father Murphy that, in fact, the attitude was far more flexible than the statement suggested.[205] Furthermore, Murphy and Philbin were to visit the Falls area to encourage the voluntary removal of the barricades. Michael Farrell records that there was strong opposition behind the barricades to this, and that Philbin was publicly abused by some members of his flock on the Falls Road.[206] Given the delicacy of the situation, the Cardinal was anxious that there be no words spoken which might be interpreted as an ultimatum. Wilson informed both London and Harold Black of Conway's concerns. To the Cardinal's regret, statements were issued. On the evening of 15 September the Northern Ireland government reiterated these essential points and ended with the fiction that Callaghan supported their attitude in the matter, when in fact Callaghan was very much a moderating influence and dictated the Northern Ireland government's response.[207]

Wright called on Cardinal Conway on 19 September 1969. His report of their one and a half hour conversation makes clear the decisive role the Catholic Church played in resolving the crisis of the previous week. Conway revealed that, from his perspective, the agreement to bring down the barricades on 15 September represented 'a very considerable act of faith in the British forces' by the Catholic community.[208] By the beginning of October, Wright was able to report that the number of barricades in Belfast and Derry had fallen from a figure of 300 to 400, at the end of August, to between thirty and forty. Those that remained did not have the same symbolic significance.[209] The situation in Derry was very different to that in Belfast. When Wright visited there on 24 September, his first visit since accompanying the Home Secretary in August, he regarded the atmosphere as much less sectarian. The problem, as he saw it, was that paradoxically there was relative peace but no law and order. The army had nothing to offer the citizens of 'Free Derry', which was in a sort of limbo.[210]

Wright and the Cardinal remained in regular but less frequent contact after the 'crisis of the barricades' of September 1969. Conway was worried by the lukewarm enthusiasm and lack of initiative shown by the Northern Ireland government for the reform programme. He was also uneasy at mounting signs of extremist reaction and the impact this might have on the cohesion of the Unionist Party. The Cardinal regarded Westminster's role as watchdog as crucial because Stormont 'probably had little stomach for its task and . . . on all past form would shirk it if it could', a view also privately expressed by Lord O'Neill, the former

Prime Minister.[211] Wright's assessment was far more optimistic. He had seen no attempt by Stormont 'to soft pedal, retract, withdraw or squirm out of their obligations'.[212] But this was mitigated by a telling warning that everything could not be accomplished all at once.

There was growing unease among the Catholic community at the inconsistent administration of justice. One particularly sensitive case was the murder of John Gallagher, a thirty-year-old father of three, who was shot dead at the end of a Civil Rights demonstration in Armagh on 14 August. It was widely believed that a B-Special was responsible. Four months later, no charge had been preferred, not even a charge of unlawful discharge of weapons. More seriously, there was a glaring disparity in sentencing, with Protestants receiving two months suspended sentences for possession and discharge of arms, but Catholics receiving two years not suspended.[213] In November 1969, the Cardinal disassociated himself from criticisms of the Northern Ireland judiciary made by Father Denis Faul of Dungannon. But by December he revealed to Wright that he would have to modify this because failure to speak out would lead to a loss of influence among his community.[214] This was re-emphasised at a meeting on 29 January 1970, when Conway told Wright that he had been unable to sleep for worry. If the Northern bishops were to advocate moderation, then it was imperative that they be seen and heard to be at one with their people. As for the RUC, the Cardinal was dismayed to learn, in August 1970, that Arthur Young, the Chief Constable, was returning to the City of London Police, having spent just over a year implementing the Hunt reforms on policing in Northern Ireland. Conway insisted that Young's successor should be English because the selection of a member of the RUC, whatever his record or personality, would suggest to the Catholic community that Westminster had lost its impartiality.[215] In the event, Young was replaced by his deputy, Graham Shillington, from Portadown, whose tenure covered the introduction of internment and the violence which followed direct rule.

By November 1969, Wright felt that his usefulness was waning and the Foreign Office was keen to have him recalled. It was also suggested that Chichester-Clark was anxious that the mission be ended, as it led to suggestions that his government was merely a puppet.[216] Wright was recalled in March 1970. His valedictory dispatch provided an unadorned synopsis of the development of the Troubles:

> When the Catholics – whose loyalties are at best ambivalent – demanded civil rights, the Protestants saw red and started to burn down their houses. The Army stepped in to stop the bloodshed, whilst the Northern Ireland Government with the assistance of H. M. G. instituted a crash programme of reform.[217]

He was not slow to say that

> in the past Westminster was guilty of neglect and Stormont of arrogance: Westminster's sins of omission permitted Stormont's sins of commission ... Orange-Protestant ascendancy is what Ulster has been for the fifty years of its existence; ironically enough, it has been the existence of British-style democracy, based on universal adult franchise, which has guaranteed and perpetuated a most un-British style injustice towards the Catholic minority.[218]

The main danger he saw for the future was that of a Protestant backlash. He felt that Stormont could handle this, but only if given sufficient tools by Westminster, particularly financial and military assistance. While regarding the situation as immeasurably better than six months previously, when Northern Ireland was on the brink of civil war, he was concerned by ominous internal divisions within the Unionist Party and the increasing prominence and activity of its hardliners.[219] Believing the Northern situation to be particularly delicate at this time, the Irish government instructed its ambassador to the Holy See to make it known that any comment by the Holy Father, however well intentioned, would not serve any useful purpose and might even prove counterproductive.[220]

Wright was replaced by R. A. Burroughs, who, despite his lack of experience of Northern Ireland, remained UK representative for fourteen months. During this time the situation in Northern Ireland deteriorated rapidly. Within eight weeks, Burroughs identified the principal danger as lying not in the security field, but within the ranks of the Unionist Party, which he felt would inevitably split. The key questions were simply how long Chichester-Clark could retain control and where the line of fracture might occur.[221] Assuring James Callaghan that his predictions were not alarmist, Burroughs warned that if Chichester-Clark were defeated, it would be necessary to suspend the constitution and to impose direct rule from Westminster, which would create as many problems as it would solve. In the event, Chichester-Clark resigned on 19 March 1971; Stormont was prorogued one year later.

The 'Callaghan strategy' placed Cardinal Conway in an unenviable position. Having lost all faith in the Northern administration, he was nonetheless bound to it as the agency through which reforms, mandated by Westminster, would be implemented. The alternative was too dangerous to contemplate. Predictably, there was little appreciation of Conway's efforts. Roy Bradford, Minister of Commerce, contended that the Catholic community only reluctantly acquiesced in their British citizenship, at best as a second choice, and at worst rejected it by violence.[222] The Armagh Board of Social Responsibility evinced similar sentiment. It argued, unconvincingly, that if the Church of Ireland had acknowledged the constitutional position in the South in 1949 by the provision of appropriate state prayers, then the Catholic minority in Northern Ireland should do likewise in 1971.[223] To counteract Northern unionists' fears of being engulfed by a community with alien loyalties, the British government made a number of suggestions to encourage Catholics to cooperate with Stormont as full citizens of the UK. These included the acceptance by a Catholic priest of a New Year's honour; cooperation with the Crowther Commission to examine constitutional arrangements in Northern Ireland; and the appointment of a Catholic chaplain to Stormont.

In November 1969 James Callaghan dined with Cardinal John Heenan, the Catholic archbishop of Westminster and a close friend of Conway. He impressed on Heenan that the British government's commitment to Northern Ireland was the best guarantee of redressing Catholic grievances. More specifically, the need for both individual participation in the police force and corporate participation by the minority in public affairs, such as the appointment of a chaplain, was stressed. Heenan agreed to speak to Conway.[224] The Cardinals met the following week in Killarney, County Kerry. Conway subsequently informed Wright, in early December, that Father Seán Lowry would be willing to accept a New Year's honour.

To exclude the views of Cardinal Conway from the Crowther Commission would, it was contended, be akin to 'settling the affairs of Cyprus without getting the views of Archbishop Makarios'.[225] Crowther called on the Cardinal in May 1970 and raised the possibility of continuing the process of creating boards to deal with matters that would normally be the concern of ministries. These would be worthless without Catholic participation. This, Conway confirmed, would be forthcoming and, moreover, such boards would, he believed, 'do much to remove the sense of alienation'.[226] Other concerns raised by the Cardinal included the supervision of local appointments by an independent body, a bill of rights, the extension of a prohibition of discrimination to all executive acts of public bodies and the transfer to Westminster of all responsibility for electoral matters in Northern Ireland.

The appointment of a Catholic chaplain to Stormont proved more intractable. The three main Protestant denominations had a chaplain at Stormont, but, as was the case at Westminster, there was no Catholic chaplain. The matter was raised by representatives of the Protestant churches during a meeting with Callaghan in August 1969. The Home Secretary subsequently aired the issue with Cardinal Conway. It was believed that the appointment of a chaplain would demonstrate Catholic acceptance of the Northern constitutional arrangements. In 1970 the matter was brought to the attention of the British minister to the Holy See. It was hoped that Cardinal Conway's 'more forthcoming attitude' would be 'the subject of warm commendation from Rome'.[227] On 23 December 1970, the hierarchy duly announced the nomination of Father Robert Murphy, a former classmate of Conway and parish priest of Newtownards, County Down. Oliver Rafferty has argued that this appointment cemented 'the bonds of mutual tolerance between the hierarchy and the Stormont regime', but this was far from the case.[228] In the same way, growing desperation to find a peaceful solution to the violence besetting Northern Ireland, rather than any overt recognition of Stormont, was the reason behind Conway's wish to meet Chichester-Clark in February 1971. They had met once before in 1969, at a reception organised by James Callaghan, but their one-hour meeting on 25 February 1971 was the first official meeting of its kind in the history of the Northern Ireland state.

The Westminster general election in June 1970 returned a Conservative government led by Edward Heath. This did not alter the policy of reform through Stormont. However, over the next two years such a programme of reform became increasingly inadequate to halt the descent to wholesale disorder. Reginald Maulding continued the policy of taking soundings from church leaders. On his first visit to Northern Ireland, in July 1970, he met a delegation from the Protestant churches, among them Archbishop Simms. The Primate expressed his relief that Stormont would be supported from London, but pointed out that, paradoxically, the reforms were creating tension and fear. The delegation agreed that any alternative to the present government was too terrible to contemplate. Significantly, it underlined that the influence of the churches, including the Catholic Church, on the community at large was waning.[229] Maudling also separately met Cardinal Conway, but no record of this meeting appears to have been kept. A follow-up meeting with representatives of all four churches took place in London on 21 October 1970. As community leaders, Maudling believed that church leaders could buttress the efforts of secular leaders:

> There is a limit to what the Government can achieve by legislation. This can do no more than remove legitimate grievances and provide a legal framework within which only the people themselves can effect a change. To do this there must first be meeting of minds, a readiness to live in friendship with neighbours . . . The Government are doing their part, the Army and the police are doing theirs, the minority's grievances are being remedied, but little can come of this without a change of heart. It is in this field that the responsibility of the Churches lies.[230]

It is to these efforts that we now turn.

'Blessed are the peace-makers'

Writing in 1991, Eric Gallagher believed that when the history of the opening years of the Troubles came to be written 'the courageous and penetrating statements of many Churchmen will stand up to scrutiny'.[231] Theirs was no easy task. Both benches of bishops faced the dilemma of trying to maintain the confidence and respect of their communities without alienating certain sections by taking a firm stand. For Catholic bishops this was particularly evident in their trenchant condemnations of paramilitary violence. Support for reform and inter-communal reconciliation by Church of Ireland bishops was tantamount to 'selling out' in those eyes that feared the reform programme would lead inexorably to a united Ireland. While the churches were broadly united in striving for peace during the opening months of the Troubles, this unity came under strain as bishops were compelled to address the conflicting concerns of their respective flocks.

From 1970 onwards statements by the Church of Ireland bishops increasingly reflected the need to offer reassurance to their community about the integrity of the Northern Ireland state and assuage fears about their Protestant identity. For instance, in February 1972 Arthur Butler and George Quin issued an open letter pledging support for social reform. However, the bishops felt obliged to highlight 'mounting pressures aimed at altering the status, institutions and structures of Northern Ireland'. The letter continued:

> the majority of members of the Church of Ireland in our dioceses will not be coerced into the society and community of the Republic of Ireland as it is at present constituted ... forcible incorporation ... into a form of society which they cannot conscientiously accept will lead to greater division and even more suffering. What matters for the future of Ireland, North and South, is a community built on agreement and consent, understanding, trust, justice and Christian charity.[232]

The role of the security forces was another highly divisive topic. The Church of Ireland paid tribute, as did other Protestant churches, to the work of the security forces in individual utterances and in joint statements, such as that of 30 November 1971.[233] Catholic bishops viewed the British army as an important factor in saving their community from attack in the summer of 1969. But this image of protector changed in July 1970 after a thirty-six-hour curfew on the Lower Falls and house-to-house searches. The introduction of internment without trial in August 1971 and 'Bloody Sunday', the shooting dead of thirteen people by paratroopers following a Civil Rights rally in Derry on 30 January

1972, further reinforced the altered perception of the British army. The contrasting position of the churches was demonstrated at the end of 1972. On 20 November a statement on behalf of sixty-five Catholic priests in Belfast accused the British army of over-reaction. In response, 102 Protestant clergymen highlighted the efforts of the army and police to safeguard life and property.[234]

The constraints on Church of Ireland bishops led to periodic charges that they did not give a sufficiently strong lead. *Hibernia* bluntly, but discerningly, underlined the uneasy position of the Church of Ireland in Northern Ireland. The periodical contended that the church did not 'speak with the solid assurance of the Presbyterians, who more accurately reflect the ethos and mentality of Ulster, historically and today', and consequently was reluctant 'to become involved in the past and present political and religious turmoil in Ulster'.[235] In his Advent letter for 1972, Bishop Quin denied such allegations. He underlined the witness of his clergy in the community: 'They may not make political statements or shout on the street corners, but they are doing the work for which they were ordained. This is not always easy and sometimes clergy have been greatly misunderstood or misinterpreted.'[236] Bishops could also be misunderstood at great personal cost, even one as courageous and independent-minded as Arthur Butler. At a memorial service in St Anne's Cathedral, Belfast on 28 August 1973, he presented a rounded appraisal of the late Lord Brookeborough, who had died ten days earlier. The bishop quoted from *The Times* obituary that Brookeborough had been convinced that Catholics should be excluded from governmental responsibility. Despite Brookeborough's many talents, Butler contended that he had not been a political visionary and did not think of long-term solutions to community problems. But the bishop stressed that the former Prime Minister should not be made a scapegoat.[237] The balance of the sermon was lost in the tempest of protest that followed. Brian Faulkner was saddened that the service 'developed into an occasion for political comment, political charge and counter-charge'. Martin Smyth, Grand Master of the Grand Orange Lodge, labelled the sermon an 'unfounded slur on a great Ulsterman'.[238] Butler revealed to Trevor West, then a member of the Seanad, that while he received countless 'letters of violent abuse', many people wrote in support. The bishop felt that allowances had to be made because 'people here are nervy and overstrained. The support of thoughtful people means a lot to me at present.'[239] An editorial in the *Belfast Telegraph* pertinently argued that if more churchmen were like Butler, and spoke their mind, that the church would go up in many people's estimation.[240]

The introduction of internment, on 9 August 1971, which led to the arrest of over 450 people, deeply divided the churches. It was condemned by Cardinal Conway who appealed to the Catholic population 'not to allow their feelings . . . to lead them into situations where they could suffer serious injury or death'.[241] He certainly had cause for alarm as internment brought a serious upsurge in violence. Within a week, twenty-two people had been killed and almost 7,000 left homeless. The majority of these were Catholic, many of whom boarded trains to the Republic. According to an Irish army spokesperson, 4,339 people were in refugee camps on the night of 11 August.[242] In fact the Irish army's resources were hopelessly overstretched, as were those of the civil defence system. The Minister for Defence and the Dublin city manager turned to Archbishop McQuaid for help. McQuaid's response was without parallel. In a frenetic two-day period, he mobilised the religious orders in Dublin to make available accommodation in religious houses, institutions and training colleges. To the relief of the Minister, by the afternoon of 12 August McQuaid had secured 1,635 places in thirty-nine religious establishments.[243] A church gate collection for relief of distress was also held on Sunday 29 August and raised £25,000 for an appreciative Bishop Philbin.[244] By the end of August, Cardinal Conway could only ask: 'What lies ahead if the present wave of violence and violent repression continues?' He admitted to sharing the feelings of anger and frustration felt by the Catholic community but pleaded with people not to let this cloud their good judgement, lest further violence generate even greater suffering. He begged 'those people, few in number, who are seeking a solution by violent means . . . to consider what this vicious circle of which they are part is doing to innocent people, Catholic and Protestant, in terms of physical and mental suffering . . . to reflect on what is likely to be left at the end of a trail of destruction and death.'[245]

The response of the Protestant churches to internment was very different. A statement was issued on 9 August 1971 which stated that 'the Government in its duty to all citizens has no option but to introduce strong measures which must be distasteful to many'.[246] The three Protestant principals were in Donegal. Only the Moderator of the Presbyterian Church was contacted personally before the statement was released by appointed deputies. Jack Weir and Harold Sloan represented the Presbyterian and Methodist Churches respectively and Arthur Butler signed on behalf of Archbishop Simms. Eric Gallagher told Father Patrick Walsh, who informed Cardinal Conway, that subsequently both the archbishop and the President of the Methodist Church in fact agreed with the statement.[247] In an emotional interview on RTÉ, on 15 August, Simms said it was a 'hateful repugnant decision to have to make', and that those who drew up the statement did so 'with the sound of gunfire all around'.[248] It is revealing that the Primate felt unable to disassociate himself from a statement which had received large support from Northern members of his church, but was criticised by Southern members. He did so only in September, when the background to the statement became public. This suggested a church somewhat fearful of its Northern laity and raised the spectre of future disunity. The *Church of Ireland Gazette* was strongly critical and stressed that 'the Church of Ireland is the Church of Ireland, not of Northern Ireland or of the Republic. It serves nothing but a divisive purpose to think and speak regionally. What is said to church people in Northern Ireland should be capable of being said to their fellow members in the South.'[249] The statement also divided members of the ICC at its executive meeting in September. Eric Gallagher did not think he was ever party to a statement that 'caused so much agonising or gave so much difficulty'.[250]

Within days of the introduction of detention without trial, there were calls for an impartial investigation into allegations of physical brutality, particularly in Girdwood Barracks and Ballykinlar camp. This demand was supported by both Conway and Simms. A commission of inquiry, chaired by Sir Edmund Compton, former Ombudsman to the Westminster parliament, was established on 31 August. Conway agreed to give evidence but sought reassurance that hooding detainees; white noise; sleep, food and water deprivation would come under the scope of the inquiry. Such practices, if proven, would constitute a more refined and damaging form of brutality'.[251] Compton was noncommittal, claiming an inability to 'express an opinion on degrees of brutality in advance of our investigation of specific allegations related to particular persons'.[252] Nonetheless, the Cardinal met Compton on 24 September 1971 to discuss some of the oral evidence at his disposal. Compton's findings, published on 16 November 1971, were discredited because *ab initio* the commission had no statutory powers to require the production of records or take evidence under oath. Consequently, most of the detainees boycotted its proceedings. While the report admitted there had been interrogation in-depth, it maintained, semantically, that physical ill-treatment was not tantamount to brutality.[253]

The Catholic community was enraged and their bishops responded with a hard-hitting statement on 21 November. They condemned interrogation in-depth as 'shameful and contrary to the law of Christ', and the deprivations practised as 'immoral and inhuman' and 'unworthy of the British people'. They stressed their deep conviction (in words suggested by Bishop Cahal Daly) that 'the solution to our present tragic situation will never be found in violence or counter-violence. Far-reaching political initiative must be sought as a matter of great urgency if those who advocate violence are to be deprived of their chief ally – despair.'[254]

In addition, 387 priests, who comprised almost eighty per cent of the Catholic clergy in Northern Ireland, signed a statement condemning torture and brutality.[255] In December the Northern Church of Ireland bishops also expressed distress at the findings of Compton. They sympathised with the victims of terrorism and intimidation, and praised the work of the security forces. In a rather loaded final paragraph, they hoped that 'the conditions which led to internment without trial will soon cease'.[256] The contention of Lord Carrington, Secretary of State for Defence, that internment 'had lanced the boil of terrorism and brought the poison to the surface' could hardly have been more misguided, or the application of detention without trial more uneven.[257] Not only was it ineffective in security terms due to outdated intelligence, but the first loyalist internees were not detained until February 1973.[258] To the alarm of the Cardinal, the primary beneficiary of the introduction of internment, both in the short and long term, was the Provisional IRA, which was handed a powerful propaganda weapon.

The Catholic bishops were resolutely opposed to any alteration of the political border by force. Indeed, in one of his first meetings with Oliver Wright, Conway admitted that he did not expect to see any voluntary alteration of the border in his lifetime. He also made this known to James Callaghan. On 21 May 1970 a major joint statement, largely of Conway's creation, articulated an abhorrence of violence and an appreciation of its deadly consequences, both actual and moral. The bishops felt that 'it would be a betrayal of the Catholic community – a stab in the back – for any individual, or group, to take it upon themselves to deliberately provoke violent incidents' which could not be justified by provocation. The innocent had the right not to suffer or to be blamed for the actions of a 'handful of self appointed activists' who had no popular mandate.[259] The statement was welcomed unreservedly by Chichester-Clark and praised by Burroughs as 'extremely courageous and statesman-like', providing a lead which he hoped other religious and political leaders would follow.[260] In his reply, Conway revealed that the reaction from his own people had been good and he hoped that the government had taken note of the passage on reforms.[261]

In denouncing paramilitary violence, Cardinal Conway had to shoulder a far greater burden than the Church of Ireland bishops. He strove tirelessly to isolate and undermine the IRA and remove any misplaced sympathy for them. There were a number of factors behind this. Firstly, the campaign for civil rights might be discredited. Conway was anxious to underline that the Catholic community had legitimate grievances and a right to protest against social injustice. Secondly, he strove to disassociate the IRA campaign from the vast majority of the Catholic community.

This was a recurring theme in both personal and joint utterances, lest the entire Catholic community be tarred as IRA sympathisers. Increasingly, middle-class Protestants had come to identify the whole Catholic community with support for an IRA policy of violence perpetrated in their name. Patrick Mulligan, bishop of Clogher, thought that this was the case in Fermanagh, where there was intense bitterness.[262] On this point, the Church of Ireland bishops appealed to their faithful in a statement on 6 September 1971 not to confuse 'the activities of the terrorists with the whole Roman Catholic community'.[263] The Cardinal was at pains to distinguish between the majority peaceful community on one hand, and a disruptive minority, intent on holding 'whole communities up to ransom', on the other.[264] Thirdly, Cardinal Conway stressed that violence was as abhorrent to the Catholic community as it was to their Protestant neighbours. He availed of every suitable opportunity to stress that the IRA's campaign had no legitimacy. For instance, during a sermon in Drogheda on the feast of Blessed Oliver Plunkett, on 11 July 1971, he reiterated that the 'only lasting foundation for peace is justice but violence can make the road to justice much longer and can leave it strewn with innocent human lives and serious injuries and great human suffering. No one has the right to inflict this suffering on the people.'[265]

Following several weeks of escalating paramilitary activity, the foundation of the loyalist UDA and several punishment attacks including some on young girls for socialising with British soldiers, the Catholic bishops issued a forceful and compelling condemnation of the IRA on 12 September 1971. 'Who in his sane senses', they asked, 'wants to bomb a million Protestants into a united Ireland?' They dismissed any notion that such a campaign was concerned with defending the Catholic community. Instead, it brought 'shame and disgrace on noble and just causes. It is straining people's nerves to breaking point. It is destroying people's livelihood. It is intensifying sectarian bitterness. It is pushing the union of minds and hearts between men and women of all-Ireland farther and farther away.'[266] The statement emphasised that the bishops were 'painfully aware' of the contributory factors to the current state of unrest, but nevertheless condemned violence and 'the vicious evil of intimidation from whatever source and on whatever side'. These sentiments were reiterated in a statement by the entire Episcopal Conference on 29 September 1971.

The closing months of 1971 were among the bloodiest of the period. Preaching in Armagh Cathedral on 12 December, Cardinal Conway reviled as 'a foul monster' the person who could plant a bomb among innocent people. He believed that anyone who condoned this in the slightest degree, even in thought, would 'become morally soiled'.[267] In his

Christmas broadcast on RTÉ television, he cautioned against familiarity with violent death clouding the clear realisation that such things were evil, for which there was no other name. Deeply shocked by Bloody Sunday, Cardinal Conway called on the Catholic community 'to preserve calm and dignity in the face of this terrible news'.[268] At the funeral of the thirteen victims, he appealed for love, not hatred, and hoped that forgiveness rather than revenge would prevail. The leaders of the four main churches issued a statement on 3 February 1972 which shared 'the great grief and pain of our people at each injury or death in our land, no matter who is involved. We share also the desire for peace and justice, for security and liberty alike for Protestant and Catholic.'[269] In an earlier draft, Conway substantially amended a central paragraph on the reasons underlining the conflict. By scoring out the references to relations with the Republic or Britain, he squarely located the basic issue to be resolved as 'the relationship between our communities in Northern Ireland'.[270]

Cardinal Conway's exertions were supported and reinforced in particular by the vehement and articulate statements of Bishop Cahal Daly of Ardagh and Clonmacnoise, a native of County Antrim, and Bishop Philbin. In November 1971, at the annual dinner of the Longford Association in London, Bishop Daly contended that when 'the real national problem is one of establishing mutual peace and trust between different communities within Ireland, talk of violent solutions is self-contradictory. Force as a solution to the present Irish problem must be unconditionally condemned and renounced.'[271] Two months later he pointed out that the Catholic bishops had also condemned 'the brutalities and inhumanities of military repression, which provoked further violence, and [called] . . . for political reforms to remove the basic injustices out of which the violence grew'.[272] Catholic bishops were openly criticised by both wings of the IRA, at times by their own community and occasionally by their own clergy. For instance, Bishop O'Doherty of Dromore was condemned by the South Down/South Armagh Command of the Official IRA for suggesting that the military could not be blamed for all the destruction and loss of life endured in the Dromore diocese.[273] On 17 January 1971 Philbin outraged the parishioners of Ballymurphy by denouncing active IRA personnel in the area for obeying 'immoral orders'. The local IRA had helped quell serious rioting and the following week fifteen women delivered a letter of protest to the bishop's residence condemning his sermon. Ballymurphy also witnessed a very public stand-off between the diocesan authorities and Father Desmond Wilson, a local curate, who eventually resigned, in June 1975, in protest at his superiors' interference in trying to control the activities of the working-class parish.[274]

Philbin provided one of the most thorough condemnations of the IRA in an address to the Irish Association in Manchester in January 1974. He carefully outlined and then demolished the myths and fallacies surrounding IRA aims and support. He criticised financial donations from people of Irish extraction on the basis of sentiment stoked by misleading propaganda. In common with many of his episcopal colleagues, he was particularly concerned that many young people were being led astray by 'false doctrine'. Philbin did not deny that Catholic grievances had been 'studiously exploited', but neither did he deny that the rest of the Catholic population were without blame: 'Should not the whole people have found ways to dissociate themselves from what was being done, to repudiate guilt by association, as a discharge of conscience and in order to clear the reputation of the country in the eyes of the world?'[275] He concluded by summing up Ireland's problem as 'the continued existence of underground armies, not any of the issues they exploit . . . There is no middle course in meeting this challenge. It is time we made up our minds clearly about it and made our minds known without any possibility of misunderstanding.'[276] The attention paid here to episcopal pronouncements should not obscure the fact that numerous individual priests also ceaselessly condemned violence. For instance, Canon Pádraig Murphy pleaded with those 'whose hands are stained with blood' to reconsider the price their community was being asked to pay.[277]

The Northern bishops were not the only members of the hierarchy seeking peace. In addition to assisting Northern refugees, Archbishop McQuaid dramatically brokered the first Christmas truce, in December 1971, which he made clear was not 'a political initiative'.[278] The background was perhaps the most dangerous and spectacular of McQuaid's thirty-two year episcopacy. While he informed the Taoiseach and John Peck, the British ambassador, of the Christmas appeal, no state archival material has emerged, to date, to suggest that either government was aware of McQuaid's meeting with senior Official and Provisional IRA leaders. On 16 December he instructed his Press Officer, Osmund Dowling, to contact Tomás Mac Giolla, Ruairí Ó Brádaigh, Seán Mac Stiofáin, and Cathal Goulding, with a view to a meeting. McQuaid met Ó Brádaigh and Mac Stiofáin at Archbishop's House, at 2.45 p.m. on Monday 20 December; Goulding attended at 3.30 p.m.; and MacGiolla at 8.15 p.m. that evening.[279] The only account of these furtive meetings was a letter from McQuaid to Gaetano Alibrandi, the papal nuncio. The Provisionals agreed to the truce, and spoke to McQuaid at length about 'very secret aspects of their movement. It would be difficult to conceive a more cordial and friendly meeting'. The Officials explained that they were not 'engaged in warlike hostilities', and, according to the archbishop, 'were very relaxed and cordial in their discussions'. McQuaid felt that one had to be careful in calling them Marxist, 'for they confuse social justice with Marxist aims'. 'The most formidable man of this group', he informed Alibrandi, 'kissed my ring and genuflected with quite spontaneous faith.' McQuaid intimated that the 'situation gives great promise. I believe I can say that, despite appearances and the continuance of hostilities, the situation has changed and the hopes of negotiations, if not of peace at once, are substantial.'[280]

McQuaid's hopes were not fully realised. The Official IRA did permanently end their paramilitary campaign on 29 May 1972, following public outrage at the killing of nineteen-year-old Private William Best. This was welcomed by Cardinal Conway as 'the first glimmer of a new dawn of peace' fervently sought by the community at large.[281] His sense of relief was palpable at the announcement by the Provisional IRA, on 22 June 1972, that they would suspend activities on 26 June, subject to 'a public reciprocal response [being] forthcoming from the armed forces of the British crown'.[282] But the Cardinal nonetheless warned that

> we are still very close to the brink. We should keep continually before our minds also the horror of what people have been through over the past four years. We should close our eyes from time to time and imagine we could see those 386 bodies laid out in a row – young men's lives blasted almost before they had begun to live; older men, women and children.[283]

Conway was bitterly disappointed when the Provisional IRA resumed their campaign two weeks later, following failed talks with William Whitelaw in London. The Cardinal appealed 'to all responsible for God's sake to have mercy on the innocent and to bring these campaigns of violence and threats of violence to a speedy end'.[284]

In October 1972 Cardinal Conway privately admitted that the *fratres separati* had not 'spoken out sufficiently strongly about the threat posed by their own paramilitary groups. There has been a deafening silence.'[285] He referred to the increasing activity of loyalist paramilitaries since the prorogation of Stormont in March 1972. In particular, mounting sectarian assassinations throughout 1972 and 1973 greatly perturbed the Cardinal. He compiled an extensive list of the names, particulars and circumstances of those assassinated through detailed correspondence with individual priests and news reports. Between 8 January 1972 and 21 July 1973, he catalogued 183 such deaths, of which an overwhelming majority of 118 (sixty-five per cent) were Catholic. Sixty others were Protestant and five were not known.[286] Furthermore, he revealed that most of the assassinations were localised in Portadown and in Belfast, where the Catholic population comprised a minority of around twenty-five per cent. Conway also monitored the number of cases in which an arrest was made and charges pressed. His covert fear was that the campaign of assassination aimed to end a Catholic presence in one quarter of Belfast. He was dismayed that 'the authorities and the media seem to have played down the fact that the backlash has begun'.[287] Research by Fay, Morrissey and Smith has confirmed that over one third of all deaths during the Troubles occurred in the five postal districts located in North and West Belfast.[288]

The Cardinal, therefore, took it on himself to draw attention to such murders. He felt that they should outrage the public conscience in exactly the same manner as the callous murder of three Scottish soldiers the previous March at which Conway was horrified.[289] In August 1972 other church leaders joined the Cardinal in expressing 'horror and utter condemnation of the terrible assassinations which have added a new dimension to the violence in this community in recent months'.[290] At his own request, Conway met William Whitelaw on 6 November to express his anxiety about the safety of the Catholic population. This was followed, a week later, by a major statement which highlighted two campaigns of violence in Northern Ireland. The first – the IRA campaign – was well known and from its inception in 1970 utterly condemned by the Catholic bishops. The Cardinal felt that 'public opinion in Britain and throughout the world' should realise the existence of a second campaign waged 'against the Catholic population as such'. As proof, he cited sixty Catholic deaths since the beginning of the year, a thousand families burned or bombed out of their homes and several Catholic churches which were singled out for attack.[291] His concern was shared by the Church of Ireland bishops of Connor, and Down and Dromore. When Conway and Philbin met Whitelaw on 5 December 1972, as part of the consultations prior to the publication of the White Paper, they took the opportunity to urge him again to take immediate action to end the spate of sectarian assassinations.[292]

The New Year opened with the murder of John Mooney, a Catholic father of three, at the Rolls Royce factory in Belfast on 3 January. In response, church leaders unambiguously deemed 'a crime before God' sectarian and political murders, whether of civilians or security personnel, which brought 'shame to our land and tragedy to countless homes'.[293] They urged the Secretary of State to act and implored the whole community to 'root out this evil'. The Cardinal estimated that in the first six months of 1973, there had been twice as many assassinations as in the corresponding period for 1972. At the beginning of February, he again condemned assassinations and spoke of 'the anguish of mind of whole communities who now find themselves engulfed in pessimism and despair'.[294] On 6 July 1973 he urged the news media in Northern Ireland and throughout the world to focus public attention on assassinations, believing that 'if the relevant statistics and circumstances are studied a very sinister pattern can be clearly seen'.[295] As in the previous year, in early November, he made an incisive statement treating assassinations (of which there had been 150 in 1973) as a facet of the violence in Northern Ireland which was being 'swept under the carpet'. In no uncertain terms, he argued that the 'base deeds of the IRA' did not justify 'the campaign of slaughter and intimidation' against the Catholic community, which only desired peace and an end to violence. He felt bound to say that the Catholic population was 'disturbed by the fact that official concern to stamp out this "second campaign", or even clearly to acknowledge its existence, appears to be less than adequate' in terms of official statements and the extent of measures to combat assassinations.[296] Dismay was recorded in government circles at Cardinal Conway's outburst. It predictably drew the wrath of the Orange Order, which condemned the statement as a propaganda piece 'to absolve the Roman Catholic Church from involvement in the campaign of violence'.[297] An editorial in the *Irish Independent* judged the Cardinal to be in a very strong position to condemn bloodshed from non-Roman Catholic quarters, given his unreserved condemnation of republican violence.[298] On the Church of Ireland side, the Down and Dromore diocesan council spoke of the 'shameful and tragic new development [of] sectarian and political assassinations'.[299] Archbishop Simms also strongly condemned assassinations in his presidential addresses to the Armagh diocesan synod in October 1973 and 1974.

On 30 October 1972, the Northern Ireland Office published a discussion paper, *The Future of Northern Ireland*, which was to have a seminal influence on British policy towards Northern Ireland. It reaffirmed that there would be no change in the constitutional status of Northern Ireland without the consent of a majority of the population. It also floated the concept of power-sharing and introduced 'to the political lexicon the phrase "Irish dimension" in acknowledgement of the South's interest'.[300] The following month, Edward Heath met the four church leaders at Stormont for informal discussions. He subsequently wrote to Simms that it would be 'of enormous value if, over the coming months, church leaders can, both individually and collectively, reiterate their total rejection of violence, from whatever quarter it may come, and their support for a just, peaceful and lasting settlement in the interests of all the people of Northern Ireland'.[301]

It was with great earnestness that the leaders of the four main churches rose to this task. In November 1972 the Lord Mayor of Belfast called a meeting of church representatives which was attended by Bishop Butler, Bishop Quin, Monsignor P. J. Mullally (on behalf of Bishop Philbin), Harold Sloan and R. V. Lynas, Moderator of the Presbyterian Church. It was suggested that church leaders prepare their congregations for the arrival, on 20 March 1973, of the White Paper, *Northern Ireland Constitutional Proposals*, 'so that they will consider it carefully and not just throw it out if it does not contain exactly what they want it to contain'.[302] One week before the publication of the proposals, nine church leaders urged Northern politicians as well as the print and broadcast media in Northern Ireland, the Republic and Britain to avoid sensationalism and to provide instead balanced and constructive comment. Church leaders were apprehensive that ordinary people might not study in full, or properly grasp, the implication of such a complex document. The danger existed that people might instead 'act upon the snap judgements of politicians and others . . . in Ulster's perilous situation it is terribly true that . . . "words can kill".'[303] On 18 March Conway asked all the people of Ireland to pray on bended knee for an end to the scourge of violence, while Cardinal Heenan appealed to both communities to stop looking backwards.[304]

The White Paper provided for a seventy-eight member Assembly, elected by proportional representation in multi-member constituencies, from which a power-sharing executive would be formed. London was to retain control over matters such as security and the legal system. While Northern Ireland's constitutional status remained unaltered, the White Paper made provisions for North-South links.[305] The proposals were welcomed by Archbishop Simms as 'a fair and workable basis from which to move forward towards overcoming the problems of Northern Ireland'. He reiterated the appeal for all people to 'adopt a constructive approach and to avoid words and actions that would wreck the present attempt to take us out of our violence and instability . . . Let us build, not destroy.'[306] In addition, he welcomed the firm resolve of the White Paper to establish the rule of law and to recognise fundamental freedoms. Cardinal Conway warned that Northern Ireland faced 'a choice between a path of peace and reconciliation, on the one hand, or a continuing nightmare of violence and death, on the other'.[307] The General Board of the Presbyterian Church felt that nothing in the White Paper violated Christian conscience or justified any section holding the community to ransom or resorting to violence.[308] On 24 March the leaders of the four main churches said that an opportunity now existed for the people of Northern Ireland to break out of the vicious circle of violence and death.

After a long series of talks at Stormont, an executive was eventually formed in November 1973. Throughout this decisive year, church leaders lent their support at various important stages. Prayers were offered in advance of the Assembly elections which were held on 28 June 1973. Whitelaw believed that the agreement on power-sharing 'had broken the mould of Northern Ireland politics based on sectarian division'.[309] In this light, Cahal Daly warned that those who obstructed power-sharing, and tried to sabotage the new political institutions, were sabotaging the future of both communities in Northern Ireland.[310] Bishops Quin and Heavener, as well as Archbishop Simms, made similar pleas. The last stage was the meeting between the political parties and the two governments at Sunningdale in December 1973. The Sunningdale communiqué was supported by the House of Bishops as a 'basis for building a fair and peaceful society, both in Northern Ireland and in the Republic'. The Church of Ireland statement warned, however, that it would succeed only if 'interpreted and implemented in a trusting and generous spirit ... at this critical juncture of our history, we urge everyone to weigh carefully the alternative'.[311] In his 1973 Christmas broadcast on RTÉ, Cardinal Conway urged everyone to 'pray, pray every day, pray and mean it, pray from your heart, get your children to pray. This scourge of violence, with its utter disregard for the sacredness of human life, is now in its fifth year.'[312] In a sermon broadcast on BBC 1, in early January 1974, Bishop Butler similarly appealed to ordinary people that, whatever their personal political opinion, it was their Christian duty to support and give power sharing a chance.[313] History would prove otherwise.

The Troubles have divided the post Second World War history of Northern Ireland into two phases. In the 1950s and 1960s the Northern Catholic bishops viewed the Northern Ireland state dichotomously. Abject suspicion of local government coexisted with guarded confidence in central government. With the advent of the welfare state, the bishops moved from highlighting the injustice of the state to emphasising injustices within it. While not selling out on the national question, they no longer wore their history like a hairshirt and instead sought parity in practical terms. This resembled the *Paritätsfrage* ('parity question') – the articulation by German Catholics of demands for equality as citizens *within* the German *Kaiserreich* from the 1890s, rather than protests against an unjust state during the *Kulturkampf* of the 1870s.[314] Relations between the bishops and the Northern Ireland administration were frequently uneasy and bordered at times on antagonistic. There was an element of a tug-of-war in the implementation of the educational and health advances under the welfare state. But the Catholic bishops had to be pragmatic, as their welfare state objectives could not be achieved in isolation from central government. There was a genuine closeness between the hierarchy and their people, for whom the bishops engaged in a process of incremental gain. Following the advent of the Troubles, the years of preoccupation with health and education seemed halcyon. Led forcefully by Cardinal Conway, the Northern bishops were implacably opposed to violence which jeopardised not only life and limb, but also the hard-won socio-economic gains. The bishops tried to moderate and channel the deep frustrations of their community. In their advocacy of the peaceful attainment of justice, they supported the British government's underpinning of Stormont, through which it was believed social and economic reform could be implemented and stability restored. The 'structural approach' to the Northern Ireland problem, as political scientists have come to describe it, failed. The problem could not be conceived solely in socio-economic terms. The White Paper in 1973 sought therefore to provide new political arrangements. If the bishops' outspoken denunciation of violence increasingly fell on deaf ears this did not reflect a lack of earnestness, but rather the declining influence of the churches on the men of violence. The bishops continually underlined that these were a minority and that the vast majority of their flock sought peace. In this, no less than heretofore, the Northern Catholic bishops stood with their people.

Notes

1 *ICD 1954*, p. 717.
2 *Ibid.*
3 OFMLA, D'Alton Papers, Box 8, NI Government A, Folder 5, Letter Maginess to D'Alton, 20 January 1953.
4 Sabine Wichert, *Northern Ireland since 1945* (2nd edn, London and New York, 1999), p. 49.
5 NAI, DFA 305/14/303/Pt II, Letter Cremin to Molloy, 23 March 1962.
6 See Liam Ryan, 'Church and politics: the last twenty-five years', *The Furrow*, 30: 1 (1979), p. 3.
7 Whyte, *Church and State*, p. 366.
8 Kennedy, *Cottage to Crèche*, p. 176.
9 *Quadragesimo anno*, §§ 78–80 cited in Christopher McOustra, *Love in the Economy. Catholic Social Doctrine for the Individual* (Slough, 1990), p. 46.
10 OFMLA, D'Alton Papers, Box 18, Lenten pastoral: 'The church and freedom', 15 February 1952, p. 9.
11 UCDA, de Valera Papers, P150/2895, Letter Browne to de Valera, 20 January 1939. On vocationalism see J. J. Lee, 'Aspects of corporatist thought in Ireland: the Commission on Vocational Organisation 1939–43', in A. Cosgrove and D. McCartney (eds), *Studies in Irish History Presented to R Dudley Edwards* (Dublin, 1979), pp. 324–46.
12 See Frank J. Coppa, *The Modern Papacy since 1789* (London, 1998), p. 219.

13 *Mater et magistra*, §§ 218–21 cited in McOustra, *Love in the Economy*, p. 57.
14 DCDA, Mageean Papers, Lenten pastoral: *A Crisis in Christian Civilisation*, p. 8 (read on 11 February 1945).
15 OFMLA, D'Alton Papers, Box 25, Organisations, Folder: Catholic Truth Society, Address by the Cardinal at AGM, 10 October 1951.
16 *Ibid.*, Box 18, Lenten pastoral: 'The church and freedom', 15 February 1952, pp. 16–17.
17 Dromore Diocesan Archives (henceforth DroDA), O'Doherty Papers, Box 18, Lenten pastoral (no title), 12 February 1947, p. 9.
18 *JSA*, President's address, 26 October 1948, p. 15.
19 *Ibid.*, President's address, 7 October 1952, p. 13.
20 *Irish Amsterdam. Reports of the Conference of the Irish Churches* (Belfast, 1949), pp. 16–17.
21 Donald Harman Akenson, *Education and Enmity. The Control of Schooling in Northern Ireland, 1920–50* (Newton Abbot, 1973).
22 Harris, *The Catholic Church*, p. 199.
23 *Ibid.*, p. 243.
24 This episode is discussed by Kevin Haddick-Flynn, *Orangeism. The Making of a Tradition* (Dublin, 1999), pp. 331–2 and M. W. Dewar, John Brown and S. E. Long, *Orangeism. A New Historical Appreciation* (Belfast, 1967), pp. 174–80.
25 Akenson, *Education and Enmity*, p. 180.
26 DCDA, Mageean Papers, E. 11/46, Copy 'Statement on education reconstruction in Northern Ireland', [Signed by Cardinal MacRory, Daniel Mageean, Patrick Lyons, Neil Farren, Eugene O'Callaghan and Eugene O'Doherty], 28 March 1945.
27 DCDA, Mageean Papers, Lenten pastoral: *A Crisis in Christian Civilisation*, part 2: 'Educational Reconstruction in N. Ireland', p. 13 (read on 18 February 1945).
28 *Ibid.*, p. 14.
29 *Ibid.*, p. 16.
30 DCDA, Mageean Papers, Lenten pastoral: *On Security*, p. 15 (read on 10 March 1946).
31 *ICD 1960*, p. 713.
32 Pastoral of the American hierarchy: 'The dignity of man', 22 November 1953, *The Furrow*, 5: 3 (1954), p. 179.
33 DroDA, O'Doherty Papers, Box 18, Lenten pastoral, 22 February 1949, p. 10.
34 Elliott, *The Catholics of Ulster*, p. 431.
35 *DRDS*, President's address, 27 June 1951, pp. 67–8.
36 For example, *DRDS 1949*, 'Derry Diocesan Board of Education Report to Synod', p. 11.
37 Akenson, *Education and Enmity*, p. 166.
38 *Ibid.*, p. 180.

39 *ICD 1955*, p. 642.
40 *ICD 1964*, p. 730.
41 OFMLA, D'Alton Papers, Box 9, NI Education C, Folder 1, figures compiled by Father Francis Lenny, April 1957.
42 In the event, the Education (Amendment) Act 1951 postponed raising the school leaving age until 1 April 1953, and in 1953 it was further postponed until 1 April 1957.
43 *ICD 1956*, p. 658.
44 The figures for other denominations were: Presbyterian 51,211 (27.92 %); Church of Ireland 45,104 (24.59 %); Methodist 7,031 (3.83 %); Others 5,016 (2.73 %), *ICD 1953*, p. lxxiii; *ICD 1961*, p. 666.
45 DroDA, O'Doherty Papers, Box 17/2–3/5 B2, Primary [Schools] Report 1957; Schools Report 1967.
46 DCDA, Mageean Papers, E.5/2/2, Letter R. S. Brownell (permanent secretary Ministry of Education) to Mageean, 29 June 1945.
47 *Ibid.*, Copy letter Mageean to Brownell, 2 July 1945.
48 *Ibid.*, Copy letter Mageean to Monsignor Coghlan, 7 August 1945.
49 *Ibid.*, Copy letter Father P. J. Mullally (diocesan secretary) to Major J. Glen (assistant secretary Ministry of Education), 7 February 1946.
50 *Ibid.*, Letter D'Alton to Mageean, 2 March 1949.
51 Public Record Office of Northern Ireland (henceforth PRONI), CAB/4/1192, Secret memo by Ivan Neill (Minister of Education) 'New Voluntary Training College for Men Students', 27 March 1962.
52 *ICD 1963*, p. 674. St Joseph's was amalgamated with St Mary's in 1985.
53 OFMLA, D'Alton Papers, Box 9, NI Education B, Folder 5, Letter D'Alton to Lord Brookeborough, 7 September 1953; Copy letter Brookeborough to Mageean, 15 January 1954.
54 Michael McGrath, *The Catholic Church and Catholic Schools in Northern Ireland. The Price of Faith* (Dublin, 2000), p. 246.
55 Westminster Diocesan Archives (henceforth WDA), Godfrey Papers, 3/3/14, Memo of telephone conversation between Conway and Monsignor Derek Worlock, 13 February 1962.
56 McGrath, *Catholic Schools*, p. 239.
57 Patrick Shea, *Voices and the Sound of Drums* (Belfast, 1981), p. 160. Brownell was permanent secretary from 1939 to 1958. He succeeded A. N. Bonaparte Wyse, who had the distinction of being the only Catholic to attain that rank in the Northern Ireland Civil Service.
58 OFMLA, D'Alton Papers, Box 8, NI Education A, Folder 3, Statement by D'Alton, n. d. [but 1 January 1950].
59 Graham Walker, *The Politics of Frustration. Harry Midgley and the Failure of Labour in Northern Ireland* (Manchester, 1985), p. 218, 182.
60 *Ibid.*, p. 186.
61 Shea, *Voices*, p. 166.
62 PRONI, Harry Midgley Papers, D/4089/4/1/32, Electoral manifesto Willowfield division, October 1953.

63 *IP*, 2 February 1955.
64 NI House of Commons Debates, vol. 35, col. 2286, 22 November 1951.
65 McGrath, *Catholic Schools*, p. 159.
66 OFMLA, D'Alton Papers, Box 8, NI Education A, Folder 8, Copy letter D'Alton to Dean Quinn, 16 May 1956.
67 *Ibid.*, Draft statement by northern bishops, 2 April 1957.
68 *Spectator*, 20 November 1959; *IT*, 10 December 1959.
69 *ICD 1963*, p. 734.
70 *Northern Whig*, 16 August 1962.
71 PRONI, Cahir Healy Papers, D/2991/B/15/17, Copy letter H. Burdge (grand secretary to Grand Orange Lodge of Ireland) to Gerry Lennon, 19 January 1963; NAI, DFA 305/14/342, Confidential memo Cremin to McCann, 16 April 1963; *BT*, 18 June 1963.
72 DerDA, Farren Papers, Father Toner (diocesan secretary Down and Connor) to Farren, 31 July 1965 enclosing copy memorandum of meeting between Philbin and Governor of Northern Ireland on 29 July 1965.
73 *Derry Journal*, 11 February 1966; on the university controversy in Derry see Marc Mulholland, *Northern Ireland at the Crossroads* (Basingstoke, 2001), pp. 53–57.
74 NAUK, FO 1109/171, Copy memorandum: 'Voluntary Schools and the Education Act, 1944', n.d. The two other categories were 'controlled' and 'special arrangement' schools. In the former, the Church had minority representation on the managing body with the entire cost borne by the local education authority. Of 4,828 schools in this category in 1959, 4,519 were Church of England, two Catholic and 307 other. Special Agreement Schools allowed the church majority representation on the governing body but the power to appoint and dismiss teachers rested with the local education authority. The grant scheme was the same as for aided schools. Of ninety-one such schools, twenty-five were Church of England and sixty-six Catholic.
75 NAUK, PREM 13/870, Confidential copy statement by Anthony Crosland (Secretary of State for Education and Science), 14 February 1965.
76 McGrath, *Catholic Schools*, pp. 160–6.
77 DCDA, Philbin Papers, E. 11/67, Copy letter Conway to Long, 8 May 1967.
78 PRONI, CAB/4/1351/4, Secret memo by Minister of Education, 17 November 1966.
79 Paul Bew, Peter Gibbon and Henry Patterson, *Northern Ireland 1921–1966. Political Forces and Social Classes* (revised edn, London, 1996), p. 114. See also Henry Patterson, *Ireland since 1939* (Oxford, 2002), p. 192; Edward Daly, *Mister, Are You a Priest?* (Dublin, 2000), p. 132. However, Mulholland is more sympathetic see *Northern Ireland at the Crossroads*, pp. 152–3.
80 McGrath, *Catholic Schools*, p. 171.
81 DCDA, Philbin Papers, E. 11/67, Copy letter Cardinal Conway to J. M. Benn (permanent secretary Ministry of Education), 28 July 1967.

82 *Ibid.*, Copy letter Long to Conway, 6 October 1967.
83 *Ibid.*, Copy statement by Philbin on White Paper on Education, 19 October 1967.
84 *Hibernia*, 31: 11 (1967), p. 5; *Irish News* (henceforth *IN*), 29 November 1967.
85 *BT*, 11 December 1967.
86 McGrath, *Catholic Schools*, p. 247.
87 William Conway, *Catholic Schools* (Dublin, 1971), p. 16.
88 DCDA, Philbin Papers, E. 11/67 Copy letter Conway to Long, 25 November 1967.
89 PRONI, CAB/4/1377, Conclusions of a meeting of the cabinet, 23 November 1967.
90 DCDA, Philbin Papers, E. 11/67, Copy letter Long to Conway, 27 November 1967.
91 *Ibid.*, Copy confidential letter Long to Conway, 21 December 1967.
92 DerDA, Farren Papers, Pastoral Letters/Sermons, 'The Education Bill (Northern Ireland) 1968. A Statement by the Catholic Bishops', January 1968. Printed in *IN*, 8 January 1968.
93 McGrath, *Catholic Schools*, p. 173.
94 NAI, DFA 2002/19/423, Copy Northern Ireland Government press release. Extracts of a speech by the Minister of Education at UTA Annual Conference, 14 April 1971.
95 KDA, Quinn Papers, AQ\80, Statement by Catholic bishops, 23 May 1968.
96 OFMLA, D'Alton Papers, Box 8, NI Government A, Folder 3, Letter Conway to D'Alton, 29 March 1957.
97 PRONI, CAB/4/1038/10, Secret report of Committee on Projected Northern Ireland Bill, April 1957.
98 WDA, Godfrey Papers, 3/3/14, Letter D'Alton to Godfrey, 8 February 1962.
99 *Ibid.*, Copy memorandum by Worlock on Northern Ireland Bill 1962, 7 March 1962.
100 WDA, Godfrey Papers, 3/3/14, Copy confidential letter Worlock to Conway, 12 February 1962.
101 OFMLA, D'Alton Papers, Box 8, NI Government A, Folder 9, Copy of press statement by ecclesiastical authorities of Armagh, Clogher, Derry, Down and Connor, Dromore and Kilmore, 11 February 1962.
102 *Ibid.*, Copy letter D'Alton to Shane Leslie, 13 February 1962.
103 *Times*, 12 February 1962; *BT*, 12 February 1962.
104 NAUK, DO 130/129, Confidential letter Cremin to Maclennan, 7 February 1962.
105 *Ibid.*, Letter John Wakely (CRO) to George Crombie, 22 February 1962.
106 PRONI, CAB/4/1187/1, Memorandum ('secret') on Northern Ireland Bill by A. J. Kelly (secretary to NI cabinet), 19 February 1962.
107 PRONI, CAB/4/1187/3, Copy letter Rev. J. H. R. Gibson (clerk of General Assembly) to cabinet, 19 February 1962; *HB*, vol. ii, meeting of 19 February 1962, p. 239.

108 OFMLA, D'Alton Papers, Box 8, NI Government A, Folder 9, Letter Conway to D'Alton, 21 February 1962.
109 WDA, Godfrey Papers, 3/3/14, Letter Conway to Worlock, 27 February 1962.
110 OFMLA, D'Alton Papers, Box 8, NI Government A, Folder 9, Copy letter D'Alton to Lord Longford, 5 March 1962; Box 3, Apostolic Nunciature, Folder: Archbishop Riberi 1959–62, Copy letter D'Alton to Antonio Riberi, 26 February 1962.
111 PRONI, CAB/4/1187/5, Memo: 'Northern Ireland Bill – Amendment to Clause 13', considered at cabinet meeting, 20 February 1962.
112 PRONI, HO/5/150, Memo on Family Allowance, 6 June 1956.
113 OFMLA, D'Alton Papers, Box 8, NI Government A, Folder 8, unpublished letter by D'Alton, n.d.
114 Denis P. Barritt and Charles F. Carter, *The Northern Ireland Problem. A Study in Group Relations* (London, 1962), p. 111.
115 OFMLA, D'Alton Papers, Box 8, NI Government B, Folder 3, Copy letter D'Alton to E. H. Jones (secretary NIHA), 10 September 1958; Copy letter D'Alton to Mageean, 27 November 1958
116 *Ibid.*, Letter O'Doherty to D'Alton, 28 November 1958.
117 OFMLA, D'Alton Papers, Box 8, NI Government C, Folder 4, 'The Northern Ireland Hospitals Authority and Catholics', paper by Michael Kelly delivered to a meeting of the Guild of St Luke, Belfast, 3 December 1961.
118 *Ibid.*, Michael Kelly, *Belfast's Mater Hospital Why?* (Belfast, 1954), p. 3.
119 Eamon Phoenix, 'Mater: Hospital that shines in a bright constellation,' *IN*, 31 October 1983.
120 *IN*, 20 November 1947.
121 DCDA, Mageean Papers, MH 6/51, Legal opinion of Geoffrey Bing, 23 February 1951.
122 WDA, Griffin Papers 2b, Copy statement by hierarchy of England and Wales, 8 May 1946. See also Michael de la Bedoyere, *Cardinal Bernard Griffin Archbishop of Westminster* (London, 1955), p. 67.
123 WDA, Griffin Papers 3b, Copy letter Cardinal Griffin to Bevan, 22 October 1947.
124 *Ibid.*, Letter Bevan to Griffin, 23 December 1947.
125 DCDA, Mageean Papers, MH 6/54, Draft memorandum on Tanner Committee, n.d.
126 *Ibid.*, Memo of meeting of deputation from Board of Management with Health Services Investigating Committee, 29 November 1954.
127 *Ibid.*, MH 1/7, Confidential circular letter to priests of Down and Connor, 15 May 1955.
128 *Ibid.*, MH 6/48, Letter Peter Gormley to Monsignor James Hendley, 10 December 1948.
129 *ICD 1961*, p. 710.
130 DCDA, Philbin Papers, Copy letter Philbin to William Morgan (Minister for Health and Social Services), 28 April 1965.

131 DCDA, Mageean Papers, MH 6/54, Letter Thomas Cairns to Mageean, 16 July 1954.
132 *BT*, 18 February 1964.
133 PRONI, CAB/4/1253/9, Conclusions of meeting of the cabinet, 22 January 1964; CAB/4/1268/10, Conclusions of a meeting of the cabinet, 28 May 1964.
134 *Ibid.*, CAB/4/1290/14, Conclusion of meeting of the cabinet, 27 January 1965.
135 DCDA, Philbin Papers, Copy letter Philbin to Morgan, 28 April 1965.
136 NAI, DT 96/6/644, Letter Philbin to Lemass, 26 April 1965.
137 *Ibid.*, Letter Philbin to Lemass, 5 May 1965.
138 *Ibid.*, Report J. G. Molloy (Irish ambassador) to Seán Ronan (assistant secretary DEA), 10 May 1965.
139 PRONI, HO/5/56, Memo by Secretary of State on proposed bill on racial relations, 3 March 1965; letter Cecil Bateman to R. J. Guppy (HO), 10 March 1965.
140 PRONI, CAB/4/1311/6, Memo by Minister of Health and Social Welfare, n.d.
141 DCDA, Philbin Papers, Speech by Philbin at Nurses' Prize Giving, Mater Hospital, 24 November 1966.
142 *Ibid.*, Letter Morgan to Philbin, 24 December 1968; PRONI, CAB/4/1419/26, Conclusion of a meeting of the cabinet, 21 November 1968.
143 DCDA, Mageean Papers, 1/2/64–69, 'Mater Infirmorum Hospital: Income and Expenditure Accounts', 31 December 1969.
144 PRONI, CAB/4/1622/26, Conclusions of a meeting of the cabinet, 12 October 1971. The original date of 1 November 1971 was postponed for two months.
145 John H. Whyte, 'How much discrimination was there under the unionist regime, 1921–68?', in Tom Gallagher and James O'Connell (eds), *Contemporary Irish Studies* (Manchester, 1983), pp. 1–35.
146 *ICD 1960*, p. 681. For a more detailed discussion of O'Callaghan, see Ó Corráin, '*Semper fidelis*: The episcopacy of Eugene O'Callaghan, 1943–1969', in Henry A. Jefferies (ed.), *History of the Diocese of Clogher* (Dublin, 2005), pp. 223–44.
147 Sydney Elliott, 'The Northern Ireland electoral system: A vehicle for disputation', in Patrick J. Roche and Brian Barton (eds), *The Northern Ireland Question. Nationalism, Unionism and Partition* (Aldershot, 1999), p. 126.
148 *DRDS*, President's address, 25 June 1952, pp. 68–9.
149 CDA, O'Callaghan Papers, Letter Cahir Healy to O'Callaghan, 21 January 1964 with memorandum: 'Is there discrimination in Enniskillen'.
150 *Northern Standard*, 10 January 1964.
151 *Ibid.*, 31 January 1964; *Fermanagh Herald*, 8 February 1964.
152 *IN*, 14 October 1964.

153 Whyte, 'How much discrimination was there', p. 20; OFMLA, D'Alton Papers, Box 19, D'Alton Plan 1957, Points appended to handwritten draft of interview given to Douglas Hyde, n.d. [these points did not feature in the published interview].
154 Cited in Peadar Livingstone, *The Fermanagh Story* (Enniskillen, 1969), p. 373.
155 *BT*, 27 November 1964.
156 OFMLA, Conway Papers, 18/8–1, Copy statement in Dungannon, 30 May 1965.
157 *Ibid.*, Sermon by Cardinal Conway in Portadown, 18 May 1969.
158 See Michael Cunningham, *British Government Policy in Northern Ireland, 1969–2000* (Manchester, 2001), p. 8.
159 Ciarán de Baróid, *Ballymurphy and the Irish War* (revised edn, London, 2000), p. 61. See Bob Purdie, *Politics in the Streets. The Origins of the Civil Rights Movement in Northern Ireland* (Belfast, 1990), ch. 4 for a discussion of the origins of the Northern Ireland Civil Rights Association.
160 See Thomas H. O'Connor, *Boston Catholics. A History of the Church and Its People* (Boston, 1998), pp. 275–6.
161 OFMLA, Conway Papers, 18/8–1, Statement of Northern bishops, January 1968.
162 McElroy, *The Catholic Church and the Northern Ireland Crisis*, pp. 17–18.
163 OFMLA 18/8–1, Joint statement by Northern bishops, 20 January 1969.
164 DerDA, Farren Papers, Letter Farren to J. W. Russell (Solicitor to Commission of Enquiry), 1 May 1969 enclosing statement.
165 *IT*, 26 October 1968.
166 *Fermanagh Herald*, 5 October 1968.
167 *Londonderry Sentinel*, 6 November 1968.
168 *II*, 11 November 1968.
169 RCBL, Simms Papers, MS 238 Copy, 'The Irish Council of Churches and the Irish Crisis'.
170 *II*, 29 August 1969.
171 NAI, DFA 2000/5/45, 'Refugees in the state', 25 August 1969.
172 OFMLA, Conway Papers, 18/8–1, Statement by Cardinal Conway, 14 August 1969.
173 RCBL, Simms Papers, MS 238/1/12, Letter Jenkins to Simms, 15 July 1969.
174 Whiteside, *Simms*, p. 156.
175 *Hibernia*, 33: 15 (1969), p. 6.
176 See, for instance, *Report of Armagh Diocesan Council 1972*, 'Diocesan Board of Social Responsibility – Annual Report', p. 51.
177 *JGS 1970*, President's address, 12 May 1970, p. xlvii.
178 OFMLA, Conway Papers, 18/8–1, Sermon in Armagh Cathedral, 17 August 1969.
179 *Londonderry Sentinel*, 3 November 1971.

180 NAI, DFA 2000/5/45, Letter J. F. Shields (Irish ambassador to Holy See) to secretary DEA, 25 August 1969; DDA, McQuaid Papers, AB8/B/XVIII/04, 'Northern Ireland', donation by McQuaid 12 August 1969.
181 OFMLA, Conway Papers, 18/8–1, Joint statement by Northern bishops, 23 August 1969.
182 *Ibid.*
183 PRONI, CAB/4/1465/13, Copy of Downing Street Communiqué, 20 August 1969; Paul Bew and Gordan Gillespie, *Northern Ireland. A Chronology of the Troubles 1968–1993* (Dublin, 1993), p. 20.
184 Ken Bloomfield, *Stormont in Crisis. A Memoir* (Belfast, 1994), p. 118.
185 James Callaghan, *A House Divided: The Dilemma of Northern Ireland* (London, 1973), p. 65.
186 NAUK, CJ 3/18, Confidential report Wright to Callaghan, 6 March 1970.
187 Peter Rose, *How the Troubles came to Northern Ireland* (Basingstoke, 2000), p. 178.
188 OFMLA, Conway Papers, 18/8–1, Press release by Cardinal Conway, 29 August 1969.
189 HB, vol. iii, meeting of 11 May 1970, p. 156.
190 PRONI, CAB/4/1467/13, Conclusions of a meeting of the cabinet, 26 August 1969.
191 NAUK, CJ 3/18, Copy confidential record of conversation with Cardinal Conway, 4 September 1969.
192 OFMLA, Conway Papers, 18/8–1, Unpublished draft statement by Conway, September 1969.
193 NAUK, CJ 3/18, Secret report Wright to James Callaghan, 13 September 1969.
194 *Ibid.*, Copy confidential report by W. K. K. White (Western European Department) of visit to Dublin and meeting with Seán Ronan, Dennis Holmes and Éamon Gallagher (DEA) 2–4 March 1970, 16 March 1970.
195 NAUK, CJ 3/18, Secret report Wright to Callaghan, 13 September 1969.
196 NAUK, CJ 3/53, Copy of memo 'Northern Ireland: The Belfast Barricades', 15 September 1969; CJ 3/18, Secret report Wright to Callaghan, 13 September 1969. A much less informative account is provided by Callaghan, *A House Divided*, p. 103.
197 OFMLA, Conway Papers, 16/3–4, Copy letter Conway to Farren, 3 September 1969; DCDA, Philbin Papers, Lenten pastoral 1970, 3 February 1970, p. 5.
198 OFMLA, Conway Papers, 18/8–1, Unpublished draft statement by Conway, September 1969.
199 NAUK, CJ 3/18, Secret report Wright to Callaghan, 13 September 1969.
200 NAUK, PREM 13/2845, Copy letter ('confidential') Derek Andrews to Brian Cubbon (HO), 10 September 1969.
201 NAUK, CJ 3/53, Copy of memo 'Northern Ireland: The Belfast Barricades', 15 September 1969.

202 NAUK, CJ 3/18, Confidential record of conversation with Cardinal Conway, 10 September 1969.
203 PRONI, CAB/4/1475/13, Conclusions of a meeting of the cabinet, 15 September 1969.
204 NAUK, CJ 3/18, Confidential narrative of events by Wright, 15 September 1969.
205 *Ibid.*, Confidential record of conversation between A. P. Wilson (Office of the UK Representative in Northern Ireland) and Cardinal Conway on 15 September 1969, 16 September 1969.
206 Michael Farrell, *Northern Ireland: The Orange State* (London, 1976), p. 267.
207 PRONI, CAB/4/1475, Copy of statement by NI government, 15 September 1969.
208 NAUK, CJ 3/18, Copy confidential record of conversation with Cardinal Conway, 19 September 1969.
209 *Ibid.*, Copy letter Wright to James H. Waddell (HO), 1 October 1969.
210 *Ibid.*, Confidential letter Wright to Waddell, 25 September 1969.
211 NAUK, CJ 3/18, Copy confidential record of conversation with Cardinal Conway, 19 September 1969; CJ 3/8, Minute of conversation with Lord O'Neill by Neil Cairncross (Northern Ireland Department HO), 29 June 1970.
212 NAUK, CJ 3/18, Copy confidential record of conversation with Cardinal Conway, 6 November 1969.
213 *Ibid.*, Copy confidential record conversation with Cardinal Conway, 4 December 1969.
214 *Ibid.*
215 NAUK, CJ 3/11, Confidential telegram R. A. Burroughs to Cairncross, 22 August 1970.
216 NAUK, CJ 3/82, Copy of memo on Northern Ireland, 11 November 1969.
217 NAUK, CJ 3/18, Summary of Oliver Wright's 'Ulster: Valedictory despatch', 6 March 1970.
218 *Ibid.*, Confidential report Wright to Callaghan, 6 March 1970.
219 NAUK, CJ 3/11, Memo on political situation for Home Secretary, 11 March 1970.
220 NAI, DFA 98/3/73, Copy letter ('urgent and confidential') Sean Ronan to ambassador to Holy See, 11 February 1970.
221 NAUK, CJ 3/18, Secret report Burroughs to Callaghan, 28 April 1970.
222 *IT*, 23 January 1971.
223 RCBL, Simms Papers, MS 238, Copy circular D. J. Crozier (general secretary Armagh Board of Social Responsibility) to the board, 4 September 1971.
224 NAUK, CJ 3/88, Copy memo regarding meeting with Cardinal Heenan Cairncross to D. E. R. Faulkner, 4 November 1969; note on Heenan by Faulkner, 7 November 1969.
225 NAUK, HO 221/358, Copy letter Professor F. H. Newark (Queen's University Belfast) to Crowther, 10 February 1970.

226 *Ibid.*, Copy note of a meeting with Cardinal Conway, 5 June 1970.
227 NAUK, CJ 3/23, Copy letter White to M. Williams (minister to Holy See), 5 June 1970.
228 Oliver Rafferty, 'God and Ulster', *IN*, 19 September 1994.
229 NAUK, CJ 4/21, Note for the record of Home Secretary's meeting with representatives of the Protestant churches, 30 June 1970, 22 July 1970 with supplementary note 24 July 1970.
230 NAUK, CJ 4/3, Briefing notes for Secretary of State's meeting with church leaders, 20 October 1970.
231 Eric Gallagher, 'Northern Ireland – The record of the churches', *Studies*, 80: 318 (1991), p. 174.
232 *IT*, 4 February 1972.
233 *Ibid.*, 1 December 1971.
234 *IN*, 21 November 1972; *IT*, 1 December 1972.
235 *Hibernia*, 33: 15 (1969), p. 6.
236 *Report of the Down and Dromore Diocesan Council for 1971*, 'The Church in the Community', p. 10.
237 LHL, Church of Ireland Press release: Address by Bishop Butler at Memorial Service for Lord Brookeborough, 28 August 1973.
238 *IT*, 29 August 1973; 3 September 1973.
239 TCD, Trevor West Papers, MS 11034/1/3/15, Letter Butler to West, 4 September 1973.
240 *BT*, 29 August 1973.
241 *IN*, 10 August 1971.
242 *IT*, 12 August 1971.
243 DDA, McQuaid Papers, AB8/B/XVIII/04, Note by McQuaid, 12 August 1971.
244 *Ibid.*, Letter Philbin to McQuaid, 1 October 1971.
245 OFMLA, Conway Papers, statement, 31 August 1971.
246 RCBL, Simms Papers, MS 238, Copy statement on internment.
247 OFMLA, Conway Papers, 15/8–9, Letter Patrick Walsh to Conway, 20 August 1971.
248 *BNL*, 16 August 1971.
249 *CoIG*, 27 August 1971, p. 2.
250 Cited in Norman W. Taggart, *Conflict, Controversy and Co-operation. The Irish Council of Churches and "The Troubles" 1968–1972* (Dublin, 2004), p. 56.
251 NAUK, CJ 4/109, Letter Conway to Compton, 14 September 1971.
252 *Ibid.*, Copy letter Compton to Conway, 16 September 1971.
253 *Compton Report* (Cmnd. 4823), p. 71.
254 OFMLA, Conway Papers, 18/8–2/2, Joint statement by bishops, 21 November 1971.
255 *II*, 2 November 1971.
256 RCBL, Simms Papers, MS 238, Statement by Northern Church of Ireland bishops; *IT*, 1 December 1971.

257 NAUK, PREM 15/472, Secret note of a meeting between the Secretary of State for Defence and four Northern Ireland Ministers held on 1 October 1971, 4 October 1971.
258 Bew and Gillespie, *Chronology*, p. 58.
259 OFMLA, Conway Papers, 18/8–2/2, Joint statement, 21 May 1970.
260 *IN*, 22 May 1970; OFMLA, Conway Papers, 18/8–2/2, Letter Burroughs to Conway, 21 May 1970.
261 OFMLA, Conway Papers, 18/8–2/2, Copy letter Conway to Burroughs, 25 May 1970.
262 OFMLA, Conway Papers, 16/3–1, Letter Mulligan to Conway, 2 November 1971.
263 RCBL, Simms Papers, MS 238, Statement by North of Ireland bishops, 6 September 1971.
264 OFMLA, Conway Papers, 18/8–1, Statement by Cardinal Conway, 2 April 1970.
265 OFMLA, Conway Papers, Bound volume of statements on Northern Ireland situation, sermon in Drogheda, 11 July 1971.
266 *Ibid.*, Joint statement by Northern bishops, 12 September 1971.
267 *Ibid.*, Sermon Armagh Cathedral, 12 December 1971.
268 *Ibid.*, Statement by Cardinal, 30 January 1972.
269 OFMLA, Conway Papers, 15/8–2, Copy statement by the heads of churches, 3 February 1972.
270 *Ibid.*, Draft of statement of 3 February 1972 with Conway's amendments.
271 *IN*, 11 November 1971.
272 *IT*, 3 January 1972.
273 *BT*, 6 January 1972. See *IN*, 23 April 1973 for condemnation of Cahal Daly by the Official IRA, and *IN*, 21 March 1974 by Provisional IRA.
274 See de Baróid, *Ballymurphy*, pp. 56, 63, 194–6.
275 William J Philbin, *Ireland's Problem* (Belfast, 1974), p. 6.
276 *Ibid.*, p. 8.
277 *IN*, 21 May 1973.
278 DDA, McQuaid Papers, AB8/B/XVIII/04, 'A Christmas Appeal', 20 December 1971.
279 *Ibid.*, Memo by James Ardle MacMahon (diocesan secretary), Dec 1971.
280 *Ibid.*, Draft letter ('personal') McQuaid to Alibrandi, 23 December 1971.
281 OFMLA, Conway Papers, Bound volume of statements on Northern Ireland situation, Sermon in Middletown, Co. Armagh, 30 May 1972.
282 Quoted in Bew and Gillespie, *Chronology*, p. 53.
283 OFMLA, Conway Papers, Bound volume of statements on Northern Ireland situation, Sermon in Clonard Monastery, Belfast, 25 June 1972.
284 *Ibid.*, Statement, 10 July 1972.
285 OFMLA, Conway Papers, 15/8–9, Copy letter Conway to Walsh, 13 October 1972.
286 OFMLA, Conway Papers, 26/20–7, 'Assassinations.'

287 OFMLA, Conway Papers, 15/8–9, Copy letter Conway to Walsh, 26 September 1972.
288 Marie Therese Fay, Mike Morrissey and Marie Smyth, *Mapping Troubles-Related Deaths in Northern Ireland 1969–1998* (2nd edn, Derry, 1998), p. 32.
289 OFMLA, Conway Papers, Bound volume of statements on Northern Ireland situation, Statement 10 March 1971.
290 OFMLA, Conway Papers, 15/8–2, Press release by Conway, Simms, Lindsay (Methodist President), Lynas (Presbyterian Moderator), 18 August 1972.
291 *IT*, 15 November 1972.
292 *II*, 6 December 1972.
293 OFMLA, Conway Papers, 18/8–3, Joint statement, 3 January 1973.
294 OFMLA, Conway Papers, 26/20–7, 'Assassinations'
295 *IN*, 6 July 1973.
296 NAI, DFA 2000/14/460, Copy statement by Cardinal Conway, 9 November 1973.
297 *BNL*, 10 November 1973, *BT*, 14 November 1973.
298 *II*, 10 November 1973.
299 *Report of the Down and Dromore Diocesan Council to the Diocesan Synod 1973* 'The Church in the Community', p. 10.
300 David McKittrick and David McVea, *Making Sense of the Troubles* (Belfast, 2000), p. 88.
301 RCBL, Simms Papers, MS 238, Letter Edward Heath to Simms, 20 November 1972.
302 OFMLA, Conway Papers, 15/8–2, Letter Lynas to Conway, 27 November 1972.
303 *Ibid.*, 15/8–3, 'Representation to the News Media from Churches in Ireland', 12 March 1973.
304 *IN*, 19 March 1973; *Times*, 19 March 1973.
305 See Seán Farren and Robert F. Mulvihill, *Paths to a Settlement in Northern Ireland* (Gerrards Cross, 2000), p. 73.
306 RCBL, Simms Papers, MS 238, Draft of statement on White Paper, 22 March 1973.
307 *IN*, 26 Mar 1973.
308 *IT*, 23 March 1973.
309 William Whitelaw, *The Whitelaw Memoirs* (London, 1989), p. 120.
310 *II*, 21 November 1973.
311 HB, vol. iii, meeting of 11 December 1973, p. 280.
312 OFMLA, Conway Papers, 18/9–3, RTÉ Broadcast Christmas, 1973
313 *IN*, 7 January 1974.
314 David Blackbourn, *Class, Religion and Local Politics in Wilhelmine Germany: The Centre Party in Württemberg before 1914* (New Haven and London, 1980), p. 33.

5

'That they may be one': inter-church relations and religious borders in Ireland

> Some windows, once opened, can never be closed again. (Lawrence Elliott, *I will be called John*)

The political border aside, the Irish churches faced a second form of partition, in the 1949 to 1973 period, namely the denominational border between Catholic and Protestant. The unfolding of the ecumenical story in Ireland was something of a *longue durée*. A silent *konfessionskrieg* gradually gave way from the 1960s onwards to ecumenical activity unprecedented in tone and scope. A period that began with the infamous Fethard-on-Sea boycott ended with the first official inter-church meeting at Ballymascanlon Hotel, Dundalk in September 1973.

Ballymascanlon, as the meeting was colloquially known, became 'a synonym for ecumenical dialogue'.[1] Derived from the Greek word *oikumene*, meaning the whole of the inhabited world, in the twentieth century ecumenism described the movement aspiring towards the unity of all Christians. This aspiration, as unity may or may not occur at some unspecified point in the future, has existed in various forms for centuries. But it had never been as effective as in the twentieth century. The method of achieving unity, the omega point of ecumenism, has been inter-church dialogue with an emphasis on resolving divisive issues through consensus achieved by clearer understanding and exchange of insight. Consequently, such dialogue has increased the complexity and understanding of the term ecumenism. Before the Second Vatican Council, the main ecumenical impetus came from the Protestant churches. With the convocation of the Council, new ground was broken and a new language of possibility and promise was spoken. Its decrees provided the context for a new phase of inter-church relations and facilitated official dialogue at an international level, the impact of which was not lost on Ireland. Particularly significant in the Irish case was the influence of unofficial local level contact between the churches through, among others, the historically neglected Churches' Industrial Council as well as the Glenstal and Greenhills conferences. Incrementally, they helped to overcome the churches' mutual ignorance of and isolation from one another, and to generate a momentum for reconciliation as divisive issues such as mixed marriage, hitherto rich soil for rancour, were discussed. Misconceptions of a religious war in Northern Ireland provided a pressing rationale for entente at the end of the 1960s. However, therein lurked new dangers for the churches, as ecumenism became a lightning-rod for the ill-will of those opposed to Rome. Intra-Protestant dialogue, the Second Vatican Council, *rapprochement* between Rome and Canterbury, small-scale Irish ecumenical efforts and the catalysing impact of the Troubles in Northern Ireland were both causative and reactive agents. For the sake of clarity they are outlined separately in this chapter. However, this should not conceal the often complex interaction between them.

'Cold War'

In character with the prevailing international political climate of Cold War, official relations between the Catholic Church and the Church of Ireland were glacial throughout the 1950s. There were virtually no points of contact as both churches competed in sanctimonious sniping from sandbags of ancient mistrust. They were represented towards one another by rival self-righteousness. Little had changed since Cardinal MacRory urged de Valera, to no avail, not to allow the title 'Church of Ireland' stand in Bunreacht na hÉireann because it would be 'a very great mistake to seem to approve or accept such an arrogant assumption'.[2] The official response of the Vatican to nascent ecumenism was simply *non possumus* – we cannot. In December 1949, the Holy Office issued an instruction warning bishops to 'employ altogether exceptional watchfulness and control' over meetings between Catholics and other Christians.[3] For Archbishop Gregg this *ipse dixit* merely reaffirmed that 'discussions with any other object than surrender to the Roman position need not be considered'.[4]

The proclamation of the dogma of the Assumption, on 1 November 1950, provides a good example of how far apart the churches were. For the first time since papal infallibility was promulgated in 1870, Pius XII infallibly defined the doctrine of the Assumption. Eamon Duffy argues that this embarrassed Catholic theologians since it was unsupported in scripture. It also further damaged inter-church relations even for those such as the Orthodox Church who shared the doctrine but rejected the unilateral right of the pope to define it.[5] The House of Bishops viewed with alarm what the *Irish Catholic Directory* trumpeted as the 'greatest Catholic event of the century'.[6] Greatly exercised by the gravity of the doctrinal issue involved and with the backing of the House of Bishops, Gregg wrote a pastoral which was read on 10 December 1950.[7] 'To define this dogma as an Article of its Faith', was, the pastoral argued, to misrepresent 'the Catholic Faith and expose it to ridicule'. Moreover, such a definition revealed 'the penalty, both for the Pope and for his Church, of the absoluteness of the Papal claim to Infallibility'.[8]

While official relations between the churches were confrontational, at a personal level bishops were courteous and respectful. In Armagh the two Primates lived less than two miles apart. When John D'Alton became archbishop of Armagh in 1946, Gregg wrote to welcome him and sought permission to call to Ara Coeli.[9] From their limited correspondence it appears that both men had a warm personal regard for one another. When Gregg retired in February 1959, D'Alton wished that he would 'enjoy and benefit from the rest which you have well earned after your many years of faithful service. I can assure you that you will be leaving with the highest esteem of my priests and people'.[10] For his part, Gregg was happy to have enjoyed the Cardinal's acquaintance although they 'could not meet very often'.[11] D'Alton was even approached by George Seaver, Gregg's biographer, to write a few lines of personal reminiscence. Seaver remarked that it 'is a happiness to us that your relations with him were so friendly over a long period of years, and this despite his known opposition to the Roman Catholic Church, in certain respects'.[12] D'Alton penned a warm-hearted note praising Gregg's scholarship and intellectual abilities. Admittedly, there was far less evidence of contact between D'Alton and James McCann, even though both had served their episcopal apprenticeships in the diocese of Meath. The same personal respectfulness was evident in Dublin. McQuaid and Simms expressed sympathy on the death of church dignitaries, exchanged Christmas and Easter greetings, and before the advent of postal districts in 1962, returned any post mistakenly delivered to the wrong archbishop of Dublin.

The *Ne Temere* decree and mixed marriage

The conditions imposed by the *Ne Temere* decree on 'mixed marriages' between Catholics and Protestants poisoned inter-church relations. Even after the Second Vatican Council, this remained *the* major point of contention at diocesan, national and international level. Michael Ramsey, Fisher's successor as archbishop of Canterbury, believed that there was no other subject which 'causes so much soreness, or does more damage to the growth of ecumenical relations'.[13] Pope Pius X's *Ne Temere* (1908) was in essence a housekeeping measure, providing, for the first time, one uniform set of marriage regulations for all Catholics. *Ne Temere* was incorporated into the *Codex Inuris Canonici*, the Code of Canon Law, on 19 May 1918, ten years after the decree was first applied in Ireland.

At the most fundamental level, the dispute to which *Ne Temere* gave rise stemmed from the doctrinal division between the churches. Marriages between members of the Protestant churches are also interchurch marriages but raise only minor difficulties. By contrast, the divisions between the Protestant churches and the Catholic Church are much greater. They have different positions with regard to what constitutes a valid marriage and to the extent of church authority over such a marriage. The *Codex* drew a distinction between a marriage to a non-Roman Catholic Christian and a non-Christian. The latter was invalid unless a dispensation from the impediment was attained. Marriage to another Christian was regarded as irregular rather than invalid. A dispensation from this irregularity was made conditional on the promise that any children of a mixed marriage would be baptised and brought up as Catholics. The promise stemmed from the belief that the Catholic Church was the one true church. For this reason also, it was hoped that the non-Roman Catholic partner might be converted. The penalty for non-observance of the promise by a Catholic was excommunication. Other stipulations also caused much bitterness and sorrow. Under canon 1094, an inter-church marriage had to be conducted by a Catholic priest in an unconsecrated building without religious celebration, hence the infamous 'sacristy weddings'. The *Codex* disapproved of mixed marriages and tried to prevent them, but ensured they would be strictly controlled should they occur.[14]

Ne Temere was deeply resented by the Church of Ireland. It is revealing to recall initial Church of Ireland reaction to *Ne Temere* and how little this changed. Addressing members of the Young Men's Association on 17 March 1911, Gregg, then incumbent of Blackrock parish in Cork, attacked *Ne Temere* for what he regarded as the dishonourable bartering of Protestant children, the very life blood of any church whose purpose is to hand on the faith. 'Every Protestant who has children, and consents to let them go to the other side, is a traitor to the cause . . . Mixed marriages tend to rob us of the next generation, and we need to band ourselves together to stop the leakage.'[15] In addition to the danger posed to the religious upbringing of children, the inter-church marriage was undesirable due to the threat it posed to the religious faith of the partners, the integrity of the marriage, and the solidarity of the church community. As White put it, for a Protestant to convert to Catholicism ('to turn') was 'a social lapse, a weakening of the tribe, a desertion from the post of duty'.[16] The Church of Ireland viewed *Ne Temere* as an instrument of slow strangulation or even extermination, particularly in the Republic where the church was demographically weak. Robert MacCarthy argues that it decimated many rural parishes.[17] This canon of ecclesiastical law was certainly one of a number of contributory factors to population decline. But to claim that it *alone* was responsible for something as complex as population decline is an exaggeration. It fails to take into account marriage late in life and consequent low marriage fertility, emigration, self-choice in terms of marriage partners and strenuous Church of Ireland warnings to create, in Gregg's words, 'a deep-rooted prejudice . . . against such marriages on Roman Catholic terms'.[18] In May 1951 the House of Bishops approved a notice warning against the dangers of *Ne Temere* which was placed in all church porches. The Dublin, Glendalough and Kildare Committee on Youth Activities recommended that conditions governing entry to parochial dances should be tightened up so as to ensure Protestant young people 'meet only those of their own persuasion'. This was still a concern for the same committee almost a decade later.[19]

The promise to raise children of a mixed marriage as Catholics was highlighted during the 1950s in two very public examples: the Tilson case and the Fethard-on-Sea boycott. In 1950 the High Court ruled against Ernest Tilson's absolute right to determine the religious education of his children after his marriage to a Catholic woman had failed. This interpretation referred to Articles 41 (The Family), 42 (Education) and 44 (Religion), and not solely Article 44.1.2 (the special position of the Catholic Church) as Bowen suggests.[20] As Kennedy points out, the ruling, which was upheld in the Supreme Court, favoured the principle of joint guardianship. This meant that a decision could not be unilaterally altered by one parent.[21] This was also the nub of the Fethard-on-Sea boycott in 1957.

The boycott undoubtedly represented the lowest point of the Irish inter-church cold war. As outlined in chapter three, the government's condemnation was unambiguous. By contrast the Catholic hierarchy neither officially intervened nor condemned the boycott of the religious minority.[22] The *Gazette* aimed its accusations squarely at the Catholic authorities: 'their silence can be taken to mean only approval, and any subsequent expression of disapproval will be put down to pressure of opinion or consideration of policy'.[23] The abrasive Bishop Michael Browne of Galway defended the boycott in inflammatory terms at the Congress of the Catholic Truth Society in Wexford on 30 June 1957:

> There seems to be a concerted campaign to entice or kidnap Catholic children and deprive them of their Faith. Non-Catholics, with one or two

honourable exceptions, do not protest against the crime of conspiring to steal the children of a Catholic father. But they tried to make political capital, when a Catholic people made a peaceful and moderate protest.[24]

Despite widespread condemnation, the bishop could see no reason to modify his position. Browne's argument rested on the proposition that the protest was not directed at the Protestant inhabitants of Fethard-on-Sea because they were Protestant. Rather, it was a demonstration against the crime of abducting the children from their father and denying them the one true faith. The locus of injustice was thus shifted from the boycotted villagers to the children themselves and the implicit breaking of the promise.

This position was also representative of many members of the Church of Ireland. For instance, Bishop Tyndall of Kilmore stated that though his church did not like the *Ne Temere* decree, it certainly did not encourage or condone the breaking of a solemn and binding promise.[25] Where the sides differed, of course, was in acknowledging that the method of protest employed, and the subsequent consequences, created an even greater injustice. Reaction by members of the Church of Ireland in the Republic ranged from outright condemnation, with a wish to take action, to one of stoically seeing out the storm. Bishop Phair initially played down the boycott, deplored the consequences of mixed marriages, publicly stated that Mrs Cloney acted wrongly and criticised the excessive press publicity given to the boycott. However, increasing disquiet by the laity forced him to take some sort of action. Accompanied by Senator Stanford, he met the President on 10 July 1957 to brief him on the situation. Writing in the local diocesan magazine the following month, the bishop felt that the boycott had become a national issue, but appealed for restraint. This was condemned as merely 'counsell[ing] appeasement' by Hubert Butler.[26] Other members of the Church of Ireland used their position, or the letters pages of the press, to make known their denunciation. One church member suggested to Alberto Levame, the papal nuncio, that the Vatican Secretariat of State be informed of the events in Fethard-on-Sea. The Clogher diocesan synod, presided over by Bishop Tyner, passed a unanimous resolution on 21 June 1957 which regarded 'with the gravest concern and distress the boycott at Fethard-on-Sea of the members of our Church'. A copy was sent to de Valera.[27]

What were the responses of Cardinal D'Alton, Archbishop McQuaid and Bishop Staunton? Under canon law, neither D'Alton nor McQuaid could intervene directly in the diocesan jurisdiction of another bishop. It is perhaps for this reason that there is no copy of any correspondence between McQuaid and Staunton with regard to the boycott.

Eilín Barrington, a teacher in Gorey, County Wexford, urged the Cardinal 'to speak out once and for all against this terrible thing and so put an end to it'.[28] D'Alton had a reputation for moderation. The previous year, he made known to the secretary of the Methodist Church his abhorrence of 'any restriction on the freedom of religious worship' in Spain.[29] It was therefore peculiar that he remained silent and allowed his church to be tarnished by bad publicity at home and overseas. His reply to Barrington reiterated Browne's essential argument – the return of the children should be regarded as the first and essential act of justice. It also revealed his concern at the implications of the boycott in Northern Ireland, while underscoring the issue of episcopal jurisdiction: 'It is of course a matter not for me, but for the bishop of Ferns to deal with events in Fethard-on-Sea, which unfortunately are being used here in the North to stir up further hatred against the Catholics.'[30] Following a visit from a group of prominent Northern Catholics, D'Alton wrote to Staunton, who denied that the boycott originated from any instruction from him. He agreed to issue a statement but seemed oblivious to the barrage of protest.[31] Staunton was deeply suspicious of supposed anti-Catholic propaganda in the press. In a revealing letter to McQuaid, shortly after the boycott petered out, addressing the issue of public relations, he wrote:

> The lay public, in general, accept without criticism or even any thought, what they read, including, in too many cases, attacks on the Catholic Church, its teaching and leaders . . . I felt this in the Fethard-on-Sea case. The Protestant propaganda, in my opinion successful, was in fact an attack on the Catholic Church, under the guise of an attack on the people of Fethard-on-Sea.[32]

That Fethard-on-Sea so embittered relations between the churches makes the achievements of ecumenical *rapprochement* in the following years all the more remarkable.

At an official level the Second Vatican Council brought about a new attitude towards inter-church marriage. Though modified, the underpinnings of *Ne Temere* were not completely abolished, and while not forbidden inter-church marriages remained unpalatable. Unlike the *Codex*, the *Declaration on Religious Freedom* recognised the need to respect the conscience of the individual. In November 1964 a special *Votum on Mixed Marriages* replaced the *Codex*. This was implemented in two stages. In March 1966 an *instructio* entitled *Matrimonii sacramentum* was issued. This was followed in 1970 by a *motu proprio*[33] entitled *Matrimonia mixta*. The *instructio* was described as 'No Advance' by the *Gazette*, whereas the *Irish Catholic* aptly described it as a 'cautious experiment rather than of any shifting of fundamental outlook on mixed marriages'.³⁴ This was how Bishops McAdoo and Wyse Jackson saw it when they reported to the House of Bishops in June 1966. While clearly more conciliatory in tone, the *instructio* remained 'quite unsatisfactory', because 'there is an insuperable moral problem in making the promise which has to be given almost as heretofore. That the promise may be made verbally rather than in writing is no real concession: the enforceable contract still remains.'³⁵ The House of Bishops prepared a pastoral letter on the subject, copies of which were sent to all the bishops of the Anglican Communion. Read on Sunday 20 November 1966, the pastoral regarded the lack of movement on the promise as 'a grave disappointment'. It reiterated the belief that

> it is a fundamental right of parents freely to decide for themselves the religion in which their children are to be brought up . . . We must therefore with great regret make it clear to our people that in all essentials the position of the Roman Catholic Church in respect of mixed marriages remains unaltered. The *Ne Temere* decree still remains a serious obstacle to closer relationships on all but the superficial level.³⁶

If the promise was still demanded, the House of Bishops instructed clergy not to attend such a wedding, either as an officiant or as a guest in the body of the church.³⁷ The Catholic Church's position on mixed marriages remained an affront to the Church of Ireland.

In January 1970 *Matrimonia mixta* provided a more comprehensive treatment of inter-church marriage. It was a mixture of intransigence on some points and notable advances on others. This edict consciously recognised the Christian faith of other churches and Pope Paul VI directed clergy to cultivate relations with other ministers so that proper pastoral support could be given to inter-church couples. Small though this conciliatory admission may be, it would have been unthinkable ten years previously. The wedding in the Catholic church was no longer to be regarded as inferior and full religious rites were to be celebrated before the altar rather than in the sacristy. The penalties outlined in the *Codex* were relaxed. For instance, marriage before a minister of another church was no longer a cause for excommunication. Accordingly, Archbishop Simms told the General Synod in 1970 that

> There are helpful and welcome features in the document which indicate that thinking on the problem goes on . . . This is not to encourage mixed marriage – neither Church wishes to do so. We know there is still stress on the consciences of the keen church member in spite of the easings.³⁸

The promise remained the key sticking point. The Catholic Church seemed immutable on the matter. For Cardinal Conway, it was 'not possible for any human authority, Pope, bishop or anyone else, to release a

Catholic from the duty of preserving his faith and handing it on to his children'.[39] Changes to the regulations governing the religious upbringing of children were largely formulaic. A mandatory promise was no longer required from the non-Roman Catholic partner, who was entitled to a say in that upbringing. However, the obligations incumbent on the Catholic partner to do all in their power to raise children in the Catholic faith remained. Heron suggests that doing 'all in their power' was an advance over 'making absolutely sure', as set down in the *Codex*. Furthermore, he argues that by changing the form of the promise, the Catholic Church recognised that the children might not in fact be brought up as Catholics.[40] Nonetheless, the House of Bishops regarded the changes to the promise as little more than a modified insistence that children be brought up as Catholics. Commenting on this at the joint diocesan synod of Dublin, Glendalough and Kildare, in October 1970, Archbishop Buchanan felt that 'if people are mature enough to marry, they are capable of deciding the upbringing of their children without dictation from any quarter'.[41]

The reception and implementation of *Matrimonia mixta* in Ireland was complicated by three additional factors. Firstly, *Humanae vitae*, Paul VI's divisive encyclical of 1968, which reaffirmed the traditional position of the Catholic Church on birth control, was viewed as a disservice to the cause of Christian unity. This was still fresh in the minds of the Church of Ireland community before, during and after the publication of *Matrimonia mixta*. *Humanae vitae* was further seen to increase pressure on inter-church marriages which now had to 'reconcile the conflicting teachings of their respective Churches in the matter of family limitation'.[42] It painted a picture of a reactionary and obscurantist Catholic Church. The second complicating factor was the outbreak of the Troubles. Coloured by the situation in Northern Ireland, Catholic marriage regulations were dressed in new clothes and factored in as a cause of Northern fears. For instance, the report of the Committee on Christian Unity adopted at the diocesan synod of Dublin, Glendalough and Kildare on 22 October 1969, blamed *Ne Temere* for sectarian division.[43] For this reason, in his paper on mixed marriages at Ballymascanlon, Cahal Daly insisted that 'the Catholic Church's attitude can never be understood if it is interpreted in political or demographical or sociological terms. It is a question of doctrine, of ecclesiology, of how the Church understands herself.'[44]

Lastly, implementation was exacerbated by Paul VI's decision to let national Episcopal Conferences decide on the precise form of the promise and the conditions for granting dispensations. This was an understandable attempt by the Pope to mollify conservative unease. Like Ireland, Switzerland has a large Protestant and a large Catholic population. But the response of the respective Episcopal Conferences to *Matrimonia mixta* was very different. The Swiss bishops referred to the possibility that inter-church marriage could contribute to the restoration of Christian unity. They also emphasised that the religious convictions of the other partner should be respected. Moreover, the religious upbringing of the children was explicitly declared to be a matter of conscience for *both* partners.[45] Catholic bishops in Switzerland, France, Germany and the Benelux countries accepted in principle that they could no longer insist on all children being Catholic. The French bishops made explicit allowances for not asking for the promise in difficult cases. The Dutch never asked for the promise.[46] By contrast, the Irish Episcopal Conference was coldly juridical. At a general meeting in March 1970, an almost pre-conciliar line was retained. The Irish bishops resolved that 'the Catholic party be normally asked to make the necessary promise and declaration in writing in the presence of the non-Catholic party and the parish priest', the non-Roman Catholic party being asked 'not to impede'.[47] In Cork, Bishop Lucey still demanded promises from the Protestant party also. At the October meeting of the Episcopal Conference, it was decided not to grant a dispensation 'in cases where it is clear – either from explicit statements or on other grounds – that some or all of the children would be brought up as non-Catholics'.[48] Over half of the priests of the Dublin arch diocese, interviewed by John Fulton, saw the Catholic upbringing of the children of an inter-church marriage as a serious obligation for the Catholic partner.[49] The hierarchy also pushed for inter-church marriages to be conducted by Catholic priests. In any event the number of such marriages remained low. Only sixty-seven were recorded for the diocese of Derry in 1970 compared to 1,135 marriages among Catholics.[50] While inter-communal tension in Northern Ireland may account to some extent for such low figures, of 7,400 marriages in the archdiocese of Dublin during 1972, only 388 involved a partner of another church. By comparison, mixed marriages accounted for 27.5 per cent of all marriages in West Germany in 1970.[51] That inter-church marriage was the subject of frank discussion at Ballymascanlon was, in light of the above, a notable advance towards addressing the most intractable ecumenical obstacle.

Intra-Protestant *rapprochement*

During the first half of the twentieth century ecumenism was almost exclusively concerned with intramural divisions between the Protestant churches. The Edinburgh Missionary Conference in 1910 is conventionally regarded as the birth of twentieth-century ecumenism. In its aftermath, two separate organisations as well as an International Missionary

Council emerged. The 'Life and Work' Conference, created in 1925, was concerned with the application of Christian principles to matters of social justice and international peace. Two years later, the first World Conference on 'Faith and Order' addressed doctrinal matters. The three organisations converged with the founding of the World Council of Churches (WCC) in Amsterdam in 1948.[52] The WCC represented about 480 million members of the reformed churches. It was not a super church. Archbishop Fisher told a meeting of the British Council of Churches in Belfast, in April 1952, that it was a fellowship designed to help the members 'know each other better, to co-operate so far as cooperation is possible, to grow in charity and understanding of one another, to reach out to find the will of Christ which each of them imperfectly as yet can read'. It was the business of individual churches, not the WCC, to frame schemes of reunion. 'If progress in the search is slow', Fisher continued, 'that is due not to the Council but to the churches; and at least the Council keeps barking at their heels to keep them moving'.[53] Until the Second Vatican Council, the WCC was the most tangible expression of ecumenism.

The response in Ireland to these events and others, such as the unofficial Malines Conversations between Anglican and Catholic theologians in the 1920s, was the foundation in January 1923 of the United Council of Christian Churches and Religious Communions in Ireland (UCCC). Members included: the Church of Ireland, Presbyterian Church, Methodist Church, United Free Church of Scotland, Baptists, Congregationalists, Moravians, Society of Friends and the Salvation Army. This watershed development in Irish intra-Protestant collaboration was less a reflection of the tense Irish political situation than of an industrious ecumenical decade internationally.

Involvement in international bodies such as 'Life and Work' or the WCC was a very different matter from domestic intra-Protestant cooperation, or so-called 'Home Reunion', between the trenchantly denominational Protestant churches. As Michael Hurley has pointed out, the main problem 'was not Rome's unwillingness to cooperate with the Protestant Churches or the Protestant Churches' unwillingness to cooperate with Rome but the Protestant Churches' unwillingness to cooperate with each other'.[54] Such efforts were fitful. Although the General Synod established a Home Reunion Committee as early as 1905, 'Home Reunion' was not discussed with Presbyterian representatives until January 1931. This led to the establishment of an officially approved joint committee which considered the question between 1932 and 1934. These exploratory talks foundered on the key issue of episcopacy. A resolution calling on each church to declare that 'it fully and freely recognises, as a basis for further progress towards Union, the validity, efficacy and spiritual reality of both ordination and sacraments, as administered in the other Church' was successfully opposed by Archbishop Gregg at the General Synod in 1935. Discussions were subsequently discontinued. Presbyterian-Methodist discussions also petered out in 1947, not because of a failure to recognise one another's sacraments and orders but due to a lack of consensus on the itinerancy of ministers.[55]

Gregg's antipathy towards ecumenism was well known. According to his biographer, he disliked 'being, or of being seen, in the company of Presbyterians or of non-conformists'.[56] During his incumbency he was more interested in establishing inter-communion between the Church of Ireland and the Old Catholic Churches in Holland, Germany and Switzerland, in line with the Church of England, than in conversations with Irish Presbyterians and Methodists, let alone Catholics. In a revealing commentary on the Anglican-Methodist conversations in England during the 1950s, he dismissed any 'irregular form of limited inter-Communion' and believed that '"friendly relations" are as far as we in Ireland can go at present'.[57] As late as November 1959, caution was advocated by the House of Bishops in the formation of clubs involving members of the Church of Ireland and other denominations.[58]

The case for better relations was boosted by the appearance in January 1958 of *Focus*, a short-lived interdenominational Protestant monthly review. Inspired largely by Risteard Ó Glaisne, a broadcaster, Irish language enthusiast and member of the Methodist Church, *Focus* sought to provide a forum for liberal, intellectual views on religion and society while eschewing references to the partition question.[59] It aimed to provide a platform for the different Protestant traditions on the island of Ireland to engage honestly with each other and make their voices heard. As proof of this intention, the Church of Ireland, Presbyterian Church, Methodist Church and Society of Friends were represented on the editorial council. It also sought to promote a spirit of goodwill between Catholics and Protestants. The journal received critical praise. However, it never achieved a widespread circulation due to difficulty in securing advertising revenue and lack of expertise in administration and distribution.[60] While it is difficult to gauge precisely to what extent *Focus* cultivated intra-Protestant harmony, it signalled, and was a manifestation of, a marked change of atmosphere.

In this regard, Archbishop McCann was far more disposed to pan-Protestantism than his predecessor. Along with Bishop Frederick Mitchell, he served on the Lambeth committee on church unity in 1958. McCann was vice-president. Somewhat surprisingly, Mitchell, who was regarded as a conservative, instituted a series of informal Anglican-Methodist-Presbyterian conferences at Murlough House near Dundrum, County Down. With the consent of the House of Bishops, the first such meeting was held on 26 September 1961. It was suggested that provision be made for non-Anglicans to receive Holy Communion in Anglican churches in special circumstances or on special occasions. Secondly, in areas with few Presbyterians or Methodists it was mooted that they worship with the Church of Ireland congregation. Thirdly, it was suggested that permission be given for regular united evening services in places where there were two or three churches of different denominations but where total Protestant numbers were small.[61] This groundbreaking contact prepared the way for resumption, in 1964, of triple-track official conversations between the Church of Ireland and Methodists; Church of Ireland and Presbyterians; and Methodists and Presbyterians. The minutes of the House of Bishops make clear that their initial approach to the Methodist Church was heavily influenced by the example and form of dialogue between the Church of England and the Methodist Church in England, of which Henry Stanistreet, Church of Ireland bishop of Killaloe, requested that his Church be kept appraised.[62] Neither was the Church of Ireland immune to the impact of the Second Vatican Council and international entente between Rome and Canterbury.

Official level contact between the Protestant churches was reinforced by diocesan and local level efforts. For instance, in January 1963 a Derry and Raphoe diocesan committee was appointed. It held meetings with Presbyterian and Methodist representatives. The result was the establishment of the North-West Council of Churches in December 1964.[63] Such a development echoed resolution thirteen of the 1920 Lambeth Conference which sought the establishment of councils of churches. These were by no means solely a Northern phenomenon. In January 1960, a council of churches was established in Dún Laoghaire, County Dublin to draw its members 'into greater understanding and to enable them to share more fully in the ecumenical movement, carrying on a united witness and service in the community'.[64] At the diocesan synod of Derry and Raphoe in 1965, Bishop Tyndall pointed out that the function of the North-West Council was not to unite the churches, but to create a climate in which there could eventually be unity of the Protestant churches.[65] However, this should not obscure a very definite change of mentality. At the Clogher diocesan synod in September 1960, Bishop Buchanan asked 'for forgiveness for our share in the division of Christ's church. All churches are at fault. There is no room today for mutual recriminations. There can be no re-union without repentance.' He hoped that the Church of Ireland would be in the van of the ecumenical movement and called for 'mutual study and frank courteous discussion'.[66] Behind such fresh thinking lay the challenges to organised religion of the television age, urbanisation, the sexual revolution, growing secularism as well as the general questioning of traditional structures and authority in Western society. Hence at the General Synod in 1966, Archbishop McCann felt that 'denominationalism is outmoded. Sectarianism is no longer relevant. The major issues of evangelisation in a secular and largely non-Christian world completely eclipse the relatively minor subjects debated by our fore-fathers.'[67] He repeated this sentiment at the Armagh diocesan synod the following year but warned that 'any reunion of the Churches cannot come about for reasons of expediency. There must be honest agreement on fundamental principles'.[68]

Eighteen meetings were held between the Church of Ireland and the Methodist Church and fourteen between the Church of Ireland and the Presbyterian Church. These sets of conversations were deemed sufficiently fruitful, in April 1966, for the discussions to merge, something the House of Bishops had previously rejected in October 1964 and March 1966.[69] The first session of tripartite discussions took place in January 1968. A Declaration of Intent, issued on 20 March 1968, sought 'to discover how our churches may do together at all levels those things which conviction does not require us to do separately'.[70] It also welcomed approaches from other churches wishing to join the quest for unity. On a more practical level, a bill regarding the use of Church of Ireland buildings by non-Church of Ireland ministers was passed at the General Synod in 1966. Remarkably, the first instances of shared buildings between the Church of Ireland and the Methodist Church took place not in the Republic, as one might have expected, but in the diocese of Connor at Monkstown near Newtownabbey and at Glengormley, County Antrim in 1968.[71] The Moderator of the Presbyterian Church and the President of the Methodist Church were invited to address the General Synod on its opening day in May 1968. Similarly, the Presbyterian Church requested that the House of Bishops send two representatives to a meeting of the General Assembly in 1971. Eighteen months of tripartite discussion led to four Agreed Statements on the Divine Revelation and the Scriptures; the Church; the sacraments of Baptism and Holy Communion; the Creeds and later Historical Statements of Belief. However, the churches remained divided on the threefold order of bishop, presbyter and deacon, and on the appointment of lay members to pastoral office.[72] A major 215–page report, *Towards a United Church*, was produced in 1973. Nevertheless, the tripartite talks faded out under the shadow of traumatic events in Northern Ireland

and the ripple effect of the failure of the Anglican-Methodist scheme of union to obtain the necessary three-quarters majority at the Church of England Synod in 1972. By June 1974, the Presbyterian and Methodist view that federation had become the goal rather than merely a stage had in the mind of the House of Bishops 'sabotaged the talks'.[73]

Canterbury and Rome

Angelo Giuseppe Roncalli called an Ecumenical Council (in the traditional sense of the word as a gathering of the universal church), the first since 1870, on 25 January 1959, barely two and a half months after becoming Pope John XXIII.[74] He sought *aggiornamento*, that the Catholic Church be brought up to date and adapt itself to meet the challenging conditions of modern times, that the windows be opened to let in a draught of fresh air to an all too medieval and monarchical institution. This became the trademark of John XXIII's pontificate. But he also intended the Council to be 'an invitation to the separated communities to seek unity' and coined the phrase 'brothers in Christ' to refer to Christians not as yet in communion with the Catholic Church.[75] This phrase signalled a decisive change of Vatican mentality. As early as February 1959, an editorial in the *Irish Catholic* suggested that 'one of the ways in which the success of the Council will be judged will be the extent to which it furthers Christian unity'.[76] In June 1960, John XXIII established a Secretariat for the Promotion of Christian Unity under the presidency of Cardinal Augustin Bea SJ, who had been rector of the Pontifical Biblical Institute and confessor to Pius XII. The following year, five Catholic observers attended the third assembly of the WCC in New Delhi. To add firm conviction to his ecumenical sentiment, Pope John called on these churches to send observers to the Council. As President of the Lambeth Conference, Archbishop Ramsey was invited to appoint three observers in June 1962. He selected Frederick Grant of the Protestant Episcopal Church in the USA; Charles de Soysa, archdeacon of Columbo, from the Church of India, Pakistan, Burma and Ceylon; and John Moorman, Church of England bishop of Ripon. While they could not vote, the observers were able to comment on conciliar documents and Bea assured Ramsey that they had 'helped to create a better understanding and deeper esteem between brothers in Christ'.[77] At the end of the Council, Ramsey thanked Pope Paul VI for 'the constant kindness given to all the Anglican Observers who have been privileged to be present at the Council. Our Observers have frequently told me of the wonderful opportunities given to them for ecumenical discussion and friendly relationships.'[78]

John XXIII also extended the hand of friendship to Canterbury. On 22 November 1960 Geoffrey Fisher set out on a symbolic journey first to Jerusalem to meet Campbell MacInnes, the Anglican archbishop; then to Istanbul to meet Athenagoras I, the Ecumenical Patriarch of Constantinople; and, lastly, to the Vatican to meet the Pope.[79] On 2 December 1960 the first meeting of an archbishop of Canterbury and a pope since the Reformation took place. It seemed an unlikely encounter given Fisher's well-known Low Church credentials and robust opposition to Catholicism. Only four years previously, Con Cremin, Irish ambassador to the Holy See, had heard Fisher described by English clergy as 'violently and almost blindly anti-Catholic'.[80] In his last months of office before retirement, Fisher was conscious of history's shadow. In a letter to Queen Elizabeth, who herself had visited Pope John in 1959, he confided that if the visit came off, it would be 'not only important', but 'revolutionary'. That the visit could take place was attributed to Pope John and many in the Vatican who had shown a special interest in the Church of England 'but conspicuously *not* the Hierarchy here in England'. Moreover, Fisher informed the Queen that 'they want to be on friendly terms with us; and we have long desired to be on happier terms with them'.[81] He was willing to face down any protestors. The archbishop did not seek prior government approval. The British administration was greatly surprised when it learned of the planned visit and indeed Harold Macmillan, the Prime Minister, felt hurt that Fisher did not inform him.[82] Fisher's boldly conceived meeting with the Pope, though unofficial, was deeply symbolic. The very fact that it took place at all was no small achievement. In the words of Pope John, even though he and the archbishop had gone 'only as far as the threshold of great problems', crucially, as Peter Hebblethwaite notes, contact had been re-established.[83]

That the high walls separating Anglicans and Catholics were being lowered was not lost on the Church of Ireland. The final entry in Gregg's diary described it as possibly one of the greatest events in the history of Christendom.[84] The *Gazette* led with the editorial comment: 'A Door Opened'.[85] No mention of the historic encounter was made in the *Irish Catholic Directory* or in the minutes of the Episcopal Conference. The reaction of Catholic authorities in England was anything but enthusiastic. Hugh McCann, the Irish ambassador, reported from London that Cardinal Godfrey, Gerald O'Hara (the apostolic delegate) and Bishop Cashman, the auxiliary bishop of Westminster, felt nothing would come of Fisher's visit. Public utterances made by Fisher since his return were regarded as offensive to the Catholic Church in England. There was also a feeling among English Catholic authorities that Fisher was 'more politician than churchman'.[86] Further unease at perceived Anglican manoeuvrings and one-upmanship was detected by Con Cremin when he met Cardinal Godfrey and his secretary, Monsignor Derek Worlock, at a dinner in Áras an Uachtaráin, on 19 March 1961, to mark the Irish Patrician Year. Cremin was left with the general impression that both men were 'extremely apprehensive of the dangers of the apparent rapprochement between the Church of England and Rome being abused to the disadvantage of the Catholic Church in England'.[87]

There were further symbolic journeys which conditioned the international climate of ecumenism. Pope Paul VI led a pilgrimage to the Holy Land in January 1964, the first since Saint Peter left Jerusalem for Rome, to pray for Christian unity. He met Athenagoras, the first meeting between Pope and Patriarch since the schism of 1054. The following year they nullified the Catholic-Orthodox exchange of excommunication at the time of the schism. Not only did this maintain the momentum towards Christian unity, but as Peter Scarlett, British minister to the Holy See, observed, it modified 'in a slight but important manner the claims to primacy which the Bishop of Rome has so long asserted'.[88] Pope Paul's concern that Archbishop Ramsey visit Rome and that this should be of 'the greatest significance both on the official and on the private level' can be seen as part of the same impetus for greater understanding and friendship between denominations.[89] The Pope dispatched Bishop Jan Willebrands and Monsignor Jean-François Arrighi to Lambeth to work on the details of the visit. On the morning of 23 March 1966, Paul VI and Archbishop Ramsey met in the Sistine Chapel where they exchanged gifts. As Owen Chadwick notes, their formal addresses were realistic in speaking of a goal that was far off.[90] Some of the knottier issues such as recognition of Anglican orders, mixed marriages, the rebaptism of converts and the possibility of a joint commission on theology were raised privately that afternoon in a meeting in the papal library.[91] Although these topics were merely aired, during his visit Ramsey 'formed more than a respect, he formed an affection for Pope Paul . . . this was a new stage in the history of the Churches since the Reformation'.[92] The following morning they worshipped together in St Paul-without-the-walls, at which service a Common Declaration was read. Afterwards, they exchanged the kiss of peace and the Pope gave his episcopal ring to Ramsey (this the latter wore until his death in 1988).[93] Thanking the Pope on returning to London, Ramsey looked forward to 'the practical plans . . . for theological dialogue, and to the growth of acts of charity and co-operation in every country'.[94] Remarking on the Common Declaration, in Dublin the following year, Ramsey believed that the hope of eventual unity would help the churches 'treat one another not as enemies and rivals but as allies in Christendom in the war against materialism and secularism, and as brethren together in our response to Christ's call to a holiness which none of us has attained'.[95] Similarly, Bishop O'Doherty highlighted the tireless work of Pope Paul for ecumenism:

> His advice to examine what is common rather than to argue about what is different has given great support to those who feel the urgent need for better community relations. We must all realise that at the present time it is not one creed or another that is being called into question; it is the very concept of religion that is being attacked.[96]

The Second Vatican Council and Irish responses

That the Catholic Church in Ireland was not completely unprepared for the new thinking and renewal of the Second Vatican Council was due in no small measure to two pioneering journals and, more especially, to their editors: *The Furrow* under J. G. McGarry and *Doctrine and Life* under Austin Flannery.[97] Commenting on the establishment of *The Furrow*, in 1950, Cardinal D'Alton thought that it would 'provide a forum for the discussion of practical pastoral problems, and will contain informative articles on matters which fall within the Church's sphere of influence, and have a bearing on Catholic life'.[98] It far exceeded this. Both journals translated and communicated the ideas of European theologians and Catholic intellectual thought to Irish readers. They thus helped enlarge the vision of the Church and play a providential role in preparing for the Second Vatican Council.[99] *Doctrine and Life* published the texts of conciliar documents and with *The Furrow* helped transmit the teaching of the Council to Ireland. These journals were complemented by the Milltown Park public lectures, sponsored by the Society of Jesus, which in addition facilitated interdenominational contact. Inaugurated in 1960, these meetings attracted large audiences of up to 700 in their first decade. In 1968 Mercy Simms, wife of Archbishop Simms, was the first non-Roman Catholic to address the group at a meeting attended by President de Valera. Popular interest in, and knowledge of, religious affairs was bolstered by developments in the broadcast and print media. Particularly significant was the advent of a national television service and specialist religious affairs correspondents – the first being John Horgan in the *Irish Times* in 1965.

The Irish hierarchy dutifully followed the new ecumenical direction. In the lead up to the Council, their Lenten pastorals departed abruptly from the theme of moral warning which typified their pronouncements during the 1950s. Both the laity and the hierarchy had to prepare for what Bishop O'Doherty presciently described as 'one of those momentous events which may well change the face of the world'.[100] Despite a narrow conception of what the labours of the Council would entail, it is possible to detect a tone in the hierarchy's pastorals suggesting that the road to unity could be widened. This was stronger among some bishops than others. In his 1959 Lenten pastoral, Cardinal D'Alton dismissed any idea of a 'super church' because 'unity among bodies holding incompatible beliefs on essential points of faith is surely illusory'. His interpretation of the movement as it affected the Catholic Church was conservative and, while welcoming efforts at reunion, towed the traditional line of the one true church formula:

> the true Church of Christ has never lost this unity and never can. In all movements towards "re-union", therefore, there is no question of restoring a unity which has been lost, since Christ can not be divided, but rather of a return of separated brethren to the flock which has always been one.[101]

Yet, cautious and unprecedented references to reunion were in evidence. Daniel Mageean was less trenchant than D'Alton. In February 1961, in his last Lenten pastoral before his death, he warned that 'no quick and easy solution can be anticipated. The factors of misunderstanding, ignorance and prejudice, the growth of centuries, constitute a formidable obstacle.' But he continued 'at this historic moment in the history of the Church, we Christians are all called to play our part, for by Baptism we were made members of the Mystical Body. This unity of the Church is our concern: an injury to the body affects all the members of that body'.[102] Similarly, Bishop O'Doherty reflected:

> if we are separated from friends by a very long distance so that we cannot come to them in a day, we can, even in a day, make the distance a little bit less. The whole journey may take a long time, but as soon as we start out on the journey the way has been shortened by that amount.[103]

So great was the emphasis on unity that Bishop Farren, while hoping that misunderstandings would be removed and unity restored, felt it necessary to explain, in 1963, that the Council's work was greater than unity alone, that 'the sacred deposit of Christian doctrine should be guarded and taught more efficaciously'.[104]

The extent of the hierarchy's contribution to the Council can be gauged from their input to the preparatory commissions and, secondly, from their interest in and participation at the Council sessions. The Irish hierarchy were not unaware of what the agenda would contain. In May 1959, Pope John created an Ante-Preparatory Commission charged with consulting the bishops and archbishops of the world, the superiors of religious orders, and the theological faculties of Catholic universities regarding the matters to be considered at the Council. Preparatory commissions proper were established in June 1960. Cardinal D'Alton was a member of the Central Theological Commission which had the power of veto over its ten sub-commissions.[105] However, ill health, which plagued the last years of his incumbency, prevented him from attending several meetings. Other Irish prelates were members of the various preparatory sub-commissions. For instance, Philbin served on the Commission for the Discipline of Clergy and Christian People, and Archbishop Joseph Walsh of Tuam was a Consultor on the Commission on Sacred Liturgy.[106] These commissions received some thirty-five submissions from Ireland. As Fuller has observed, the general thrust of these was pre-conciliar in seeking clarification of the certainties of faith, rather than seeking innovation and change.[107] The Pope had very different ideas. However, before commenting on the hierarchy's attitude to the Council, it is appropriate to sketch an overview of the Council itself.

Cardinal D'Alton led the Irish delegation to Rome for the opening session which commenced on 11 October 1962, the date of his eightieth birthday. The architect of the Council, John XXIII, spoke for thirty-eight minutes after which the 2,600 assembled bishops continued for three years over four three-month sessions. By the Council's conclusion on 7 December 1965, four constitutions, nine decrees and three declarations had thoroughly scrutinised every aspect of church life and transformed the Catholic Church. While the fundamentals of faith remained immutable, their adaptation to, and presentation in, the modern world crucially did not. The first session ended on 8 December 1962. D'Alton did not live to see the second as he died on 1 February 1963. Neither did John XXIII, who died of stomach cancer at the age of eighty-one on 3 June 1963. His successor Cardinal Giovanni Battista Montini, the cardinal archbishop of Milan, took the name Paul VI on his enthronement on 30 June 1963. Described in Vatican circles as a dynamic progressive, Paul was politically more conservative that Pope John, but shared 'his predecessor's taste for imaginative departures from Papal tradition', and was deeply committed to Christian unity.[108] If John was the man to inaugurate the Council, then Paul was the pontiff to guide and conclude it. In parenthesis, Montini was the first Pope to have visited Ireland both officially, as Chief of the Vatican Secretariat of State when returning from a trip to the US in September 1951, and privately in a visit to Dublin in August 1961.[109]

The second session related to the church itself and opened, after a ten-month interval, on 29 September 1963 with an appeal by Paul VI for Christian unity. Turning to the sixty-two observers from other Christian churches, in their special place of honour near the papal throne, he begged God's forgiveness 'if we are in any way to blame for our prolonged separation'.[110] William Conway, to whom the episcopacy of Armagh had devolved just over two weeks earlier, headed the Irish delegation for the remainder of the Council. It was at the second session that some of the most famous decisions were taken. For example, the Constitution on the Liturgy (*Sacrosanctum concilium*) was promulgated on 4 December 1963, the last day of the session. Among other things, it replaced the Latin Mass with the vernacular. This was officially introduced in all Irish churches on 7 March 1965.[111]

The third session opened on 12 September 1964. On 21 November 1964, the Decree on Ecumenism (*Unitatis redintegratio*) and the Dogmatic Constitution on the Church (*Lumen gentium*) were promulgated. These were revolutionary. The Decree on Ecumenism stressed the unifying elements between Christians, while at the same time emphasised that truth could not be compromised. Traditional Catholic ecclesiology before the Council was exclusivist in that it identified the one true Church of Christ with the Catholic Church. As Duffy comments, the Decree on Ecumenism 'broke decisively with the attitude of supercilious rejection of the ecumenical movement which Pius XI had established in *Mortalium annos* [1928], and placed the search for unity among Christians at the centre of the Church's life'.[112] *Lumen gentium* recognised the presence of the Church of Christ outside the Catholic Church by stating that the former 'subsisted in' and not simply that it 'was' the Catholic Church.[113] This was a crucial nuance. It was held that the one true church exists, but is only imperfectly realised in each separate denomination. Therefore, each has something to contribute to and something to learn from dialogue with other Christians, thereby leading to mutual understanding.[114] The Second Vatican Council thus erected the dogmatic scaffolding to support ecumenical relations with other Christian churches. Three years of work were completed at the fourth session between 14 September and 7 December 1965. The Declaration on Religious Liberty (*Dignitatis humanae*) was promulgated on the last working day of this session. It is difficult to overemphasise how great an advance in principle this was. Since the reign of Constantine, it was held that error had no right, thus it seemed 'that religious freedom was something the Roman Catholic Church claimed for itself but refused to others'.[115] In contrast, the Declaration, which was largely drafted by the American theologian John Courtney Murray and supported by Cardinal Cushing of Boston on behalf of the American hierarchy, recognised the universality of religious freedom.[116] The magnitude of this change of stance was captured in a comment by the British legation to the Holy See: 'Even the most rabid anti-Catholics must surely regard this declaration as a step in the right direction, and might – one may perhaps hope – inspire a movement towards greater tolerance among the Protestant Churches.'[117]

Throughout the Council, the majority of the Irish hierarchy stayed cocooned in the Irish College in Rome. Bishop Browne insisted on this for ease of conferring, despite initial fears from some of his colleagues that the College would not be comfortable enough. In the event, the rector had running water installed in each room. Cardinal D'Alton and Bishop James MacNamee of Ardagh and Clonmacnoise were guests of the nursing order of 'the Blue Nuns'.[118] Eugene O'Callaghan left the first session due to ill health and did not return. Tommy Commins, Irish ambassador to the Holy See, reported to Hugh McCann, secretary of the Department of External Affairs, that no one in Rome, not even the Irish *periti* (experts) who were in daily contact with the Irish bishops, could tell whether as a collective group they had any policy on any particular question. This, he felt, was 'an extraordinary situation which reflects an oyster-like and thus far completely impenetrable attitude and one which is apparently uniquely characteristic of the Irish Hierarchy'. The ambassador continued: 'it has always been evident that their whole attitude to the Council itself has been the reverse of exuberant and the only thing which one can deduce with certainty from contact with them, is that their first reactions to any given problem within the Council will be supremely conservative'.[119]

The conservative, even reactionary, attitude of the Irish hierarchy is in part revealed by the topics, all too few, on which they spoke. The only exception seemed to have been Philbin's progressive contribution, on 13 October 1963, to the debate on the role of the laity. He stressed that the Council should be mindful of the fact that the laity had to live in the world of today.[120] He was also the only Irish bishop to speak on the Schema on Divine Revelation in October 1964. It was hardly surprising that during the debates on collegiality Archbishop McQuaid, in the first session, and Bishop Browne, in the second, weighed in against any attempt to limit the power and autonomy exercised by individual prelates within their own diocese.[121] However, it is impossible to infer that this was 'the line' of the Irish bishops as a body. McQuaid, speaking on his own behalf, also made a short and clinical intervention on the ecumenical schema on 19 November 1963, as did Cardinal Heenan on behalf of the bishops of England and Wales. It was McQuaid's second and last contribution to the Council debates. Commins provides a fascinating appraisal of the difference in approach and style, but not substance, of the Irish and English contributions. Both archbishops were at one 'in requiring from the separated brethren, as a condition of unity, unqualified adherence to every iota of Catholic doctrine as it exists'. From his encounters with Heenan, Commins was fully aware of how critical the archbishop of Westminster was of European bishops soft-pedalling 'the gravity of the doctrinal difference between Catholics and Protestants'. But unlike McQuaid, Heenan was deeply conscious of presiding in a country where the Catholic Church had an uphill struggle to gain acceptance. Consequently, he had, in Commins's view, 'acutely developed political antennae and a rare sensitiveness to atmosphere' which made him aware of the 'political necessity for him in his public utterances to avoid any appearance of waving the Roman sceptre'.[122] In this regard, he was successful. By contrast, McQuaid had little use for subtleties and appeared far more unbending, even though communicating essentially the same message. To Commins, McQuaid seemed 'temperamentally incapable of "padding" a statement in the interest of making its essential import more easily acceptable ... [which] naturally must tend to make the average person interpret his crisp style as reflecting an unrelenting and dogmatic attitude'.[123]

Before the beginning of the third session, Commins further considered the hierarchy's attitude to the Council. He found little evidence that 'the Hierarchy as a body, or indeed by and large as individuals, has moved from the rather supine and reserved approach to the Council and Council problems which has characterised their participation in the last two sessions'.[124] The minutes of the general episcopal meeting held in the Irish College in November 1964, at which the question of *communicatio in sacris* (worship in common) with people of other faiths was considered, corroborate the ambassador's view. The bishops concluded that 'special consideration should be given to the historical and social circumstances of the various countries and to the fact that what might be tolerated in one country might not be advisable in another'. As for Ireland, somewhat against the spirit of the Council, it was considered that the advisable degree of *communicatio* 'would be much less than that contemplated in some other countries'.[125] The Irish delegation followed rather than set the pace, with the French, German and American hierarchies in the vanguard of *aggiornamento*.[126]

The myopic general attitude of the Irish hierarchy to the Council was reflected in its paltry contribution to the inter-sessional commissions. These think-tanks had operated since March 1964 and formed the engine room of the Council where proposals and schemata were initially devised. Ireland was represented by Archbishop Conway who sat on the Commission for Priests, Archbishop Thomas Morris for Lay Apostolate, and Bishop Browne for Bishops. Irish *periti* on the Commissions included Father Kerrigan (guardian of St Isidore's) for Theology; Monsignor Dónal

Herlihy (rector of the Irish College Rome and future bishop of Ferns) for Training of Priests, Catholic Schools and Bishops; Dr Francis Cremin of Maynooth for Priests and Matrimony; and Monsignor Dominic Conway (spiritual director of the Irish College and future bishop of Elphin) for Missions.[127] Despite the central importance of the work of the commissions, Conway attended once, Morris twice and Browne not at all. Of the *periti*, Herlihy, Conway and Kerrigan were all resident in Rome and worked steadily. Cremin resided in Ireland, and Commins was given to understand that he was not permitted by the hierarchy to leave his duties in Maynooth, even though an international expert on canon law. This summed up for the ambassador the 'degree to which the Irish hierarchy as a whole seem to be outside the climate of the Council' possibly due to the centrality of the unappealing ecumenical concept.[128] Irish apathy was compounded by the fact that, unlike the French hierarchy, the Irish bishops refused to consult or draw on the expertise of the *periti*, who were not even allowed to attend episcopal meetings in the Irish College at which conciliar matters were discussed.[129] Commins could only conclude pessimistically that the Irish hierarchy did not appear abreast of modern thought in the Church, and only 'a very sanguine man indeed could entertain the expectation that for Ireland Vatican II will parallel Vatican I by turning up modern versions of Cullen, McHale [*sic*] or Moriarty!'[130]

A confidential letter from William Conway to the bishops in January 1965 bears out Commins's observations of the Irish hierarchy's conservatism. Though ostensibly concerned with informing the Holy See of the hierarchy's fear that teaching on contraception would be revised, the logic behind such apprehension is most revealing. The bishops were wary of change lest it endanger the faith and morals of the laity, or indeed undermine their *magisterium* or teaching authority. It was believed that uncertainty in the expression of the church's official teaching could lead 'many people to question not merely the traditional teaching on birth-control, but the very foundations of the Church's ordinary teaching authority and indeed, the very principle of the immutability of the Church's doctrine'.[131] Conway suggested that 'people may well say, "if the Church can change her doctrine on birth-control, she can change her doctrine on anything"'.[132] What if the Irish Catholic child of the earlier part of the twentieth century came of age by questioning many of the old certitudes including the authority of the hierarchy? Philbin's first Lenten pastoral after the Council warned against misreading the new aspects of conciliar decrees. These, he stressed, had altered 'relatively little':

> there appears to be a concept of a Church in which change and evolution are bigger factors than the preservation of what has been revealed once and for

all ... Let no one mislead us into thinking that the Church has been cut adrift from its moorings by the Vatican Council. It can never be so cut adrift.[133]

Similarly, McQuaid reassured a congregation in Dublin's Pro-Cathedral that 'no change will worry the tranquillity of your Christian lives'.[134] This reflected a distinct unease with the departure from the integralist view of the church as unchanging, but did such traditionalism retard the implementation of the conciliar decrees in Ireland?

Notwithstanding the issue of inter-church marriage described above, the hierarchy's attitude towards executing the decrees of the Council can most aptly be described as obedient without great enthusiasm. Vincent Twomey puts it more strongly: 'unthinking to the end, a provincial and submissive Church simply and obediently carried out the instructions coming from Rome that unintentionally but effectively dismantled their own deeply cherished version of Catholicism'.[135] It would be wrong to conclude that the attitude of the hierarchy remained completely unaltered, but the Council exposed a marked generation gap within it. While McQuaid and, to a lesser extent, Philbin were sceptical and belonged to the old school of integralist thinking, they were much the exception. By the mid-1960s, there was a much younger and more progressive cohort of bishops, chief among them Cardinal Conway. He combined a more positive, though cautious, attitude towards change with a more populist, energetic and less dogmatic style of leadership. As MacRéamoinn notes, Conway's fundamental conservatism was tempered by a sharp sense of reality, that the wind of change 'was no passing blast and that the Church in Ireland must bend to it'.[136] In January 1966 Pope Paul VI himself outlined the various discernible attitudes among Catholics towards ecumenism. These ranged from complete indifference, to naïve optimism, to suspicion and scepticism that ecumenism would disrespect the church's tradition.[137] While McQuaid fitted into the third category, this was, in the Pope's view, opposed to the spirit of the times. The Decree on Ecumenism underlined that there could be no ecumenism worthy of the name without a change of heart. The background to the formulation of the *Irish Directory on Ecumenism* illustrates McQuaid's waning influence within the Episcopal Conference.

It was resolved at the Council that the application of the Decree on Ecumenism would be explained by the Secretariat for Promoting Christian Unity in a detailed directory. This was produced in two parts: the first was approved by the Pope in 1967, the second three years later. The Vatican Directory was the template for national directories. Part I called for the setting up of commissions on ecumenism at both diocesan and Episcopal Conference level. The Irish hierarchy duly established an

Ecumenical Commission in 1965, with Archbishop Morris of Cashel as chairperson and Bishop Herlihy of Ferns as secretary. Following the Vatican lead, a statement was issued on 15 March 1966 indicating that Catholics could attend the baptism, marriage and funerals of non-Roman Catholics. Public representatives and civic officials could also be present at non-Roman Catholic services on official occasions.[138] McQuaid's lengthy observations on the Vatican Directory provide not only a barometer, if one were needed, of his distaste for ecumenism, but a revealing contrast with the tone and language of the eventual *Irish Directory on Ecumenism* prepared by Morris's commission. In his covering note to Herlihy, McQuaid quipped: 'Cardinal Bea is a very zealous man, but he is not the Archbishop of Dublin where the situation needs very delicate handling.'[139] He continued:

> Non-Catholics represent to us the people who deliberately strove for centuries to destroy the one true Faith, who till very recently occupied the dominant position in our economic and cultural life and who to-day stand for the English remnant that still holds a very great share of the sources of economic life, and is firmly masonic in outlook and activity. For these reasons, ecumenism is with us in Dublin a gravely delicate process, which requires careful preparation and very tactful execution. It cannot be hastened, no matter what a minimal group may urge.[140]

He feared joint prayer meetings would lead to indifferentism and saw little evidence in Dublin to suggest that non-Roman Catholics wished to draw nearer the Catholic faith. Unlike Ireland, there was a traditionalist counter-offensive in France against both the ideology and liturgy of the Council. This focused on the schismatic Archbishop Marcel Lefebvre, head of the Holy Ghost Order, who considered the Declaration on Religious Liberty 'a betrayal of the Syllabus of Errors (1864) of Pius IX and a mortal blow to the Catholic Church'.[141] McQuaid, himself a member of the Holy Ghost Order, would have known both Lefebvre and France, but for the archbishop of Dublin extreme distaste did not amount to disobedience.

A draft of the *Irish Directory on Ecumenism* was completed in the later part of 1968 and finalised in January 1969. This twenty-four-paragraph document acknowledged that there 'is in Ireland a new endeavour among Christians of different denominations to live in harmony and peace'. However, it underlined that Catholics and other Christians were divided on many issues, some of major doctrinal importance, and warned against 'unity at the expense of truth'.[142] Even so, the document was a significant advance and, in the light of McQuaid's comments, markedly more liberal than the archbishop of Dublin would have wished. The key provisions included an acknowledgement of the validity of Baptism conferred in Christian communions not of the Catholic Church as a bond linking all Christians. Secondly, a certain *communicatio in spiritualibus*, or prayer offered in common, was allowed. Thirdly, participation by Christians of other churches in Catholic liturgy was welcomed. While they were allowed to assist at Mass, they were not admitted to Communion 'since this requires belief in Christ's real presence in the Eucharist and is the sign that unity in faith and worship is already realised'.[143] The bishops concluded with the admission that although 'the road to unity is long and arduous', little by little 'the obstacles to perfect ecclesiastical communion' could be overcome.[144] The sharp divergence with McQuaid's earlier comments revealed a stranded archbishop, Ozymandias-like, the Irish bishop of bishops overtaken by the changing context of church life. What remains to be explored is how the Church of Ireland perceived the Second Vatican Council.

The Church of Ireland watched the Council with curiosity and hope. In Ireland, the papacy of John XXIII became the springboard for a new found ecumenical *élan*. In contrast to the austere sanctities of Pius XII's pontificate, Pope John showed a novel willingness to depart from old ways. His humanity, humour and personal warmth made him the first people's pope and swept away much of the suspicion of Rome. Indicative of this spirit was a resolution at the General Synod in 1962 which noted 'with much interest and prayerful anticipation the new approach to the relationship amongst Christians which appears to animate the minds of Pope John XXIII and his Consultants in preparation for the forthcoming Vatican Council'.[145] George Simms wrote the official Church of Ireland prayer for the Council and convinced Archbishop McCann that it should be carried in the *Gazette* on 24 August 1962, a point omitted in Whiteside's biography.[146] The death of Pope John after a pontificate of only five years, the shortest for two centuries, prompted an unprecedented outpouring of tributes from the Church of Ireland. Bishop Moore praised his courage, warm-heartedness and enterprise; Bishop Buchanan spoke of his 'simple goodness'.[147] Expressing more than a conventional expression of sympathy, the *Gazette* conveyed a genuine sense of loss:

> It is true to say that all Christians and millions who are outside the faith have drawn hope in the future from the life and death of a good and great man whom his own Church, even if she would, cannot keep to herself. From the earliest days of his papacy men recognised in him the characteristic of intense love for his fellowmen . . . A Pope who was eccentric enough to break bounds and pray in parish churches, relax with children in hospital and himself to go to the prisoners who were not allowed to come to him was bound to catch the imagination of the world.[148]

The Decree on Ecumenism was welcomed by the UCCC and this was conveyed to McQuaid and Conway.[149] On a more practical level, the Church of Ireland was directly involved in the Anglican-Roman Catholic Joint Preparatory Commission of which Bishop Henry McAdoo was a member. Established in November 1966, this grew out of Paul VI's meeting with Archbishop Ramsey. The Commission gathered at Gazadda in Italy in January 1967, Huntercombe in Buckinghamshire from 31 August to 4 September 1967, and Malta from 30 December to 3 January 1968. The outcome was the *Malta Report* which was largely based on papers submitted by McAdoo and Christopher Butler, auxiliary bishop of Westminster. Accepting that full organic unity lay in the future, the *Malta Report* anticipated, in the phrase of McAdoo and Butler, 'unity by stages'.[150] The report's main recommendation was to establish a permanent commission to examine historically divisive issues between the two churches. Thus came into being the Anglican-Roman Catholic International Commission (ARCIC I), co-chaired by McAdoo and Alan Clarke, the Catholic bishop of East Anglia. It met between 1969 and 1981, and published Agreed Statements in the form of discussion documents, rather than official declarations by the churches, on the Eucharist (Windsor 1971); on Ministry and Ordination (Canterbury 1973); and on Authority in the Church (Venice 1976). ARCIC delivered its *Final Report* for consideration in 1982. It was a great source of disappointment to McAdoo that this was coldly received by the General Synod with what Richard Clarke termed 'a grudging and graceless assent'.[151]

Ecumenism from the grassroots

The Second Vatican Council did not bring about any immediate change in institutional church relations in Ireland. Official contact came to fruition slowly in the decade after 1963 as a result of international factors and, in the Irish context, low-key ecumenical moves and the galvanising impact of the Troubles. The first inter-church body in Ireland to be recognised by the four main churches was the Churches' Industrial Council in Belfast. This grew out of a common concern at industrial conditions and mounting unemployment which cut across traditional lines of demarcation in terms of religion and social class. Throughout the 1950s, unemployment in Northern Ireland averaged 7.4 per cent (four times the national average) and in 1958 rose to ten per cent. This was exacerbated greatly in Belfast by the depressed state of the textile industry and a steep reduction in shipbuilding and repair. Between 1960 and 1964, employment in this sector fell by 11,500 or 40 per cent.[152] Coming as it did before the Second Vatican Council, the Churches' Industrial

Council was therefore a significant but historically neglected breakthrough.

In May 1957 a Church of Ireland Industry Committee was established. Six months later this became the Church of Ireland Diocesan Industrial Council – a joint effort by the dioceses of Down and Dromore and Connor, with a membership composed of the two bishops, clergy and those active in both management and trade unions.[153] Notably, together with a primary aim of promoting better understanding of industrial problems was the desire 'to promote cooperation in this field among the various branches of the Christian Church'.[154] To this end, an approach was made in 1958 to other Christian bodies with a view to an exchange of ideas and eventual joint action. Thus the Churches' Industrial Council came into being in February 1959, the representation being six members of the Presbyterian Church, six Church of Ireland and three Methodist. Two months later Gordon Hannon, chairperson of the Council and rector of Rostrevor, informed a meeting of the Council that he had met Bishop Mageean of Down and Connor who was willing to appoint Catholic representatives. Five Catholic nominees duly attended the October 1959 meeting.[155] The Council's aims were: to make employers and employees aware of their Christian responsibility; to undertake serious study of the problems of industry; to consider ways of helping young people entering industry; to take united action where possible and appropriate; and to encourage consultation between church members and others engaged in industry.[156] On 1 May 1961 the five patrons – Bishop Mageean, Frederick Mitchell (Church of Ireland bishop of Down and Dromore), Robert Elliott (Church of Ireland bishop of Connor); A. A. Fulton (Moderator of the Presbyterian Church) and R. W. McVeigh (President of the Methodist Church) – issued a statement which highlighted the need to break down barriers, for all classes and creeds to co-operate fully for the common good.[157] At the time, the Churches' Industrial Council was the only inter-church body with Catholic participation and marked the possibility of further common action. A similar council with an annually rotating chairmanship was formed in Derry in 1966, under the patronage of the leaders of the four main religious denominations in that city.[158]

Several ecumenical initiatives from the grassroots helped open the way for the first official inter-church meeting at Ballymascanlon in 1973. Hurley places particular significance on a UCCC conference at Greystones in Wicklow in 1963, at which he believes the first reference by the Irish Protestant churches to the desirability of a new relationship with Catholics was made.[159] Even before the Decree on Ecumenism, an ecumenical conference was held at Glenstal Abbey in June 1964. This novel development originated as a lay-clerical group of Dublin Catholics interested in religion and theology which became known as Flannery's Harriers after the noted Dominican Austin Flannery. With the help of Archbishop Simms they cultivated contacts with Church of Ireland clergy. It was left to Michael Hurley to invite Methodist and Presbyterians he had come to know. Thus, about forty people, drawn from the four main denominations, attended a two-day conference on liturgy. At the end of the first conference, Abbot Joseph Dowdall stressed that the meeting was a private gathering and not an official or representative one. 'The multilateral character of the conferences which beforehand may have seemed too bold for a beginning, too likely to be an obstacle to real dialogue proved rather to be a help and an enrichment.'[160] Though initially a departure 'into the unknown' Glenstal became an annual event.[161] In 1965 the custom developed whereby if a paper was read by a member of one denomination, then the discussants would be of a different denomination. Over the years Glenstal addressed a variety of theological issues. John Armstrong, who became Church of Ireland bishop of Cashel in 1968 and later Primate, regularly attended both before and after becoming a bishop. In 1969, Simms spoke on 'Prayer in the New Testament', and in 1971 Bishop Richard Hanson also gave a paper. The first Catholic bishop to attend was Cahal Daly, who chaired a session on Christian marriage in 1972. The residential character of the Glenstal conferences, as well as the topics discussed, played a crucial role in establishing trust and friendship across the denominational divide, where previously there was mutual ignorance.[162] It allowed participants to gain a fuller understanding of what they held in common and of their differences.

In 1966 a one-day conference was held at Greenhills Presentation Convent outside Drogheda. This was originally suggested by J. G. McGarry, who thought that such a location would be more amenable to participants from Northern Ireland. While Cardinal Conway approved of the conference, Archbishop McCann was initially reluctant to allow such an event in his diocese, but Simms prevailed on him. Gallagher and Worrall stress that 'had it not been for Glenstal in particular and to a lesser extent Greenhills, it is doubtful if the Ballymascanlon meetings would have come into being with so little opposition'.[163] In 1967 the General Synod's Church Unity Committee reported that while there had been no official talks with the Catholic Church, there had been many unofficial dialogues: 'It is one of the encouraging signs in our island that such dialogues can take place in a spirit of Christian goodwill.'[164]

There were countless other examples indicative of a sense of ecumenical *glasnost*. By the mid-1960s, Church of Ireland dignitaries were attending Catholic services and vice versa. At a civic reception on his first official visit to Ballycastle, County Antrim, in June 1964, Bishop Philbin regarded as 'heart warming' the presence of representatives of the Church of Ireland and the Presbyterian Church and further commented: 'even when differences remain we can recognise and respect them as being honestly and sincerely held'.[165] Kevin McNamara, at that time professor of Theology at Maynooth, addressed the Church of Ireland Clerical Society of Ireland on 15 November 1967.[166]

While McQuaid did not reciprocate Simms's level of interest in ecumenism, even such a doughty traditionalist was not unresponsive to the post-conciliar atmosphere. He presented Simms with copies of Council documents both before and after the infamous public meeting on ecumenism in the Mansion House. The archbishops had previously met socially and privately, but the Mansion House meeting on 18 January 1966, during Church Unity Week, was their first public meeting and was attended by the nuncio, President, Taoiseach, Lord Mayor and members of the diplomatic corps. It was not remembered for the lecture by Monsignor Arthur Ryan or the significance of a joint recitation of the Lord's Prayer, but for a symbolically empty chair on the dais beside McQuaid, while Simms sat in the second row of the audience. As Cooney reveals, this was by no means a calculated snub. The original plan was that both archbishops were to sit at either side of the President in the front row, but chaotic organisation allowed the reserved seats to be taken by the crowd.[167] It was an unfortunate outcome, for which McQuaid suffered opprobrium. He made known to Archbishop and Mrs Simms his sorrow for any embarrassment caused.[168]

The visit of Archbishop Ramsey for the centenary of St Bartholomew's, Dublin in June 1967 illustrates the degree to which the atmosphere had changed. In 1961 McQuaid refused to meet the archbishop of Canterbury.[169] But six years later, representatives of both the Church of Ireland and the Catholic Church greeted the archbishop at Dublin airport, which Ramsey regarded as a 'sign of growing brotherly relations'.[170] While McQuaid could not attend a lecture by Ramsey on Canterbury and Rome, he was only too happy to meet him at Archbishop's House in Drumcondra on 24 June, before Ramsey had lunch with President de Valera.[171] For photographs of the occasion, McQuaid insisted that Ramsey, as guest of honour, take his own large chair in the library.[172] Ramsey later praised McQuaid's 'delightful hospitality', mentioned how moving he found his visit to Maynooth and how touched he was that McQuaid had come to Dublin airport to wave him off.[173]

Opposition to ecumenism

Yet while outwardly these ecumenical developments were progressive, they were not welcomed in all quarters. Ecumenism was a chameleonic word capable of changing its colours depending on the user. Just as Pope Paul outlined a range of attitudes to ecumenism among Catholics, the same was true among Irish Protestants. Many were suspicious of even intra-Protestant *rapprochement*. Bishop Buchanan revealed his astonishment at continuous sniping at the WCC in his address to the Clogher diocesan synod in 1966. Citing the example of Macmillan and Wilson visiting Moscow and de Gaulle crossing the Rhine, he called for neighbourliness: 'Each man should decide in his own conscience whether he stands for co-operation or division, peace or violence, love or bitterness. Let us cease looking over our shoulders.'[174] Others were sceptical. One Church of Ireland correspondent to the *Irish Times*, in March 1965, warned against getting lost 'in a fog of geniality', and pressed for principle and prudence rather than 'pious piffle'. Similarly, Cecil Williams, rector of St Luke's in Dublin, wondered 'where and when does one draw a line of demarcation? . . . Roman doctrine has not yet altered one iota'.[175]

However, in Northern Ireland criticism of the so-called 'Romeward trend', of ecumenism being simply a euphemism for absorption by Rome, was far more deep-seated, rambunctious and organised than Williams' fears of denominational Esperanto. This was so before the outbreak of the Troubles. For instance, Samuel Long (rector of Dromora and Garvaghy, and Deputy Grand Chaplain) wrote in his contribution to *Orangeism. A New Historical Appreciation*: 'No single thing has contributed more to the unrest of the Province [Ulster], so religion conscious, than the pressures of an ecumenism which too often turns Romeward.'[176] Gallagher and Worrall similarly remarked that ' "Romanism" is a word to fan many a smouldering ember of Ulster Protestant suspicion into the strongly burning flame of "No Surrender" and no truck with the Roman Catholic Church.'[177] For those of Ian Paisley's ilk, ecumenism meant capitulation to Rome and provided a *raison d'être* for extreme forms of political and religious conservatism. In the *Revivalist*, the organ of the Free Presbyterian Church, the intra-Protestant meetings at Murlough House in the early 1960s were described by Paisley as 'the training school of the pro-Romanist 'protestant' ministers of Ulster'.[178] Terence O'Neill's public letter of condolence to Cardinal Conway on the death of Pope John XXIII and the Lord Mayor's decision to fly the flag on City Hall at half-mast in June 1963 infuriated Paisley who excoriated these 'Iscariots of Ulster'.[179] Unsurprisingly then, Archbishop Ramsey, an Anglo-Catholic, was deeply suspect in anti-ecumenical eyes. Indeed Paisley shot to prominence on the back of Ramsey's visit to Rome in 1966. He and four companions, who were on the same flight as the archbishop, caused a scene at the airport by opening waistcoats revealing slogans such as 'Archbishop Ramsey traitor to Protestant Britain'.[180] Precautions were taken by Scotland Yard, the RUC and the Gardaí to ensure that there was no repeat demonstration when Ramsey came to Dublin the following year. But when Ramsey visited Northern Ireland in May 1973, Free Presbyterians protested in Ballycastle. Paisley was a bitter and implacable opponent of all aspects of ecumenism. His incessant polemic was freighted with anti-Rome invective. He attacked Northern Ireland's church leaders for selling their Protestant heritage with characteristic Vesuvian rage and vitriol:

> This is not a time for a velvet tongue. It is a day of war and war to the death. The enemy we fear is the enemy within . . . If they want to go to Rome, then let them go, but they are not taking Ulster with them.[181]

Catholicism was as far removed from his brand of Christianity as heaven was from hell, and a deep well from which to extract political capital.

The religio-political symbiosis which Paisley's emergence represented placed the Church of Ireland in an invidious position, as 'no surrender' had complicating political as well as religious connotations. To Buchanan's credit, he was one of the few Church of Ireland bishops to publicly challenge Paisley's claim to represent Northern Protestants. In an open letter in October 1969, he warned the Free Presbyterian leader that he 'may unwittingly start a blaze which you cannot extinguish'.[182] This came too late perhaps to be effective and in the intervening years the House of Bishops was guilty of constantly looking over its shoulder. It is little known that this fearfulness was such that it nearly prevented Bishop McAdoo becoming a member of ARCIC, despite being regarded, as his obituary noted, as 'one of the most distinguished scholars of his generation'.[183] In June 1966 McAdoo accepted Ramsey's invitation to join the Anglican-Roman Catholic Preparatory Commission. But two weeks later he apologetically withdrew. Having confidentially consulted his fellow bishops, McAdoo informed Ramsey that 'in the light of the present deterioration in the situation in the North of Ireland . . . the presence of a bishop of the Church of Ireland on the Commission might be a serious embarrassment to the Church in the North'. 'In deference to the feelings expressed', and recognising 'the serious difficulties in the present Northern situation', the bishop underlined that he had 'no choice in the matter'.[184] Resolutions passed at Orange Order demonstrations in July 1966 vigorously attacked ecumenism. Bishop Elliott of Connor, a Grand Chaplain of the Grand Lodge, felt compelled to absent himself from the main gathering of the County Grand Lodge of Belfast at Finaghy. On foot of this, McCann informed Ramsey that 'relations have worsened owing to Paisley's campaign . . . we as Irish bishops are a target for Paisley, and two of our brethren – Connor and Down and Dromore – have suffered from Press attacks in the last fortnight because of their firm stand against the Paisley misrepresentation'.[185] The House of Bishops did not mind a priest serving on the Commission and suggested Thomas Salmon, vicar of St Anne's in Dublin and future dean of Christ Church Cathedral. Ramsey regretted the non-participation of McAdoo, but was chary of including priests on the Commission.[186]

A second letter from McCann on 20 July 1966 revealed even greater levels of anxiety. Ostensibly writing on the subject of *Ne Temere*, this letter in fact threw into sharp relief the depth and breadth of Northern hostility towards ecumenism. 'A distrust', McCann wrote, 'is now arising in quarters hitherto loyal. We must at all costs keep our laity with us. We are now being told that the leaders are far ahead of the led, and that the progress is too rapid.' Fearful of being isolated from his flock, or losing members to the gospel halls or indifferentism, he appealed to Ramsey for restraint in any pronouncements concerning Anglican-Roman Catholic *rapprochement* lest confidence in church leadership be damaged. A sense of panic and pressure to maintain the loyalty of laity was palpable:

> We here [Northern Ireland] must "walk delicately" in the immediate future, and do all in our power to keep the confidence of our people. I hope Your Grace will understand that I am trying to express the feelings of a large number of our community who are perturbed and upset by so much that has happened in recent months.[187]

The fear of being out-bred in Northern unionist circles lent a quasi-political dimension to opposing *Ne Temere*, in particular, and ecumenism in general. By 1968, the Derry and Raphoe diocesan committee on Christian Unity observed a growing 'militancy amongst those in our Country who are opposed to the Ecumenical Movement'.[188] In this light, as discussed in chapter one, it was scarcely surprising that the Church of Ireland bishops caved in during the 'Ripon affair' in February 1967. The third resolution put by the Orange Order in July 1967, 'resolutely oppose[d] any alliance or union of Churches which involves any sacrifice of Protestant truth or freedom of conscience'.[189] For his part, Ramsey understood that many in Northern Ireland could 'feel alarmed, often without a proper grasp of the facts'. But he was resolute in his desire both to meet those within the Catholic Church anxious 'for a brotherly relationship with mutual respect and co-operation', and to resist any 'aggressive tactics on the Roman Catholic side' should they occur.[190]

It was several months later, in March 1967, ironically in the aftermath of the damaging 'Ripon affair', before the House of Bishops seemed to have recovered their nerve. McCann informed Ramsey that the Irish bishops 'now feel that we must take a stronger line and we are happy that so many of our people are with us in this determination'.[191] The resolve of the House of Bishops had been strengthened by resolutions received from the Irish Church Association and the Kilmore Clerical Association.[192] It was requested that the invitation to McAdoo be renewed. As the Commission had already been in operation, it had to be enlarged by two members per delegation before a fresh invitation could be extended in April 1967. McCann requested that McAdoo's nomination not be made public until after the General Synod in May, thereby 'prevent[ing] a certain "difficult" section from raising a discussion which we would prefer not to take place'.[193] McAdoo's appointment was simply reported in the *Journal of the General Synod* in 1968.[194] The Church of Ireland was not the only Protestant church to grow cautious. In 1964 thirty-two members of the General Assembly of the Presbyterian Church recorded their opposition to continued membership of the WCC and in the following years some presbyteries passed resolutions calling for disaffiliation.[195] However, Gallagher and Worrall make the pertinent point that 'the fact that ecumenical activity of any kind exist[ed] in the province [was] far more remarkable than any failure to develop it fully'.[196] Yet, such trenchant opposition to ecumenism was hardly encouraging as the storm clouds burst over Northern Ireland.

The galvanising impact of the Troubles and new structures

It was sadly ironic that 1968, declared a Peace Year by Pope Paul VI, saw the onset of the Troubles in Northern Ireland. The eruption of unrest in October fundamentally altered the landscape of inter-church relations. It narrowed the scope for self-satisfied denominational bickering at a time when there was increasing polarisation between the communities at the secular level. The Troubles induced inter-church cooperation in three ways: meetings of church leaders and their representatives; intercessions for peace, which became a *zeitgeist*; and meetings of the Joint Group on Social Problems. All contributed to the meeting at Ballymascanlon in 1973.

A large obstacle to inter-church cooperation in the late 1960s was simply the lack of consultative structures. In 1966 the UCCC was reconstituted as the Irish Council of Churches (ICC) which was the official ecumenical body of eight member churches: the Church of Ireland, Congregational Union (who subsequently dropped out and were later replaced by the Lutheran Church), Methodist Church, Moravian Church, Non-Subscribing Presbyterian Church, Presbyterian Church, Religious Society of Friends and the Salvation Army.[197] From 1967 to 1969, Eric Gallagher, Superintendent of the Methodist Belfast Central Mission, served as chairperson and in 1968 Norman Taggart, Minister of Greenisland Methodist Church, was appointed organising secretary. Both were instrumental in building bridges with the Catholic Church. According to Hurley nothing 'of any significance for the cause of reconciliation in post-World War II and post-Vatican II Ireland [has happened] without the active encouragement if not the actual participation of Eric Gallagher'.[198] On 21 October 1968 the ICC called for consultation with the Catholic Church to explore how they might contribute to improving community relations. However, it was the attack on Civil Rights marchers at Burntollet Bridge in January 1969 that spurred the churches into urgent action. Gallagher wrote to Cardinal Conway, on behalf of the ICC, informing him that sixteen heads or representatives of Protestant churches had signed a letter to the government on 9 January which called for 'a judicial and public enquiry into all the events and decisions which surround the present controversy'.[199] Gallagher also put before the Cardinal a suggestion to establish 'some type of joint consultative body' to enable mutual understanding, 'for bridges to be built and to be kept open'.[200] Conway was 'deeply moved' and informed Gallagher of his 'appreciation of the genuine spirit of Christianity shown by the Protestant Churches in these difficult days'.[201] The Cardinal lost no time in consulting his brother bishops. On 23 January 1969 he informed Archbishop McCann that the idea was positively received and suggested a meeting of the heads of the churches to explore the matter in greater detail. This took place one week later at Ara Coeli.

The outcome was the appointment of a secret and informal *ad hoc* committee composed of representatives of the church leaders or principals. The committee would not issue any public statements but would serve as 'a clearing-house for views which could be communicated to the "principals"'.[202] Despite increasingly trying circumstances, the *ad hoc* committee became a significant means of keeping, in Cardinal Conway's words, 'the lines of communication open'.[203] The first meeting was held on Wednesday 23 April 1969. Father Denis Faul of St Patrick's Academy, Dungannon and Father Patrick Walsh, the Catholic dean of residence at Queen's University and future bishop of Down and Connor, represented the Cardinal, who carefully monitored the meetings and personally read all correspondence from his representatives. Conway also was in frequent contact with Eric Gallagher, whom he regarded as always 'very reasonable'.[204] Gallagher attended on behalf of the Methodist Church and acted as chairperson; Harold Allen represented the Presbyterian Church and Eric Elliott the Church of Ireland. The smaller Protestant churches were unable to attend the opening meeting. It was only in June 1969 that John Radcliffe attended on behalf of the Non-Subscribing Presbyterian Church. Both Faul and Walsh found him 'most agreeable and fair-minded, with a sense of history and a sensitivity which is very refreshing'.[205] Discussion at the opening meeting was 'friendly and frank'.[206] Eric Elliott vaguely outlined the fears and apprehensions of liberal Protestants of the possible denial of certain liberties if Catholics were in control of central or local government. There was also general agreement that there had been a hardening of attitudes among Protestants. This was largely in response to numerous attacks on public buildings and utilities during April 1969. Conway revealed to Walsh that he found it 'impossible to be convinced that our people are in any way responsible for these explosions and . . . infuriating that the Minister and the police should be almost "pinning" them on us against a background of circumstances which point very much the other way'.[207] In the event, the Scarman Tribunal disclosed that the attacks were perpetrated by the Ulster Volunteer Force, a loyalist paramilitary group, in an attempt to destabilise Terence O'Neill's government and end the reform programme.

Walsh's commentary on the third meeting is instructive. He thought that Eric Gallagher was 'prepared to do all he can to ensure that the grievances felt by the Catholic Community are fairly met'.[208] To this end, Gallagher called for an independent commission to redraw local government boundaries taking into account geographical, social and economic considerations. He also condemned the Special Powers Act as 'a terrible Act' and was opposed to the use of the B-Specials. By contrast, Eric Elliott brought up 'the bogey men of the IRA and conditions in the Republic' at every turn, to the extent that the chairperson had to remind him that their primary concern was with Northern Ireland! Subverting the perceived logic, Elliott suggested that a points system for the allocation of housing would favour large families and discriminate against smaller ones. He also alleged that there was discrimination in employment in Strabane and in the Republic. Unlike Gallagher, both he and Harold Allen also tended to absolve the police from any blame in recent disturbances.[209] Criticism of conditions in the Republic was for Elliott both a blind spot and an *idée fixe*, but was also demonstrative of similar misgivings among Northern Church of Ireland clergy. Elliott repeated these fears and insecurities with monotonous regularity and unwaning conviction not only at future meetings of the *ad hoc* committee, but also prominently in the reports of the Church of Ireland's influential Role of the Church Committee of which he was honorary secretary.

The *ad hoc* committee continued to meet regularly without really addressing the root causes of the situation in Northern Ireland. But such consultation was regarded by the Catholic representatives as 'most enlightening in regard to the thinking of the other members of the committee who would generally be considered as holding liberal views'.[210] The widespread rioting during the summer of 1969, and subsequent intervention by Westminster, added a dose of realism to the meetings. The report to Cardinal Conway of the meeting on 5 September stated that

> for the first time . . . members seemed prepared to admit that the real root cause of all the present troubles must be laid at the feet of the ruling Unionist Party. The Reverend John Radcliffe was the most outspoken about the present regime and all except the Reverend Harold Allen, who is a member of the Unionist Party, agreed that the statement of the Unionist Parliamentary Party on the Callaghan proposals and the performance of the Unionist Chief Whip were a disaster and that the publication of 'Ulster-the Facts' [a government pamphlet] was a disgrace for a party which is supposed to be governing.[211]

Faul and Walsh recommended that John Radcliffe be invited to any meeting of Church principals. Walsh's optimism at more productive meetings was reversed by the two subsequent gatherings which he described as 'disturbing and distressing'.[212] Eric Elliott, harking back to his favourite hobby-horse, believed

> the key to the North lies with the South and if our group is going to make any contribution to community relations in the North then we must certainly examine the denial of civil rights to Protestants in the South. Almost all the demands of the minority in the North were now being met and the back lash from the extremists is only explicable in terms of their genuine fears of what would happen if they were absorbed into an All-Ireland Republic.[213]

Though undoubtedly discouraging, the Cardinal reassured Walsh: 'I suppose we must continue to be patient; these meetings are useful at least in that they give us an idea as to what they are thinking. I realise it must be an awful bore for you and I am very grateful to you for attending.'[214] The meetings continued intermittently along somewhat predictable lines for another three years with Walsh admitting that they were 'almost just talking for the sake of talking'.[215] From its inception, the *ad hoc* group remained secret, although its existence was admitted, with the consent of the principals, in Eric Gallagher's submission to the Scarman Tribunal. Only at a meeting on 13 December 1971 was it deemed opportune to make the existence of the committee known publicly. Although the committee continued to meet until 12 January 1973, by 1972 it was superseded by the emergence of the Joint Group on Social Problems and more open contact between church leaders and bishops, to which we now turn.[216]

For Church of Ireland and Catholic bishops teacup ecumenism was all very well, but united action for peace was quite another matter. Particularly in those dioceses with their ecclesiastical seats in Derry and Belfast, the bonds soldered by shared horror of sectarian violence resulted in bishops working together. At a time of deep mistrust and tension in the Derry diocese, both bishops – Neil Farren and Charles Tyndall – led by example and worked together assiduously for community peace. In his presidential address to the diocesan synod in October 1968, Tyndall spoke of keeping 'an open door to dialogue at all levels – parochial and central – with the Roman Church'.[217] He and Farren arranged an all-night vigil for peace in the city's cathedrals on 15 November 1968, the night before a major march organised by the Derry Citizen Action Committee. In April 1969, with other church leaders they made a deeply symbolic peace tour of the Bogside and the Fountain Estate areas, where they were warmly received. Tyndall, who had been bishop of Derry and Raphoe for twelve years, was gravely ill at this time and retired in September 1969. On his death on 3 April 1971, Farren paid generous and sincere tribute to his counterpart's efforts to establish peace and harmony in Derry. Farren continued to work with Tyndall's successor, Cuthbert Peacocke, and in February 1973 they issued a joint statement attacking the 'futility' of the campaign of violence.[218] In Belfast private contact was similarly maintained between Bishops Arthur Butler and William Philbin.

In tandem with the *ad hoc* committee, the principals met together as secretly but not as regularly. It is striking to recall that it was only in 1968 at the official opening of the Armagh Planetarium that they met together for the very first time. Events in the latter part of that year forced church leaders to be far more resolute in seeking cooperation and appealing for reconciliation from all who abhorred violence. Archbishop Simms made this clear in his enthronement address on becoming Primate in October 1969: 'in the context of differing religious traditions there is much that can be done together without abandoning convictions or sacrificing principles'.[219] In the opening years of the Troubles, meetings of church leaders tended to be held in Armagh in either the residence of the Cardinal or the archbishop. Systematic minutes of these meeting were not kept, but memoranda prepared by the *ad hoc* committee and some major points of inter-church disagreement, such as mixed marriages, were discussed. Whether there was a full exchange of views is unknown. By May 1970, Conway was able to report to Father Walsh that he had met the other heads several times in recent months.

One of the most pressing issues facing church leaders was the need to refute the misrepresentation of the situation in Northern Ireland as a religious war between Catholics and Protestants. They were confronted with the frustrating problem that religious labels were applied to what were basically divided political aspirations or loyalties. This was exacerbated by the fact, as Bishop Hanson put it, that 'Ulster is cursed with strident pedlars of dishonest religion.'[220] In an interview on the BBC at the end of August 1969, Conway described the conflict as essentially political or communal, rather than in any sense doctrinal. Simms agreed with him and told Malcolm Muggeridge that church leaders were striving to remove the hyphen between the word 'religion' and 'political'.[221] That they, along with John Carson, the Presbyterian Moderator, were televised together on the BBC and again talking to Kenneth Harris on Ulster Television would have been inconceivable even six months before. Nonetheless, the international image of the churches continued to be sullied by assertions that Christians of different denominations in Northern Ireland could not live in peace with one another. In early May 1970 Conway proposed a joint statement to correct this. He drafted a statement emphasising that the true nature of the Troubles was misconceived. This was circulated to Simms, Carson and George Good, the President of the Methodist Church, for comments and suggestions. Conway's initiative was, he revealed to Patrick Walsh, enthusiastically received. Any fears he had that his draft might be watered down proved unfounded as only minor, mostly cosmetic, changes were made.[222] George Good realised 'how much easier it is to work on a statement that is already made rather than compile one from the beginning. I would like to express my own personal gratitude to you for doing the most difficult part of this work.'[223] The statement was finalised at a meeting at Ara Coeli on 27 May and issued three days later. The first joint statement by church leaders had

> no wish to deny that there are serious and deep divisions, which we deplore, in the Northern Ireland community but we wish to assert that these divisions are not primarily of a religious character. They arise from deep and complex causes – historical, political and social – but the religious differences between professing Christians are not a primary cause.[224]

The statement also underlined that the image of violence was created by a very small proportion of the people, but that the vast majority yearned for peace. Denying that the situation in Northern Ireland was a religious conflict became a constant theme, collectively and individually, for both sets of bishops in subsequent years. For instance, while admitting that the divisions in Northern Ireland at times coincided with denominational groupings, Bishop Philbin firmly reiterated in an address to the Irish Association in January 1974 that 'nobody in Ireland conceives of our dissensions as a power-struggle between different concepts of Christianity'.[225] Archbishop Ramsey also reaffirmed that the Troubles were not caused by religion, but by religion distorted by political and social prejudice.[226]

The joint statement of May 1970 was signed by the four principals in alphabetical order, lest it seem one church was being ranked above another. It set a precedent for further collaborative pronouncements. However, such statements were by necessity safe and non-controversial. Conway privately expressed the belief that, however valuable they were, statements from the Northern bishops carried more weight with the Catholic community.[227] This left church leaders open to criticism for not doing enough to promote harmony and counter bigotry. Richard Hanson, the former bishop of Clogher, launched a stinging attack on what he termed the captive churches in November 1973. He argued that all the major denominations in Northern Ireland had long ago surrendered their independence to the active or passive support of political ideologies in order to maintain the support of their people:

> the trouble with Northern Ireland is perhaps that religion has gone sour. Instead of being a point from which we can understand, interpret and even criticise . . . it is dragged helplessly at the wheels of political chariots. The churches are captive churches in a humiliating and disgracing position whether they recognise it or not.[228]

The consequence of this situation was, to his mind, a deep rift bisecting society in Northern Ireland where Christianity meant division. Catholics, he maintained, kept intact their separate Catholicism and Protestants preserved their existence against this, despite lip service to the contrary. Notably, Hanson was speaking from the safety of Cambridge. As outlined in chapter one, his experience in Clogher demonstrated the negative consequences of being so forthright in Ireland.

Church leaders faced the ongoing dilemma of appealing for moderation and peace, but at the same time being ever watchful for fear of moving too far ahead of their flocks and becoming isolated from their communities. The hostility with which the bishops had to contend can be judged from the verbal attack visited on Arthur Butler for attending the funeral of Hugh Mullan, the first Catholic priest to be killed during the Troubles in the rioting that followed the introduction of internment in August 1971. The select vestry of St Michael's parish, Belfast condemned Butler for conduct incompatible with the teaching of the Church of Ireland.[229] The daughter of Bishop Tyndall recalled that her parents received abusive telephone calls at the See House in Derry night after night from those angered by her father's ecumenical stance.[230]

It is therefore not surprising that, in the main, joint statements were concerned with condemnation of violence, expressions of sympathy with the bereaved and intercessions for peace. At the end of June 1970 church leaders were saddened at the renewed outbreak of violence and appealed to people of goodwill not to lose heart. On 18 February 1971 over 8,000 Protestants and Catholics went to the Ulster Hall to unite in prayer for peace.[231] The House of Bishops designated a special 'Hour of Prayer for Peace' on Sunday 19 September 1971 throughout the province of Armagh. To Cardinal Conway the situation was 'quite grave' and called for 'a striking demonstration of prayer'.[232] A similar interdenominational meeting was held in Newry the following month with prayers led by Bishop O'Doherty and Bishop Quin as well as the local heads of the Methodist and Presbyterian Churches.[233] A united act of intercession for peace by the main religious denominations in each local area was proposed for 1 October 1972, as an expression of the 'will of the silent majority', during a year which witnessed 467 deaths, the highest of the Troubles.[234] However, Conway privately revealed his disappointment that in Armagh both Presbyterian and Methodist ministers refused to attend; reports were similar from County Tyrone.[235] The tradition of joint appeals for peace at Christmas also developed. Simms typified the thinking of church leaders in this regard, by urging people to believe in prayer as a means of holding 'far away any thought of provocation. The contribution of each one of us to the restoration of order can be of great significance if we care enough for the calming and healing of community relationships wherever we find ourselves.'[236] Despite the great strain imposed on church leaders during the opening years of the Troubles, it is worth noting that this increased their mutual friendship and concern on a personal level.

The example given by church leaders was complemented by interdenominational initiatives at parish and diocesan level, of which there were numerous examples in the early years of the Troubles. For instance, PACE (Protestant and Catholic Encounter) was a non-political organisation, established in the autumn of 1968 and publicly inaugurated in March 1969, which aimed to promote harmony and goodwill between the religious and political communities in Northern Ireland. Desmond Mock, the honorary secretary, felt that one of its most important functions was to act as 'peace committee' if needed at times of high feeling. By 1973, PACE had a membership of 1,639 in a federation of thirty-seven local branches.[237] Both Catholic and Church of Ireland clergy worked side by side, together with lay members, on relief organisations such as 'Movement for Peace in Ireland', established on 30 November 1970.[238] Two youth camps for Protestants and Catholics were held in Castlerock, County Londonderry in 1970 and 1971, and a joint Catholic-Protestant conference was held at Benburb Abbey in May 1970. Clergy of all denominations were among the volunteers who helped clean up St Anthony's Catholic church in Willowfield, Belfast, after it had been sacked by loyalist rioters in February 1973. Bishop Quin opened a Church of Ireland fund which raised £600 towards the cost of repair.[239] Similarly, Catholics helped repair Spamount Congregational church in central Belfast after it had been vandalised in July 1973.[240] An approach by the Ministry of Community Relations, in 1970, to the four main church leaders resulted in the formation of the Central Churches Committee for Community Work in association with the Northern Ireland Council of Social Service. During the summer of 1973, the ICC and Cardinal Conway established an inter-church committee charged with the allocation of £9,000 donated by European Churches to help in practical reconciliation work.[241] Qualifying projects for grants included those aimed at improving interdenominational understanding, such as Corrymeela, which had been opened in October 1965 by Ray Davey; educational and research projects, including holidays for children and the aged; visits and exchanges between congregations.

The third strand of inter-church cooperation was the Joint Group on Social Problems. In March 1970 the ICC and the Irish Episcopal Conference decided to set up a group on specific common problems such as poverty and drug addiction. Conway and Simms formally announced the ICC/Roman Catholic Joint Group on 8 May 1970. Twenty-eight representatives, mostly from Northern Ireland, fifty per cent Catholic and fifty per cent Protestant, attended the first meeting on 8 September 1970 at the Windsor Hotel in Belfast. Norman Taggart and Father Gerard McConville, of St Mac Nissi's College, Garron Tower, County Antrim, were appointed joint secretaries. Eric Gallagher and Robert Murphy, parish priest of Newtownards, chaired alternate meetings. Between September 1970 and 9 January 1974, twelve meetings were held at various intervals mostly in Belfast and Dublin with occasional meetings in Dundalk and Derry.[242] The Group worked through specialist working parties of which three were initially appointed: Drug Abuse, The Use of Alcohol Among Young People, and Housing. These were composed of experts, drawn from North and South, who were not normally members of the Joint Group. In 1972, the Working Party on Drug Abuse published *Drug Abuse: A Report to the Churches in Ireland*, and in 1974 the Working Party on Alcohol produced *Young Drinkers*. In early 1972 Eric Gallagher and Norman Taggart pushed for a further working group to be established on violence.[243] This was formed in 1973. Chaired by Cahal Daly and Eric Gallagher, after fourteen plenary sessions it produced *Report on Violence* in 1976. For one Catholic bishop, this report was far better than anyone had any right to expect from a joint group, despite some of the conclusions being necessarily of the lowest common denominator variety. He was in no doubt that these had been reached with difficulty, 'because no one can easily side-step convictions, or, if you like, the prejudices in which they have been reared'.[244]

Father McConville routinely sent copies of the minutes to Cardinal Conway, who took an active interest in its work and, as for the *ad hoc* committee, regarded as 'very valuable' that 'it keeps Catholics and Protestants talking and working together'.[245] Taggart met the Cardinal on 23 February 1972 and suggested a joint working party on pastoral problems such as mixed marriages.[246] From this stemmed the decision at a general meeting of the Episcopal Conference in June 1972 to issue a formal invitation to the ICC for a joint meeting of representatives from the member churches with the Episcopal Conference 'on the entire range of ecumenical questions in Ireland'.[247] The decision to broaden the field of discussion was almost entirely that of Cardinal Conway.[248] This invitation to the Protestant churches was issued by Bishop John McCormack of Meath, secretary of the hierarchy, through the ICC on 17 July 1972.[249] Conway and McCormack were given responsibility for further arrangements, and only in October 1972 was the invitation made public. The House of Bishops warmly welcomed it at their September meeting and Archbishop Simms was mandated to accept and reply on his colleagues' behalf.[250] The full committee of the Irish Council of Churches considered this *demarche* at the beginning of November 1972. The outcome was the encounter at Ballymascanlon.

Ballymascanlon

Even before Ballymascanlon there were positive signs of *rapprochement* between the Church of Ireland and the Catholic Church at an official level. In March 1971, the hierarchy appointed Kevin McNamara as Catholic observer to the Irish Tripartite Conversations. On 5 November 1972 Archbishop Ryan became the first Catholic archbishop to attend a service in Christ Church Cathedral since the Reformation. The following year, the Standing Committee of the General Synod passed a resolution inviting Catholic representatives to the General Synod. These were small reminders of how far relations had progressed. The Irish School of Ecumenics also helped clear the way for Ballymascanlon with its emphasis on a multilateral approach to inter-church relations and joint study.

The first official meeting of all the member churches of the ICC and the Episcopal Conference took place at the Ballymascanlon Hotel, Dundalk on 26 September 1973. This was a red-letter day in the history of inter-church relations, for it was the first time that the Catholic Church in Ireland became involved in ecumenical dialogue at an official level. Cardinal Conway described the meeting as marking a 'most significant advance', Archbishop Simms as an altogether 'encouraging event'.[251] Ballymascanlon differed from previous ecumenical encounters not only because the hierarchy approved of it, but because delegates were 'mandated' by the Episcopal Conference.[252] Indeed the Catholic party consisted of the twenty-eight Catholic bishops, four Maynooth professors, two diocesan priests from Belfast, two members of religious communities and six lay people.[253] The thirteen members of the Church of Ireland delegation consisted of the two archbishops, four bishops, four clergy and three prominent lay people.[254] What Gallagher and Worrall describe as 'non-theological factors', the shared horror of communal strife, added urgency and momentum to Catholic-Protestant cooperation and forced the churches to come together. Also integral was, according to Cahal Daly, the fear that ecumenism could become identified exclusively with a number of specific practical problems, such as mixed marriage, and the fear that this would be both an oversimplification of such problems and of ecumenism in general.[255] Hence the emphasis placed on a wide-ranging discussion. The meeting was predictably opposed by Ian Paisley, who requested that a protest in writing be received. Having consulted with Archbishop Simms, Conway agreed. The Free Presbyterian leader was joined by about 120 members of his church; the protest passed off without incident. The response of the inter-church meeting to Paisley's letter of protest was a public statement which stated that his objection was based on 'a complete misunderstanding' of the nature and purpose of the meeting.[256] How, an editorial in the *Irish News* wearily asked, would Paisley et al. be convinced 'that when church leaders set out to promote the investigation of theology on an ecumenical basis, there are no plots involved; no takeovers by Rome; no attacks on the Reformed Church; no power ploys and, certainly, no Jesuitical tricks'.[257]

Conway and Simms chaired the meeting attended by eighty-three representatives. Bishop McCormack and Ralph Baxter prepared the format for the opening prayers. The agenda was deliberately broad, 'a tour of the horizon', with the intention of setting down a framework within which to begin discussion.[258] To this end four working parties were established, one for each of the pre-agreed sessions. Archbishop Dermot Ryan and Dean Salmon read introductory papers on the 'Church, Scripture and Authority'. Professor John Barkley of the Presbyterian

Church introduced the second working group on 'Baptism, Eucharist and Marriage' with Bishop Philbin replying. Eric Gallagher and Bishop Éamonn Casey addressed 'Social and Community Problems'. Lastly, Bishop Cahal Daly presented a paper on 'Christianity and Secularism' with Bishop McAdoo replying. Interim reports from the working parties were presented at the following inter-church meeting on 1 May 1974. The working party on Baptism, Eucharist and Marriage reported on the Eucharist in 1975 and on Baptism in 1977. Those on Christianity and Secularism, and Social and Community Problems submitted final reports in 1975. From the latter emerged a joint standing committee on Mixed Marriages, which produced a report in 1977 and is still in existence.[259]

The portrayal of the nature and objectives of the meeting by the media differed markedly from that of the actual participants. The churches viewed the gathering as ecumenical, with pastoral, scriptural and doctrinal facets. But in media eyes, Ballymascanlon was some sort of religious antidote to the political friction of the time. Editorials and columnists, such as T. P. O' Mahony of the *Irish Press* and John Cooney of the *Irish Times*, used the term 'summit', as did the Department of External Affairs' file on the meeting. By treating religious issues in political terms, this misnomer created unrealistic expectations in some quarters and great anxiety in others. Bishop Peacocke of Derry and Raphoe and Archbishop Simms pointedly had to reassure their respective diocesan synods that the meeting in Dundalk was not 'a sell out', but, as Peacocke pronounced, 'a way to express in truth and charity the positions held sincerely by the various Churches'.[260] However, the press did welcome the putting aside of denominational rivalry in the face of four years of bloodshed in Northern Ireland. An editorial in the *Belfast Telegraph* commented: 'today's conference at Dundalk is proof that churchmen accept that they have a partial responsibility for what has gone wrong and for charting the way forward'.[261] But in such a view lay the inherent danger of evaluating the progress of ecumenical dialogue in terms of the resolution of the Northern Ireland problem. Though having a bearing on one another, both were distinct. To measure one against the other did a great disservice to both.

Hurley's comment that 'Ballymascanlon 1973, however historic, was hardly dramatic – it produced no other agreement except to meet again' is certainly true.[262] But in the exchange of courtesies and shared prayers and readings at Ballymascanlon, there was something deeply symbolic. Official inter-church relations had to begin on the ground floor with, as Gallagher and Worrall wryly observed, 'the Irish ecumenical dilemma of negotiating with regard to the apparently non-negotiable'.[263] Although a small beginning, Ballymascanlon was, as Simms told the Armagh diocesan synod, 'an opportunity for a personal interchange of information about our beliefs, our convictions, our thoughts on the problems which concern us all and often cause suffering, strains and stresses'.[264] It laid the foundation for mutual trust. Moreover, that controversial subjects, such as mixed marriages, featured on the agenda and were charitably treated, began the process of defining a glossary of understanding. Before the Second Vatican Council listening to the theological convictions of Protestant denominations would have constituted the sin of indifferentism for Catholics. Ballymascanlon epitomised the advice of Cardinal Mercier: 'In order to unite you must love one another. In order to love you must know one another. In order to know you must meet one another.'[265] The hopefulness of ecumenical rhetoric was palpable, given the fortitude the participants would have to show in the trying years ahead. That it took place was, as Cardinal Conway noted in his opening address, the fundamental point.

If the state of inter-church relations during the Fethard-on-Sea boycott is juxtaposed with Ballymascanlon, the intervening years witnessed unquestionable development from a perspective where Catholic bishops regarded Protestants as heretics, to recognition of their ecclesial communities. To paraphrase what G. K. Chesterton said of Christianity, at the outset it was not that ecumenism had been tried and found wanting, rather it had been found difficult and left untried. The provenance of growing inter-church relations in Ireland was varied. The product of intra-Protestant ecumenism, the Second Vatican Council and local ecumenical outreach seemed to be a hot-house plant – flourishing inside the house, but with an uncertain future in the inhospitable Northern air made bitter by Paisley's biblical flow of condemnation. Gallagher and Worrall make the interesting assertion that had the political crisis occurred ten years before it did, the churches would have taken sides as they did in the Home Rule crisis.[266] By highlighting the dualism between political and religious partition, the Troubles re-orientated inter-church relations and forced church leaders to question whether they were prisoners of the cultural and political polarities of Irish life, and in part responsible for the anguish in Northern Ireland. Their answer was a somewhat hesitant but expiatory yes. Eric Gallagher captured the paradox of ecumenical success in an address to the Irish Association in March 1973:

> There are probably more inter-denominational bridges in existence at this time than at any other time in my memory. We are looking at the problem at a moment when the leaders of our Churches are probably – even certainly – having more contacts, and intimate contacts at that than ever before. And at the same time the rank and file never had less and they never wanted less.[267]

However, the establishment of the *ad hoc* committee, Joint Group and, crucially, the inter-church conference gave Irish inter-church *rapprochement* a necessary structural basis. This led to real, if limited, benefits in inter-communal relations in the North, as church leaders constructed a quiet reconciliation by unlocking the denominational impasses of the past with meaningful communication. They hoped that this would filter downwards because, as the Book of Proverbs warned, where the leaders have no vision, the people perish. Bound together by a web of shared concern and an aversion to sectarian conflict, the churches could only reject Brian Moore's pun that in the beginning was the word and the word was 'no'.

Notes

1 Cahal Daly and Stanley Worrall, *Ballymascanlon. An Irish Venture in Inter-church Dialogue* (Belfast and Dublin, 1978), p. 9.
2 UCDA, de Valera Papers, P150/2867, Letter MacRory to de Valera, 28 May 1937.
3 OFMLA, D'Alton Papers, Box 1, Holy See I, Folder: Holy Office, 'Instruction to Local Ordinaries about the *Ecumenical Movement*', 20 December 1949, p. 4.
4 *JGS 1950*, President's address, 9 May 1950, p. lxxxviii.
5 Eamon Duffy, *Saints and Sinners. A History of the Popes* (2nd edn, New Haven and London, 2001), p. 353.
6 *ICD 1951*, p. 765.
7 HB, vol. ii, meeting of 14 November 1950, p. 99.
8 RCBL, Simms Papers, MS 238/1/7, 'The Roman Catholic Dogma of the Assumption', 14 November 1950.
9 OFMLA, D'Alton Papers, Box 34, Miscellaneous B, Letter Gregg to D'Alton, 22 June 1946.
10 *Ibid.*, Copy letter D'Alton to Gregg, 17 February 1959.
11 *Ibid.*, Letter Gregg to D'Alton, 3 March 1959.
12 *Ibid.*, Letter George Seaver to D'Alton, 23 October 1961.
13 LPL, Ramsey Papers, vol. 106, fol. 145, 'Memorandum on points to be raised in Ramsey's private meeting with Pope Paul VI', n.d.
14 See Alasdair Heron, *Two Churches – One Love* (Dublin, 1977), p. 44; Raymond M. Lee, 'Intermarriage, conflict and social control in Ireland: the decree *Ne Temere*', *Economic and Social Review*, 17: 1 (1985), pp. 15–16.
15 J. A. F. Gregg, *The Ne Temere Decree* (Dublin, 1911), p. 22.
16 Heron, *Two Churches*, pp. 4–5; White, *Minority Report*, p. 6.
17 R. B. MacCarthy, *Ancient and Modern: A Short History of the Church of Ireland* (Dublin, 1995), p. 53.
18 *JGS 1951*, President's address, 8 May 1951, p. lxxxiv.

19 *Diocesan Synod of Dublin, Glendalough and Kildare 1954*, 'Report of the Diocesan Committee on Youth Activities 1953–54', p. 2; 'Report of the Diocesan Committee on Youth Activities 1961–62', p. 2.
20 See Gerard Hogan, 'A fresh look at Tilson's case', *Irish Jurist* 33 (1998), pp. 315–16; Bowen, *Protestants in a Catholic State*, p. 43.
21 Kennedy, *Cottage to Crèche*, p. 94.
22 At an inter-church service to mark the 200th anniversary of the 1798 Wexford Rising in June 1998, Bishop Brendan Comiskey publicly apologised for the events in Fethard-on-Sea. See *CoIG*, 19 June 1998, p. 2.
23 *CoIG*, 14 June 1957, p. 1.
24 *IP*, 1 July 1957.
25 *AC*, 6 July 1957.
26 UCDA, Fisher Papers, P164/22, *The Diocesan Magazine Ossory, Ferns and Leighlin*, 27: 26 (1957), p. 3; Butler, 'Boycott Village', in *Escape from the Anthill*, p. 139.
27 UCDA, Fisher Papers, P164/9, Letter Levame to Price, 13 August 1957; *IP*, 22 June 1957; NAI, DT S 16247, Letter W. W. Magee (honorary secretary diocesan council of Clogher) to de Valera, 24 June 1957.
28 OFMLA, D'Alton Papers, Box 33, Custody of Children, Folder: Fethard-on-Sea, Letter Eilín Barrington to D'Alton, 10 July 1957.
29 *Ibid.*, Non-Catholic Bodies, Folder: Persecution of Protestants in Columbia, Copy letter D'Alton to J. Lynham-Cairns (secretary Methodist Church in Ireland), 15 June 1956.
30 *Ibid.*, Custody of Children, Folder: Fethard-on-Sea, Copy letter D'Alton to Barrington, 15 July 1957.
31 RCBL, PC 52, Grant, *The Fethard Boycott*, p. 6.
32 DDA, McQuaid Papers, AB8/B/XV/b/04, Hierarchy Meetings 1958, Letter Staunton to McQuaid, 21 January 1958.
33 ('Of his own accord'), a type of papal rescript in which the pope personally decides on the provisions.
34 *CoIG*, 25 March 1966, p. 2; *Irish Catholic*, 24 March 1966.
35 HB, vol. ii, meeting of 13 June 1966, p. 395.
36 RCBL, Simms Papers, MS 238, 'Church of Ireland Pastoral Letter on Marriage 1966'.
37 HB, vol. iii, meeting of 17 June 1969, p. 116.
38 *JGS 1970*, President's address, 12 May 1970, p. xlviii.
39 OFMLA, Conway Papers, 18/8–1, Copy press release, 29 April 1970.
40 Heron, *Two Churches*, pp. 54–5.
41 *IT*, 28 October 1970.
42 *CoIG*, 9 August 1968, p. 2.
43 *IT*, 23 October 1969.
44 Cahal Daly, 'Interchurch marriages: The position of the Irish Episcopal Conference', *The Furrow*, 25: 1 (1974), p. 30.
45 Declan Deane, 'Mixed marriage: Irish and Swiss bishops' statements compared', *The Furrow*, 25: 10 (1974), pp. 544–8; Felix Trösch, 'Positions and

46 Eoin de Bhaldraithe, 'The ecumenical marriage', *The Furrow*, 32: 10 (1981), p. 644.
47 KDA, Quinn Papers, AQ\57, Minutes of General Meeting of Irish Hierarchy, 9–11 March 1970.
48 *Ibid.*, 12–14 October 1970.
49 John Fulton, 'Intermarriage and the Irish clergy: a sociological study', in *Beyond Tolerance*, p. 161.
50 DerDA, Farren Papers, Annual Statistics–General Statistical Questionnaire for the Year 1970.
51 White, *Minority Report*, p. 133; Joachim Lell, 'Position and trends in Germany', in *Beyond Tolerance*, p. 137.
52 For a detailed history of these developments see Ruth Rouse and Stephen Charles Neill (eds), *A History of the Ecumenical Movement 1517–1948* (London, 1954), chs 8, 9 and 11.
53 LPL, Fisher Papers, vol. 102, fols 285, 291, British Council of Churches Meeting, Belfast, 23 April 1952.
54 Michael Hurley, 'The preparatory years', in Ian Ellis and Michael Hurley, *The Irish Inter-Church Meeting. Background and Development* (Belfast, 1998), p. 7.
55 See Ellis, *Vision and Reality*, pp. 76–82; Megahey, *Irish Protestant Churches*, pp. 126–8.
56 Seaver, *Gregg*, p. 248.
57 RCBL, Simms Papers, MS 238/1/7, Letter Gregg to Simms, 1 December 1955.
58 HB, vol. ii, meeting of 17 November 1959, p. 197.
59 *Focus*, 1: 1 (1958), pp. 3–7.
60 Interview with Risteard Ó Glaisne, April 2002.
61 RCBL, Simms Papers, MS 238, Copy memorandum ('private and confidential') of meeting at Murlough House by T. C. Patterson, 29 September 1961.
62 HB, vol. ii, meeting of 23 April 1963, p. 271; Special meeting of 16 October 1963, p. 286; LPL, Ramsey Papers, vol. 40, fol. 293, Copy letter Henry Stanistreet to Faulkner Allison (bishop of Winchester and honorary secretary of Church of England House of Bishops), 27 November 1963.
63 *DRDS 1965*, 'Report of the Diocesan Committee on Christian Unity', p. 9.
64 *Report of the Dublin Diocesan Council and the Glendalough and Kildare Diocesan Councils to the Diocesan Synods 1960*, 'Report of Diocesan Committee on Christian Unity 1959–60', pp. 1–2.
65 *Londonderry Sentinel*, 3 November 1965.
66 *IR*, 29 September 1960.
67 *JGS 1966*, President's address, 10 May 1966, pp. xlvii-iii.
68 *JSA*, President's address, 10 October 1967, p. 12.
69 HB, vol. ii, meeting of 19 October 1964, p. 332; meeting of 7 March 1966, p. 384; meeting of 18 April 1966, p. 385.

70 *JGS 1968*, 'Church Unity Committee', Appendix 3, p. 154.
71 HB, vol. iii, meeting of 22 April 1968, p. 73; meeting of 14 October 1968, p. 89.
72 *JGS 1969*, 'Church Unity Committee', Appendix A, pp. 130–1.
73 HB, vol. iii, meeting of 18 June 1974, p. 293.
74 For background to announcement, see Peter Hebblethwaite, *John XXIII. Pope of the Council* (London, 1984), ch. 14.
75 *ICD 1960*, p. 660.
76 *Irish Catholic*, 5 February 1959.
77 LPL, Ramsey Papers, vol. 26, fol. 135, Letter Bea to Ramsey, 14 December 1962.
78 *Ibid.*, vol. 86, fol. 357, Copy letter Ramsey to Paul VI, 1 December 1965.
79 For background to these visits see Edward Carpenter, *Archbishop Fisher. His Life and Times* (Norwich, 1991), pp. 713–44.
80 NAI, DFA 313/31B, Copy letter Con Cremin (Holy See) to secretary DEA, 21 May 1956.
81 NAUK, PREM 11/4594, Extract from letter ('strictly confidential') Fisher to Queen Elizabeth, 18 October 1960. Fisher's emphasis.
82 NAUK, HO 304/11, Copy confidential minute by Prime Minister to Home Secretary, 3 September 1960.
83 *Irish Catholic*, 8 December 1960; Hebblethwaite, *John XXIII*, p. 383.
84 OFMLA, D'Alton Papers, Box 34, Miscellaneous B, Letter George Seaver to D'Alton, 23 October 1961 in which Seaver conveys final diary entry to Cardinal D'Alton.
85 *CoIG*, 9 December 1960, p. 1.
86 NAI, DFA 313/31F, Secret report Hugh McCann to secretary DEA, 29 December 1960.
87 NAI, DFA 313/31G, Confidential note by Cremin, 29 March 1961.
88 NAUK, FO 371/178051, Minute by W. B. L. Ledwidge, 6 February 1964.
89 NAUK, FO 380/194, Telegram ('restricted') Michael S. Williams (British legation to Holy See) to FO, 3 February 1966.
90 Owen Chadwick, *Michael Ramsey. A Life* (Oxford, 1990), p. 320.
91 Under Leo XIII's papal bull, *Apostolicae Curae* (1896), Anglican ordinations were regarded as invalid.
92 Chadwick, *Ramsey*, pp. 321–2.
93 Michael De-la-Noy, *Michael Ramsey. A Portrait* (London, 1990), p. 152.
94 LPL, Ramsey Papers, vol. 106, fol. 174, Copy letter Ramsey to Paul VI, 4 April 1966.
95 RCBL, Simms Papers, MS 238, *Rome and Canterbury* (London, 1967), p. 12 [public lecture by Ramsey delivered at RDS, Dublin on 23 June 1967].
96 DroDA, O'Doherty Papers, Box 18, Lenten pastoral, 19 February 1968, p. 7.
97 Conveyed in an interview with Seán MacRéamoinn, October 2003.
98 OFMLA, D'Alton Papers, Box 33, Publications, '*The Furrow* and its programme', November 1949.

99 For background to establishment of *The Furrow* and the influence of McGarry, see Fuller, *Irish Catholicism*, pp. 82–8 and Enda McDonagh, *Between Chaos and New Creation: Doing Theology at the Fringe* (Dublin, 1986), pp. 174–82.
100 DroDA, O'Doherty Papers, Box 18, Lenten pastoral, 26 February 1962, p. 4.
101 OFMLA, D'Alton Papers, Box 18, Lenten pastoral: 'The unity of the Church', 27 January 1959, pp. 17–19.
102 DCDA, Mageean Papers, Lenten pastoral, 'That they all may be one', 18 January 1961, p. 13 (read on 26 February 1961).
103 DroDA, O'Doherty Papers, Box 18, Lenten pastoral, 26 February 1962, p. 8.
104 DerDA, Farren Papers, Pastorals/Sermons, Lenten pastoral, 17 February 1963, p. 3.
105 OFMLA, D'Alton Papers, Box 2, Holy See II, Ante-Preparatory Commission, Letter Pericles Felici (general secretary Central Preparatory Commission) to D'Alton, 24 June 1960.
106 NAI, DFA P330, List of Irish ecclesiastics and clergy on preparatory commissions for Ecumenical Council, n.d.
107 Fuller, *Irish Catholicism*, pp. 105–6.
108 NAUK, FO 371/178051, Minute by W. B. L. Ledwidge, 6 February 1964.
109 *ICD 1964*, p. 732.
110 Peter Hebblethwaite, *Paul VI. The First Modern Pope* (London, 1993), p. 350.
111 *ICD 1966*, p. 719. For an in-depth treatment of changes in the liturgy as applied in Ireland, see Fuller, *Irish Catholicism*, pp. 109–23.
112 Duffy, *Saints and Sinners*, p. 362.
113 *Ibid.*, p. 361.
114 See Victor Griffin, *Anglican and Irish: What We Believe* (Dublin, 1976), p. 47.
115 Hurley, *Christian Unity*, p. 214.
116 See O'Connor, *Boston Catholics*, p. 264.
117 NAUK, FO 371/183259, Minute on Vatican Council Declaration on Religious Freedom, 18 December 1965.
118 OFMLA, D'Alton Papers, Box 4, Hierarchy I, Folder: Correspondence – Secretaries Irish Hierarchy 1946–63, Letter Bishop Fergus to D'Alton, 13 March 1962; Cahal Daly, *Steps on my Pilgrim Journey* (Dublin, 1998), p. 118.
119 NAI, DFA P330, Letter ('secret) Commins to McCann, 18 November 1963.
120 *ICD 1964*, p. 770.
121 NAI, DFA P330, Copy letter ('secret') Commins to McCann, 23 Nov 1963; Xavier Rynne, *The Second Session: The Debates and Decrees of Vatican Council II, September 29 to December 4, 1963* (London, 1964), pp. 98, 208.
122 NAI, DFA P330, Copy letter ('secret') Commins to McCann, 23 November 1963.

123 *Ibid.*
124 NAI, DFA P353/1, Secret report Commins to secretary DEA, 29 July 1964.
125 DDA, McQuaid Papers, AB8/B/XV/b/05, Minutes of Extraordinary General Meeting, 10 and 18 November 1964.
126 On the contribution of the French hierarchy see Pierre Pierrard, *Un Siècle de L'église de France, 1900–2000* (Paris, 2000), p. 175.
127 NAI, DFA P353/1, Secret report Commins to secretary DEA, 29 July 1964.
128 *Ibid.*
129 NAI, DFA P330, Letter ('secret') Commins to McCann, 18 November 1963; Pierrard, *Un Siècle*, p. 175.
130 NAI, DFA P353/1, Secret report Commins to secretary DEA, 29 July 1964. The ambassador alluded to the prominent role played by Cardinal Paul Cullen (archbishop of Dublin, 1852–78), John MacHale (archbishop of Tuam 1834–1881) and David Moriarty (bishop of Kerry 1856–1877) at the First Vatican Council in 1869. Cullen presented the basic formulation of papal infallibility which was eventually accepted by the council fathers and promulgated by Pope Pius IX in 1870. MacHale and Moriarty were among the minority which argued against the definition. Though Moriarty regarded it as inopportune, he accepted papal infallibility when it was defined.
131 DerDA, Farren Papers, 'Letters to/from Bishops', Copy confidential letter Conway to bishops, 23 January 1965.
132 *Ibid.*
133 DCDA, Philbin Papers, Lenten pastoral, 14 February 1966, pp. 8–10.
134 Cooney, *McQuaid*, p. 371.
135 D. Vincent Twomey, *The End of Irish Catholicism?* (Dublin, 2003), p. 35.
136 Seán MacRéamoinn, 'Renewal or revision?', in Alan Falconer, Enda McDonagh and Seán MacReamoinn (eds), *Freedom to Hope? The Catholic Church in Ireland Twenty Years after Vatican II* (Dublin, 1985), p. 9; interview with MacRéamoinn, October 2003.
137 Cahal Daly, 'Ecumenism in Ireland now: problems and hopes', *The Irish Theological Quarterly*, 45: 1 (1978), p. 10.
138 DDA, McQuaid Papers, AB8/B/XV/b/06, Hierarchy Meetings 1966(1), Letter Bishop Herlihy to McQuaid, 21 March 1966, enclosing minutes of meeting of the Commission on Ecumenism, 15 March 1966.
139 *Ibid.*, Letter McQuaid to Herlihy, 26 April 1966.
140 *Ibid.*, Comments by the archbishop of Dublin on the *Directorium de re oecumenica*, 21 April 1966.
141 Pierrard, *Un Siècle*, p. 197.
142 *Irish Directory on Ecumenism* (Dublin, 1969), para.3, p. 3; para. 5, p. 4.
143 *Ibid.*, para. 20, p. 11.
144 *Ibid.*, para. 24, p. 12.
145 *JGS 1962*, p. cxvi.
146 RCBL, Simms Papers, MS 238/1/15, Letter McCann to Simms, 1 August 1962; Hurley, *Christian Unity*, p. 92.

147 *AC*, 6 July 1963; *IR*, 20 June 1963.
148 *CoIG*, 7 June 1963, p. 1.
149 *JGS 1965*, 'Church Unity Committee', report of UCCC, pp. 187–8.
150 Alan C. Clarke and Colin Davey (eds), *Anglican/Roman Catholic Dialogue. The Work of the Preparatory Commission* (London, 1974), pp. 84–115.
151 Quoted in Hurley, 'In memoriam Henry Robert McAdoo', *Doctrine and Life*, 49: 6 (1999), p. 351. See also obituary comment by Professor Henry Chadwick, *Church Times*, 24 December 1998.
152 See Bew *et al.*, *Northern Ireland*, pp. 117, 127.
153 Letter Robin Gibson (former honorary secretary Church Industry Committee and honorary treasurer of Churches' Industrial Council) to author, 20 May 2003; 8 June 2003.
154 Robin Gibson collection, 'Church of Ireland Dioceses of Down and Dromore and of Connor Industrial Council Principles and Aims'.
155 Letter Gibson to author, 8 June 2003. Numbers of representatives were later increased as follows: Catholic (6), Church of Ireland (6), Presbyterian Church (6), Methodist (4), Quaker (1), nominees of UCCC (2).
156 'The Churches Industrial Council (Northern Ireland)', *Christus Rex*, 19: 3 (1965), p. 226.
157 *ICD 1962*, p. 692.
158 *DRDS 1966*, 'Report of the Committee on Christian Unity', p. 15; *ICD 1967*, p. 758.
159 Interview with Michael Hurley, April 2002.
160 Michael Hurley, *Church and Eucharist* (Dublin, 1966), p. 12.
161 Joan Turner, *Glenstal Abbey Ecumenical Conferences 1964–1983* (Belfast, 1983), p. 3.
162 Interview with Cardinal Cahal Daly, February 2004.
163 Eric Gallagher and Stanley Worrall, *Christians in Ulster 1968–1980* (Oxford, 1982), p. 30.
164 *JGS 1967*, 'Church Unity Committee', p. 129.
165 *ICD 1965*, p. 733.
166 RCBL, Clerical Society of Ireland, MS 142/3, Minute Book 1938–71, entry for 1967.
167 See Cooney, *McQuaid*, pp. 373–5.
168 Mercy Simms Papers, Letter McQuaid to Mercy Simms, 15 April 1966.
169 Deirdre McMahon, 'John Charles McQuaid, archbishop of Dublin, 1940–72', in James Kelly and Dáire Keogh (eds), *History of the Catholic Diocese of Dublin* (Dublin, 2000), p. 374.
170 *IT*, 24 June 1967.
171 RCBL, Simms Papers, MS 238/1/18, Letter McQuaid to Simms, 3 May 1967.
172 *Sunday Independent*, 25 June 1967.
173 LPL, Ramsey Papers, vol. 116, fol. 172, Copy letter Ramsey to McQuaid, 27 June 1967.

174 *IR*, 29 September 1966.
175 *IT*, 30 March 1965; *CoIG*, 27 August 1965, p. 4.
176 Dewar *et al*, *Orangeism*, p. 190.
177 Gallagher and Worrall, *Christians*, p. 23.
178 Robin Gibson Collection, *The Revivalist*, November 1959.
179 Terence O'Neill, *The Autobiography of Terence O'Neill* (London, 1972), p. 50; Dennis Cooke, *Persecuting Zeal. A Portrait of Ian Paisley* (Dingle, 1996), p. 141.
180 NAUK, FO 380/194, Copy confidential report Michael S. Williams to Michael Stewart (Secretary of State for Foreign Affairs), 29 March 1966; *The Times*, 23 March 1966.
181 Quoted in John D. Brewer and Gareth I. Higgins, *Anti-Catholicism in Northern Ireland, 1660–1998. The Mote and the Beam* (Basingstoke 1998), p. 106.
182 *IP*, 10 October 1969.
183 *The Times*, 15 December 1998.
184 LPL, Ramsey Papers, vol. 107, fols 138–40, Letter McAdoo to Ramsey, 18 July 1966.
185 *Ibid.*, fols 142–3, Letter McCann to Ramsey, 19 July 1966.
186 *Ibid.*, fol. 146, Copy letter Ramsey to McCann, 21 July 1966.
187 *Ibid.*, fols 88–9, Letter McCann to Ramsey, 20 July 1966.
188 *DRDS 1968*, 'Report of the Diocesan Committee on Christian Unity', p. 16.
189 *BNL*, 23 June 1967.
190 LPL, Ramsey Papers, vol. 107, fol. 90, Copy letter Ramsey to McCann, 25 July 1966.
191 *Ibid.*, vol. 120, fol. 325, Copy letter ('private') McCann to Ramsey, 15 March 1967.
192 HB, vol. iii, meeting of 14 March 1967, p. 27; RCBL, Kilmore Clerical Association, MS 403, 'Minutes 1963–77', 28 February 1967.
193 LPL, Ramsey Papers, vol. 120, fol. 332, Copy confidential letter Ramsey to McCann, 17 April 1967; fol. 334, Confidential letter McCann to Ramsey, 27 April 1967.
194 *JGS 1968*, 'Report of Proceedings of Standing Committee of the General Synod', p. 60.
195 Gallagher, 'Northern Ireland – The record of the churches', p. 170; the Ruling Elders Fellowship Presbytery of Tyrone called for disaffiliation in 1971, *BNL*, 2 September 1971.
196 Gallagher and Worrall, *Christians*, p. 23
197 See Taggart, *Conflict*, p. 19; see also John M. Barkley, *The Irish Council of Churches 1923–1983* (Belfast, 1983).
198 Hurley, 'The preparatory years', p. 28.
199 PRONI, CAB/4/1427/11, Copy letter Eric Gallagher to Terence O'Neill, 9 January 1969.
200 OFMLA, Conway Papers, 15/8–9, Letter Gallagher to Conway, 8 January 1969. For background to ICC decision see Taggart, *Conflict*, pp. 27–32.

201 OFMLA, Conway Papers, 15/8-9, Copy letter Conway to Gallagher, 10 January 1969.
202 *Ibid.*, Copy letter Conway to Walsh, 21 March 1969.
203 *Ibid.*, Copy letter Conway to Patrick Walsh, 20 August 1971.
204 *Ibid.*, Letter Conway to Walsh, 25 June 1969.
205 *Ibid.*, Letter Walsh to Conway, 9 September 1969.
206 *Ibid.*, Letter Walsh to Conway, 24 April 1969, enclosing minutes of first meeting.
207 *Ibid.*, Copy letter Conway to Walsh, 26 April 1969.
208 *Ibid.*, Letter Walsh to Conway, 26 May 1969 enclosing minutes of third meeting.
209 *Ibid.*
210 OFMLA, Conway Papers, 15/8-9, Letter Walsh to Conway, 10 July 1969.
211 *Ibid.*, Letter Walsh to Conway, 9 September 1969.
212 *Ibid.*, Letter Walsh to Conway, 17 September 1969.
213 *Ibid.*, Letter Walsh to Conway, 2 October 1969 enclosing minutes of eleventh meeting on 25 September 1969.
214 *Ibid.*, Copy letter Conway to Walsh, 18 September 1969.
215 *Ibid.*, Letter Walsh to Conway, 20 August 1971.
216 See Taggart, *Conflict*, p. 114.
217 *Londonderry Sentinel*, 6 November 1968.
218 *BNL*, 27 February 1973.
219 *IR*, 2 October 1969.
220 *CoIG*, 26 March 1971, p. 1.
221 *II*, 1 September 1969.
222 OFMLA, Conway Papers, 15/8-9, Copy letter Conway to Walsh, 25 May 1970; RCBL, Simms Papers, MS 238, Draft of statement received on 4 May 1970 with amendments by Simms.
223 OFMLA, Conway Papers, 15/8-2, Letter Good to Conway, 15 May 1970.
224 *Ibid.*, 18/8-1, Copy joint statement by church heads, 30 May 1970.
225 Philbin, *Ireland's Problem*, p. 3.
226 *BT*, 1 May 1971.
227 OFMLA, Conway Papers, 15/8-9, Letter Walsh to Conway, 22 May 1970; copy letter Conway to Walsh, 25 May 1970.
228 RCBL, Simms papers, MS 238, 'Reflections of Reality. Northern Ireland – The Captive Churches' preached at Great St Mary's, Cambridge, 25 November 1973.
229 *BT*, 25 August 1971.
230 Norah Good, 'Charles Tyndall 1900–1971: "The peace bishop',", *Search*, 20: 1 (1997), pp. 52–3.
231 *BNL*, 19 February 1971.
232 DDA, McQuaid Papers, AB8/B/XV/b/09, Hierarchy Standing Committee Minutes 1971, Letter Conway to members of the Episcopal Conference, 10 September 1971.
233 *BT*, 1 November 1971.

234 OFMLA, Conway Papers, 16/2, Copy letter Conway to Philbin, 1 September 1972; Bew and Gillespie, *Chronology*, p. 57.
235 OFMLA, Conway Papers, 15/8–9, Copy letter Conway to Walsh, 26 September 1972.
236 RCBL, Simms papers, MS 238, draft statement, n.d.
237 PRONI, PACE Papers, D/4098/4/1, Circular Mock to Group Secretaries, 14 June 1972; D/4098/1/1, Minutes of meeting held on 18 Dec 1973; D/4098/1/1, Minutes of meeting of management committee, 26 September 1973.
238 NAI, DFA 2002/19/396, Copy constitution of Movement for Peace in Ireland; *IN*, 1 December 1970.
239 *BNL*, 10 February 1973; *BT*, 5 June 1973.
240 *IT*, 3 July 1973.
241 OFMLA, Conway Papers, 15/8–3, Letter Ralph Baxter to Conway, 25 June 1973; *BT*, 28 August 1973.
242 OFMLA, Conway Papers, 15/8–8, First Report of the Joint Group, March 1972.
243 *Ibid.*, Letter McConville to Conway, 2 March 1972.
244 Private information.
245 OFMLA, Conway Papers, 15/8–8, Copy letter Conway to McConville, 21 December 1971.
246 See Taggart, *Conflict*, pp. 109–11.
247 KDA Quinn Papers, AQ\59, Minutes of General Meeting of Irish Hierarchy, 19–22 June 1972.
248 Confirmed in conversation with Cardinal Cahal Daly, February 2004.
249 HB, vol. iii, meeting of 18 September 1972, p. 248; copy letter Bishop McCormack to secretary of ICC, 17 July 1972.
250 HB, vol. iii, meeting of 18 September 1972, p. 248.
251 *IP*, 27 September 1973; OFMLA, Conway Papers, 15/8–4/1, Letter Simms to Conway, 12 October 1973.
252 Confirmed in conversation with Cardinal Cahal Daly, February 2004.
253 KDA, Quinn Papers, AQ\60, Minutes of the Standing Committee of the Irish Hierarchy, 21 September 1973.
254 These were: Bishops Armstrong, Butler, Caird and McAdoo; Dean Tom Salmon; Canon Eric Elliott, Canon John Barry, Reverend Robin Eames, Miss E. Coulter, Mr J. L. B. Deane and Dr Kenneth Milne. Letter Donald Caird to author, 14 June 2003.
255 Gallagher and Worrall, *Christians*, p. 36; Cahal Daly, 'Ecumenism in Ireland now', p. 4.
256 OFMLA, Conway Papers, 16/8–1, Letter Paisley to Conway, 24 September 1973; copy letter Conway to Paisley, 25 September 1973; *IP*, 27 September 1973.
257 *IN*, 26 September 1973.
258 OFMLA, Conway Papers, 18/8–3/1, Opening statement by Cardinal Conway, 26 September 1973.

259 See Ian Ellis, 'The period since 1973', in Ellis and Hurley, *The Irish Inter-church Meeting*, pp. 41–50.
260 *JSA*, President's address, 9 October 1973, p. 7; *Londonderry Sentinel*, 31 October 1973.
261 *BT*, 26 September 1973.
262 Hurley, 'The preparatory years', p. 28.
263 Gallagher and Worrall, *Christians*, p. 140.
264 *JSA*, President's address, 9 October 1973, p. 7.
265 Cited in S. G. Poyntz, *Journey Towards Union* (Dublin, 1976), p. 23.
266 Gallagher and Worrall, *Christians*, p. 38.
267 Eric Gallagher, 'Interdenominational trust', *Doctrine and Life*, 23: 5 (1973), p. 228.

Conclusion

This study was motivated by the question of how the Church of Ireland and the Catholic Church, as all-Ireland institutions, coped with the political reality of operating on a partitioned island during the quarter century from 1949 to 1973. Such an environment demanded a testing dual loyalty as the churches attempted to honour Christ's injunction to render to both God and Caesar. This was no simple accomplishment. By 1949, the existence, for almost thirty years, of contiguous political jurisdictions magnified the importance of the border. This fact had overarching repercussions for the churches. It reinforced the inherent importance to them of maintaining religious unity across the state boundary. In addition to rendering to God in a corporate denominational sense, the influence of international ecumenism and the Second Vatican Council in conjunction with a shared revulsion of violence in Northern Ireland compelled the churches to improve inter-church relations. The border cut across denominational constituencies. The churches were consequently part of a local majority and a local minority religious community. A basic challenge then for church authorities was to reconcile the Church of Ireland in the South and the Catholic Church in Northern Ireland to living in those jurisdictions. A dual loyalty to God, on one hand, and Caesar, on the other, required adroit leadership from both sets of church authorities. Theirs was a delicate balancing act. Bishops played a dual role. They were both churchmen, and, in a civic society sense, leaders of their communities. As we have seen, realism and pragmatism characterised their interaction with both governments just as the provision of sensible direction and solid guidance marked relations with their laities.

Ecclesiastical unity remained indispensable and symbolically important for both churches. The terms 'hands across the border' and 'indivisible island' were as applicable to one as to the other in terms of their all-Ireland nature. This was expressed by their ecclesiastical geography alone. Both had dioceses and parishes which straddled the political border. But for each, there was only one church and one people, undivided by political jurisdiction and indivisible in the faith. An all-Ireland framework served as an important constitutional constant for the Catholic and Church of Ireland faithful throughout the island. However, such ties of creed were tested. Given the demographic and political disparity between its Northern and Southern members, this was particularly so for the Church of Ireland. Withdrawal from the British Commonwealth in 1949 forced the Church of Ireland bishops to alter the state prayers for those of their laity residing in the Republic. This was opposed in some quarters because expressions of loyalty to the crown and indeed membership of the Commonwealth were seen as unifying factors between North and South. Firm church leadership found a way through. New archival material has revealed that the 'Ripon affair' in 1967 exposed divergent Northern and Southern responses to nascent ecumenism. Civil strife in Northern Ireland, from 1969 onwards, similarly threatened to fracture the Church of Ireland's religious unity. The Catholic bishops faced a different set of challenges which had international and domestic dimensions. The archbishop of Armagh was seen to represent Catholic interests in both parts of the island. Similarly, the papal nuncio in Dublin, though accredited to the Southern government, had ecclesiastical jurisdiction over the entire island. By this highly unusual arrangement the Vatican recognised partition politically, but not ecclesiastically. The Catholic hierarchy, no less than the government in Dublin, strongly resisted any alteration in the standing of either the archbishop of Armagh or the jurisdiction of the nuncio. Domestically, the bishops had to contend with attacks on the border itself. Their vehement opposition to any alteration of the border by violent means contributed to an evolution in mainstream Irish nationalist discourse and helped alter the valency of the national question. Challenges to the churches' internal peace and religious unity were moderated by their organisational structure and tenacity in the faith. Bishops and laity were not compartmentalised by diocese or political jurisdiction. The border did not undercut their all-Ireland basis. Neither did it fissure their religious unity.

Obeisance to Caesar was less straightforward. For members of the Church of Ireland in the South and Catholics in the North, denomination lent cohesion to their respective communities. Arriving at a *modus vivendi* with central government in each state, on behalf of their people, was essential. In this regard, both sets of bishops were pragmatic in adapting to political realities. Each engaged in the politics of incremental gain with, as has been seen, developments in education serving as a model example. The Northern Catholic bishops and the House of Bishops served as anchor to their respective community and spiritual barques and, in their own contrasting way, reconciled their flocks to the two states.

Probing a combination of state and new church archival material has shaken some of the myths that have grown up around the Church of Ireland in the Republic and the Catholic Church in Northern Ireland. Far from being the alienated minority of caricature, the Church of Ireland in the Republic was more aptly described in the words of Bishop Arthur Butler as a 'confident minority' in the 1950s and 1960s. From the outset, the House of Bishops, ably led by Archbishop Gregg, demonstrated their integrity by altering the state prayers to fit the political circumstances of living in a republic. The Church of Ireland bishops enjoyed a cordial relationship with the government in Dublin. This was indicated in small but telling ways. For instance, a state reception was held to mark the visit of the British Council of Churches in 1961 and the centenary of Disestablishment was similarly honoured. In education, that most sensitive area of church–state relations, the Irish government met the concerns of the House of Bishops with sincerity and generosity.

Neither should monolithic assumptions be made about the Northern Catholic bishops. Unlike their Church of Ireland counterparts in the Republic, there was a greater sense among them of being in, but not of, the Northern Ireland state. But this did not prevent pragmatism from prevailing, as appropriate. In these years there was a quiet decoupling of the national question from practical socio-economic issues occasioned by the advent of the welfare state. Under the leadership of Cardinal John D'Alton and his successor William Conway, the Northern Catholic bishops moved decisively from highlighting the injustice of the state to emphasising injustices within it. In general, relations were less harmonious than those between the Church of Ireland and the Irish government. It would be manifestly unjust to allege (and there is no evidence to suggest) that the Southern government could afford to be more munificent simply because the Church of Ireland formed a smaller proportion of its citizens than Catholics did in Northern Ireland. Relations between the Catholic Church and the Northern state were coloured by a clash of religious and national identities. For this reason, the Northern Catholic bishops were anxious to maintain their voluntary and semi-autonomous status in education and health. A profound distrust of local government reinforced the need for a working relationship with central government. As stewards of their people, the Catholic bishops tried to moderate the fears and anxieties of their laity when the political temperature increased in Northern Ireland in the late 1960s. In the opening years of the Troubles, Cardinal Conway provided a key source of leadership. He and his brother bishops supported Westminster's policy of reform implemented through Stormont because the alternative was too terrible to contemplate. They excoriated paramilitary violence and sectarian assassination. That all men of God were increasingly ignored did not reflect any lack of sincerity on their part. Despite his discipline, the historian, nonetheless, remains human and cannot but be cognisant of the pathos of the dire situation which confronted Cardinal Conway and Archbishop Simms as Northern Ireland slipped further into conflict, death and fear.

The churches' earnestness for peace and justice in Northern Ireland manifested itself in ecumenical striving. That the old discourse of mutual ignorance and hostility, sadly demonstrated during the Fethard-on-Sea boycott, could give way to inter-church dialogue would have been unimaginable in the early 1950s. For centuries the churches were emblematic of division but the twentieth century, in particular, witnessed an upsurge in ecumenical ferment. As a member of the Anglican Communion, the Church of Ireland was involved in the development of intra-Protestant *rapprochement* epitomised by the World Council of Churches. As a part of the Universal Church, the Catholic Church in Ireland was not as insular as its critics, at times, maintain. The Irish hierarchy were not in the van at the Second Vatican Council. Although they accepted the new thinking without great enthusiasm, crucially they did so obediently. Growing friendship between the Vatican and Canterbury provided a firm lead to the Irish churches in the *terra incognita* of Anglican-Roman Catholic dialogue. Ecumenical endeavours at a grassroots level coalesced with, and were influenced by, these international efforts. But the advent of the Troubles provided a crucial catalyst. At a time when their respective communities were becoming ever more polarised, church leaders took great risks in establishing a secret *ad hoc* committee to keep channels of communication open as they tried to move beyond the sterile controversies of the past. Ecumenical entente drew bitter criticism from ill-affected detractors who equated Ireland's political and religious borders. Nonetheless hands were stretched across the denominational border. Pope John XIII called for a new Pentecost and the Spirit moved as it willed. The outcome was the historic first official Irish inter-church meeting at Ballymascanlon in 1973.

It was never a certainty that the division of an island into 'two Irelands' politically would not also induce ecclesiastical partition. That such a situation did not come to pass was due to the watchful eyes of Church of Ireland and Catholic Church authorities. Both ardently safeguarded their communities' cross-border religious unity and, at the same time, were attuned to the realities of living in the two Irish states. This was a delicate equilibrium to attain. But by transcending the political border in worship and adapting to life in both jurisdictions, the Catholic Church and Church of Ireland did just that, they rendered to both God and Caesar.

Appendix 1: Church of Ireland archbishops of Armagh and Dublin; bishops of cross-border and Northern Ireland dioceses

Diocese	Bishop	Accession	Resignation/Death
Armagh	John A. F. Gregg (b. 1873, Gloucestershire)	trs. from Dublin el. 15/12/1938	r. 18/02/1959 d. 02/05/1961
	James McCann (b. 1897, Grantham)	trs. from Meath el. 19/02/1959	r. 17/07/1969 d. 18/07/1983
	George O. Simms (b. 1910, Lifford, Co. Donegal)	trs. from Dublin el. 17/07/1969	r. 11/02/1980 d. 15/11/1991
Dublin Glendalough and Kildare	Arthur W. Barton (b. 1881, Dublin)	trs. from Kilmore el. 07/02/1939 conf. 15/02/1939	r. 15/11/1956 d. 22/09/1962
	George O. Simms	trs. from Cork el. 04/12/1956 conf. 11/12/1956 trs. to Armagh 17/07/1969	
	Alan A. Buchanan (b. 1907, Fintona, Co. Tyrone)	trs. from Clogher el. 10/09/1969 conf. 14/10/1969	r. 10/04/1977 d. 04/02/1984
Clogher	Richard Tyner	el. 09/11/1943 cons. 06/01/1944	d. 6/04/1958
	Alan A. Buchanan	el. 17/06/1958 cons. 29/09/1958 trs. to Dublin 14/10/1969	
	Richard P. C. Hanson (b. 1916)	el. 09/12/1969 cons. 17/03/1970	r. 31/03/1973 d. 23/12/1988
	Robert Heavener	el. 04/05/1973	r. 31/05/1980

Diocese	Bishop	Accession	Resignation/Death
	(b. 1905, Redcross Co. Wicklow)	cons. 29/06/1973	d. 08/03/2005
Connor	Charles King Irwin (b. 1874)	trs. from Limerick el. 17/06/1942* conf. 02/09/1942	r. 31/05/1956 d. 15/01/1960
	R. Cyril H. G. Elliott (b. 1890, Dublin)	el. 28/06/1956 cons. 21/09/1956	r. 31/07/1969 d. 03/04/1977
	Arthur H. Butler (b. 1912, Dublin)	trs. from Tuam el. 16/09/1969 conf. 14/10/1969	r. 30/09/1981 d. 06/07/1991
Derry and Raphoe	Robert McNeill Boyd (b. 1890, Kilkee, (Co. Down)	trs. from Killaloe el. 20/03/1945	d. 01/07/1958
	Charles J. Tyndall (b. 1900)	trs. from Kilmore el. and conf. 14/10/1958	r. 30/09/1969 d. 03/04/1971
	Cuthbert I. Peacocke (b. 1903, Dublin)	el. 16/10/1969 cons. 06/01/1970	r. 31/03/1975 d. 10/04/1994
Down and Dromore	William Kerr (b. 1873)	el. 9/12/1944 cons. 25/01/1945	r. 31/07/1955 d. 03/02/1960
	Frederick J. Mitchell (b. 1901)	trs. from Kilmore el. and conf. 18/10/1955	r. 07/11/1969 d. 03/06/1979
	George A. Quin (b. 1914, Stradbally, Co. Laois)	el. 26/11/1969 cons. 06/01/1970	r. 31/03/1980 d. 08/08/1990
Kilmore, Elphin and Ardagh	Albert E. Hughes (b. 1878)	el. 14/12/1938 cons. 25/04/1939	r. 12/05/1950 d. 11/05/1954
	Frederick J. Mitchell	el. 28/07/1950 cons. 21/09/1950 trs. to Down 18/10/1955	
	Charles J. Tyndall	el. 16/12/1955 cons. 02/02/1956 trs. to Derry and Raphoe 14/10/1958	

Diocese	Bishop	Accession	Resignation/Death
	Edward F. B. Moore (b. 1906, Cootehill, Co. Cavan)	el. 28/11/1958 cons. 06/01/1959	r. 31/05/1981 d. 13/12/1997

*When Connor separated from Down and Dromore in 1944, Irwin retained Connor

Notes: b. = born; conf. = confirmed in office; cons. = consecrated; d. = died; el. = elected; r. = retired; trs. = translated

Sources: various entries from *Church of Ireland Directory/Irish Church Directory*; *Church of Ireland Gazette*; *Church Times*; F. W. Fawcett, and D. W. T. Crooks, *Clergy of Derry and Raphoe* (Belfast, 1999); W. E. C Fleming, *Armagh Clergy 1800–2000* (Dundalk, 2001); *Irish Times*; W. J. R. Wallace, (ed.), *Clergy of Dublin and Glendalough* (Belfast, 2001); Ulster Historical Foundation, *Clergy of Connor from Patrician Times to the Present Day* (Belfast, 1993), *Clergy of Down and Dromore* (Belfast, 1996).

Appendix 2: Catholic bishops of the Armagh province

Diocese	Bishop	Accession	Resignation/Death
Armagh	John D'Alton (b. 1882, Claremorris, Co. Mayo)	cons. coadj. of Meath 29/06/1942 Succeeded 16/06/1943 trs. to Armagh 25/04/1946 inst. 13/06/1946 Cardinal 12/01/1953	d. 01/02/1963
	William Conway (b. 1913, Belfast)	app. aux. bp. 04/06/1958 cons. 27/07/1958 app. Archbishop 10/09/1963 Cardinal 22/02/1965	d. 17/04/1977
Ardagh and Clonmacnoise	James J. McNamee (b. 1876, Fintona, Co. Tyrone)	app. 02/06/1927 cons. 31/07/1927	d. 24/04/1966
	Cahal B. Daly (b. 1917, Loughguile, Co. Antrim)	app. 02/06/1967 cons. 16/07/1967 trs. Down and Connor 08/09/1982 inst. 17/10/1982 trs. Armagh 06/11/1990 inst. 16/12/1990 Cardinal 28/06/1991	r. 01/10/1996
Clogher	Eugene O'Callaghan (b. 1888, Camlough, (Co. Armagh)	app. 03/02/1943 cons. 04/04/1943	r. 03/12/1969 d. 21/05/1973

Diocese	Bishop	Accession	Resignation/Death
	Patrick Mulligan (b. 1912, Lisbellaw, Co. Fermanagh)	app. 03/12/1969 cons. 18/01/1970	r. 02/09/1979 d. 21/01/1991
Derry	Neil Farren (b. 1893, Buncrana, Co. Donegal)	app. 05/08/1939 cons. 01/10/1939	r. 13/04/1973 d. 07/05/1980
Down and Connor	Daniel Mageean (b. 1882, Saintfield, Co. Down)	app. 31/05/1929 cons. 25/08/1929	d. 17/01/1962
	William Philbin (b. 1907, Kiltimagh, Co. Mayo)	trs. from Clonfert 09/06/1962 inst. 30/08/1962	r. 24/08/1982 d. 22/08/1991
Dromore	Eugene O'Doherty (b. 1896, Moville, Co. Donegal)	app. 11/03/1944 cons. 28/05/1944	r. 22/11/1975 d. 24/03/1979
Kilmore	Patrick Lyons (b. 1875, Collon Co. Louth)	app. 06/08/1937 cons. 03/10/1937	d. 27/04/1949
	Austin Quinn (b. 1892, Derrynoose, Co. Armagh)	app. 19/07/1950 cons. 10/09/1950	r. 10/12/1972 d. 24/09/1974
Meath	John Kyne (b. 1904, Longwood Co Meath)	app. 17/05/1947 cons. 29/06/1947	d. 23/12/1966
	John McCormack (b. 1923, Moynalty Co. Meath)	app. 30/01/1968 cons. 10/03/1968	r. 16/05/1990 d. 21/09/1996
Raphoe	William MacNeely (b. 1888, Donegal Town)	app. 21/04/1923 cons. 22/07/1923	d. 11/12/1963
	Anthony C. McFeely (b. 1909, Ballybofey, Co. Donegal)	app. 20/05/1965 cons. 27/06/1965	r. 16/02/1982 d. 07/10/1986

Notes: b. = born; conf. = confirmed in office; cons. = consecrated; d. = died; el. = elected; r. = retired; trs. = translated

Sources: Bernard J. Canning, *Bishops of Ireland 1870–1987* (Ballyshannon, 1987); *Irish Catholic Directory* various years.

Bibliography

Religious and diocesan archives

Catholic

Cardinal Tomás Ó Fiaich Memorial Library and Archive, Armagh
Papers of William Conway
Papers of John D'Alton

Clogher Diocesan Archives, Monaghan
Papers of Eugene O'Callaghan
The Witness

Derry Diocesan Archives, Derry
Papers of Neil Farren

Down and Connor Diocesan Archives, Belfast
Papers of Daniel Mageean
Papers of William Philbin

Dromore Diocesan Archives, Newry
Papers of Eugene O'Doherty

Dublin Diocesan Archives, Drumcondra
Papers of John Charles McQuaid

Kilmore Diocesan Archives, Cavan
Papers of Austin Quinn

Westminster Diocesan Archives, London
Papers of William Godfrey
Papers of Bernard Griffin

Church of Ireland/Church of England

Armagh Diocesan Office, Armagh
Armagh Diocesan Magazine
Journal of the Synod of Armagh

Derry Diocesan Office, Derry
Derry and Raphoe, diocesan synod reports
Diocese of Raphoe, reports of rural deans

Dublin Diocesan Office, Church of Ireland House, Dublin
Dublin, Glendalough and Kildare, diocesan reports

Lambeth Palace Library, London
Diaries of John Moorman
Papers of Geoffrey Fisher
Papers of Lambeth Conference 1958
Papers of Michael Ramsey

Representative Church Body, Dublin
Diocesan council reports for: Armagh, Clogher, Connor, Down and Dromore, and Kilmore
House of Bishops, minutes of meetings

Representative Church Body Library, Dublin
Minutes of Clerical Society of Ireland
Minutes of Kilmore Clerical Union
Papers of Association for the Promotion of Christian Knowledge
Papers of William R. Crawford
Papers of J. L. B. Deane
Papers of General Synod Standing Committee Sub-Committee on State Prayers
Papers of *Irish Anglicanism*
Papers of Irish Guild of the Church
Papers of Hugh Maude
Papers of George Otto Simms (by permission of the Simms family)
Typescript: *The Fethard Boycott 1957 – Recollection and Reflections of Rev. Edward Francis Grant, Rector of Fethard Union, Mar. 1946–Nov. 1956*

State and local government archives

Cavan County Council
Minutes of County Council

Dublin City Archives
Minutes of the Municipal Council of the City of Dublin

Monaghan County Council
Minutes of County Council

National Archives of Ireland, Dublin
Department of Foreign Affairs
Department of Justice

Department of the Taoiseach
Minutes of Cabinet Meetings
Minutes of Government Meetings

National Archives, London
Dominions Office
Foreign and Commonwealth Office
Foreign Office
Home Office
Northern Ireland Office
Prime Minster's Office

Public Record Office of Northern Ireland, Belfast
Cabinet Conclusions
Home Office
Papers of Cahir Healy
Papers of Harry Midgley
Papers of PACE

Libraries and university archives

Linen Hall Library, Belfast
Northern Ireland Political Collection
Northern Ireland Political Ephemera
Papers of Eric Gallagher

National Library of Ireland
Papers of Shane Leslie
Papers of Seán T. Ó Ceallaigh

University College Dublin Archives Department
Papers of Frank Aiken
Papers of Ernest Blythe
Papers of Eamon de Valera
Papers of Adrian Fisher
Papers of Seán MacEntee
Papers of Patrick McGilligan

Trinity College Dublin Manuscripts Room
Papers of Trevor West

Private collections

Robin C. Gibson
Papers of Mercy Simms

Printed church sources

Catholic

Flannery, Austin (ed.), *Vatican Council II. The Conciliar and Post Conciliar Documents* (revised edn., Dublin, 1992 [1st edn., 1975])
Irish Catholic Directory
Irish Directory on Ecumenism (Dublin, 1969)

Church of Ireland

Administration 1967
Church of Ireland Directory (until 1967 *Irish Church Directory*)
Commission for the Sparsely Populated Areas. Reports to the General Synod 1957–65
Irish Amsterdam. Reports of the Conference of the Irish Churches (Belfast, 1949)
Irish Evanston – A Conference of the Irish Churches
Journal of the General Synod

Official sources

Belfast and Northern Ireland Directory
Compton Report (Cmnd. 4823)
Dáil Debates
Hansard
Hansard Northern Ireland
Report of the Committee on the Constitution Pr. 9817 (Dublin, 1967)
Report of the Ministry of Education 1954–55 (NI) Cmd. 351 (Belfast, 1956)
Seanad Debates
Thom's Directory
University Statistics 1938–39 and 1948–49 to 1952–53 Pr. 2617 (Dublin, 1954)

Newspapers, periodicals and journals

Anglo-Celt
Belfast News-Letter
Belfast Telegraph
Catholic Herald
Christus Rex
Church of Ireland Gazette
Church of Ireland Magazine
Church Times
Daily Telegraph
Derry Journal
Doctrine and Life
Evening Mail
Evening Press
Fermanagh Herald
Feasta
Focus
Furrow
Hibernia
Impartial Reporter
Irish Catholic
Irish Economic and Social History
Irish Historical Studies

Irish Independent
Irish News
Irish Press
Irish Times
Leader
Londonderry Sentinel
Northern Standard
Northern Whig
Search
Spectator
Sunday Independent
Sunday Observer
Sunday Press
Standard
Times
Ulster Herald

Interviews and correspondence

Rt Rev. Donald Caird
Very Rev. Martin Clarke
Cardinal Cahal Daly
Most Rev. Edward Daly
J. L. B. Deane
Very Rev. Victor Griffin
Rev. Michael Hurley, SJ
Rev. Gabriel Kelly
Very Rev. Robert MacCarthy
Rt Rev Mgr. Liam MacDaid
Most Rev. Francis MacKiernan
Seán MacRéamoinn
Rev. Peter McAnenly
Dr Kenneth Milne
Most Rev. Joseph Duffy
Professor Michael Gallagher
Robin C. Gibson
Rev. Edward F. Grant
J. Montgomery
Risteard Ó Glaisne
Geoffrey Perrin
Rt Rev. Samuel G. Poyntz
Rev. Canon Robin Richey
Rev. Canon Albert Stokes
Rt Rev. R. A Warke
Professor Trevor West

Secondary sources

Acheson, Alan, *A History of the Church of Ireland 1691–1996* (Dublin, 1997).
Agee, Chris (ed.), *Unfinished Ireland. Essays on Hubert Butler* (Belfast, 2003).
Akenson, Donald Harmon, *Education and Enmity. The Control of Schooling in Northern Ireland, 1920–50* (Newton Abbot, 1973).
—— *A Mirror to Kathleen's Face. Education in Independent Ireland* (Montreal and London, 1975).
Barkley, John M., *The Irish Council of Churches 1923–1983* (Belfast, 1983).
Bartlett, Thomas, 'Church and state in modern Ireland, 1923–1970. An appraisal reappraised', in Brendan Bradshaw and Dáire Keogh (eds), *Christianity in Ireland. Revisiting the Story* (Dublin, 2002), pp. 249–58.
Barrington, Dónal, *Uniting Ireland*, Tuairim Pamphlet 1 (Dublin, 1959).
Barritt, Denis P. and Charles F. Carter, *The Northern Ireland Problem. A Study in Group Relations* (London, 1962).
Bew, Paul and Gordan Gillespie, *Northern Ireland. A Chronology of the Troubles 1968–1993* (Dublin, 1993).
Bew, Paul, Peter Gibbon and Henry Patterson, *Northern Ireland 1921–1996. Political Forces and Social Classes* (revised edn., London, 1996 [first published in 1995 as *Northern Ireland 1921–1994*]).

Blackbourn, David, *Class, Religion and Local Politics in Wilhelmine Germany. The Centre Party in Württemberg before 1914* (New Haven and London, 1980).
Blanshard, Paul, *The Irish and Catholic Power* (London, 1954).
Bloomfield, Ken, *Stormont in Crisis. A Memoir* (Belfast, 1994).
Bonner, Brian, *Derry. An Outline History of the Diocese* (2nd edn., Pallaskenry, 1995 [1st edn., Dublin 1982]).
Bowen, Kurt, *Protestants in a Catholic State. Ireland's Privileged Minority* (Dublin, 1983).
Bowman, John, *De Valera and the Ulster Question, 1917–1973* (Oxford, 1982).
Brewer, John and Gareth Higgins, *Anti-Catholicism in Northern Ireland, 1660–1998. The Mote and the Beam* (Basingstoke 1998).
Brown, Terence, *Ireland. A Social and Cultural History 1922–1979* (London, 1981).
—— 'Religious minorities in the Irish Free State and the Republic of Ireland 1922–1995', in *Building Trust in Ireland. Studies Commissioned by the Forum for Peace and Reconciliation* (Belfast, 1996), pp. 215–53.
Buchanan, Audrey, 'In retrospect. Alan Alexander Buchanan', *Search*, 17: 1 (1994), pp. 34–9.
Butler, Hubert, *Escape from the Anthill* (revised edn., Mullingar, 1986 [1st edn., 1985]).
Callaghan, James, *A House Divided. The Dilemma of Northern Ireland* (London, 1973).
Canning, Bernard J., *Bishops of Ireland 1870–1987* (Ballyshannon, 1987).
Carpenter, Edward, *Archbishop Fisher. His Life and Times* (Norwich, 1991).
Cave, Stephen A., *Our Church in History* (Dublin, 1954).
Chadwick, Owen, *Michael Ramsey. A Life* (Oxford, 1990).
Clarke, Alan C. and Colin Davey (eds), *Anglican/Roman Catholic Dialogue. The Work of the Preparatory Commission* (London, 1974).
Connolly, S. J. (ed.), *The Oxford Companion to Irish History* (2nd edn., Oxford, 2002).
Conway, William, *Catholic Schools* (Dublin, 1971).
Cooke, Dennis, *Persecuting Zeal. A Portrait of Ian Paisley* (Dingle, 1996).
Cooney, John, *The Crozier and the Dáil. Church and State 1922–1986* (Cork, 1986).
—— *John Charles McQuaid. Ruler of Catholic Ireland* (Dublin, 1999).
Coppa, Frank J., *The Modern Papacy since 1789* (London, 1998).
Cunningham, Michael, *British Government Policy in Northern Ireland, 1969–2000* (Manchester, 2001).
Daly, Cahal B., *Violence in Ireland* (Dublin, 1973).
—— 'Interchurch marriages. The position of the Irish Episcopal Conference', *The Furrow*, 25: 1 (1974), pp. 29–33.
—— 'Ecumenism in Ireland now. problems and hopes', *The Irish Theological Quarterly*, 45: 1 (1978), pp. 3–27.
—— *Steps on my Pilgrim Journey* (Dublin, 1998).

Daly, Cahal and Eric Gallagher, *Violence in Ireland* (Belfast, 1976).
Daly, Cahal and Stanley Worrall, *Ballymascanlon. An Irish Venture in Inter-Church Dialogue* (Belfast and Dublin, 1978).
Daly, Edward, *Mister, Are You a Priest?* (Dublin, 2000).
—— 'The "Troubles"', in Henry A. Jefferies and Ciarán Devlin (eds), *History of the Diocese of Derry from Earliest Times* (Dublin, 2000), pp. 259–96.
De Baróid, Ciarán, *Ballymurphy and the Irish War* (revised edn., London, 2000 [1st edn., 1989]).
De Bhaldraithe, Eoin, 'The ecumenical marriage', *The Furrow*, 32: 10 (1981), pp. 639–48.
De Blaghd, Earnán, *Briseadh na Teorann* (Dublin, 1955).
De La Bedoyere, Michael, *Cardinal Bernard Griffin Archbishop of Westminster* (London, 1955).
Deane, Declan, 'Mixed marriage. Irish and Swiss bishops' statements compared', *The Furrow*, 25: 10 (1974), pp. 544–8.
Deane, J. L. B., *Church of Ireland Handbook* (Dublin, 1962).
—— 'General Synod. Retrospect and prospect', *New Divinity*. 1: 1 (1970), pp. 13–24.
De-la-Noy, Michael, *Michael Ramsey. A Portrait* (London, 1990).
Delaney, Enda, *Demography, State and Society. Irish Migration to Britain, 1921–1971* (Liverpool, 2000).
—— 'Political catholicism in post-war Ireland. The Revd Denis Fahey and Maria Duce, 1945–54', *Journal of Ecclesiastical History*, 52: 3 (2001), pp. 487–511.
Dewar, M. W., John Brown and S. E. Long, *Orangeism. A New Historical Appreciation* (Belfast, 1967).
Dooley, Terence, *The Plight of Monaghan Protestants 1912–26* (Dublin, 2000).
Duffy, Eamon, *Saints and Sinners. A History of the Popes* (2nd edn., New Haven and London, 2001 [1st edn., 1997]).
Dunlop, John, *A Precarious Belonging. Presbyterians and the Conflict in Ireland* (Belfast, 1995).
Dunn, Joseph, *No Lions in the Hierarchy – An Anthology of Sorts* (Dublin, 1994).
Elliott, Marianne, *The Catholics of Ulster. A History* (London, 2000).
Elliott, Sydney, 'The Northern Ireland electoral system. A vehicle for disputation', in Patrick J. Roche and Brian Barton (eds), *The Northern Ireland Question. Nationalism, Unionism and Partition* (Aldershot, 1999), pp. 122–38.
Ellis, Ian, *Vision and Reality. A Survey of Twentieth Century Irish Inter-Church Relations* (Belfast, 1992).
Ellis, Ian and Michael Hurley, *The Irish Inter-Church Meeting. Background and Development* (Belfast, 1998).
Erskine, John, 'The Presbyterian Church in Ireland', in Norman Richardson (ed.), *A Tapestry of Beliefs. Christian Traditions in Northern Ireland* (Belfast, 1998), pp. 45–65.
Fagan, Seán, '*Humanae vitae* 30 years on', *Doctrine and Life* 49: 1 (1999), pp. 51–4.

Falconer, Alan, Enda McDonagh and Seán MacReamoinn (eds), *Freedom to Hope? The Catholic Church in Ireland Twenty Years after Vatican II* (Dublin, 1985).
Fallon, Brian, *An Age of Innocence. Irish Culture 1930–1960* (Dublin, 1999).
Farrell, Michael, *Northern Ireland. The Orange State* (London, 1976).
Farren, Seán and Robert F. Mulvihill, *Paths to a Settlement in Northern Ireland* (Gerrards Cross, 2000).
Fay, Marie Therese, Mike Morrissey and Marie Smyth, *Mapping Troubles-Related Deaths in Northern Ireland 1969–1998* (2nd edn., Derry, 1998 [1st edn., 1997]).
Fawcett, F. W. and D. W. T. Crooks, *Clergy of Derry and Raphoe* (Belfast, 1999).
Ferriter, Diarmaid, *The Transformation of Ireland 1900–2000* (London, 2004).
FitzGerald, Garret, *Towards a New Ireland* (London, 1972).
—— *Reflections on the Irish State* (Dublin, 2003).
Fitzpatrick, David, *The Two Irelands 1912–1939* (Oxford, 1998).
—— 'The Orange Order and the border', *Irish Historical Studies*, 33: 129 (2002), pp. 52–67.
Fleming, Lionel, *Head or Harp* (London, 1965).
Fleming, W. E. C., *Armagh Clergy 1800–2000* (Dundalk, 2001).
Foster, R. F., *The Irish Story. Telling Tales and Making It Up in Ireland* (London, 2001).
Fuller, Louise, *Irish Catholicism since 1950. The Undoing of a Culture* (Dublin, 2002).
Fulton, John, 'Intermarriage and the Irish clergy: a sociological study', in Michael Hurley (ed.), *Beyond Tolerance. The Challenge of Mixed Marriage* (London, 1975), pp. 157–74.
—— *The Tragedy of Belief. Division, Politics and Religion in Ireland* (Oxford, 1991).
Gallagher, Eric, 'Interdenominational trust', *Doctrine and Life*, 23: 5 (1973), pp. 227–39.
—— 'Northern Ireland – The Record of the Churches', *Studies*, 80: 318 (1991), pp. 169–77.
Gallagher, Eric and Stanley Worrall, *Christians in Ulster, 1968–1980* (Oxford, 1982).
Gallagher, Frank, *The Indivisible Island. The History of the Partition of Ireland* (London, 1957).
Garvin, Tom, *Preventing the Future. Why was Ireland so Poor for so Long?* (Dublin, 2004).
Good, Norah, 'Charles Tyndall 1900–1971. "The peace bishop"', *Search*, 20: 1 (1997), pp. 46–53.
Gregg, J. A. F., *The Ne Temere Decree* (Dublin, 1911).
Griffin, Victor, *Anglican and Irish What We Believe* (Dublin, 1976).
—— *Mark of Protest. An Autobiography* (Dublin, 1993).
Girvin, Brian, *From Union to Union. Nationalism, Democracy and Religion in Ireland – Act of Union to EU* (Dublin, 2002).

Haddick-Flynn, Kevin, *Orangeism. The Making of a Tradition* (Dublin, 1999).
Harkness, D. W., *Northern Ireland since 1920* (Dublin, 1983).
—— *Ireland in the Twentieth Century Divided Island* (Baskingstoke, 1996).
Harris, Mary, *The Catholic Church and the Foundation of the Northern Ireland State* (Cork, 1993).
Hastings, Adrian, *A History of English Christianity 1920–1990* (3rd edn., London, 1991 [1st edn., 1986]).
Hayes, Maurice, *Community Relations and the Role of the Community Relations Commission in Northern Ireland* (London, 1972).
Heath, Edward, *The Course of My Life. My Autobiography* (London, 1998).
Hebblethwaite, Peter, *John XXIII. Pope of the Council* (London, 1984).
—— *Paul VI. The First Modern Pope*. (London, 1993).
Hennessey, Thomas, *A History of Northern Ireland 1920–1996* (Dublin, 1997).
Heron, Alasdair, *Two Churches – One Love* (Dublin, 1977).
Heslinga, M. W., *The Irish Border as a Cultural Divide* (3rd unrevised edn., Assen, 1979 [1st edn., 1962]).
Hogan, Gerard, 'A fresh look at Tilson's case', *Irish Jurist*, 33: 311 (1998), pp. 311–32.
Holmes, R. F. G., *Presbyterianism and Orangeism 1795–1995* (Belfast, 1996).
Horgan, John, *Seán Lemass. The Enigmatic Patriot* (Dublin, 1997).
—— *Noël Browne. Passionate Outsider* (Dublin, 2000).
Hurley, Michael, *Church and Eucharist* (Dublin, 1966).
—— *Christian Unity. An Ecumenical Second Spring?* (Dublin, 1998).
—— 'In memoriam Henry Robert McAdoo', *Doctrine and Life*, 49: 6 (1999), pp. 350–5.
—— 'Northern Ireland and the post-Vatican II ecumenical journey', in Brendan Bradshaw and Dáire Keogh (eds), *Christianity in Ireland. Revisiting the Story* (Dublin, 2002), pp. 259–70.
Hurley, Michael (ed.), *Irish Anglicanism 1869–1969* (Dublin, 1970).
—— *Beyond Tolerance. The Challenge of Mixed Marriage* (London, 1975),
Inglis, Tom, *Moral Monopoly. The Catholic Church in Modern Irish Society* (Dublin, 1987).
Jackson, Alvin, 'J. C. Beckett. politics, faith, scholarship', *Irish Historical Studies*, 33: 130 (2002), pp. 129–50.
Keane, Thomas, 'Demographic trends', in Michael Hurley (ed.), *Irish Anglicanism*, pp. 168–78.
Kennedy, Denis, *The Widening Gulf* (Belfast, 1988).
Kennedy, Finola, *Cottage to Crèche. Family Change in Ireland* (Dublin, 2001).
Kennedy, Michael, *Division and Consensus. The Politics of Cross-Border Relations in Ireland, 1925–1969* (Dublin, 2000).
Keogh, Dermot, 'Church, state and society', in Brian Farrell (ed.), *De Valera's Constitution and Ours* (Dublin, 1988), pp. 103–22.
—— *Ireland and the Vatican* (Cork, 1995).

Keogh, Dermot, 'The role of the Catholic Church in the Republic of Ireland 1922–1995', in *Building Trust in Ireland. Studies Commissioned by the Forum for Peace and Reconciliation* (Belfast, 1996), pp. 85–213.

Kissane, Bill, 'The illusion of state neutrality in a secularising Ireland', in John T. S. Madeley and Zsolt Enyedi (eds), *Church and State in Contemporary Europe. The Chimera of Neutrality* (London, 2003), pp. 73–94.

Küng, Hans, 'Catholics and Protestants. An ecumenical inventory', in Alberic Stacpoole (ed.), *Vatican II by Those Who Were There* (London, 1986).

Lee, J. J., 'Aspects of corporatist thought in Ireland: the Commission on Vocational Organisation 1939–43', in Art Cosgrove and Donal McCartney (eds), *Studies in Irish History Presented to R. Dudley Edwards* (Dublin, 1979), pp. 324–46.

—— *Ireland 1912–1985. Politics and Society* (Cambridge, 1989).

Lee, Raymond M., 'Intermarriage, conflict and social control in Ireland. The decree Ne Temere', *Economic and Social Review*, 17: 1 (1985), pp. 11–27.

Lell, Joachim, 'Position and trends in Germany', in Michael Hurley (ed.), *Beyond Tolerance*, pp. 135–44.

Livingstone, Peadar, *The Fermanagh Story* (Enniskillen, 1969).

—— *The Monaghan Story* (Enniskillen, 1980).

Logue, Paddy (ed.), *The Border. Personal Reflections from Ireland North and South* (Dublin, 1999).

Lynn, Brendan, 'Nationalist Politics in Derry 1945–1969', in Gerard O'Brien (ed.), *Derry and Londonderry. History and Society* (Dublin, 1999), pp. 601–24.

MacCarthy, R. B., *Ancient and Modern. A Short History of the Church of Ireland* (Dublin, 1995).

MacDermott, Eithne, *Clann na Poblachta* (Cork, 1998).

MacDonagh, Oliver, *States of Mind. A Study of Anglo-Irish Conflict 1780–1980* (London, 1983).

McAdoo, Henry Robert, *No New Church* (Dublin, 1945).

—— *Marriage and the Community. The Inter-Church Marriage* (Dublin, 1974).

—— *Being an Anglican* (Dublin, 1977).

McCabe, Ian, *A Diplomatic History of Ireland, 1948–49. The Republic, the Commonwealth and NATO* (Dublin, 1991).

McDonagh, Enda, *Between Chaos and New Creation* (Dublin, 1986).

McDowell, R. B., *The Church of Ireland 1869–1969* (London, 1975).

McElroy, Gerald, *The Catholic Church and the Northern Ireland Crisis 1968–86* (Dublin, 1991).

McGrath, Michael, *The Catholic Church and Catholic Schools in Northern Ireland: The Price of Faith* (Dublin, 2000).

McKay, Susan, *Northern Protestants. An Unsettled People* (Belfast, 2000).

McKittrick, David and David McVea, *Making Sense of the Troubles* (Belfast, 2000).

McKittrick, David, Seamus Kelters, Brian Feeney and Chris Thornton, *Lost Lives* (Edinburgh, 1999).

McMahon, Deirdre, *Republicans and Imperialists. Anglo-Irish Relations in the 1930s* (New Haven and London, 1984).

—— 'A larger and noisier southern Ireland. Ireland and the evolution of dominion status in India, Burma and the Commonwealth, 1942–9', in Michael Kennedy and Joseph Morrison Skelly (eds), *Irish Foreign Policy 1919–1966. From Independence to Internationalism* (Dublin, 2000), pp. 155–91.

—— 'John Charles McQuaid, archbishop of Dublin, 1940–72', in James Kelly and Dáire Keogh (eds), *History of the Catholic Diocese of Dublin* (Dublin, 2000), pp. 349–80.

McOustra, Christopher, *Love in the Economy. Catholic Social Doctrine for the Individual (Slough*, 1990).

Maclear, J. F. (ed.), *Church and State in the Modern Age* (Oxford, 1995).

Madden, Finbar, J. and Thomas Bradley, 'The diocese of Derry in the twentieth century, c. 1900–1974', in Henry A. Jefferies and Ciarán Devlin (eds), *History of the Diocese of Derry from Earliest Times* (Dublin, 2000), pp. 240–58.

Maguire, Martin, 'The Church of Ireland and the problem of the protestant working-class of Dublin, 1870s–1930s', in Alan Ford, James McGuire and Kenneth Milne (eds), *As by Law Established. The Church of Ireland since the Reformation* (Dublin, 1995), pp. 195–203.

Manktelow, Michael, *John Moorman. Anglican, Franciscan, Independent* (Norwich, 1999).

Mansergh, Diana (ed.), *Nationalism and Independence. Selected Irish Papers by Nicholas Mansergh* (Cork, 1997).

Megahey, Alan, *The Irish Protestant Churches in the Twentieth Century* (Basingstoke, 2000).

Mehaffey, James, *One Family* (Dublin, 1983).

Milne, Kenneth, 'Brave new world', in Stephen R. White, *A Time to Build. Essays for Tomorrow's Church* (Dublin, 1999), pp. 15–27.

—— 'The Church of Ireland since partition', in Brendan Bradshaw and Dáire Keogh (eds), *Christianity in Ireland. Revisiting the Story* (Dublin, 2002), pp. 220–30.

—— 'The Protestant churches in independent Ireland', in James P. Mackey and Enda McDonagh (eds), *Religion and Politics in Ireland at the Turn of the Millennium* (Dublin, 2003), pp. 64–83.

Moorman, John, *Vatican Observed. An Anglican View of Vatican II* (London, 1967).

Mulholland, Marc, *Northern Ireland at the Crossroads. Ulster Unionism in the O'Neill Years 1960–9* (Basingstoke, 2000).

Murphy, Colin and Lynne Adair (eds), *Untold Stories. Protestants in the Republic of Ireland 1922–2002* (Dublin, 2002).

Murphy, John A., *Ireland in the Twentieth Century* (Dublin, 1975).

Murray, Gerard, *John Hume and the SDLP. Impact and Survival in Northern Ireland* (Dublin, 1998).

Murray, Patrick, *Oracles of God. The Roman Catholic Church and Irish Politics, 1922–37* (Dublin, 2000).

O'Brien, Gerard (ed.), *Derry and Londonderry. History and Society* (Dublin, 1999).
Ó Buachalla, Séamas, *Education Policy in Twentieth Century Ireland* (Dublin, 1988).
O'Connor, Fionnuala, *In Search of a State. Catholics in Northern Ireland* (Belfast, 1993).
O'Connor, Seán, *Troubled Sky. Reflections on the Irish Educational Scene 1957–1968* (Dublin, 1986).
O'Connor, Thomas H., *Boston Catholics. A History of the Church and Its People* (Boston, 1998).
Ó Corráin, Daithí, 'Semper fidelis. The episcopacy of Eugene O'Callaghan, 1943–1969', in Henry A. Jefferies (ed.), *History of the Diocese of Clogher* (Dublin, 2005), pp. 223–44.
—— 'Ireland in his heart north and south'. The contribution of Ernest Blythe to the partition question', *Irish Historical Studies*, 35:137 (2006).
O'Halloran, Clare, *Partition and the Limits of Irish Nationalism* (Dublin, 1987).
O'Leary, Don, *Vocationalism and Social Catholicism in Twentieth-Century Ireland* (Dublin, 2000).
O'Neill, Terence, *The Autobiography of Terence O'Neill* (London, 1972).
Patterson, Henry, *Ireland since 1939* (Oxford, 2002).
Philbin, William J., *Patriotism* (Dublin, 1958).
—— *Ireland's Problem* (Belfast, 1974).
Phoenix, Éamon, *Northern Nationalism. Nationalist Politics, Partition and the Catholic Minority in Northern Ireland 1890–1940* (Belfast, 1994).
Pierrard, Pierre, *Un Siècle de L'église de France, 1900–2000* (Paris, 2000).
Pilkington, Lionel, 'Religion and the Celtic tiger. The cultural legacies of anti-Catholicism in Ireland', in Peadar Kirby, Luke Gibbons and Michael Cronin (eds), *Reinventing Ireland. Culture, Society and the Global Economy* (London, 2002), pp. 124–39.
Poyntz, Samuel G., *Journey Towards Union* (Dublin, 1976).
Proctor, W. C. G., *A Dublin Theological Scrapbook* (Dublin, 1973) [Printed for private circulation only].
Purdie, Bob, *Politics in the Streets. The Origins of the Civil Rights Movement in Northern Ireland* (Belfast, 1990).
Rafferty, Oliver, *Catholicism in Ulster 1603–1983* (London, 1994).
Refaussé, Raymond, *Church of Ireland Records* (Dublin, 2000).
Rose, Richard, *Governing without Consensus. An Irish Perspective* (London, 1971).
Rose, Peter, *How the Troubles came to Northern Ireland* (Basingstoke, 2000).
Rouse, Ruth and Stephen Charles Neill (eds), *A History of the Ecumenical Movement 1517–1948* (London, 1954).
Ryan, Dermot, *Marriage and Pastoral Care* (Dublin, 1973).
Ryan, Liam, 'Church and politics. the last twenty-five years', *The Furrow*, 30: 1 (1979), pp. 3–18.

Ryan, Michael (ed.), *The Church and the Nation. The Vision of Peter Birch Bishop of Ossory 1964–1981* (Dublin, 1993).
Rynne, Xavier, *The Second Session. The Debates and Decrees of Vatican Council II, September 29 to December 4, 1963* (London, 1964).
Sacks, Paul Martin, 'Bailiwick, locality, and religion. Three elements in an Irish Dáil constituency election', *Economic and Social Review*, 1: 4 (1970), pp. 531–54.
Seaver, George, *John Allen Fitzgerald Gregg Archbishop* (London, 1963).
Sexton, J. J. and Richard O'Leary, 'Factors affecting population decline in minority religious communities in the Republic of Ireland', in *Building Trust in Ireland. Studies Commissioned by the Forum for Peace and Reconciliation* (Belfast, 1996), pp. 255–332.
Shea, Patrick, *Voices and the Sound of Drums* (Belfast, 1981).
Simms, George, 'Richard Patrick Crosland Hanson, 1916–1988. Bishop, writer, teacher', *Search*, 12: 1 (1989), pp. 42–7.
—— 'In retrospect – Frederick Julian Mitchell (1901–1979)', 14: 2 (1991), pp. 18–22.
Stanford, William Bedell, *Stanford. Regius Professor of Greek, 1940–80, Trinity College, Dublin. Memoirs* (Dublin, 2001).
Staunton, Enda, *The Nationalists of Northern Ireland 1918–1973* (Dublin, 2001).
Stewart, A. T. Q., *The Narrow Ground. Aspects of Ulster, 1609–1969* (London, 1977).
—— *The Shape of Irish History* (Belfast, 2001).
Storey, Earl, *Traditional Roots. Towards an Appropriate Relationship between the Church of Ireland and the Orange Order* (Dublin, 2002).
Taggart, Norman W., *Conflict, Controversy and Co-operation. The Irish Council of Churches and 'The Troubles' 1968–1972* (Dublin, 2004).
Tanner, Marcus, *Ireland's Holy Wars. The Struggle for a Nation's Soul, 1500–2000* (New Haven and London, 2001).
Twomey, D. Vincent, *The End of Irish Catholicism?* (Dublin, 2003).
Trösch, Felix, 'Positions and trends in Switzerland', in Michael Hurley (ed.), *Beyond Tolerance*, pp. 127–34.
Turner, Joan, *Glenstal Abbey Ecumenical Conferences 1964–1983* (Belfast, 1983).
Wallace, W. J. R. (ed.), *Clergy of Dublin and Glendalough. Biographical Succession Lists* (Belfast, 2001).
Walker, Brian M., *Parliamentary Election Results in Ireland 1918–1992* (Dublin, 1992).
Walker, Graham S., *The Politics of Frustration. Harry Midgley and the Failure of Labour in Northern Ireland* (Manchester, 1985).
Walsh, Brendan M., *Religion and Demographic Behaviour in Ireland* [ESRI Paper No. 55] (Dublin, 1970).
—— 'Trends in the religious composition of the population in the Republic of Ireland, 1946–71', *Economic and Social Review*, 6: 4 (1975), pp. 543–55.

Warke, Roy, *Ripples in the Pool* (Dublin, 1993).
—— 'A Sixties Man. Some Reflections on the Primacy and Retirement of The Most Reverend James McCann' (typescript, 2001).
White, Jack, *Minority Report. The Protestant Community in the Irish Republic* (Dublin, 1975).
Whitelaw, William, *The Whitelaw Memoirs* (London, 1989).
Whiteside, Lesley, *George Otto Simms. A Biography* (Gerrards Cross, 1990).
Whyte, John H., 'Political life in the South', in Michael Hurley (ed.), *Irish Anglicanism*, pp. 143–53.
—— *Church and State in Modern Ireland 1923–70* (Dublin, 1971).
—— 'How much discrimination was there under the Unionist regime, 1921–68?', in Tom Gallagher and James O'Connell (eds) *Contemporary Irish Studies* (Manchester, 1983), pp. 1–35.
—— *Interpreting Northern Ireland* (Oxford, 1990).
Wichert, Sabine, *Northern Ireland since 1945* (2nd edn., London and New York, 1999 [1st edn., 1991]).
Wilson, W. G., *How the Church of Ireland is Governed* (Dublin, 1963).
Yeats, Michael B., *Cast a Cold Eye. Memoirs of a Poet's Son and Politician* (Dublin, 1998).
Ulster Historical Foundation, *Clergy of Connor from Patrician Times to the Present Day* (Belfast, 1993).
—— *Clergy of Down and Dromore* (Belfast, 1996).

Index

Note: 'n.' after a page number indicates the numer of a note on that page.

ad hoc committee 217–20, 229
Administration 1967 22, 24–6
Agagianian, Cardinal Gregorio Pietro 91
Aiken, Frank 19, 60, 62, 76
Akenson, Donald Harman 120
Alibrandi, Archbishop Gaetano 77, 163–4
Allen, Revd Harold 218–19
All-Party Anti-Partition Conference 45
All-Party Oireachtas Committee on the Implication of Irish Unity 35
Alport, C. J. 54
Ancient Order of Hibernians 129
Anglican Communion 16, 29, 79, 98, 189, 243
Anglican-Roman Catholic International Commission (ARCIC) 209, 214, 216
Anglican-Roman Catholic Joint Preparatory Commission 209, 214
Anglo-Irish negotiations (1938) 44
Anti-Partition Campaign 45, 47, 117
Anti-Partition League 45, 127
Apprentice Boys 145
Ara Coeli 8, 148, 150, 184, 217, 221
Armagh (Roman Catholic archdiocese of) 4, 44, 60–3, 124
   archbishop of 7, 43, 56–7, 61, 241, 247
   province of 4, 8
Armagh (Church of Ireland diocese of) 3, 26, 72 195
   archbishop of 8, 73, 244
   Board of Social Responsibility 34–5, 146, 153–4
   diocesan synod of 90, 119, 166, 195, 228
   province of 3, 9 n.3, 223
Armstrong, Bishop John 211
Arnold, Bruce 102
Athenagoras I, Patriarch 197–8

Baker, Alex 147
Ballykinlar camp 159
Ballymascanlon 182, 190–1, 210–11, 216, 225–8, 243
Ballymurphy 162
Bandon Grammar School 79, 89
Barkley, Revd Professor John 226
barricades 148–51
Barrington, Dónal 95
Barrington, Eilín 188
Barton, Archbishop Arthur 13, 18, 71, 73, 90, 244
Barton, Robert 91
'Battle of the Bogside' 145
Baxter, Revd Ralph 226
Bea, Cardinal Augustin 196, 207

Beckett, Professor J. C. 36
Beere, Thekla 88
Belfast Central Defence Committee 150–1
Berry, Peter 27
Best, Private William 164
Bevan, Aneurin 138
Beveridge Report (1942) 118
Birch, Bishop Peter 77
Bird, J. A. D. 30–1
Black, Harold 150–1
Blackrock College 60
Blake, Archbishop Anthony 44
Bloody Sunday 156, 162
Blythe, Ernest 45–6, 55
Boggs, Bertie 91
Boland, Frederick H. 19, 49, 58
Book of Common Prayer 14, 17, 19
Booth, Lionel 74, 91
border 1–5, 9, 12–14, 27, 31, 34–6, 43–4, 46, 48, 50–3, 55–7, 63, 105, 160, 182, 240–1, 243
  see also partition
Bowen, Kurt 72, 186
Bowman, John 10 n.4, 45, 54
Boyd, Bishop Robert McNeill 19, 90, 123, 141, 245
Bradford, Roy 153
Briseadh na Teorann 46
British army 150–2, 155–7
British Commonwealth 6, 12, 14–18, 52–5, 91, 241
British Council of Churches (BCC) 30, 75–6, 192, 242
Brown, Professor Terence 81
Browne, Bishop Michael 82, 92, 118, 186–8, 203–5
Browne, Dr Noël 5, 73, 96
Brownell, Reginald 126
Brooke, Basil (Lord Brookeborough) 53, 123, 126, 128, 132, 157
Bryson, W. F. 142
Buchanan, Archbishop Alan 33–4, 74–5, 98, 103, 144, 190, 194, 208, 213–14, 244

Bunreacht na hÉireann 13–14, 73, 78, 97, 183
  All-party committee on 98–100
  Article 44 of 96, 98–101, 186
Burntollet Bridge 143, 217
Burroughs, R. A. 153, 160
Bunting, Major Ronald 144
Bunworth, Lieutenant-Colonel R. W. 74–5
Butler, Bishop Arthur 70, 98, 105, 145–6, 156–8, 167–8, 220, 222, 242, 245
Butler, Bishop Christopher 209
Butler, Hubert 70–1, 90, 187
Butler Education Act (1944) 121

Caird, Bishop Donald 72, 81
Cairns, Thomas 139
Callaghan, James 148–51, 153–5, 160
Callaghan strategy 147–8, 153
Cameron, Lord 144
Canterbury 28, 59, 183, 194, 196–7, 212, 243
Carrington, Lord 160
Carson, Revd Dr John 221
Casey, Bishop Éamonn 227
Cashman, Bishop David John 197
Catholic Action 93, 96, 118
Catholic Church 1, 5, 240, 242
  Church of Ireland, relations with 77, 182–4
    see also Ballymascanlon; inter-church relations
  condemnation of IRA 156, 161–2
  diocesan boundaries 1–2, 4, 9 n.3
  Episcopal Conference of 7–8
  episcopal committees 7–8
  Standing Committee of 7–8, 49
  in England 58, 60, 197–8
  inter-church marriage *see* mixed marriage
  IRA border campaign 6, 43, 27
  local government (Northern Ireland) 115, 133, 143

moral teaching 103–4, 117, 205
Northern Ireland administration 115–17, 140, 147, 168–9, 242
Northern Ireland Civil Rights Association 143
opposition to physical force nationalism 46–9, 51
Orange Order 31, 128
Second Vatican Council 199–200, 203–6
'special position' of *see* Bunreacht na hÉireann, Article 44
social injustice 140–1, 143
social teaching 101, 117
Troubles 116–17
Catholic Truth Society 186
Catholic Union 59
censorship 97, 103
Central Churches Committee for Community Work 224
Cheke, Sir Marcus 59
Chesterton, G. K. 228
Chichester-Clark, James 149–50, 152–3, 155, 160
Childers, Erskine 19, 78, 91
children's allowance 135
Christ Church Cathedral 18, 25, 73–4, 93, 215, 225
Church and State in Modern Ireland, 1923–1970 5–6
see also Whyte, John H.
Churches' Industrial Council 182, 209–10
Churchill, Sir Winston 19
Church of England 22, 71, 76, 129, 193–4, 196–8
Church of Ireland 1–2, 5–6, 9, 240–3
administrative structure 8, 25
Catholic Church 183–4
see also Ballymascanlon; inter-church relations
church property 22–3
clerical mobility 23
clerical stipends 23
condemnation of IRA 49
diocesan boundaries 1–3, 9 n.3
discrimination 93
see also Fethard-on-Sea boycott; Meath Hospital
episcopal enthronements 72–3
House of Bishops 8, 13–14, 16–18, 25, 29, 31, 33, 70–2, 78–9, 81–2, 92, 97–8, 103–5, 135, 148, 168, 183–4, 186, 189–90, 193–6, 214–16, 223, 225, 241–2
House of Representatives 8
Irish government, relations with 5, 70, 72, 105, 242
Irish language 88
labour force, representation 88–9
population decline 20–2, 25, 186
Second Vatican Council 208–9
social grievances in Northern Ireland 144, 148
state prayers 12–20, 36, 70, 154, 241–2
unity 12–13, 23, 27, 34–6
vocations, shortage of 22–3
welfare state 119
Church of Ireland Gazette 25–6
Cicognani, Cardinal Amleto Giovanni 62
City and Town Parishes Commission 24
Civil Rights campaign 101, 104, 141, 143–5
Clark, George 128–9
Clarke, Bishop Alan 209
Clarke, Bishop Richard 209
Clerical Society of Ireland 212
Clogher (Roman Catholic diocese of) 4, 44, 49, 124, 141, 161, 247–8
Clogher (Church of Ireland diocese of) 3, 17, 25, 31–2, 34, 80, 83, 145, 222, 244–5
diocesan synod of 84, 144, 187, 194, 213

Cloney, Sheila 94, 187
  see also Fethard-on-Sea boycott
Clonfert (Roman Catholic diocese of) 4, 51, 56, 248
Clutterbuck, Sir Alexander 53–4
Code of Canon Law (*Codex Inuris Canonici*) 185, 188–90
Cohalan, Bishop Daniel 92
Cole, John 90
Cole, John C. 82, 90
Colley, George 82–3, 99–100
Colthurst, Revd Joseph Riversdale 18
Commins, Thomas 60–3, 101, 203–5
Commission on Vocational Organisation 118
communism 119
community relations 12, 32, 34, 146, 199, 217, 219, 224
company vote (*Northern Ireland*) 141
Compton Report 159–60
Connor, (Church of Ireland diocese of), 3, 22–4, 33, 145, 165, 195, 210, 215, 245
Constitution on the Liturgy (*Sacrosanctum concillium*) 202
contraception 97, 101–4, 205
Conway, Monsignor Dominic 205
Conway, Cardinal William 6, 43, 53, 56–7, 62–3, 85, 100, 126, 128, 133, 155, 189, 202, 204–6, 209, 211, 217–21, 224–6, 242–3, 247
  Article 44 101
  assassinations 164–6
  barricades 148–51
  Callaghan strategy 148, 151, 153–4
  Civil Rights campaign 143
  condemnation of violence 145–6, 160–2, 167–9, 223
  Crowther Commission 154
  education in Northern Ireland 130–2
  housing 142
  integrated schooling 131

internment 158–60
joint statement by church leaders on nature of the Troubles 221–2
Northern Ireland Bill 133–5
Official IRA 164
Provisional IRA 164–5
Cooney, John 10 n.5, 212, 227
Cork, Cloyne and Ross (Church of Ireland diocese of) 23
  diocesan synod of 30, 33, 71
Corrymeela 224
Cosgrave, Liam 59, 89, 104
Costello, John A. 14–15, 89–91, 139
Council of Europe 45
Craigavon, Lord 132
Craigmyle, Lord 133–4
Cremin, Con 54, 58–9, 76, 116, 134, 197–8
Cremin, Dr Francis 205
Criminal Law Act (1935) 101, 103
Crowther Commission 154
Crozier, Archbishop John 20
Crozier, Bishop John Wintrop 92
Cumann Gaelach na hEaglaise, see Irish Guild of the Church
Cunningham, Charles 134
Curran, Revd Lodge 47
Cushing, Cardinal Richard James 202

D'Alton, Cardinal John 6, 43–4, 46–51, 118–19, 125–6, 128–9, 136, 142, 184, 199, 242, 247
  D'Alton plan 46, 51–6
  death and succession of 60–2
  Fethard-on-Sea 187–8
  leadership style 56–7
  Northern Ireland administration 115–16
  Northern Ireland Bill 133–5
  Second Vatican Council 200–1, 203
Dáil Éireann 15, 19, 60, 77–8, 90
Daly, Bishop Cahal 159, 162, 168, 190, 211, 225–7

Davey, Revd Ray 224
Day, Archbishop John Godfrey Fitzmaurice 13
Deane, J. L. B. 29, 33
de Baróid, Ciarán 143
de Blaghd, Earnán see Blythe, Ernest
Declaration on Religious Freedom 188
Decree on Ecumenism (*Unitatis redintegratio*) 74, 202, 206, 209–10
Decree on Religious Liberty (*Dignitatis humanae*) 98, 202, 207
Delaney, Enda 97
Dell'Acqua, Monsignor Angelo 58–9
Derry (Roman Catholic diocese of) 4, 48, 123–4, 144, 191, 220, 248
Derry and Raphoe (Church of Ireland diocese of) 3, 13, 15, 18, 25, 194, 220, 223, 245
   diocesan synod of 90, 144, 146, 194, 227
   Donegal Education Committee of 83
de Soysa, Archdeacon Charles 196
detention without trial see internment
de Valera, Eamon 19, 43, 45, 48, 54, 56, 60, 73–4, 76, 78, 81, 89–90, 118, 183, 199, 212
   Fethard-on-Sea boycott 95–6, 187–8
Dignan, Bishop John 56
Dignitatis humanae, see Decree on Religious Liberty
Dillon, James 50
direct rule 152–3
Disestablishment 8, 13, 25
   centenary of 6, 30, 76, 105, 242
divorce 97–103
Dobbin, Maurice 25
Dobbs, Revd Harry 20
Dockrell, Henry 91
Dockrell, Maurice 91
Doctrine and Life 199

dogma of the Assumption 183–4
Dogmatic Constitution on the Church (*Lumen gentium*) 202
Douglas, James Green 89–90
Dowdall, Abbot Joseph 211
Dowling, Osmund 163
Down and Connor (Roman Catholic diocese of) 4, 56, 124, 248
Down and Dromore (Church of Ireland united dioceses of) 3, 23–4, 33, 146, 165, 210, 215, 245–6
   diocesan council of 20, 166
   diocesan synod of 26
Downing Street Declaration (1969) 147
Dromore (Roman Catholic diocese of) 4, 124, 131, 162, 191, 248
Dublin, Glendalough and Kildare, (Church of Ireland united dioceses of) 24, 26, 72, 80–2, 90, 186
   diocesan council of 15
   diocesan synod of 18, 190
   Temperance and Social Welfare Society of 97
Duffy, Eamon 183, 202

Eames, Revd Robin 33
ecumenism 2, 182–3, 191–3, 198–9, 202–3, 205–7, 212, 220, 226, 228, 240–1
   opposition to 28, 213–16
Edinburgh Missionary Conference 191
education 7, 241
   (*England and Wales*) 129–30
      see also Butler Education Act (1944)
   (*Northern Ireland*) 117
      'conscience clause' 123
      Education Act (1923) 120–1
      Education Act (1947) 120, 123, 125–7, 132
      Education Act (1968) 126, 132

education (cont.)
   (Northern Ireland) (cont.)
      Educational Amendment Act (1930) 121, 132
      Educational Reconstruction in Northern Ireland (1944) 121–2
      'four and two' committees 120, 123, 128, 130–1
      Local Education Authorities and Voluntary Schools (1967) 130–2
      local education authorities/committees 120–1, 126–8, 130–2
      Lynn Committee 120–1
      provision of school places 126–7
      school leaving age 124
      shortage of teachers 124–5
      teachers' National Insurance contribution 126
      voluntary status 120–3, 125–9, 132
   (Republic of Ireland) 70
      Church of Ireland Board of 26, 79, 81–5
      community schools 84
      comprehensive schools 83–8
      Council of 78
      denominational 7, 78, 84
      grants 80–1, 83, 85–8
      Irish language 80
      primary schools, reorganisation of 82–3
      school transport scheme 79–80, 82, 87–8
      secondary education 83–4
      Secondary Education Committee 85–7
      teacher training 80, 126
      textbooks 81
      vocational school 83–4, 87–8
Education and Enmity 120
elections, local (Northern Ireland) 141

Elliott, Canon Eric 33, 35, 218–19
Elliott, George 142
Elliott, Marianne 123
Elliott, Bishop Robert 29–30, 210, 214, 245
Elizabeth, Queen 19–20, 58, 60, 115–16, 197
Ervine, St John 14–15

Fahey, Revd Denis 96–7
Fallon, Brian 97
family planning 35, 101, 103
   see also contraception
Farrell, Michael 151
Farrell, Archdeacon R. T. 80
Farren, Bishop Neil 44, 48, 51, 120, 122, 124, 129, 144, 200, 220, 248
Faul, Revd Denis 152, 217–19
Faulkner, Brian 53, 157
Faulkner, Pádraig 77, 84–5
Ferguson, Dick 29
Fethard-on-Sea boycott 6, 93–7, 182, 186–8, 228, 243
Fianna Fáil 15, 50, 56, 89–91
Fianna Uladh 47
Fine Gael 14–15, 50, 89, 91–2, 99, 104
Fisher, Revd Adrian 94–5
Fisher, Archbishop Geoffrey 14, 76, 184, 192, 197
Fitt, Gerry 150
FitzGerald, Garret 100
Fitzgibbon, Frank 18
Fitzpatrick, David 80
Fitzsimmons, William 130
Flanagan, Monsignor P. J. 142
Flannery, Revd Austin 199, 211
Focus 193
Fox, Billy 89, 91
Freeland, General Sir Ian 150
Freemasons 93
Free Presbyterian Church 213–14, 226
Fuller, Louise 6, 201

Fulton, Revd A. A. 210
Fulton, John 191
Furrow, The 199
Future of Northern Ireland, The 166

Gallagher, Revd Eric 30, 156, 158–9, 211, 213, 216–19, 224–8
Gallagher, Frank 63
Gallagher, John 152
Garrett, Revd F. H. 16
Gazette, see Church of Ireland Gazette
General Synod 8–9, 12, 15, 17–20, 24–7, 33, 35, 82–3, 87, 90, 146, 189, 192–3, 195, 208–9, 216
   Board of Education *see* Education, (*Republic of Ireland*)
   Church Unity Committee 211
   committees of 26–8
   Standing Committee of 9, 18, 24, 29, 33, 148, 225
George VI, King 16, 19
gerrymandering 52, 141
Girdwood Barracks 159
Glenstal 182, 210–11
Godfrey, Archbishop William 58, 60–1, 133, 197–8
Good, Revd George 221
Goulding, Cathal 163
Government of Ireland Act (1920) 133–4
Graham, Sir Clarence 128
Grant, Revd Edward 94
Grant, Frederick 196
Grant, William 138
Greenhills conference 183, 211
Gregg, Archbishop John 6, 12–14, 17–20, 22, 24, 30, 56, 71–3, 75, 89–90, 93, 119, 136, 242, 245
   Cardinal John D'Alton and 184
   dogma of the Assumption 183–4
   ecumenism, opposition to 193, 197
   Ne Temere decree 185–6

Griffin, Archbishop Bernard 60
Griffin, Revd Victor 15, 23, 30, 33
Guinness, Henry Eustace 90

Hall-Thompson, Samuel 121, 123, 126, 130
Hannon, Revd Gordon 210
Hanson, Bishop Richard 31–2, 84, 145, 211, 221–2, 244
Harris, Mary 10 n.4, 121
Harvey, Brian 28
Haughey, Charles J. 35, 86, 104
Health Services (*Northern Ireland*) Act (1948) 136–7
   Advisory Committee 138
   Amendment Bill 140
   voluntary hospitals 137
Healy, Cahir 127
Hearn, Bishop Thomas R. 71, 92
Heath, Edward 59, 155, 166
Heavener, Bishop Robert 32, 75, 80, 168, 244–5
Hebblethwaite, Peter 197
Heenan, Cardinal James 154, 167, 203–4
Herlihy, Bishop Dónal 204–5, 207
Heron, Alasdair 190
Heron, Archie 91
Heslinga, M. W. 63
Hillery, Dr Patrick 83, 102
Hodges, Bishop Charles Evelyn 79–80, 96, 98
Holy See *see* Vatican
'Home Reunion' 192–3
   see also intra-Protestant *rapprochement*
Horgan, John 101, 199
housing 30, 134, 141–4, 218, 224
Humanae vitae 190
Hume, John 35
Hunt case (1945) 99
Hunt Committee 148
Hunt reforms 152

Hurley, Revd Michael 77, 192, 210–11, 217, 227
Hyde, President Douglas 73, 75

inter-church marriage *see* mixed marriage
inter-church relations 5–7, 182–4, 216, 225, 227–8, 240
  see also Ballymascanlon
interdepartmental unit on Northern Ireland 35, 103
internment 152, 156–60, 222
inter-nunciature question 58–9, 61, 63
intra-Protestant *rapprochement* 183, 191–5, 213, 228, 243
Investment in Education 82
Ireland, Denis 89
Irish Anglicanism 1869–1969 77
Irish Association 31, 52, 163, 222, 228
Irish Church Association 28, 216
Irish College, Rome 203–5
Irish Council of Churches (ICC) 145, 159, 216–17, 224–6
Irish Directory on Ecumenism 206–8
Irish Guild of the Church (*Cumann Gaelach na hEaglaise*) 81
Irish Medical Association 5
Irish National Teachers Organisation 131
Irish Republican Army (IRA) 62
  border campaign 6, 27, 43, 45–8, 49, 128
    see also Official IRA; Provisional IRA
Irish School of Ecumenics 225
Irwin, Bishop Charles King 13, 245–6

Jackson, Bishop Robert Wyse 76, 189
Jacob, Frank 71, 87
Jenkins, Revd Raymond 146
Jenkins, Roy 148
Jessop, Professor W. J. 102
Jewish Congregation 77

John XXIII, Pope 59, 118, 128, 196–7, 200–1, 208, 213, 243
Johnson, Dean F. K. 34
Joint Group on Social Problems 216, 220, 224–5, 229

Keery, Neville 91
Kelly, Eddie 50
Kelly, John 140
Kelly, Liam 47
Kelly, Revd Michael 136, 139–40
Kennedy, Finola 186
Kennedy, Michael 46
Kilmore (Roman Catholic diocese of) 4, 44
Kilmore Clerical Association 35, 216
Kilmore, Elphin and Ardagh (Church of Ireland diocese of) 3, 27, 75, 79–80, 93, 96, 145, 245–6
  diocesan synod of 82, 85
Kilmuir, Lord 133–5
Kinane, Archbishop Jeremiah 49
King-Harmon, Sir Cecil 16
Knights of St Columbanus 93
Knocknagoney, parish of 23

Laithwaite, Sir Gilbert 49
Lamb, Canon Henry 27
Lambeth Conference 79, 96, 98, 193–4, 196
Larmor, Sir Graham 52
Lefebvre, Archbishop Marcel 207
Legion of Mary 49
Lemass, Seán 27, 46, 51, 60, 74–6, 78, 99, 101, 139
Lenihan, Brian 35, 86–7, 99
Lennon, Gerry 129
Leo XIII, Pope 118
Leonard, R. G. L. 90
Leslie, Sir Shane 53, 62, 134
Levame, Archbishop Alberto 57, 187
Lewis-Crosby, Dean Ernest H. 18
licensing laws (*Republic of Ireland*) 97

Limerick (Church of Ireland diocese of) 3, 9 n.3 22, 245
Lincoln Theological College 71
Lloyd, Geoffrey 129
Londonderry, Lord 120
Long, Revd Samuel 213
Long, William 126, 130–2
Longford, Lord *see* Pakenham, Frank
Longley, Edna 90
Lowry, Revd Seán 154
Luce, Professor A. A. 14
Lucey, Bishop Cornelius 56, 92, 118, 191
Lumen gentium, *see* Dogmatic Constitution on the Church
Lynas, Revd R. V. 167
Lynch, Jack 74, 77, 85–6, 91, 100–1, 103
Lynn Committee *see* Education, (*Northern Ireland*)

McAdoo, Bishop Henry 71, 74, 81, 87, 189, 209, 214–16, 227
MacBride, Seán 73–4
McCall, Séamus 45
McCann, Hugh 55, 60–1, 63, 197, 203
McCann, Archbishop James 6, 24–5, 28, 30, 83, 90, 96–8, 146, 184, 193, 195, 208, 211, 215–17
MacCarthy, Very Revd Robert 186
McCauley, Leo 59
McConville, Revd Gerard 224–5
McCormack, Bishop John 225–6
MacDermott, Eithne 45
McElroy, Gerald 10 n.8, 143
MacEntee, Seán 91
McGarry, Canon J. G. 199, 211
McGee v Attorney General (1973) 104
Mac Giolla, Tomás 163
McGrath, Michael 126–7, 130–1
McHugh, Bishop Charles 44
MacInnes, Archbishop Campbell 197

McKevitt, Revd Peter 118
McKinney, Revd J. W. 89
Maclennan, Sir Ian 134
Macmillan, Harold 54, 197, 213
McNamara, Revd Kevin 212, 225
MacNamee, Bishop James 203
MacNeice, Bishop John 13
McQuaid, Archbishop John Charles 6–7, 47, 56–7, 61, 63, 74, 76–7, 92, 97, 147
  contraception 102–4
  divorce 100
  ecumenism 207–8
  Fethard-on-Sea boycott 95, 187–8
  IRA Christmas truce 163–4
  Northern refugees 158
    see also internment
  Second Vatican Council 203–4, 206, 209
  Simms, Archbishop George 184, 212
MacRéamoinn, Seán 206
MacRory, Cardinal Joseph 46, 115, 183
Macrory report 142–3
Mac Stiofáin, Seán 163
McVeigh, Revd R. W. 210
Maffey, Sir John *see* Rugby, Lord
Mageean, Bishop Daniel 6, 44, 46, 48, 56–7, 118, 125–6, 129, 200, 210, 248
Educational Reconstruction in Northern Ireland (1944) 121–2
  Mater Hospital, Belfast 137–9
Maginess, Brian 116, 128, 133
Malines Conversations 192
Malta Report 209
Mansergh, Professor Nicholas 13
Maria Duce 49, 96–7
marriage bar 80
Marsh, Arnold 91
Mater et magistra (1961) 118
Mater Hospital, Belfast 6, 136–40
Matrimonia mixta (1970) 188–91

Matrimonii sacramentum (1966) 188
Maude, Hugh 15–19
Maudling, Reginald 148, 155
May, Morris 127
Meath Hospital 93–4
Methodist Church 1, 72, 77, 89, 158, 188, 192–6, 210, 217, 221, 223
  see also intra-Protestant *rapprochement*
Mew, Colonel Robert 19, 74
Midgley, Harry 126–7
Milltown Park lectures 199
Milne, Dr Kenneth 10 n.4, 35
Minford, Nat 128
Mitchell, Bishop Frederick 29, 75, 93, 98, 193, 210, 245
mixed marriage 21–2, 35, 94, 183–91, 206, 220, 226–7
Mock, Desmond 223
Molloy, John 116
Molloy, Bishop Thomas 47
Montini, Giovanni Battista *see* Paul VI, Pope
Mooney, John 165
Mooney, Patrick 50
Moore, Bishop Edward 27, 75, 85, 88, 93, 208, 246
Moore, Theodore Kingsmill 92, 102
Moorman, Bishop John 28–9, 33, 196
  see also Ripon affair
Morgan, William 139–40
Morris, Archbishop Thomas 204–5, 207
Mortalium annos 202
'Mother and Child' scheme 5, 15, 127
Mothers' Union 100
'Movement for Peace in Ireland' 224
Moynihan, Maurice 95
Mullally, Revd P. J. 139, 167
Mullan, Revd Hugh 222
Mulligan, Bishop Patrick 161, 248

Murlough House 194, 213 *see* intra-Protestant *rapprochement*
Murphy, Revd Pádraig 149–51, 163
Murphy, Revd Robert 155, 224
Murray, John Courtney 202

Nationalist Party 48, 127, 129
national question 43–4, 46–7, 50, 57, 63, 101, 116, 168, 241–2
Neill, Ivan 135–6, 139
Ne Temere decree 6, 21, 94, 102, 184–90, 215
  see also mixed marriage
Newe, G. B. 32, 91
Norfolk, duke of 59
Northern Ireland Bill (1962) 133–5
Northern Ireland Constitutional Proposals (1973) 167
Northern Ireland government 5, 28, 44, 52, 56, 61, 75, 77, 91, 115–17, 124, 126, 130, 133–5, 140, 145, 147, 150, 153, 168,
  levels of 115
  reform programme 151–2
Northern Ireland Hospitals Authority (NIHA) 136
Northern Ireland Housing Executive 142
Northern Ireland Housing Trust (NIHT) 141
Northern Ireland Office 166
North-West Council of Churches 194

Ó Brádaigh, Ruairí 163
O'Brien, Conor Cruise 55
O'Callaghan, Bishop Eugene 44, 46, 50, 141–2, 203, 247
Ó Ceallaigh, President Seán T. 19, 62
O'Doherty, Bishop Eugene 10 n.9, 44, 119–20, 122, 131, 133–4, 136, 162, 199–200, 223, 248
Ó Glaisne, Risteard 193
O'Halloran, Clare 45
O'Hanlon, Fergal 49–50

Ó hAnnluain, Eineachán 50
O'Hara, Archbishop Gerald 47, 58, 197
O'Mahony, T. P. 227
O'Malley, Donagh 84–6
O'Neill, Phelim 75
O'Neill, Captain Terence (Lord O'Neill) 27, 46, 128, 130, 132, 139, 149, 151, 213, 218
Ó Nualláin, Nioclás 27
Ó Nualláin, Seán 46
Ó Raifeartaigh, Tarlach 79
Offences against the State Act 27
Official IRA 162–4
Orange-Green talks 129
Orange Order 6, 28–33, 75, 80, 126–9, 144, 166, 214–15
  Bible instruction 121
Orpen, Edward Richards 89
Orr, Lawrence Percy 30–1, 129
Orthodox Church 183, 198
Oulton, Professor J. E. L. 23

PACE *see* Protestant and Catholic Encounter
Paisley, Revd Ian 28, 144, 213–15, 226, 228
Pakenham, Frank (Lord Longford) 54–5, 133–5
papal infallibility 183
papal nuncio, jurisdiction of 57–8, 241
Paritätsfrage 168
partition
  ecclesiastical 2, 14, 34, 182, 243
  federal solution to *see* D'Alton, Cardinal John, D'Alton plan
  political 1–2, 9, 12, 27, 36, 43–9, 51–7, 59, 62–3, 100, 116, 129, 193, 228, 241
Patrician Year (1961) 43, 75, 91, 198
Paul VI, Pope 60, 63, 147, 189–90, 196, 198–9, 201, 206, 209, 213, 216

Peacocke, Bishop Cuthbert 28, 33, 145–6, 220, 227, 245
Peacocke, Bishop Joseph 13
Peck, Sir John 163
Perdue, Bishop Gordon 85–7
Phair, Bishop John Percy 15, 95–6, 187
Philbin, Bishop William 51, 57, 62, 129, 131, 143, 149–51, 158, 165, 167, 212, 220, 222, 227, 248
  condemnation of IRA 162–3
  Mater Hospital Belfast 138–40
  Second Vatican Council 201, 203, 205–6
Pilkington, Lionel 97
Pius IX, Pope 207
Pius X, Pope 184
Pius XI, Pope 53, 117, 202
Pius XII, Pope 59, 183, 196, 208
Porter, Norman 128
power-sharing 166–8
Poyntz, Bishop Samuel 33, 74, 76
prayer book *see* Book of Common Prayer
Presbyterian Church 1, 9 n.2, 72, 77, 136, 157–8, 167, 192–6, 210, 212, 216–18, 223, 227
  see also intra-Protestant *rapprochement*
Pro-Cathedral Dublin 77, 104, 206
Protestant and Catholic Encounter (PACE) 32, 223
Provisional IRA 160–6, 218

Quadragesimo anno (1931) 117–18
Quin, Bishop George 145–6, 156–7, 167–8, 223–4, 245
Quinn, Bishop Austin 44, 53, 62, 84, 248

Race Relations Bill 140
Radcliffe, Revd John 218–19
Rafferty, Revd Oliver 155

Ramsey, Archbishop Michael 184, 196–8, 209, 212–16, 222
ratepayer suffrage (*Northern Ireland*) 141
Refugees Relief Co-ordination Centre 145
Reilly, Patrick 90
Report on Violence 225
Representative Church Body (RCB) 24–5, 40 n.66, 80
Republic of Ireland Act 14, 37 n.7
Rerum novarum (1891) 118
Revivalist, The 213
Ripon affair 27–9, 33–4, 215–16, 241
Rising (1916), fiftieth anniversary of 77–8
Robinson, D. L. 73
Robinson, Howard W. 24
Robinson, Mary 101
Rodgers, Bishop Joseph 53
Role of the Church Committee 33–5, 102–3, 218
Rome *see* Vatican
Rossorry, parish of 31
Royal Ulster Constabulary (RUC) 47, 150, 152, 214
Rugby, Lord (Sir John Maffey) 15, 54
Ryan, Monsignor Arthur 212
Ryan, Archbishop Dermot 225–6
Ryan, Bishop Thomas 56, 68 n.93

Sacks, Paul 91
St Anne's Cathedral, Belfast 28, 157
St Columb's College, Derry 120
St Dorothea's, Gilnahirk 23
St Eugene's Cathedral, Derry 48
St Fin Barre's Cathedral, Cork 71
St Joseph's College, Belfast 125
St Macartan's Cathedral, Monaghan 50, 141
St Mary's College, Belfast 125–6
St Mary's College, Strawberry Hill 124
St Molua, parish of 23

St Patrick's Cathedral, Armagh 48, 161
St Patrick's Cathedral, Dublin 15–16, 19, 23, 74–5, 78, 81
Salmon, Dean Thomas 74, 215, 226
Samoré, Cardinal Antonio 62
Scarlett, Sir Peter 59, 198
Scarman Tribunal 148, 218–19
Seanad Éireann, nominations to 89–90
Seaver, Revd George 93, 184
Second Vatican Council 2, 6, 28, 74, 76, 98, 100, 117, 128, 131, 182–4, 188, 192, 194, 196, 199, 205–9, 212, 228, 240, 243
  preparatory commissions for 200–1
  sessions of 201–2
Secretariat for the Promotion of Christian Unity 196, 206
Sensi, Archbishop Giuseppi 62
Sexton, J. J. and Richard O'Leary 21
Shea, Patrick 126
Sheldon, William 15
Shillington, Graham 152
Simms, Archbishop George 6, 13, 24, 29–32, 76–8, 81–2, 92, 98, 100–1, 166–8, 189, 208, 211, 220, 223–5, 226–7, 243–4
  internment 158–9
  leadership of 71–2, 146
  McQuaid Archbishop John Charles 184, 212
  translation to Armagh 74, 145
Simms, Mercy 199, 212
Sinn Féin 48, 50
Slack, Revd Kenneth 76
Sloan, Revd Harold 158, 167
Smyth, Revd Martin 157
Social Democratic and Labour Party (SDLP) 148
Social Services Act (NI) (1949) 135
Soskice, Sir Frank 140, 148
South, Seán 49

Sparsely Populated Areas Commission (SPAC) 24–5
'special position' clause *see* Bunreacht na hÉireann, Article 44
Special Powers Act 150, 218
Stafford, Revd William 94
Stanford, Professor W. B. 94–6, 102, 187
Stanistreet, Bishop Henry 194
Staunton, Bishop James 10 n.9, 95, 187–8
Storero, Monsignor Luciano 76
Stormont
  appointment of Catholic chaplain to 154–5
  government *see* Northern Ireland government
  prorogation of 148, 153, 164
  reforms *see* Callaghan strategy
Stranmillis College, Belfast 125
Stronge, Sir Norman 74
subsidiarity 118–19, 121
Sunningdale communiqué 168
Supreme Court 92, 104, 186
Syllabus of Errors 207

Taggart, Revd Norman 217, 224–5
Tanner Report (1955) 138
  see also Health Services (*Northern Ireland*) Act (1948), Advisory Committee
Tardini, Monsignor Domenico 59, 62
Thompson, T. J. 29
Tilson case 186
Towards a New Ireland 100
Towards a United Church 195
Trench House 125, 145
Trinity College Dublin 25, 31, 71, 89
tripartite talks *see* intra-Protestant *rapprochement*
Troubles, The 2, 5–7, 34, 50, 97, 100, 116–17, 131, 143, 145–6, 152–3, 156, 165, 168–9, 183, 209, 213, 216, 222–3, 228, 242–3

administration of justice 152
inter-church relations 216, 220
mixed marriages 190
nature of 221–2
security forces 156, 160
Twomey, Revd Professor Vincent 206
Tyndall, Bishop Charles 36, 75, 96, 98, 144, 187, 194, 220, 222, 245
Tyner, Bishop Richard 17, 32, 187, 244

UK representative to Northern Ireland 147–8, 153
Ulster Special Constabulary 147, 150
Ulster Teachers' Association 132
Ulster Unionist Council 30, 128
Ulster Volunteer Force (UVF) 218
Unionist Party 35, 53, 55, 126, 128–9, 151, 153, 219
Unitatis redintegratio, *see* Decree on Ecumenism
United Council of Christian Churches and Religious Communions in Ireland (UCCC) 119, 192, 209–10, 216
  see also Irish Council of Churches (ICC)
University Colleges
  governing bodies of 92
  non-Roman Catholic students at 92
University of Ulster 129

Vatican 5, 43, 57–61, 63, 101, 153, 155, 196–8, 202–3, 205, 207, 241
  apostolic delegation in the UK 58
  Canterbury 59, 183, 194, 196–7
  nascent ecumenism 183
Vatican II *see* Second Vatican Council
Viney, Michael 82, 88, 91

Wallace, Martin 129
Walsh, Brendan 21–2

Walsh, Archbishop Joseph 53, 201
Walsh, Revd Patrick 158, 217–21
Walshe, Joseph 58
Warke, Revd Roy 23
Webb, Dr David 16, 93
Webb, Archdeacon William 19
Weir, Revd Jack 158
welfare state 115, 117–19, 140, 168, 242
West, Trevor 101, 157
White, Jack 89, 185
Whitelaw, William 148, 164–5, 168
Whiteside, Lesley 208
Whyte, John H. 5–6, 117, 140
Wichert, Sabine 116
Williams, Revd Cecil 213
Willis, Revd Andrew 26, 34
Wilson, Austin 150–1
Wilson, Dean David 16
Wilson Revd Desmond 162
Wilson, Revd John 136
World Council of Churches (WCC) 76, 98, 192, 196, 213, 216, 243
Worlock, Monsignor Derek 133–5, 198
Worrall, Stanley 211, 213, 216, 226–8
Wright, Oliver 142, 147–54, 160

Yeats, Michael B. 89
Young, Sir Arthur 152
Young, John A. 33

EU authorised representative for GPSR:
Easy Access System Europe, Mustamäe tee 50,
10621 Tallinn, Estonia
gpsr.requests@easproject.com

www.ingramcontent.com/pod-product-compliance
Ingram Content Group UK Ltd.
Pitfield, Milton Keynes, MK11 3LW, UK
UKHW021944200326
4879IPUK00004B/79